seditious
allegories

seditious allegories

john thelwall & jacobin writing

michael scrivener

the pennsylvania state university press
university park, pennsylvania

Library of Congress Cataloging-in-Publication Data

Scrivener, Michael Henry, 1948–
 Seditious allegories : John Thelwall and Jacobin writing / Michael Scrivener.
  p.   cm.
 Includes bibliographical references and index.
 ISBN: 978-0-271-02847-7
  1. Thelwall, John, 1764–1834—Political and social views. 2. Politics and literature—Great Britain—History—18th century. 3. Literature and society—Great Britain—History—18th century.   4. France—History—Revolution, 1789–1799—Influence.   5. English literature—French influences.   6. Jacobins—Great Britain—History.   7. Social problems in literature.   8. Sedition—Great Britain.   9. Radicalism in literature. 10. Allegory. I. Title.

PR3729.T4 Z88 2001
828′.609—dc21

00-064979

Copyright © 2001 The Pennsylvania State University
All rights reserved
Printed in the United States of America
Published by The Pennsylvania State University Press,
University Park, PA 16802-1003

It is the policy of The Pennsylvania State University Press to use acid-free paper for the first printing of all clothbound books. Publications on uncoated stock satisfy the minimum requirements of American National Standard for Information Sciences—Permanence of Paper for Printed Library Materials, ANSI Z39.48–1992.

*To My Mother
and in Memory of My Father*

Contents

Acknowledgments ix
Abbreviations xi
Introduction 1

Part 1 Jacobinism 19

1 Defining Jacobinism 21
2 Thelwall's Replies to Burke 43

Part 2 The Voice of the People 87

3 Thelwall's Popular Poetry and LCS Culture 91
4 Excursus: Radical Underground: Spence and Wedderburn 129
5 Intemperance, Oratory, and Voicelessness 167

Part 3 Jacobin Allegory 205

6 Peripatetic Imagination 209
7 Against Empire 233
8 Autobiographies 257

Conclusion 289
Index 297

Acknowledgments

Publication of this book has been aided by a subvention from Wayne State University. For a project that has spanned over a decade I am heavily indebted to Wayne State University—the English Department, the College of Liberal Arts, the Graduate School, the Office of Research Sponsored Programs—which has been generous in giving me a sabbatical (1997), travel grant (1995), small research grant (1996), and summer grants (1991, 1993, 1997), without which the book could not have been written. I am also indebted to fellow scholars who commented on conference papers or lectures I delivered or who provided editorial guidance on my contributions to essay collections. I wish to thank Stephen C. Behrendt, Michael T. Davis, Peter Kitson, Michael Macovski, Paul Magnuson, Peter Manning, Timothy Morton, Nicholas Roe, G. A. Rosso, Nigel Smith, Judith Thompson, and Daniel P. Watkins. For offering useful suggestions and criticism at the book's various stages I want to thank Gregory Claeys, P. J. Corfield, Damian Walford Davies, James Epstein, Anne Janowitz, and David Worrall. Among the English Department faculty at Wayne State University who contributed in some way to my thinking about Thelwall and Jacobinism I want to give special thanks to my colleague Arthur Marotti. I am grateful as well to the two readers for Penn State Press, Gregory Claeys and David Simpson. Finally, Arthur Efron and Irving Massey have helped me more than they realize. Without the assistance and guidance I have received from many people the book would not have been written, but I take full responsibility for the book's flaws.

I have used all or part of the following essays and am reprinting them with permission: "John Thelwall's Political Ambivalence: Reform and Revolution," in Michael T. Davis, ed., *Radicalism and the Threat of Revolution in Britain, 1789–1848* (London and New York: Macmillan and St. Martin's Press, 2000), 69–83 (reproduced with permission of Palgrave); "Jacobin Romanticism: John Thelwall's 'Wye' Essay and 'Pedestrian Excursion' (1797–1801)," in Peter Kitson, ed., *Placing and Displacing Romanticism* (Aldershot: Ashgate Press, 2001); "The Rhetoric and Context of John Thelwall's 'Memoir,'" in G. A. Rosso and Daniel P. Watkins, eds., *Spirits of Fire: English Romantic Writers and Contemporary Historical Methods* (Rutherford, N.J.: Fairleigh Dickinson University Press, 1990), 112–30; "The Discourse of Treason, Sedition, and Blasphemy in British Political Trials, 1794–1822," *Romantic Praxis* (March 1999), http://www.rc.umd.edu/praxis/law/scrivener/mscrv.htm; "John Thelwall and Popular Jacobin Allegory, 1793–95," *ELH* 67:4 (2000): 951–71.

Abbreviations

EB   *The Writings and Speeches of Edmund Burke.* 9 vols. Ed. L. G. Mitchell and William B. Todd. Oxford: Clarendon Press, 1989.
EHT   *Essays on His Times.* 3 vols. Ed. David V. Erdman. No. 3 of *The Collected Works of Samuel Taylor Coleridge,* ed. Kathleen Coburn. London and Princeton: Routledge and Kegan Paul, Princeton University Press, 1978.
F   *The Friend,* 2 vols. Ed. Barbara E. Rooke, No. 4 of *The Collected Works of Samuel Taylor Coleridge,* ed. Kathleen Coburn. London and Princeton: Kegan Paul and Princeton University Press, 1969.
HS   *The Horrors of Slavery and Other Writings by Robert Wedderburn.* Ed. Iain McCalman. Edinburgh: Edinburgh University Press, 1991.
LCS   London Corresponding Society
LHC   John Thelwall, *A Letter to Henry Cline, Esq. on Imperfect Developements of the Faculties, Mental and Moral, as well as Constitutional and Organic; and on the Treatment of Impediments of Speech.* London: Arch, Ridgeway, Kent, and Mackie, 1810.
LJT   Mrs. [Cecil] Thelwall, *The Life of John Thelwall.* London: John Macrone, 1837.
MWC   E. P. Thompson, *The Making of the English Working Class.* New York: Vintage, 1963.
P   John Thelwall, *The Peripatetic,* 3 vols. London: Thelwall, 1793. Rpt with intro. by Donald H. Reiman. New York and London: Garland, 1978.
PEJ   *The Politics of English Jacobinism. Writings of John Thelwall.* Ed. Gregory Claeys. University Park: Pennsylvania State University Press, 1995.
PH   *Parliamentary History of England,* 36 vols. London: T. C. Hansard, 1801–3; 1806–20.
PJC   P. J. Corfield and Chris Evans, "John Thelwall in Wales: New Doc-

umentary Evidence," *Bulletin of the Institute of Historical Research* 59 (1986): 231–39.

PL   John Thelwall, *Political Lectures. No. 1. On the Moral Tendency of a System of Spies and Informers*. London: John Thelwall, 1794.

Poems   John Thelwall, *Poems, Chiefly Written in Retirement*, 2nd edition. Hereford: W. H. Parker, 1801. Rpt. Oxford: Woodstock Books, 1989.

PR   Michael Scrivener, *Poetry and Reform. Periodical Verse from the English Democratic Press 1792–1824*. Detroit: Wayne State University Press, 1992.

PVS   John Thelwall, *Poems on Various Subjects*, 2 vols. London: John Denis, 1787.

PWTS   *The Political Works of Thomas Spence*. Ed. H. T. Dickinson. Newcastle upon Tyne: Avero, 1982.

ST   T. B. Howell, *A Complete Collection of State Trials, 33 vols*. London: Hansard, 1817.

T   John Thelwall, *The Trident of Albion, An Epic Effusion; And an Oration on the Influence of Elocution on Martial Enthusiasm; with an Address to the Shade of Nelson*. Liverpool: G. F. Harris, 1805.

TJT   John Newton, *The Trial at Large of John Thelwall for High Treason*. London: H. D. Symonds, 1795.

TR   E. P. Thompson, *The Romantics: England in a Revolutionary Age*. New York: The New Press, 1997.

TRW   Erasmus Perkins [George Cannon], *The Trial of the Rev. Robert Wedderburn*. London: E. Perkins, 1820.

WTP   Moncure Daniel Conway, ed., *The Writings of Thomas Paine*, 4 vols. 1894–96 rpt. New York: AMS Press, 1967.

Introduction

> Socrates was found, as usual, in
> the places of public resort—in the
> workshops of the artists, and
> among the labourers in the
> manufactories, uttering seditious
> allegories, and condemning the
> desolating tyranny of the
> Oligarchy.
>
> —John Thelwall, *The Rights of
> Nature*, Letter 1 (1796; PEJ 401)

From about 1792 to 1797 Jacobin and other radical writing proceeded from a vigorous public sphere, both plebeian and middle class, and mounted a challenge to aristocratic power serious enough to provoke repression and a cultural counterrevolution. Such writing, much of it experimental, mixed oral and print-culture forms, popularized literary and intellectual traditions that had long been outside the reach of middling-class and laboring-class readers, and introduced novel emphases into prose and poetry. In the 1790s Jacobins changed London cultural life with their periodicals, novels, plays, lectures, meetings, pamphlets, songs, and poetry. By the end of the 1790s, however, literary Jacobinism barely existed: Jacobin writing had been repressed and Jacobin ideas were stigmatized, and even the most moderate reform was taboo.

To be sure, not all the radicals and reformers in the 1790s were Jacobins, even though reactionaries labeled the entire left-of-center as Jacobin. True

Introduction

Jacobins were committed to republicanism and religious heterodoxy (either deism or Dissent); most also advocated with a rationalistic rigor an expanded public sphere, participatory democracy, and international solidarity. Jacobins were a minority in the parliamentary reform movement because their republicanism conflicted with the constitutionalist emphasis on a political structure balanced among monarchical, aristocratic, and democratic forces. Many Dissenters, repelled by deism and what they perceived as extreme views on marriage, kept a distance from Jacobinism and promoted a more moderate, circumscribed version of reform. Jacobin internationalism, especially at the time of the invasion scare of the late 1790s and even more so from 1803 with the resumption of war with Napoleon, was decidedly unpopular. Even in the early and middle nineties much of the reform sentiment and sympathy for the French Revolution—from the Foxite Whigs in parliament to the Dissenters in the Society for Constitutional Information—was hardly Jacobin. Authentic Jacobinism was above all systematic, theoretical, and rationalistic, so that it was to some extent immune from emotional reactions to the French Revolution's decline and turn toward tyranny. Jacobins like Thomas Spence in fact moved further left as the revolution across the channel floundered, as merely political solutions appeared less adequate than the fundamental restructuring of property. Jacobinism was not the only source of radical and reformist ideas in the 1790s; Dissent, Whig, millennialist, and constitutionalist conceptions competed with or complemented Jacobin notions. The Jacobins, however, were the most radical and, fairly or not, the most closely tied to the fate of the revolution in France; they played a representative role much larger than their numbers.

The story of the British Jacobins[1] and their writing has been passed down to us in a distorted form in part because of Wordsworth and Coleridge, at one point both Jacobins themselves. The received narrative is that the decline and fall of Jacobinism was due to its own weaknesses and intellectual errors, not repression or coercion. *The Prelude* dramatizes Wordsworth's disillusionment with Jacobin ideas but neglects the repression and loyalist violence. Coleridge was, if anything, more evasive than Wordsworth: Coleridge's

---

1. I use throughout this study the problematic word "British," which both registers and represses the coercive and complicated union between England, Scotland, and Wales. After 1800, of course, Ireland is a most reluctant part of Britain—and only after the violence of 1798. Most of the Jacobins about whom I write are English, but "British" correctly identifies the political status of people in that historical moment while it does not designate ethnic or national identity.

Introduction

essays distance himself from the Jacobins, as though he himself had never been one. Later critics, disillusioned with Soviet Communism, saw a repetition of "the God that failed" in Wordsworth's and Coleridge's experience.[2] The poets' own anxious distortions combined with modern repudiations of Bolshevism have conspired to substitute historical projection for sober analysis of the formally innovative writing of the Jacobins.

To recover another side to the narrative of British Jacobinism it is necessary to study what and how the Jacobins wrote in their own terms, not the later ones of apostates. John Thelwall's work is useful for this internal understanding of Jacobin writing. Thelwall was a gifted, courageous political thinker, a stirring orator, and energetic activist during the 1790s. He was victimized by political repression, but acquitted of treason in December 1794 after seven months in the Tower and Newgate Prison. He and Thomas Paine were the two major theorists for the Jacobin artisans in the 1790s, according to E. P. Thompson. Thelwall, who "straddled the world of Wordsworth and of Coleridge, and the world of the Spitalfields weavers," was able to offer "a consistent ideology" to Jacobin artisans, as he "took Jacobinism to the borders of Socialism" and "revolutionism" (MWC 457–60). In 1795 his popular twice-a-week political lectures, which were published in *The Tribune* after their delivery, provoked the government's passage of the Two Acts — called Gagging Acts by the radicals — that prohibited political lecturing.

Observing the letter if not the spirit of the law, Thelwall in 1796–97 lectured on classical history to sympathetic audiences in Norwich, and was invited to lecture at other provincial towns in East Anglia. These otherwise popular lectures at Lynn, Wisbech, Yarmouth, and Derby were disrupted by loyalist crowds of sailors and soldiers. Almost kidnapped and impressed, Thelwall was compelled to draw his revolver more than a few times in self-defense, while several other times only the intervention of friends saved him from harm and injury. Although the government does not seem to have plotted Thelwall's assassination, it certainly wanted him out of radical politics.[3]

---

2. M. H. Abrams, in *Natural Supernaturalism: Tradition and Revolution in Romantic Literature* (New York: W. W. Norton, 1971), and the influential essay, "English Romanticism: The Spirit of the Age" (1963) rpt. in Harold Bloom, ed., *Romanticism and Consciousness. Essays in Criticism* (New York: W. W. Norton, 1970), 91–119, identifies Romanticism with both secularizing religious millennialism and superseding revolutionary politics with Romantic imagination. Abrams came of intellectual age in the late 1930s and 1940s, when the controversy over the Soviet Union was most intense among literary intellectuals.

3. E. P. Thompson, "Hunting the Jacobin Fox," *Past and Present* 142 (1994): 103–4; TR, 165. See also Thelwall's own account in *An Appeal to Popular Opinion, Against Kidnapping*

Introduction

Prohibited from lecturing and journalism, shadowed by spies, forced to retire to a Welsh farm, discouraged by the course of the revolution in France, devastated by the death of his young daughter, Thelwall became one of the models for Wordsworth's Solitary in *The Excursion*. In E. P. Thompson's words, "Thelwall was driven into despondent solitude not only by his own weaknesses and disappointed illusions and 'the failure of the French Revolution' but by the bearing down of the whole of established culture and established power upon him" — something Wordsworth neglected to mention in his poem.[4] Repression begets repression. *The Excursion* fails to represent the loyalist violence that targeted Thelwall and other Jacobins and has not a word to spare on the effects of repressive legislation, but pronounces confidently upon the French Revolution and radical politics. Although *The Prelude* represents the French Revolution more complexly, the poem sets up radical politics as an error, to be overcome before the imagination can perform its most authentic tasks.

The failure of the Jacobin, the defeat of Jacobinism, and the verdict of "history" look quite different from the perspective of the Jacobins themselves, especially those who, like Thelwall, never recanted their radicalism. There is another story about Jacobinism that *The Excursion* and even *The Prelude* do not tell. British Jacobinism expanded and reshaped the public sphere; initiated numerous literary experiments; sustained bold inquiries into culture, embracing questions ranging from hairstyles and child rearing to theology and women's rights; captured the allegiance of many talented intellectuals; and strongly influenced the novel and the London theater. Jacobinism exerted considerable cultural power in Britain. In terms of political theory and models of political organizing, the Jacobins set a pattern and established paradigms that were sustained by an important minority into the Reform agitation of 1830–32, the war of the unstamped in the 1830s, and Chartism.[5] The most fearless investigations into political economy bring Jacobin thinking to the brink of modernity, with anticipations by Paine and

---

and Murder; Including A Narrative of the Late Atrocious Proceedings, at Yarmouth. 2nd ed. With a Postscript; Containing A Particular Account of the Outrages, At Lynn and Wisbeach (London: J. S. Jordan, 1796).

4. Thompson, "Hunting the Jacobin Fox," *Past and Present*, 129–30; TR, 201.

5. See Gareth Stedman Jones, *Languages of Class: Studies in English Working Class History, 1832–1982* (Cambridge: Cambridge University Press, 1983). J. R. Dinwiddy argues that after 1830 radicals interpreted the French Revolution as a conflict between 1789 liberals and 1793 socialists, but popular radicalism after the 1790s was not Jacobin. *Radicalism and Reform in Britain, 1790–1850* (London: Hambledon Press, 1992), 217, 228.

Introduction

Thelwall of social democracy, by Spence and Hall of socialism, by Godwin of anarchism and communism. Ideologically, according to Gregory Claeys, two tendencies emerged from the utopianism of the 1790s. One "led from a new democratic form of commercial republicanism towards the more welfare-oriented forms of liberal democracy," while the "second, scouted by Godwin and Spence, pointed towards socialist proposals for a complete community of goods in order to abolish vice and poverty, and to efforts to eliminate political conflict altogether."[6]

The Gagging Acts of December 1795, loyalist violence against Jacobin lecturers in 1796–97, and finally the outlawing altogether of the London Corresponding Society in 1799, marked the decline of political Jacobinism, while cultural Jacobinism survived somewhat longer. By the end of the anti-Jacobin cultural reaction (1797–1805), only a tiny group of writers sustained any public Jacobinism into the nineteenth century, especially from the onset of the anti-Napoleonic war in 1803–4, when even Jacobins like William Frend became British patriots against the French.[7] When national reform politics revived with Sir Francis Burdett's independent radicalism in 1809, and especially with the popular radicalism after Waterloo, even radical reform was often pointedly un-Jacobin. The most prominent leaders of the second wave of democratic reform, such as Burdett, Orator Hunt, and Cobbett, were ostentatiously not Jacobins. Those who could be called Jacobin at that time were a minority: plebeian followers of Thomas Paine (such as Richard Carlile) and of Thomas Spence (such as Robert Wedderburn), as well as the polite Jacobins: William Hazlitt, Percy and Mary W. Shelley. The old "Jacks" such as John Thelwall, William Frend, George Dyer, and Francis Place of course still bore the name. Although the second wave of reform agitation was far larger than the first, it was less Jacobin, if we compare Cobbett with Thelwall and Orator Hunt with Paine. Reacting in part to anti-Gallic loyalism and the unpopularity of Paine's deistic *Age of Reason*, the second wave of reformers projected traditional and nationalist qualities.

The central figure of this study is John Thelwall, called by Günther Lottes the prototypical Jacobin man of letters.[8] He is a usefully central figure for a

---

6. Gregory Claeys, ed., *Utopias of the British Enlightenment* (Cambridge: Cambridge University Press, 1994), xxviii.

7. J. Ann Hone, *For the Cause of Truth: Radicalism in London, 1796–1821* (Oxford: Clarendon Press, 1982), 134–35.

8. Günther Lottes, *Politische Aufklärung und plebejisches Publikum. Zur Theorie und*

number of reasons. He wrote political prose comparable in complexity and rigor to that written by Burke, Paine, and Godwin.[9] An ambitious poet before his conversion to Jacobinism, he continued to write and reflect on poetry throughout his career. Thelwall's influence on the poetry of Coleridge and Wordsworth has long been of interest to scholars.[10] He wrote two Jacobin novels, several plays, and several autobiographical narratives. As a journalist from the 1790s to the 1820s, he edited magazines and newspapers, wrote lead articles, reviewed plays, produced literary criticism, and made political commentary.[11] Although Thelwall moderated his political stance after the 1790s, he never recanted his radicalism. In 1818 he renewed his career as a political activist as editor-owner of the radical-reform *Champion* newspaper. Coming from the same "middling" class that provided members for the London Corresponding Society and that filled the ranks of Jacobin intellectuals and writers, Thelwall was outside the genteel Oxbridge culture but within the literate London intelligentsia. (According to the Marxist historian R. S. Neale, the middling class was in fact the most politically insurgent class in the early nineteenth century.)[12] Thelwall's lectures, however

Praxis des englishchen Rakicalismus im spatën 18. Jahrhundert (Munich: R. Oldenbourg Verlag, 1979), 224.

   9. Gregory Claeys in his introduction to the recent edition of Thelwall's political prose locates Thelwall's thought in the context of political theory. PEJ xiii–lvi.

   10. Judith Thompson's "An Autumnal Blast, A Killing Frost: Coleridge's Poetic Conversation with John Thelwall," *Studies in Romanticism* 36 (1997): 427–56, explores the Thelwall-Coleridge connection at the level of figurative influences. " 'A Voice in the Representation': John Thelwall and the Enfranchisement of Literature," in Tilottama Rajan and Julia M. Wright, eds., *Romanticism, History, and the Possibilities of Genre: Re-Forming Literature, 1789–1837* (Cambridge: Cambridge University Press, 1998), 142–44, discusses Wordsworth and Thelwall in relation to *The Peripatetic*. Nicholas Roe treats Thelwall with Wordsworth and Coleridge in *Wordsworth and Coleridge: The Radical Years* (Oxford: Clarendon Press, 1988), and "Coleridge and John Thelwall: The Road to Nether Stowey," *The Coleridge Connection*, ed. R. Gravil and M. Lefebure (New York: St. Martin's Press, 1990). Another treatment of Thelwall with Coleridge and Wordsworth is the fifth chapter of Vernon Owen Grumbling's dissertation, "John Thelwall: Romantick and Revolutionist" (Ph.D. diss., University of New Hampshire, 1977). E. P. Thompson writes on Thelwall, Wordsworth, and Coleridge in "Disenchantment or Default? A Lay Sermon" (1969) and "Hunting the Jacobin Fox" (1994; 1997).

   11. For his journalism, see Michael Scrivener, "John Thelwall and the Press," in Stephen C. Behrendt, ed., *Romanticism, Radicalism, and the Press* (Detroit: Wayne State University Press, 1997), 120–36.

   12. For the centrality of the "middling classes" from the late eighteenth to the mid-nineteenth century, see R. S. Neale, *Class in English History, 1680–1850* (Totowa, N.J.: Barnes and Noble, 1981). According to Neale, who develops a "five-class" sociological model—upper, middle, middling, and working class A and B, the "middling class" emerges "as the central, most unstable and most significant political class in England in the period from 1800 to the 1840s" (136–37).

briefly, addressed socially diverse audiences, thus reflecting his connections with both the radical underground of Thomas Spence and the aristocratic radicalism of Sir Francis Burdett. As both a pioneering writer and thinker in British Jacobinism's earliest days and as an anachronistic "saved remnant" in the 1820s, Thelwall provides a line of development interesting in itself and useful for contrastive purposes.[13]

The established authorities crushed British Jacobinism and the reform movement in general with a massive if also inefficient repression. Whether the movement was really as dangerous as the Pitt government thought is another question.[14] The most fearful aspect of Jacobinism, exaggerated or not, was the social radicalism attached to a growing public sphere. The stunning popularity of Paine's *The Rights of Man* (part one, 1791; part two, 1792) restructured literacy and provoked an intensive campaign of counterpropaganda by loyalist forces. The unprecedented sales of parts one and two—easily in the hundreds of thousands within two years, approaching or exceeding a million by the start of the new century—illustrated that the literary market for democratic literature was far greater than anyone at the time had imagined was possible. Whether Paine tapped into an already existing audience that was merely waiting for the right text, or whether Paine's essay in some sense created this audience, is difficult to determine. For Richard Altick the most significant result of Paine's popularity was the "reaction of the ruling class," which was alarmed by the "potentialities inherent in the press" at a time of war. Democratic propaganda had to be suppressed, but these "crowds of readers . . . could be deprived of their literacy by no device short of extermination."[15]

Jon Klancher has shown how in the nineteenth century the politically rad-

---

13. Hone, *For the Cause of Truth*, emphasizes the continuity between the 1790s and the later radicalism by pointing to the pragmatism of the radicals: "When they found one way blocked or ineffective, they tried another" (361).

14. The weight of historical commentary leans toward the view that Pitt's repression was excessive, a gross violation of human rights, but some historians view the repression as a reasonable (from the government's perspective) set of actions to prevent revolution. Paralleling modern historians, Southey and Coleridge were convinced, even when they became Tories, that the Pitt repression was immoral and unnecessary, but Walter Scott believed that the repression suppressed a truly revolutionary threat. J. R. Dinwiddy concludes reasonably that a revolution in the 1790s would have been possible only if three things coincided: a French invasion, an Irish rebellion, and severe economic distress. *Radicalism and Reform in Britain, 1780–1850*, 169–94.

15. Richard D. Altick, *The English Common Reader: A Social History of the Mass Reading Public* (Chicago: University of Chicago Press, 1957), 72–73.

ical potential of a popular audience was weakened by its differentiation into mass and radical readers, with the former group growing at the expense of the latter.[16] Moreover, the new middle-class or Romantic reader displaced an earlier middle-class reader who was a reader-*writer* aggressively struggling against aristocratic power. The earlier reader-writer assumed that reading and writing were "not fixed functions but performing roles to be exchanged." The new Romantic readers, however, did not view their periodical literature as a "portable coffeehouse" but as a source of entertainment and information to be consumed, and as an occasion for exercising "cultural power," especially in relation to the mass reader (Klancher 22–23). "The middle-class audience achieves its sense of cultural power by continually dismantling and reconstituting signs" (Klancher 73) that remain indecipherable for the mass reader (Klancher 76–97). In the four and a half decades that Thelwall was most active as a writer, he both resisted and succumbed to the pressures described by Klancher. He performed the roles of radical and Romantic writer as well as those of reader-writer.

The key text for modern studies of the popular reader is Jürgen Habermas's 1962 *Strukturwandel der Öffentlichkeit* (*The Structural Transformation of the Public Sphere*), which makes two controversial points (he has modified these to some extent recently). First, there emerged in the eighteenth century a "public sphere" outside official government institutions and critical of them; this sphere, imperfectly egalitarian, was nevertheless characterized by a high degree of effective rationality. Second, this public sphere that permitted the exercise of critical reason, however compromised by incomplete participation, was transformed by the growth of industrial capitalism; the discursive space, once free of official government control (except for acts of repression and orchestrated violence), was restructured by the mass culture that emerged in the nineteenth century and that became fully developed

---

16. Jon Klancher, *The Making of the English Reading Audiences* (Madison: University of Wisconsin Press, 1987). Scholars inspired by Foucault and Marx have argued that Romantic literature itself played an indispensable role in forming modes of popular reading that constituted social control. Long before there were mass public educational institutions capable of disciplining and punishing a newly literate population, print culture performed the role of shaping consciousness. Among the Foucaultian studies are those by Clifford Siskin, *The Historicity of Romantic Discourse* (New York: Oxford University Press, 1988), and Nancy Armstrong, *Desire and Domestic Fiction: A Political History of the Novel* (New York: Oxford University Press, 1987). Jerome McGann's *The Romantic Ideology* (Chicago: University of Chicago Press, 1983) inspired the more Marxian approaches.

Introduction

in the twentieth. Habermas's more recent ideas on the public sphere in response to his critics concede the importance of a proletarian "counter-public sphere" and the distortions of rationality effected by the exclusion of women.[17] This study of Thelwall and Jacobin writing confirms Habermas's most recent ideas on the public sphere and audience differentiation. I use the phrase "public sphere" to signify both the plebeian "counter-public sphere" and the "bourgeois public sphere," but the context will make clear the social nature of the sphere to which I am referring. The public sphere was indeed differentiated by class and gender, but at least prior to 1832 the middle-class public sphere permitted discussion critical of established power and was at times indistinguishable from the plebeian public sphere.[18]

The public sphere generated a great deal of socially critical discourse at that time, perhaps because the "middling classes" had not yet become the more monolithic "middle class" fearfully disdainful of the "working class." Artisans, tradesmen, shopkeepers, and lower- and middle-level professionals in law, journalism, medicine, and religion challenged aristocratic power. Although some Jacobins, such as Coleridge, Southey, William Frend, and Wordsworth, were from the lower regions of elite social strata, most, such as Paine, Godwin, Wollstonecraft, Thelwall, Francis Place, Thomas Spence, and William Blake, came from the "middling" classes. A second generation of Jacobins—including Wollstonecraft's daughter and Godwin's son-in-law, and the artisan followers of Thomas Spence—sustains Jacobinism into the early nineteenth century. The British Jacobins, who were neither socially nor ideologically homogeneous, pursued with logical rigor their political and religious radicalism toward feminism and plans for redistributing property. Their republicanism was not simply negative—calling for church disestablishment, the abolition of monarchy and the House of Lords—but, more important, promoted unconstrained civil discourse. The British Jacobins,

---

17. Jürgen Habermas, *The Structural Transformation of the Public Sphere: An Inquiry into a Category of Bourgeois Society* (Cambridge, Mass.: MIT Press, 1989). See also Craig Calhoun, ed., *Habermas and the Public Sphere* (Cambridge, Mass.: MIT Press, 1992). For Romanticists applying the concept of the counter-public sphere, see the essays in the special issue of *Studies in Romanticism* 33 (1994). Paul Magnuson stresses Habermas's early formulation of an exclusively educated public sphere to contrast the nonexclusive Jacobin counter-public spheres in *Reading Public Romanticism* (Princeton: Princeton University Press, 1998), chap. 1.

18. Andrew McCann, *Cultural Politics in the 1790s: Literature, Radicalism and the Public Sphere* (New York and London: St. Martin's Press and Macmillan, 1999), 3; he discusses the public sphere in the context of Marxism and poststructuralism, 1–32.

both polite and plebeian, struggled to emancipate the public sphere that sustained their critical thinking.[19]

Jacobinism reshapes literary culture in numerous ways. The specifically Jacobin public sphere—political associations, lectures, meetings, trials—generates new kinds of reading and writing—pamphlets, songs, periodicals, oratory, popularizations. Jacobins initiate a popular literary culture that undermines aristocratic assumptions about writing and is reminiscent of the radical Protestant culture of the seventeenth century.[20] Men and women from social strata whose language supposedly is outside of "learning" and the fullest expressive capacities narrate their lives in ways that challenge aristocratic control. Oral and print culture conventions are synthesized and mutually influence one another, provoking attempts to capture more faithfully the syntax and tonalities of conversational speech as writers react against poetic diction. The hierarchy of genres undergoes a kind of leveling. Jacobinism, then, alters the very institutions of reading and writing by expanding literacy, by restructuring the popular reader, and by generating a body of diverse texts that are "seditious allegories."

Literary Jacobinism's penchant for allegory might have appeared anachronistic if we had not been reminded by Walter Benjamin, Paul de Man, and others that the dominance of the Romantic symbol was less than complete. Allegory's importance in the Romantic period is now taken for granted. Even Coleridge, largely responsible for popularizing Goethe's preference for symbol over allegory, was not dogmatic about symbolism in either his theory or his poetry. Recently Theresa Kelley wrote about the Romantic *ambivalence* toward allegory.[21] The British Jacobins, far less

---

19. The extent to which the polite Jacobins and other reformers depended on what amounts to a coffeehouse culture has not been sufficiently appreciated. Horne Tooke's Wimbledon circle had biweekly Sunday dinners; the London Philomathians (Godwin, Holcroft, Thelwall) also met biweekly; the Burdettites depended on the British Forum, the Athenian Lyceum, and the Robin Hood Society (Hone, *For the Cause of Truth* [147]). Plebeian radicals depended on different sites: taverns, open-air meetings, debating clubs.

20. See Timothy Morton and Nigel Smith, eds., *From Revolution to Revolution: Liberty's Journey, 1650–1830* (Cambridge: Cambridge University Press, 2001) for essays—including my own on Thelwall ("John Thelwall and the Revolution of 1649")—that illustrate the continuity between the radical Protestantism of the seventeenth century and the later radicalism.

21. Angus Fletcher provides a critical discussion of Goethe's and Coleridge's accounts of symbol's superiority over allegory. *Allegory: The Theory of a Symbolic Mode* (Ithaca: Cornell University Press, 1964), 13–19. The influential de Man essay, "The Rhetoric of Temporality" (1969), owes a massive debt to Walter Benjamin's ideas on allegory published in *The Origins of German Tragic Drama*, trans. John Osborne (London: Verso, 1977), 159–235. John Hodgson's

Introduction

ambivalent, wrote allegories, produced allegorical texts, practiced and provoked allegorical interpretation. Allegory seems to be the inevitable literary mode to reflect the tight interdependence of Jacobinism and anti-Jacobinism that was only strengthened by the violence of twenty-two years of war (1793–1815).[22]

Marilyn Butler has written of the "war of ideas" and the inescapable ideological conflict played out by Jacobin and anti-Jacobin novelists.[23] Allegory exists at two separate but related levels: as a recognized literary form that invited allegorical interpretation, and as an effect of aggressive interpretation that turns literary texts into allegories even when the allegorical generic markers are lacking. Coleridge in 1809 cites Archdeacon Paley about the omnipresence of Jacobin allegory and subversive discourse: "political Heresy" and religious "Infidelity" are everywhere, "served up in every shape, that is likely to allure, surprise, or beguile the imagination; in a fable, a tale, a novel, a poem; in interspersed and broken hints; remote and oblique surmises; in books of Travels, of Philosophy, of Natural History; in a word, in any form, rather than the right one, that of professed and regular disquisition" (F 2:27). If there is an evil Other implied by Paley's polemic, the versatile and prolific John Thelwall might have been it. After the Gagging Acts and Church and King violence made political lecturing impossible, Thelwall still published travel essays, as well as philosophical and scientific observations, in periodicals, books, and pamphlets, all of which challenged aristocratic power, even if indirectly and allegorically.

Political repression and anti-Jacobinism were the conditions under which Thelwall and other Jacobins had to write. The Jacobins inventively circumvented the repression, exploiting trials to their advantage, comically revising anti-Jacobin constructions, and challenging the repressive authorities. A

---

lucid study of Coleridge's ideas on allegory and symbol takes, as does de Man, a rhetorical approach. "Transcendental Tropes: Coleridge's Rhetoric of Allegory and Symbol," in Morton W. Bloomfield, ed., *Allegory, Myth, and Symbol* (Cambridge, Mass.: Harvard University Press, 1981), 273–92. Chapters 5 and 6 of Theresa Kelley's recent *Reinventing Allegory* (Cambridge: Cambridge University Press, 1997) provide a rich commentary on Romantic allegory.

22. Stuart Curran has stressed the influence of the long war on British Romanticism. See his preface to *The Cambridge Companion to British Romanticism*, which he also edited (Cambridge: Cambridge University Press, 1993), xiii. Marjorie Levinson was one of the first critics to link allegory and Keats's class position in *The Origins of Keats's Style: A Life of Allegory* (Oxford: Blackwell, 1988); see esp. 125–27, where Keats's own life is seen as an allegory because of its class-determined "lack."

23. Marilyn Butler, *Jane Austen and the War of Ideas* (Oxford: Clarendon Press, 1975).

favorite toast of Thomas Paine captures the Jacobin attitude toward repression: "The best way of advertising good books—by prosecution."[24] Repression made allegory a useful literary form, the ambiguity of which was convenient at trials. Allegories also appealed to popular audiences used to interpreting biblical and Aesopian texts. Moreover, the repression was so severe, the anti-Jacobin reaction so relentless, the political conflict so sharp, that another kind of allegory was commonplace: even when Jacobins wrote about ostensibly apolitical topics, readers could find a displaced political meaning nevertheless.

The political repression was as harsh as it was because of a great fear of the popular audience. A major thrust of Jacobin culture was popularization, making texts wholly or partly accessible to a popular audience that ordinarily would never read such things because of their constrained opportunities for learning. Excerpts from older and contemporary authors were featured in Thomas Spence's *Pig's Meat* (1793–96) and Daniel Isaac Eaton's *Politics for the People* (1793–95), both of which became digests of Jacobin writing. Thelwall popularized classical and republican writing in his essays and lectures. His edition of Walter Moyle's *An Essay Upon the Constitution of the Roman Government* (1698), retitled provocatively *Democracy Vindicated* (1796), and with the Latin translated and the references explained, is yet another example of Jacobin popularization.[25] Such popularization was an extension and application of Enlightenment assumptions concerning the reader-writer. A Jacobin allegory of where popularization could lead was Godwin's *Caleb Williams* (1794), itself a popularization of the ideas in *Political Justice* (1793); the novel represents the self-education of a servant who learns to demystify the pretenses of his aristocratic master, whose crimes he exposes to the public. His daughter's *Frankenstein* is another allegory of popularization, in which the creature, versed in Volney, Plutarch, Milton, and Goethe, inflicts violently retributive justice on a world that labels him monstrous. Godwin was in fact ambivalent about popularization and anxious about the plebeian public sphere, a source of bitter controversy in the London Corresponding Society (LCS).[26]

---

24. Quoted in Gregory Claeys, *Thomas Paine: Social and Political Thought* (Boston: Unwin Hyman, 1989), 28.
25. For a more extensive treatment of *Democracy Vindicated*, see my essay "John Thelwall and the Revolution of 1649," in Timothy Morton and Nigel Smith, eds., *From Revolution to Revolution*.
26. It is possible that Godwin's qualms about the plebeian public sphere disqualify him as a true Jacobin, but I prefer to keep him under the Jacobin tent—if just barely—because of the other aspects of his radicalism that are unquestionably Jacobin.

Introduction

In two separate periods, 1792–97 and 1816–21, there were extraordinary outbursts of popular creativity that accompanied a democratic political insurgence. I agree with the historian Dinwiddy in saying that Jacobinism predominated in the first period and played a lesser role in the second.[27] Just short of a certain degree of severity, repression does not seem to have stifled creativity but to have stimulated it, to have been in fact an inspiring muse. As Terence Alan Hoagwood has pointed out, texts produced under political repression thematize their own readability by problematizing the act of reading.[28] As interpretation became inscribed within the text itself, Jacobin allegories were in fact at the very center of the most innovative literary transformations of the 1790s. Reading an ambiguous surface for meaning was a commonplace activity in Jacobin culture, assisted in no small way by Edmund Burke's "wild rhetoric."[29] Jacobin writers were also savvy ironists, revising established literary forms. Another way literary Jacobinism is indistinguishable from the most innovative dimensions of Romanticism was in how the issue of the popular became central for Romantic poetics. As Annette Wheeler Cafarelli has recently shown, the Romantics were preoccupied with but also conflicted and contradictory about popularization.[30] Just as the Jacobins were not ambivalent about allegory, they—Godwin excepted—were enthusiastic popularizers.

Thelwall's career illustrates some of the differences between Jacobin writing and Romantic literature, Jacobin writers and Romantic authors. The process that turns writing into literature and writers into authors begins with Renaissance "self-crowned laureates" and related phenomena at a time when print culture only started to become dominant. If this is true, then one has to make some careful qualifications.[31] Literature and authors did not blossom suddenly, fully developed, in the Romantic period, nor did writing and writers completely disappear after the 1830s. "Writer" and "author" designate cultural functions, not human beings as such. John Donne and George Her-

---

27. Dinwiddy, *Radicalism and Reform in Britain, 1790–1850*, 214.
28. Terence Allan Hoagwood, *Politics, Philosophy, and the Production of Romantic Texts* (DeKalb: Northern Illinois University Press, 1996), 3.
29. For the phrase "wild rhetoric" I am indebted to Henry Golemba's *Thoreau's Wild Rhetoric* (New York: New York University Press, 1990).
30. Annette Wheeler Caferelli, "The Common Reader: Social Class in Romantic Poetics," *Journal of English and Germanic Philology* 96 (1997): 222–46.
31. Following Richard Helgerson's *Self-Crowned Laureates: Spenser, Jonson, Milton and the Literary System* (Berkeley and Los Angeles: University of California Press, 1983), there has been much research describing the birth of the author and literary authority of the early modern period.

bert the writers within manuscript collections become John Donne and George Herbert the authors in single-authored books of their poetry.[32] Most famous of all is Shakespeare the writer, who becomes the author only after his death: a socially engaged and practical writer who borrowed omnivorously from multiple sources becomes the most celebrated example of the autonomous, transcendent, original author. Thelwall illustrates the constructedness of these distinctions. Prevented by political repression and cultural reaction from performing the role of Jacobin writer, he turned to the role of Romantic author in 1801 with his *Poems*. Similarly, in 1822, after four years as radical editor and orator, he was threatened with imprisonment. He then published *The Poetical Recreations of the 'Champion' and His Literary Correspondents*, which turns into Romantic *literature* what had been predominantly Jacobin *writing*. After 1822 Thelwall edited two more periodicals as both writer and author: he continued to sustain the Enlightenment discourse of the reader-writer in pursuit of impersonal Truth but he also cultivated the "leading article" in personally expressive ways, similar to the Romantic prose of Lamb, Hazlitt, and Coleridge. Even before his fame as a Jacobin activist, Thelwall the ambitious poet who earned his money as a Grub Street editor was not immune to the lure of literature and authorship, a lure reflected in one of his early pseudonyms, Wentworth Chatterton. According to legend, Thomas Chatterton had been destroyed by his Grub Street labors but not before his genius had been revealed in poetry marked by both fraud and originality. In short, Thelwall was writer *and* author who produced writing *and* literature his entire career.[33]

The first part of this book describes the origins of Thelwall's Jacobin writing by tracing the evolution of the word "Jacobin" in France and Britain, and by

---

32. Arthur F. Marotti, *Manuscript, Print, and the English Renaissance Lyric* (Ithaca: Cornell University Press, 1995), 247–50.
33. A useful way of looking at the literature/writing distinction is Anne Janowitz's discussion of individualistic and communitarian tendencies within a single Romanticism. Jacobin writing, then, would be largely communitarian, while Romantic literature would be more individualistic. " 'A Voice from across the Sea': Communitarianism at the Limits of Romanticism," in Mary A. Favret and Nicola J. Watson, eds., *At the Limits of Romanticism: Essays in Cultural, Feminist, and Materialist Criticism* (Bloomington and Indianapolis: Indiana University Press, 1994), 83–100. Janowitz's fuller treatment appears in *Lyric and Labour in the Romantic Tradition* (Cambridge: Cambridge University Press, 1998). Another recent treatment of the writing/literature contrast is Siskin's *The Work of Writing*. Siskin sees writing as a technology that is "disciplined" by the spiritualizing force of literature. Paul Magnuson (*Reading Public Romanticism*) shows, however, that even the most subjective-seeming Romantic lyrics are also public

Introduction

describing Thelwall's rebuttals of Burke's anti-Jacobin writing. Thelwall's responses to Burke, not nearly as well known as Paine's, elaborate some themes Paine never developed extensively: a defense of the expanded public sphere, an appropriation of classical culture, and a proto-Marxist theory of labor. In favor of universal suffrage, Thelwall supported both a representative democracy and a proliferation of decentralized cultural groups—scientific, literary, educational societies—whose interaction would also "speak" with legitimacy and authority.

The second part describes how Thelwall and other members of the LCS worked through a set of problems that I have linked under the phrase, "the voice of the people." As radical lecturer, journalist, activist, and essayist, Thelwall fashioned himself as a "tribune," a "champion," a mediating figure to represent his own ideas and defend the interests of the disenfranchised. Poised between plebeian and middle-class audiences, Thelwall was unique in addressing such different kinds of readers successfully, even though, as Thompson shows, he largely ignored the artisan audience after the 1790s.[34] Thelwall works with and against the conventions of spontaneous plain speaking and willfully crafted rhetoric. Strategies of self-disclosure and self-authorization punctuate discourses that often hinge on a dramatized "intemperance" yielding ultimately to moderate caution. The pattern of losing and regaining control parallels his political theme: "Without reform, revolution." The motto for *The Tribune* from Hayley, "To paint the voice, and fix its fleeting sound," becomes a suggestive metaphor for Thelwall's political writing: how exactly is the vox populi, which is the vox dei, to assume a fixed form? In Thelwall's role as editor and lead writer for periodicals in the 1790s and later, he recurrently fashioned strategies of interpreting the popular voice.

"Voice" means something else as well to Thelwall, who was a professional teacher of elocution and a practicing speech therapist so successful that he earned enough money by his efforts to purchase the newspaper *The Champion* in 1818. His scientific and therapeutic preoccupation with voice is not utterly disconnected with political radicalism. Although he became a speech therapist only after he was forced out of radical politics, he wrote on med-

---

performances by virtue of a text's location in the culture's signifying system. The first critic that I know of to have developed extensively the historical contingencies of "literature" in relation to writing was Raymond Williams.

34. Thompson, "Hunting the Jacobin Fox," *Past and Present*, 114–15; TR, 176.

ical science in the early 1790s while he was an activist, and he never ceased to regard "elocution" as a central feature of the human sciences in a democratizing political culture. Thelwall's *Letter to Henry Cline* (1810), ostensibly about speech impediments and the physiology of speaking, is also an allegory of political repression and constrained speech.

The third part of this book, on Jacobin allegory, explores the literary effects of repression, the aggressive interpretive strategies that plumb surface features for deeper meanings, the cat-and-mouse games of transparent but legally deniable seditious references in all kinds of Jacobin writing, and other instances of literary indirection. As early as his play *The Incas* (1792) and as late as his epic poem, *The Hope of Albion* (extracts of which he was publishing in 1826), Thelwall writes allegorically, his characteristic literary mode. His literary criticism and poetry from his earliest career are insistently Romantic rather than Augustan, but for Thelwall imaginative literature exists as part of a larger "truth" that includes science, politics, and unconstrained inquiry of all kinds. If he is a literary Romantic who boldly mixed genres in his *Peripatetic* (1793), who wrote some of the very first "conversation" poems (1796–97), who composed one of the first Romantic lyrical dramas (1801), he is also an unapologetic enlightener, a religious skeptic, a proponent of scientific inquiry in all fields. Appropriately Thelwall concludes his literary career in his sixties as editor-owner of the *Panoramic Miscellany*, a periodical whose community of fellow reader-writers gestures back to the previous century.

In the 1790s the "principle of universal manhood suffrage raised the spectre of mob rule and frightened most men of property," according to H. T. Dickinson.[35] The cultural experimentation and liberal tolerance that marked much of the eighteenth century prior to the 1790s were also socially conservative, even if middle-class Dissenters and landless, unpropertied plebeians could become reader-writers of the British Enlightenment. When men of property largely abandoned the Enlightenment project in 1790s, Jacobins not only sustained but deepened the project with greater egalitarianism. Indeed, the Enlightenment becomes truly radical only after the elite classes abandon it. Replacing the cosmopolitan, international, encyclopedic Enlightenment that had been a cultural consensus for the "learned" classes was the loyalist

---

35. H. T. Dickinson, *Liberty and Property: Political Ideology in Eighteenth-Century Britain* (New York: Holmes and Meier, 1977), 239.

Introduction

nationalism described so vividly by Linda Colley.³⁶ David Simpson has also shown how during the 1790s "theory" becomes suspect within a new "nationalist" consensus.³⁷ The rise of nationalism, localism, and particularism, and the decline of internationalism and rationalist rigor, took place violently and coercively in an atmosphere of panic, not reasoned discussion. The immanent weaknesses (and enduring strengths) of the Enlightenment paradigm and of Jacobinism itself would have emerged eventually, but political repression and cultural reaction silenced what was still alive with potentiality. Because of the premature abandonment of both Enlightenment and Jacobin modes of cultural expression, we find that Thelwall's oeuvre still attracts interest and requires our attention.

---

36. Linda Colley, *Britons: Forging a Nation, 1707–1837* (New Haven: Yale University Press, 1992).
37. David Simpson, *Romanticism, Nationalism, and the Revolt Against Theory* (Chicago: University of Chicago Press, 1993).

part

1

Jacobinism

> I considered [for the past four years] a general war against Jacobins and
> Jacobinism, as the only possible chance of saving Europe
> (and England as included in Europe) from a truly frightful Revolution.
> —Edmund Burke, *Observations on the Conduct of the Minority*
> (September 1793; EB 8:404)

> Jacobinism is the revolt of the enterprising talents of a country against it's [*sic*] property.
> —Edmund Burke, *Two Letters on a Regicide Peace* (1796; EB 8:241)

> I use the term Jacobinism simply to indicate *a large and comprehensive system
> of reform, not professing to be built upon the authorities
> and principles of the Gothic customary.*
> —John Thelwall, *The Rights of Nature* (1796; PEJ 454)

> If we are Jacobins, and jacobinism is a crime, the historians, the philosophers,
> the poets and the legislators of antiquity were Jacobins also.
> —John Thelwall, *Moral and Political Magazine* (1796)

> Above all, we have to crush and disable the system of jacobinism, or if we
> even fail in completely destroying that monster, we should at least persevere till
> we have weakened the instruments and engines by which it propagates its
> principles; for it is generally agreed, that there can be no safety for Europe
> as long as jacobinism remains strong and triumphant.
> —Prime Minister William Pitt, parliamentary speech, 17 February 1800

Jacobinism

In France where there were Jacobin clubs the term "Jacobin" signified a political affiliation, but in Britain "Jacobin" is both an imprecise label by which reactionaries tagged the proponents of even the mildest reform, and a useful analytical term to describe a certain kind of radical politics. Even in France the term "Jacobin" was initially forced upon some radicals by their opponents who wanted to underline—ironically, as "Jacobin" alluded to the Dominican order—the religiously transgressive nature of their ideology. "Jacobinism," then, is a sign that mediates conflicting interpretations and that embodies displacement and the rhetorical figure of catachresis (a term misapplied because of incorrect etymology). These two chapters in the first part of this book, then, describe the origins of Jacobinism—that is, the origins of the discourse about Jacobinism—and depict the fundamental parameters of Jacobin writing in Britain. Burke's *Reflections on the Revolution in France* not only provoked replies that were Jacobin but also provided a rhetorical model and discursive style that Jacobin writers both imitated and ironically undermined. The replies to Burke by Paine and then Thelwall largely constituted the ideological terrain of British Jacobinism, but Burke himself—that is, his writing—created many of the terms by means of which the Jacobins had to argue. Paine and Thelwall were not utterly free to construct a democratic ideology; rather, they had to revise and counter the powerful ideas and images that Burke had already supplied. Burke himself was hardly in control of the ideological conflict, as his famous *Reflections on the Revolution in France* inadvertently opened up an ever-expanding sphere of public discussion about revolutionary politics. Paine, Thelwall, and other writers linked with the London Corresponding Society (LCS) were so successful in exploiting the literary public sphere that the government tried to close it down. Briefly summarized, there was a revolution in France, followed by Burke's provocative criticism, an exploding democratic public sphere, a reactionary repression, and strategies to counter the repression.

Defining Jacobinism

At one point people seemed to know what Jacobinism meant: it was a political ideology with literary manifestations. In 1816 Coleridge unapologetically used the phrase "Jacobin drama" when he attacked Maturin's play *Bertram* in the *Courier* (this was later incorporated into Chapter 23 of *Biographia Literaria*). Whether writing was in the field of theater, poetry, fiction, philosophy, or theology, it might be labeled "Jacobin." But did people really know what Jacobinism meant, or was it merely sloppy name-calling? William Godwin remarks: "It is not at all clear who is to count as a proper English 'Jacobin'—if Jacobin has a more precise reference than simply to radicals in the 1790s."[1] Numerous political theorists then and now, not just Coleridge, have used Jacobinism as a foil for their anti-Jacobin politics, but logical rigor has rarely shaped these statements.[2] The category "Jacobin" was constructed first in France and then in Britain by politically motivated catachresis. The so-called Jacobins accepted the label under protest.

History of the Word "Jacobinism"

A caucus of French deputies from Brittany began, on 30 April 1789, meeting nightly at a café in Versailles. By June the group had attracted some of

---

1. Quoted by Mark Philp, *Godwin's Political Justice* (London: Duckworth, 1986), 141 n.39. On the origins and development of the term "Jacobin," see Paul Magnuson, *Reading Public Romanticism* (Princeton: Princeton University Press, 1998), 15–22.
2. The Jacobins have been harshly criticized by some theorists on the liberal left, notably Albert Camus, who distinguished between Jacobin revolutionaries and antiauthoritarian rebels. Camus saw the Jacobins as prototypical Bolsheviks, that is, as totalitarians. *The Rebel: An Essay on Man in Revolt*, trans. Anthony Bower (New York: Vintage, 1956). In the 1980s as Communism disintegrated there was a harsh retrospective look at the Jacobins, who represented all

the most distinguished revolutionaries: Robespierre, Mirabeau, Pétion, Barnave, Sieyès, and Grégoire. After political proceedings moved from Versailles to Paris in October 1789, Le Club breton began meeting as La Société de la Révolution. (The historical ironies begin to proliferate: the French revolutionaries derived the name of their group from the London organization, the Revolution Society, whose recent declarations of support they had found so inspiring; the London society was commemorating the English revolution of 1688; Richard Price's sermon for the society in November provoked Edmund Burke to write his *Reflections on the Revolution in France*.) After it began admitting members who were not deputies, La Société des amis de la Constitution began to rent space at a Dominican convent on rue St.-Honoré.[3] The building was known as "les Jacobins" because the Dominican monks were called "Jacobins," as the street at one time was called rue St.-Jacques.[4] At first their political opponents derisively called the revolutionaries who met at the Dominican convent "Jacobins," who in turn protested against the label, the ecclesiastical connotations of which ran counter to the group's insistent opposition to feudalism.[5] Indeed, following Mirabeau's proposal of 2 November 1789, property belonging to the Catholic clergy was now at the disposal of the state. As the public persisted in calling the people after the building they rented, despite numerous objections, the group finally adopted the Jacobin name in 21 September 1792: La Société des Jacobins, amis de la liberté et de l' égalité.

The initial catachresis, then, was from the accident of the building's name, itself a result of displacement. The pattern here is one of allegorical displacement, people by buildings, one name by another name, contrary to the intentions of those so named. The medieval Spanish saint Dominic—actually Domingo de Guzman—is displaced by Jacques, St. Jacques de Vitry, Spain by France. One could draw a parallel between the austere idealism of Robespierre, the most famous Jacobin, and Dominic, whose zealous pursuit of heretics characterized the Inquisition. Both Jacobins and Dominicans were

---

that was bad with failing Communism. See Ferenc Feher, *The Frozen Revolution: An Essay on Jacobinism* (Cambridge: Cambridge University Press, 1987), and Ernesto Laclau and Chantal Mouffe, *Hegemony and Socialist Strategy*, trans. Winston Moore and Paul Cammack (London: Verso, 1985).

3. Michael L. Kennedy, *The Jacobin Clubs in the French Revolution: The First Years* (Princeton: Princeton University Press, 1982), 3–5.

4. Evart S. Scudder, *The Jacobins* (London: Arthur Baker, 1936), 16.

5. Francois Victor Alphonse Aulard, *La Société des Jacobins*, Book 1 (1889; rpt. New York: AMS, 1973), xxi–xxii.

enthusiastic proselytizers, dedicated to purifying public morality, proponents of educational reforms, at times sectarian and violent. What seemed like sarcastic irony at first turns out to be prophetic, allegorically precise, as the Jacobins come to resemble in certain nontrivial ways the religious order with which they seem to be only accidentally associated. Not everyone agrees with Crane Brinton's calling the French Jacobins essentially "religious," but some recent historians say that Jacobinism was "first of all a faith."[6] Emmet Kennedy also calls the revolution a religion,[7] and Mona Ozouf has illustrated the extent to which the revolution tried to fill the cultural vacuum left by a suppressed Christianity.[8] Many of the provincial Jacobin clubs met in confiscated church buildings, just like the Paris club, and the Jacobins, following Rousseau, tried to replace Christianity with a civil religion during the unsuccessful de-Christianizing campaign.

After the appropriation of the Jacobin name in 1792 the Jacobin club was to have a violent and abrupt demise in 1794. About four months after Robespierre was executed, the revolutionary government closed down the building, at which further political meetings were prohibited (11 November 1794). The building's new name was, according to Aulard, "Neuf-Thermidor."[9] Nine Thermidor was of course the date on which Robespierre and his Jacobin colleagues were brought before the tribunal as prisoners. There seems to be no end to the ironies of this Dominican convent. In Chapter 4, Book 7 of his history of the French Revolution, Thomas Carlyle records the fall of the Jacobins in an appropriately ironic spirit. "Gone are the Jacobins; into invisibility; in a storm of laughter and howls. Their Place is made a Normal School, the first of the kind seen; it then vanishes into a 'Market of Thermidor Ninth'; into a Market of Saint-Honoré, where is now peaceable chaffering for poultry and greens."[10] Ironically, what has triumphed is not heresy-hunting idealism, religious or political, but "peaceable chaffering for poultry and greens," commerce. The revolutionary attempt to restructure time fails miserably: the building takes its name mechanistically from the street—named after yet

---

6. Crane Brinton, *The Jacobins: An Essay in the New History* (New York: Macmillan Press, 1930), 240.
7. Emmet Kennedy, *A Cultural History of the French Revolution* (New Haven: Yale University Press, 1989), 366, 330.
8. Mona Ozouf, *Festivals and the French Revolution*, trans. Alan Sheridan (1976; rpt. Cambridge, Mass.: Harvard University Press, 1988).
9. Aulard, *La Société des Jacobins*, Book 1, xxvii.
10. Thomas Carlyle, *The French Revolution: A History* (1837; rpt. New York: Random House, 1934), 710.

another Christian saint—to which it is attached. Carlyle's irony is the tragic irony of *vanitas* and the futility of revolutionary idealism. Or perhaps this is allegorical interpretation: the Jacobin revolution merely paved the way for commerce, "peaceable chaffery," the true utopia for a bourgeois revolution.

Carlyle takes note of a word play that was current in 1794 during the Jacobins' decline. "'Down with the Jacobins, the Jacoquins,' *coquin* meaning scoundrel" (709). For all practical purposes the word "Jacobin" now means just that, scoundrel, a political zealot tainted by the Reign of Terror. It is principally as an abusive term that the word "Jacobin" and its various cognates entered British political discourse.

Edmund Burke's writing and speeches nicely illustrate the word "Jacobin." His *Reflections* uses "Jacobins" on three separate occasions, all of them signifying the place where the revolutionaries met. Burke condemns the confiscation of Church property in November-December 1789, sarcastically referring to the Jacobins as one of the new revolutionary "academies" (EB 8:155). The revolutionaries seize Church property, remove the Church as the principal institution of learning and culture, and substitute revolutionary secularism. Burke exploits the connection between the revolutionary clubs and the confiscated Church property in *A Letter to a Noble Lord* (1796): "When he [Henry VIII of England] resolved to rob the abbies, as the club of the Jacobins have robbed all the ecclesiastics" (EB 9:165–66). By 1791 Burke begins to use "Jacobin" to refer to the people rather than a meeting place (EB 8:383; *Thoughts on French Affairs* 1791), but even the earlier usage implied violence and horrifying reversals. As early as 9 February 1790 Burke in the House of Commons condemned as especially dangerous the revolutionary "clubs and associations" that were utterly anathema to Burke, whether in France or Britain (PH 28:366). By August 1791 there were 400 affiliated Jacobin clubs throughout France, an increase of 250 in twelve months.[11] Nothing alarmed Burke more than the idea of popular sovereignty. The notion that "the people" were sovereign undermined at a fundamental level Burke's own conception of legitimate, constitutional, "virtual" representation. As a debating society that pressured the revolutionary government, the Jacobin club symbolized for Burke all that was evil in the revolution.

By 1791, then, "Jacobin" referred primarily to the French revolutionaries who met at the Jacobins and affiliated clubs and secondarily to those revo-

---

11. Simon Schama, *Citizens: A Chronicle of the French Revolution* (New York: Vintage, 1989), 527. Michael L. Kennedy, *The Jacobin Clubs in the French Revolution*, lists 921 cities in which Jacobin clubs existed by July 1791, but he is using a loose definition of "Jacobin" (362).

lutionaries deemed "extreme democrats." What was most fearful about the Jacobins, then, was not violence but discursive power, the emancipation of civil discourse from previous restrictions, the displacement of ecclesiastical authority. By 1792 British radicals start to be called "Jacobins" and thereafter the word "Jacobin" is applied to British supporters of the French Revolution and British parliamentary reform. After the British "Jacobin" movements are crushed by repression, around the time of the peace of Amiens, one finds the word used somewhat less frequently, but one still finds the word "Jacobin" used as a matter of course during the first three decades of the nineteenth century. As an index for the meaningfulness of the word, the politically reactionary *Anti-Jacobin Review* ran from 1797 to 1821.[12]

"Jacobin" was not an inevitable word for the radicals and democrats— words themselves considered abusive enough. There also were "republican," "leveller," and "anarchist." What made the word "Jacobin" so appealing in British political discourse? First, the word emphasized the foreign, non-British, especially Gallic qualities of the democratic movement. Among loyalists Burke was hardly alone in suggesting the British proponents of democratic reform were acting as foreign agents. David Simpson has described how the French were demonized in British culture during the 1790s.[13] Burke publicized the actual correspondence between democrats across the channel, especially by James Watt, Jr., and Thomas Cooper, both from the Manchester Constitutional Society, who visited Paris and attempted to "represent" the British people in their public statements of support for the revolution.[14] David V. Erdman has illustrated in rich detail the extent to which some Britons did in fact collaborate with the French revolutionaries and the extent to which the French Jacobins were influenced by British republicanism.[15] The Irish uprising of 1798 after Burke's death confirmed the worst fears of anti-Jacobins, as a French invasion was coordinated—very poorly, as it turned out—with a Jacobin-led revolutionary attempt.[16] In fact,

---

12. Alvin Sullivan, ed., *British Literary Magazines: The Romantic Age, 1789–1836* (Westport: Greenwood Press, 1983), 12–21.
13. David Simpson, *Romanticism, Nationalism, and the Revolt Against Theory* (Chicago: University of Chicago Press, 1993), chap. 3.
14. See, for example, the letter to Portland, *Observations on the Conduct of the Minority* (29 September 1793), EB 8: 414.
15. *Commerce Des Lumières: John Oswald and the British in Paris, 1790–1793* (Columbia: University of Missouri Press, 1986).
16. Thomas Pakenham, *The Year of Liberty: The Story of the Great Irish Rebellion of 1798* (Englewood Cliffs: Prentice-Hall, 1969).

the British democrats were inspired by the French revolutionaries, borrowing from them words, songs, concepts, symbols, and ideology. Thelwall in 1795–96, for example, lectured from a "tribune" at the Beaufort Buildings decorated with "portraits, busts, and prints of patriots" in the Parisian revolutionary manner (LJT 310).

Another reason for the word's power is that it connected democratic politics and religious transgression, signified through either the Dominican association or the deistic and atheistic reputation of the French Jacobins. Religion was arguably the most important issue after monarchy and aristocracy.[17] The French revolutionary financial system rested on the *assignats*, which in turn was secured by confiscated Church property—as early as 1789. After 27 November 1790 clergy who refused to take the oath of loyalty to the revolution either left France or remained at considerable personal risk. Burke drew out the political implications of religion in 2 March 1790 when he opposes Fox's motion for repealing the Test and Corporation Acts. Ten years earlier, Burke claims, he might have supported such a bill, but now the religious Dissenters have become politically radical, threatening to disestablish the Church of England, just as the French revolutionaries liquidated the French Church (PH 28:441). He is particularly disturbed by the politically radical catechisms drawn up by the Baptist Robert Robinson and the Unitarian Thomas Fyshe Palmer (the latter was one of the Edinburgh conventioneers, transported to Botany Bay for sedition in 1794) (PH 8:435). Priestley and Price are further examples of seditious Dissent (PH 8:438–39). It is all of a piece for Burke: the established order either holds together in all its parts or it collapses in such a way that the weakness of any single part portends disaster for the whole. Burke and other anti-Jacobins marvel nervously at the extraordinary rapidity by which France changed fundamentally. In 1788 all seemed stable. A year later the French church and aristocratic privilege were in ruins. The succession of revolutionary stages, each one more radical than the one preceding it until 9 Thermidor, suggested to anxious observers that institutions in Britain might be more fragile than they had thought before 1789.

17. Two historians hostile to Thompson's approach to the history of the period stress the centrality of the religious context for the 1790s; they both claim that the Anglican ideology was more persuasive than the Jacobin ideology, which relied greatly on antireligious arguments. J. C. D. Clark, *English Society, 1688–1832: Ideology, Social Structure, and Political Practice During the Ancien Régime* (Cambridge: Cambridge University Press, 1985); and Ian R. Christie, *Stress and Stability in Late Eighteenth-Century Britain: Reflections on the British Avoidance of Revolution* (Oxford: Clarendon Press, 1984).

Defining Jacobinism

A third reason for the popularity of "Jacobin" as a word is its similarity to the word "Jacobite." Jacobitism was the major threat to British political stability in the first half of the eighteenth century. Jacobites were also foreign agents, linked with the danger (and reality) of invasion, connected with religious conflict. Not for nothing did Walter Scott play out in the Waverley novels the Jacobite story at a time when the actual threat to the established order was Jacobinism.[18]

A fourth reason for the inevitability of "Jacobin" as a word is its allegorical reference to an expanding public sphere, popular discussion clubs, multiplying sites of critical discourse, and the decentering of discursive authority. "Jacobin" evoked the most radical developments in France, the proliferation of clubs, revolutionary *sections*, discussion groups, decentralized bodies of politicized citizens, extraparliamentary democratic oratory. The "violence" of Jacobinism, then, was more cultural than physical.

The process by which "Jacobin" signified political catastrophe began almost simultaneously with the revolution itself. One way Jacobinism became pejorative was the effect not just of Burke and the anti-Jacobins but of French Girondins and their British supporters. First, Fox and his faction of Whigs were personal friends with the Girondin leaders and accepted their version of revolutionary events. The Foxite version permitted one to condemn the regicide and revolutionary terror, but at the same time blame them on foreign invasion and counterrevolution. The Duke of Brunswick's provocative manifesto that accompanied the allied invasion of France was one such mitigating factor accounting for the regicide; the Foxites and most of the democratic reformers did not support but instead constructed apologetic narratives for the execution of Louis and his family.[19]

Fox delivered a speech on Jacobin violence during the height of the Jacobin terror, on 17 April 1794:

> The feelings of all Europe had already suffered by the repeated horrors of France; but, with regard to their cause, the French appeared to have, in a great measure, been driven to these violent scenes of bloodshed and horror. It was with a nation as with an individual; for if an individual was placed in a situation in which he felt himself abandoned by the whole world, and found that no one was his friend, that

---

18. See a recent issue of *ELH* 64 (1997) devoted to Jacobitism.
19. Irene Cooper Willis, ed., *Charles James Fox's Speeches During the French Revolution* (London and New York: J. M. Dent and Sons, E. P. Dutton, 1924), 61–62.

no one interested himself in his happiness or welfare, but that all mankind, as it were by general consent, were his enemies, he must become a misanthrope and a savage, unless he possessed a mind more heroic and exalted than we had any right to expect.[20]

Fox's explanation of revolutionary violence is the standard *British* Jacobin defense of the revolution's violence, repeated many times. Percy Shelley used it in his preface to *The Revolt of Islam*. A version of Fox's argument appears in Shelley's unpublished review of *Frankenstein*, where the creature's "crimes" are explained thus: "Treat a person ill, and he will become wicked."[21] *Frankenstein* itself plays out the ambiguities and tensions within the British Jacobin position.[22] The British Jacobin position condemns the crime but redeems the criminal, so that Jacobinism proper is both repudiated and salvaged.

The Girondin perspective was also influential through writings by British eyewitnesses sympathetic to the revolution—Helen Maria Williams especially—and by translations of sensational Girondin memoirs, especially Madame Roland's. According to Gary Kelly, Helen Maria Williams's Girondin-colored account of the French Revolution was very influential in the 1790s as her "letters" on revolution came out in dramatic installments: "Her representation of feminized Revolutionary culture was taken up by Romantic writers seeking alternatives to Revolutionary conflict."[23] Madame Roland's *An Appeal to Impartial Posterity*, written in prison shortly before her execution, was published in 1795 by the prominent publisher, Joseph Johnson, and influenced substantially Mary Wollstonecraft's unfinished novel, *Maria* (according to Gary Kelly).[24]

Although he was the most well-known British "Jacobin" participating in revolutionary politics, Thomas Paine was actually aligned with the Girondin group. He, like Condorcet, was imprisoned by the French Jacobins. Unlike

20. Willis, 163.
21. Roger Ingpen and Walter E. Peck, eds., *The Complete Works of Percy Bysshe Shelley*, 10 vols. (New York: Gordian Press, 1965), 6:264.
22. See my essay "*Frankenstein*'s Ghost Story: The Last Jacobin Novel," *Genre* 19 (1986): 299–318.
23. Gary Kelly, *Women, Writing, and Revolution: 1790–1827* (Oxford: Clarendon Press, 1993), 30–79, 77.
24. Jeanne Marie Roland de la Platière, *An Appeal to Impartial Posterity*, trans. Bosc (1795; rpt. New York: Woodstock Books, 1990). Gary Kelly, *Revolutionary Feminism: The Mind and Career of Mary Wollstonecraft* (London: Macmillan Press, 1992), 213.

Defining Jacobinism

Condorcet, he escaped being killed by them. Shelley's generation of radicals found the Girondin version appealing, as the Girondins had enough weaknesses to permit sympathetic identification without unrealistic idealization.[25]

From the September massacres of 1792 to the fall of Robespierre on 9 Thermidor (26 July 1794) the Terror did indeed kill a huge number of people, around 40,000 victims.[26] Robespierre was directly responsible for a small fraction of those casualties, and the Jacobins themselves for a larger proportion, with revolutionaries completely outside the Jacobin clubs and the "Mountain" responsible for considerably more. Marat, Hébert, and the historically nameless *enragés* of the Parisian sections were not Jacobins, although at times they influenced them. Robespierre *justified* most of the Terror, almost always after the fact, almost always downplaying the actual number of victims, but he rarely encouraged violence or glorified it.[27] Robespierre was demonized, the most familiar synecdoche for a demonized group. "Jacobinism" was figured as a contagious disease that had "spread" to England (Burke employs the "contagion" imagery for the revolution right from the start) and whose origins were the Enlightenment *philosophes*, especially Rousseau.[28]

If the main accomplishment of the French Revolution was the "explosion of politics," the unprecedented expansion of political participation (to use Simon Schama's terms), one can also see that in Britain too the revolutionary decade of the 1790s entailed unprecedented political activity. The British Jacobins were demonized because they represented truly fearful cultural

---

25. Schama, *Citizens*, 724–25. Schama has pointed out that the Girondins have been the occasion for Marxist contempt and social-democratic and liberal projection. He reminds us that however flawed they were, the Girondins had a great deal of support outside Paris, as they attracted revolutionaries hostile to Paris and jealous of local autonomy (728). Nevertheless, the Girondins were vigorous proponents of war, had tolerated certain acts of terror (notably the September massacres of 1792, which Roland could have stopped but did not—632), and were fearful of the revolutionary crowd and the Parisian sections. If the Jacobins had not removed them from power, some other group might have done so, and at the time there were no nonviolent means of transferring power. Moreover, it is not clear that the slide toward Bonaparte's military dictatorship would have been slowed by the Girondins triumphing over the Jacobins. The "moderates" governing after Robespierre did not have much success in that area.
26. Feher, *The Frozen Revolution*, 111.
27. David P. Jordan, *The Revolutionary Career of Maximilien Robespierre* (New York: Free Press, 1985), 61, 111, 120, 143, 175, 180, 208.
28. On English Jacobin representations of Robespierre, see Nicholas Roe, *Wordsworth and Coleridge: The Radical Years* (Oxford: Oxford University Press, 1988), 199–233, and Brooke Hopkins, "Representing Robespierre," in Stephen C. Behrendt, ed., *History and Myth: Essays on English Romantic Literature* (Detroit: Wayne State University Press, 1990), 116–29.

developments, not just political ones. One takes for granted the lack of historical accuracy embedded in the word "Jacobin," but as Ferenc Feher says of Abbé Barruel's "history" of Jacobinism: it is "worthless" as factual history but "invaluable" as a "document of contemporary perception."[29]

Jacobinism and Ideology: E. P. Thompson and S. T. Coleridge

When "Jacobin" signifies something other than just any kind of British democratic or reformist expression, the word describes primarily a republican, religiously heterodox position that threatens aristocratic property. The French Revolution controversy, according to Gregory Claeys, was really about the problematics of "leveling" even when the actual debate was on ephemeral political matters. Were extreme inequality and harsh poverty the inevitable consequences of a prosperous commercial society led by a "cultured" elite?[30] Apparently so, answered Burke and Malthus. The Jacobins, from Paine to Thelwall, challenged the new aristocratic consensus at fundamental levels, economic, political, and cultural.

Literary Jacobinism, which begins with the pamphlet war sparked by Burke's *Reflections on the Revolution in France* in late 1790, takes many forms: radical periodicals aligned with the London Corresponding Society; the novels of Godwin and Wollstonecraft; the poetry of Blake and the early poetry of Coleridge, Southey, and Wordsworth; the political lectures and essays of Paine, Thelwall, Godwin, Coleridge, Frend, and Spence. This cultural insurgence at the popular and polite levels was checked but not entirely blocked by severe political repression and cultural reaction. In 1805 Godwin published *Fleetwood*, a Jacobin novel in many respects, but the targets of its criticism had become bourgeois (industrialism, child labor) rather than aristocratic. Moreover, the novel deprecates a bourgeois cultural *style* — mechanistic, utilitarian, "commercial and arithmetical" — like Burke and Carlyle. Godwin's strategic shifts tried to retain some Jacobin social criticism in the new cultural terrain from which Jacobinism has been expelled.[31] In the same year, 1805, the popularity of Scott's *Lay of the Last Minstrel* marks the turn-

---

29. Feher, *The Frozen Revolution*, 162 n. 1.
30. Gregory Claeys, "The French Revolution Debate and British Political Thought," *History of Political Thought* 11 (1990): 59–80.
31. William Godwin, *Fleetwood: Or, The New Man of Feeling*, rev. ed. (London: Richard Bentley, 1832), 173.

ing away of elite and middle-class culture from political controversy toward cultural nostalgia and escapism. *Political* Jacobinism did not disappear entirely by 1805 because it was sustained by laboring-class activists in the radical underworld described by Iain McCalman, Malcolm Chase, and David Worrall, and it would be revived, if in a revisionist form, by a second generation of polite intellectuals, including Hazlitt, Shelley, and Byron. According to Southey in 1812, "jacobinism, having almost totally disappeared from the educated classes, has sunk down into the mob."[32]

For examining the emergence, rise, and decline of Jacobinism, I want to look at two writers, one a very sympathetic modern historian (E. P. Thompson) and the other a former Jacobin (Coleridge). I am probably not the only literary scholar who first became interested in the British Jacobins after I read Thompson's *The Making of the English Working Class*. In English studies no critic of Jacobinism has more authority than Coleridge. These two writers come at Jacobinism from very different places, but insofar as "Jacobin" means anything within literary history, it is mostly because of what Thompson and Coleridge have written. I want, accordingly, to explore the adequacy of both Thompson's history and Coleridge's analysis.

Thompson's narrative about the Jacobins in *The Making of the English Working Class* and other texts, which has provoked a lively controversy, identifies them as primarily artisans and middling-class tradesmen and professionals who created their own political culture inspired by the example of revolutionary France, the ideas of Thomas Paine, and the lectures of John Thelwall. Most distinctively Jacobin, according to Thompson, is the commitment to social equality that shaped political life: "*Every* citizen on a committee was expected to perform some part, the chairmanship of committees was often taken in rotation, the pretensions of leaders were watched, proceedings were based on the deliberate belief that every man was capable of reason and of a growth in his abilities, and that deference and distinctions of status were an offence to human dignity." Other noteworthy Jacobin qualities are "self-education," "rational criticism of political and religious institutions," "conscious republicanism," and "internationalism" (MWC 183). Recent research, however, requires some nuanced revisions, especially in the "rationalism" of the Jacobins. Some Jacobins, as Jon Mee has reminded us, also used an apocalyptic idiom of religious enthusiasm, and, as James Epstein

---

32. Robert Southey, *Essays, Moral and Political*, 2 vols. (London: John Murray, 1832), 1:126.

has illustrated, most of the Jacobins (including Thelwall) employed at least some version of a constitutionalist idiom even though they had read their Paine carefully and had entertained the ideas of Godwin, both of whom repudiated constitutionalist precedent for presuppositionless rationality.[33] Thelwall, however, both a rationalist and constitutionalist, uses a constitutionalist rhetoric of "rights," moral economy, and ancient democracy to argue for universal suffrage, limits on farm size, cultivating the wastes, and guaranteeing the laborer a decent standard of living. As we will see, his constitutionalism is more strategically rhetorical than theoretically rigorous, because his logic rarely depends on appeals to constitutional precedent alone. Moreover, although Thelwall never wavers from an unyielding skepticism, his style at times is as enthusiastic as the most prophetically inspired Jacobin. The new emphases of Mee and Epstein complement rather than undermine Thompson's overall treatment: pure Jacobinism was rare.

Thompson laments the demise of Jacobinism and charts its trajectory of decline. After the 1790s "Jacobinism had become indigenous in working-class communities at exactly the same time as it had lost any national centre as well as most middle-class support" (MWC 498). Napoleon's becoming First Consul (1802) and then "Emperor" (1804) eroded the morale of the surviving Jacobins. "The First Empire struck a blow at English republicanism from which it never fully recovered" (MWC 454). Afterward, "Jacobinism, as a movement deriving inspiration from France, was almost dead." Although radicalism survived in the early nineteenth century, "the terms of argument shifted beyond recognition" (MWC 456). The notable radicals of the Waterloo and Peterloo period are not Jacobins: Cobbett, Orator Hunt, Cartwright, Burdett, and Hobhouse. None of these leaders was a republican or a religious dissident, and two did not even support universal suffrage. As described by both Thompson and James Epstein, the dominant reform ideology after the 1790s is traditionalist, deriving its justification from customary sources, even though those sources are employed often (but not always) to establish universal suf-

33. Jon Mee, "Apocalypse and Ambivalence: The Politics of Millenarianism in the 1790s," *South Atlantic Quarterly* 95 (1996): 687–93; James Epstein, *Radical Expression: Political Language, Ritual, and Symbol in England, 1790–1850* (Oxford: Oxford University Press, 1995); Günther Lottes, "Radicalism, Revolution, and Political Culture: An Anglo-French Comparison," in Mark Philp, ed., *The French Revolution and British Popular Politics* (Cambridge: Cambridge University Press, 1991), all show that despite Paine and other rationalists, the 1790s reform movement employed a largely constitutionalist idiom that ultimately weakened the movement (84–85).

frage.³⁴ Thompson mostly ignores the Jacobins after the 1790s. His too-curt dismissal of Thelwall's 1818–21 Westminster radicalism is typical;³⁵ the Jacobins at that time were at least a minority within the overall reform movement. There has been no credible challenge to the narrative of decline, but perhaps it was not as absolute as Thompson's version makes it.

Some of Thompson's critics on the left have focused on the artisanate, the social group that all agree most strongly supported Jacobinism. Critics on the left find Thompson neglects gender and blurs to some extent the decisive difference between the workshop and the factory. The nearly all-male narrative Thompson writes does indeed require the correcting commentary of feminist historians such as Anna Clark and Joan Landes. Clark, who supplements Thompson's work with information about the domestic and work life of women, also portrays the artisans as self-serving, exclusionary men whose political culture was much poorer than that created by a later industrial working class of wage earners. Landes traces the insidious dichotomy of feminine domesticity and masculine public life to the republican public sphere of the French Jacobins. Clark's harsh portrait of artisan culture is reinforced by Craig Calhoun, who accents the differences between the British Jacobins and the dominant artisan culture, as Thompson never did, to bring out some weaknesses in Marxist theory itself. Artisan political culture, tradition-bound and communitarian, was a problematic legacy for a later working class of factory workers who would have been better served by the lessons of a more rationalistic Jacobinism.³⁶ Thompson's narrative could have benefited

---

34. Thompson's historical work develops this radical traditionalism in numerous studies, most notably *The Making of the English Working Class* and *Customs in Common* (New York: The New Press, 1993). James Epstein has recently shown that the reformers of the late eighteenth and early nineteenth centuries were largely traditionalists employing a constitutionalist rather than a rationalist rhetoric. *Radical Expression*.

35. In both *The Making of the English Working Class* and the more recent essay on Thelwall, "Hunting the Jacobin Fox," Thompson ignores the three years of Thelwall's activism on behalf of radical reform when he was editor-owner of *The Champion*.

36. Thompson answers some of his critics in "The Moral Economy Reviewed" in *Customs in Common*, 259–351, and *The Poverty of Theory and Other Essays* (New York: Monthly Review Press, 1978). Francis Hearn, *Domination, Legitimation, and Resistance: The Incorporation of the Nineteenth-Century Working Class* (Westport: Greenwood Press, 1978); Anna K. Clark, *The Struggle for the Breeches: Gender and the Making of the British Working Class* (Berkeley and Los Angeles: University of California Press, 1995); Joan Landes, *Women and the Public Sphere in the Age of the French Revolution* (Ithaca: Cornell University Press, 1988); Craig Calhoun, *The Question of Class Struggle: Social Foundations of Popular Radicalism During the Industrial Revolution* (Chicago: University of Chicago Press, 1982).

from accenting some discontinuities between Jacobinism, more open to feminism and rational discussion, and traditional, more authoritarian artisan culture. Highlighting the differences between Paine and Cobbett, for example, would have opened up lines of inquiry into the ideology of the artisanate that Thompson did not pursue. Although there never was a women-centered salon culture in Britain as there was in France, Landes's analysis still applies to Britain: Gary Kelly argues that on the left writers such as Helen Maria Williams countered the masculine bias of Jacobinism with an emphasis on sensibility.[37] In Britain at least, however, Jacobinism opened up opportunities for women to question gender hierarchies. It is unclear how much one can infer from the several poems written by "F.A.C."—"Female Citizen"—in Thelwall's *Tribune* and the LCS's *Moral and Political Magazine* (PR 122-23; 129-30), but it seems that some women were part of the radical artisanate. Thompson's narrative is vulnerable to feminist critique, but the Jacobins themselves were much less so, as their rationalism and hostility to tradition opened paths to feminism.

Francis Hearn, Geoff Eley, Gareth Stedman Jones, and Craig Calhoun are some who have insisted upon the discontinuity between artisans and factory workers: that the artisanal radicalism was in fact superior to the reformist "labourism" of industrial workers that followed it (Hearn); that the artisanal public sphere is essentially different from the working-class public sphere (Eley); that Chartism failed because of its Jacobin ideology based in the artisanate, undermining a potential socialist ideology that could have emerged only from factory workers (Jones); that artisan radicalism was so strong (but largely irrelevant to socialism) because it depended upon traditional, preindustrial communities (Calhoun).[38] The most sustained critique of Thompson on the artisanate is by Perry Anderson who, following Tom Nairn, stresses the *remaking* of the British working class in the passage from the artisanate to the factory proletariat.[39] Thompson was either insufficiently rig-

37. Gary Kelly, *Women, Writing, and Revolution: 1790–1827*, 77. For a vigorous defense of sensibility and its ideology, see Jerome McGann, *The Poetics of Sensibility: A Revolution in Literary Style* (Oxford: Clarendon Press, 1996).
38. Geoff Eley, "E. P. Thompson, Social History, and Political Culture: The Making of a Working-Class Public," in Harvey J. Kaye and Keith McClelland, eds., *E. P. Thompson: Critical Perspectives* (Philadelphia: Temple University Press, 1990), 12–49; Gareth Stedman Jones, *Languages of Class: Studies in English Working Class History 1832–1982* (Cambridge: Cambridge University Press, 1983); Calhoun, *The Question of Class Struggle*.
39. Perry Anderson, *Arguments Within English Marxism* (London: NLB and Verso, 1980), 44–45.

Defining Jacobinism

orous or excessively sentimental when he stressed continuity between artisans and factory workers, Jacobinism and socialism. Against these arguments one can counter on Thompson's behalf that artisanal Jacobinism truly anticipated working-class socialism in these areas: its internationalism, its egalitarianism, its cultural project of self- and mutual education, its counter-hegemonic public sphere, its cooperative sociality, and its urban style. Thompson does not insist upon an identity between artisan and factory worker, only continuity, so that he and his critics are disputing a gray area of relative emphases, on the one hand, and political preferences (labourism versus revolution) on the other. R. S. Neale finesses the controversy over continuity by asserting that "the contending groups are always the oppressors and the oppressed who conflict with each other over matters of power and authority."[40] It is a vexed controversy too complex to explore adequately here, but lending support to Neale's point is that now, with the absolute decline of the industrial proletariat, there is still anticapitalistic, even postindustrial socialism. Labor and capital are perhaps slots in a conflicting scenario rather than socioeconomic essences tied once and for all to industrialism rather than handicrafts.

Thompson's rich appreciation for the artisan William Blake is matched by his unstinting hostility to William Godwin, a middling-class intellectual. He characterizes Blake as a lucid "witness" against the "hegemony" of working-class ideology. Jacobinism "struck root most deeply among artisans," but there was also, according to Thompson, "a small intellectual coterie" of Jacobins who advocated feminism and sexual liberation—"Mary Wollstonecraft, Godwin, Blake," and Shelley (MWC 193, 162).[41] In the case of Godwin, Thompson scapegoats the bad Jacobin to make way for the good. The artisan Blake carried forward from the seventeenth century a religiously inspired radicalism that was both innovative and customary, partaking of both the Enlightenment and popular culture. Godwin, however, a "bourgeois radical," constructed a bloodless rationalism of "self-satisfied philosophical benevolence and contempt for all received opinion and custom." Although he acted courageously in 1794 with the timely rebuttal of Judge Eyre's interpretation of the treason law and nobly in 1801 with his public refusal to disavow radicalism in the face of attacks by Samuel Parr, James Mackintosh,

---

40. R. S. Neale, *Class in English History 1680–1850* (Totowa, N.J.: Barnes and Noble, 1981), 121.
41. E. P. Thompson, *Witness Against the Beast: William Blake and the Moral Law* (New York: New Press, 1993).

and other anti-Jacobins, Thompson's Godwin is an unsympathetic figure who "cannily" avoids going to prison and who crafts an intellectually elitist position hostile to popular culture and actual politics (TR 96–106, 120). Thompson defends the anti-Godwinism of the young Wordsworth and Coleridge as penetrating critical moves to the *left* of Godwin and toward deeper egalitarianism. Thompson's argument on Wordsworth and Coleridge sharply conflicts with the New Historical emphasis on ideological displacement of politics by Romantic nature and feeling, and counters as well the central role Nicholas Roe assigns Godwin in his study of the young radical poets. Jon Mee's recent suggestion that Wordsworth's Romantic apocalypse of the imagination is not so much an evasion of history as a disciplining and privatizing of apocalypse is a helpful approach in the spirit of Thompson's arguments.[42] Thompson's appreciation of the democratic Wordsworth and Coleridge has been a salutary counter to the Althusserian ideological demolition of the two poets, while Thompson also portrayed Godwin as a prototype of the intellectual arrogance he himself associated with Althusser.[43] Thompson, who counters a baneful tendency on the left to scorn the mere "trade-union consciousness" (Lenin) of ordinary workers, does indeed seem to prefer radicalism that arises from popular culture—such as food riots—to radicalism that arises from rational inquiry.

42. Thompson, TR, 33–95 ("Disenchantment or Default? A Lay Sermon," 1969); 75–95 ("Wordsworth's Crisis," 1988); 108–32 ("Bliss Was It In That Dawn—The Matter of Coleridge's Revolutionary Youth," 1971). Nicholas Roe convincingly makes both Godwin and Thelwall central to the radicalism of Coleridge and Wordsworth, *Wordsworth and Coleridge: The Radical Years*. In line with Thompson's perspective on Wordsworth is David Simpson's recent commentary that the New Historicists have gone too far in attacking Wordsworth, neglecting his genuinely "democratic" aspects. *Romanticism, Nationalism, and the Revolt Against Theory*, 154. Jon Mee, "Apocalypse and Ambivalence: The Politics of Millenarianism in the 1790s," *South Atlantic Quarterly* 95 (1996): 687–93.

43. Both Jerome McGann, *The Romantic Ideology: A Critical Investigation* (Chicago: University of Chicago Press, 1983), and Marjorie Levinson, "The New Historicism: Back to the Future," in Marjorie Levinson, Marilyn Butler, Jerome J. McGann, and Paul Hamilton, eds., *Rethinking Historicism: Critical Readings in Romantic Studies* (Oxford : Basil Blackwell, 1989), acknowledge Althusser as an important theoretical presence behind their critique of the Romantic ideology. Thompson criticizes Althusser in his *The Poverty of Theory and Other Essays*. Although not Althusserian in any sense, Kenneth Johnston's case for Wordsworth's spying in the 1790s effectively vindicates the New Historicist critique and weakens Thompson's argument. *The Hidden Wordsworth: Poet, Lover, Rebel, Spy* (New York: W. W. Norton, 1998). Johnston's case, however, is circumstantial and based on evidence that can be interpreted in other ways, as Johnston himself admits, despite the implicit claim of the book's title. In addition to Roe's study, Philp's *Godwin's Political Justice* is an exemplary treatment of Godwin in the 1790s.

Defining Jacobinism

For Thompson the Jacobins are a chapter in the long story of the working class as it made itself, a moment in the rebellion against social deference. Thompson's critics on the left dispute what they perceive as his complacency about the ideological trajectory of the English working class, its essential "labourism" and lack of revolutionary will. Thompson's critics on the right, such as J. C. D. Clark and Ian Christie, similarly quarrel with Thompson's description of the popular consciousness and insist upon a high degree of popular consent to the aristocratic defeat of Jacobinism. They also deny continuity between the artisanate and the industrial proletariat, emphasizing the weight of the past and tradition, the resistance to change.[44] Their criticisms cannot be dismissed, but one has to ask: if there was so much consent to aristocratic hegemony in the 1790s, and if the Jacobins were such a minor nuisance, why then did the government pursue a strategy of harsh repression? Either the government was irrationally sadistic or it misperceived the threat of the Jacobins. The issue of popular consent resists verification because as soon as extensive repression is introduced, how can one later infer such a high degree of consent? Did people in fact agree with the authorities or did they only appear to do so in order to avoid harsh treatment as a hated Jacobin?

Whatever revisions are necessary in Thompson's account of the Jacobins — and some serious adjustments seem to be required — one cannot ignore the rhetorical persuasiveness of Thompson's narrative. Perhaps he tells a story too well, so that when we should be asking critical questions we are affectively engaged instead.

One of Jacobinism's most intriguing critics, on whom Thompson has written a great deal, was the one-time Jacobin Samuel Taylor Coleridge. Coleridge's treatment of Jacobinism is both useful and distracting, because his insightful rigor competed with his desire for personal exoneration from political sin. Coleridge's argument that pure Jacobinism leads inevitably to revolution, republicanism, and communism is perceptive in showing the ultimate conclusions toward which a rigorously Jacobin logic leads, even though actual British Jacobins were more moderate than the ideal type. Nevertheless, Coleridge's ideal typology charts the degrees of Jacobinism that any single text might express. Coleridge also clarifies the discourse of sedition by which

---

44. Clark, *English Society, 1688–1832*, and Christie, *Stress and Stability in Late Eighteenth-Century Britain*.

Jacobinism was identified. What distinguished a legally permissible discourse from one that invited prosecution as Jacobin was not so much the more or less radical content but the more or less popular form and the more or less deferential attitude toward established authorities. Coleridge's early attempt to treat Jacobinism analytically and not just polemically was, even after factoring out self-justification and nervous autobiographical refashioning, extremely impressive. He treated Jacobinism as political discourse that depends on rapidly shifting and ephemeral events, *and* as something truly philosophical, a style of thinking and expression that is distinctive.

Coleridge first defines Jacobinism as both specific to France and universal (4 January 1800, *Morning Post*). A nation in danger that mobilizes a politicized populace enjoying full democratic participation is "Jacobin." Such a nation's collective interest supersedes merely individual self-interest and considerations of property. "Jacobinism," then, describes how the actual Jacobins responded to the crisis brought on by the king's flight, foreign invasion, the Vendée revolt, and aristocratic subversion; it also describes the general category of revolutionary mobilization provoked by extraordinary disorder (EHT 1:74–75).

Coleridge's initial definition lacks the moral emphasis prominent two years later in a *Morning Post* article of 21 October 1802 entitled "Once a Jacobin Always a Jacobin." From the idea of universal suffrage Coleridge infers that Jacobinism requires also popular sovereignty and the subordination of absolute property rights to the criteria of social justice. Everyone "has an equal right to that quantity of property, which is necessary for the sustenance of his life, and health" (EHT 2:369). Property that exceeds a minimum is subject to legislative will governed by social equity. In short, Jacobinism leads to some form of what we would now call socialism. Moreover, popular sovereignty implies a republican form of government and the right of revolution.

In addition to this perceptive analysis of Jacobinism, he also writes some self-justifying arguments that extricate himself from his Jacobin past. "Whoever builds a Government on personal and natural rights, is so far a Jacobin. Whoever builds on social rights, that is, hereditary rank, property, and long prescription, is an Anti-Jacobin, even though he should nevertheless be a Republican, or even a Democrat" (EHT 1:370). Later, in the *Friend* (1809; 1818) and the *Biographia Literaria* (1818), Coleridge reworks the essay, establishing the Jacobin/anti-Jacobin binary as a key category in two opposing traditions and cultural identities. Coleridge spares his own former radicalism the venal label by identifying as Jacobin only a radical kind of individualism or abstract rationalism. By this definition Coleridge the Unitarian was never a Jacobin in the 1790s. As Thelwall remarked in the marginalia of *Biographia Literaria*, it is absurd to say Coleridge was never a Jacobin because, in fact, he was an extreme Jacobin on the issue of property.[45] Southey too commented wryly that if Coleridge was not a Jacobin in the 1790s "in the common acceptation of the name," then "who the Devil was?" (F 2:26 n.1). Coleridge's having been a Jacobin was inconvenient for the more conservative Coleridge writing later. According to Thompson, Coleridge was not only a Jacobin in the 1790s but was at the very center of provincial activism in 1795–97.[46]

Yet there is more than a grain of truth in Coleridge's analysis after one factors out the self-serving emphasis. Jacobins did indeed subordinate tradition to reason, but the rational criteria were social, not individualistic. Coleridge's own Unitarians and other Rational Dissenters retained Christian concepts but also aggressively dismantled what they viewed as superstition and prejudice. Paine, Thelwall, and Godwin were religious skeptics, but their political arguments also assumed traditional concepts: nature for Paine and Thelwall, the right of private judgment and civic virtue for Godwin. Coleridge's emphasis on Jacobin rationalism, however, is useful when one recalls another radical tradition that is not Jacobin: a constitutionalist rhetoric justified reform as restoration to an earlier state of justice that existed as Saxon liberty, before the Norman yoke, or perhaps as a vaguer merry old England that was not as tyrannical.[47] Coleridge's distinction between traditional and rationalistic logic is meaningful, as it also accounts for the difference between food rioters and LCS members: the food rioters acted according to customary notions of moral economy, but the LCS "citizens" made arguments, appealed to evidence, and offered rationalistic validity claims.[48] Coleridge

---

45. Burton R. Pollin and Redmond Burke, "John Thelwall's Marginalia in a Copy of Coleridge's *Biographia Literaria*," *Bulletin of the New York Public Library* 74 (1970): 73–94.

46. Thompson, TR, 108–32.

47. Thompson's historical work develops this radical traditionalism in numerous studies, most notably *The Making of the English Working Class* and *Customs in Common*. James Epstein has recently discussed the constitutionalist idiom of the reform movement in *Radical Expression*.

48. Thompson discusses the food riots in *Customs in Common*, 185–351. The distinction between customary and rational political arguments is discussed throughout Jürgen Habermas's *The Theory of Communicative Action*, 2 vols., trans. Thomas McCarthy (Boston: Beacon Press, 1984).

usefully reserves the Jacobin label for the most rationalistic and antitraditional radicalism, although, as he well knew, the Jacobins were not uniformly rationalistic or utterly without traditions. On religion all Jacobins were anticlerical and heterodox, while some, like Thelwall, Paine, and Godwin, were deistic, and others, like Coleridge, Blake, and Frend, were Christian.

Coleridge's judgment on when Jacobin discourse became legally prosecutable is consistent with the broader anti-Jacobin consensus that Coleridge was helping to build in the early nineteenth century. The anti-Jacobin paradigm rests on the judicial concept of "constructive treason": if calls for "reform" can be construed as leading eventually and indirectly to a political crisis in which the king could lose his life, then "reform" is treason. In Chief Justice Eyre's famous formulation of constructive treason in 1794, the "overt acts" tied to imagining or compassing the king's death could be even more remote than those established earlier by justices Hale and Foster. Hale and Foster ruled that nonviolent deeds that only assisted the attempted regicide were treasonous. Eyre expanded the notion of remote overt acts to include actions that would initiate a process during which and because of which the king could be killed. In Eyre's own words: "The entering into Measures which, in the Nature of Things, or in the common Experience of Mankind, do obviously tend to bring the Life of the King into Danger, is also compassing and imagining the Death of the King."[49] Eyre also ruled that nonviolent associations and assemblies advocating parliamentary reform could be treasonous because only Parliament and the King have the authority to alter the Constitution: any assembly, association, or "convention" that attempts to usurp this authority is guilty of treason. Eyre also views the very nature of the public sphere, its debates and political associations, however apparently moderate, as ultimately subversive of established authority.

Coleridge himself uses the constructive treason paradigm in the 1818 *Friend* essay on libel, but he also wants to defend freedom of the press. He rejects, like Southey, even in 1818, the justification for the anti-Jacobin repression of the 1790s. Nevertheless, he concedes that government has a right to prosecute libelous expressions. Libel cannot be defined except situationally, taking into account the "malignity of intention" that can be inferred from the "style, price, mode of circulation, and so forth." Given the "state of the times," one must gauge the libelous text for its possible effect

---

49. Jack Marken and Burton R. Pollin, eds., *Uncollected Writings (1785–1822): Articles in Periodicals and Six Pamphlets. One with Coleridge's Marginalia. By William Godwin* (Gainesville: Scholars' Facsimiles and Reprints, 1968), 134.

Defining Jacobinism

on "the lower classes" for making "turbulence" (F 1:93). Discourse aimed at a polite audience cannot be seditious, a designation reserved only for discourse aimed at a popular audience.[50] Sedition, then, is more procedural than substantive, as the expanded public sphere and exponential growth of the literary market most directly threatened aristocratic domination. Although Coleridge in fact, perhaps for self-serving reasons, repudiated the Pittite anti-Jacobin repression, one could use Coleridge's own criteria to justify that repression. He comes close to saying that elite readers should enjoy a complete freedom that is not granted to less socially privileged readers who are a potential danger to social order, but this double standard, so outrageous to a contemporary sense of justice, was commonplace in the nineteenth century.[51] Coleridge's ambivalence—his desire to acknowledge and deny his former Jacobinism—is illustrated by his reprinting his earlier seditious allegories designed for a popular audience, one of which, "Fire, Famine and Slaughter," required a long apologetic note in *Sibylline Leaves*.[52]

Both Thompson and Coleridge see Jacobinism as similarly egalitarian, even explosively so. Perhaps one might think that the central political demand of the Jacobins, universal manhood suffrage, was not nearly radical enough to sustain either the government's anxiety or commentators' radical speculations. One should recall, however, what Karl Marx said about universal suffrage in 1852: "The carrying of Universal Suffrage in England would, therefore, be a far more socialistic measure than anything which has been honored with that name on the Continent. . . . Its inevitable result, here [in Britain], is *the political supremacy of the working class*."[53] If this was true in the 1850s, perhaps it was also true in the 1790s. Indeed, as the French Revolution moved rightward from its truly Jacobin character, it abolished universal suffrage and added property requirements for voting, an addition Thelwall

---

50. Mark Philp shows that William Godwin attempted to avoid legal difficulties by appealing to a "polite" readership. *Godwin's Political Justice*, 73.

51. Paul Magnuson, who has a nuanced description and analysis of Coleridge's movement in and out of Jacobinism, emphasizes Coleridge's continuity as a radical Christian Dissenter whose support for marriage and the domestic affections distinguished his Jacobinism from that of the secular radicals like Thelwall, Paine, and Godwin. *Reading Public Romanticism*, chaps. 2–4.

52. Ernest Hartley Coleridge, ed., *Coleridge, Poetical Works* (1912 rpt. Oxford: University Press, 1967), 595–606.

53. Karl Marx and Frederick Engels, *Collected Works*, 46 vols. (New York: International Publishers, 1979), 11: 336. The essay "The Chartists" was first published in the *New York Daily Tribune*, 25 August 1852.

and the LCS unequivocally criticize.⁵⁴ The LCS advocated and practiced a participatory democracy that had its finest moments in the late 1795 demonstrations against the Gagging Acts: tens of thousands of artisans, laborers and middling-class shopkeepers, professionals and tradesmen, nonviolently protested and discussed the proposed legislation. They took these actions at considerable personal risk. What they did became illegal upon the passage of the Gagging Acts, which closed down the democratic public sphere.

True Jacobinism, then, is not just religious dissidence and a preference for radical parliamentary reform; "Jacobin" also signifies participatory democracy, an expanding public sphere, activism, internationalism, and a rationalistic rigor. Although the origins of the word were established by the intentions of those who battled against the Jacobins, the initial catachresis provoked efforts to redefine and to counter the meanings generated by the anti-Jacobins. As an analytical concept it usefully describes a democratic ideology, upheld by middling-class intellectuals and the radical artisanate, that anticipates opposition—social democratic, socialistic, communist, anarchistic—to free-market capitalism. The British Jacobins depended on a public sphere within which they could develop and refine a rationalistic logic moderated by popular culture. The appeal to the stronger argument rather than to the authority of tradition was the Jacobin style of discourse.

---

54. Thelwall, who himself—not being a freeholder—could not vote (*Tribune* 45 [21 November 1995], 3: 222), held the view generally shared in the LCS that the Directory, which had imposed property qualifications on the franchise, had retreated from the more democratic universal suffrage of the Jacobin period (*Tribune* 23 [2 September 1795], 2: 179). *The Moral and Political Magazine* remarks that the Directory is less democratic than the previous Jacobin rule (1796 October), 222–29.

2

Thelwall's Replies to Burke

In opposing Jacobinism, Edmund Burke, in his *Reflections on the Revolution in France*, perhaps assisted it by sparking a controversy that greatly expanded the public sphere.[1] The very style of Burke's essay—exuberant, metaphorical, excessive, personal, emotional, extreme, hermeneutically aggressive, figuratively rich with hyperbole and hyperbaton, rhetorically "wild" and emphatically oratorical—was occasion for imitation, parody, and antithetical negation. If Burke inadvertently enlivened democratic publicity, he did everything in his power to suppress it as well. Although he wanted to persuade members of parliament and the "political nation," he tried to silence the Jacobins and their public sphere. I am following historians like Mark Philp who argue that

---

1. The Unitarian Society, for example, gave "Thanks to Mr. Burke, for the important discussions he has provoked." See "History of Europe," *Annual Register, 1792* 34: 369. Burke himself takes notice in *Letter to William Elliot* (1797) of the reform societies that have thanked him. See EB 8: 30.

Jacobinism

the Jacobins were defeated by the government's superior power and not by the effectiveness of anti-Jacobin arguments.[2]

The chapter has three focuses: a brief examination of Burke's provocative writing, a somewhat longer discussion of Paine's central role in expanding the public sphere, and a concentrated inquiry into Thelwall's replies to Burke. Because Burke and his Jacobin opponents read each other as symptomatic of ideological distortion, aristocratic or individualistic, their conflicting appeals to authority—an ancient constitution, European culture, popular sovereignty, emancipated reason—have little common ground and reflect a conflict that will be resolved in the short term not by the stronger argument but by the power of coercion.

Although Paine is a well-known antagonist of Burke, Thelwall and his extensive arguments have been neglected. Thelwall did not have the same popularity as Paine but he too exploited the new literary market for radical pamphlets. For Burke Thelwall was one of many dangerous radicals; for Thelwall, however, Burke is a dominating presence in at least two major essays in the 1790s—*Sober Reflections* and *The Rights of Nature*—and colors to some extent everything he wrote after 1790.[3] In a *Tribune* lecture of 1795 he alludes sarcastically to Burke as "the great father and first propagator of the principles of democracy" for having inspired responses to the *Reflections on the Revolution in France*, "one of the first active causes of the growth of democracy in this country" (PEJ 221). In another *Tribune* lecture, he mockingly recommends that his audience read "every aristocratic book that is published" to get a good democratic education: "Begin with *Burke's Reflections*, for I declare to you, that it was not *Tom Paine* but *Edmund Burke* that made me so zealous a reformer, and convinced me of the necessity of annual Parliaments and universal suffrage" (PEJ 309). Thelwall was not alone in crediting Burke with authoring British Jacobinism, as the reform

---

2. Mark Philp, "Introduction," in Mark Philp, ed., *The French Revolution and British Popular Politics* (Cambridge: Cambridge University Press, 1991), disputes the views of Ian Christie and H. T. Dickinson, whose historical work asserts that the loyalist argument defeated the Jacobins in a real debate (1–17). Christie's essay, "Conservatism and Stability in British Society" (169–87) argues for the popularity of loyalism, but even if, as Christie is surely correct in saying, the general population was not "terrorized" by the government, the Jacobins were, and the general population knew about it. John Dinwiddy's "Interpretation of Anti-Jacobinism" (38–49) is a judicious meditation on the historiographical issues.

3. Andrew McCann shows how Burke influences the style and structure of one of Thelwall's published lectures in *Cultural Politics in the 1790s: Literature, Radicalism and the Public Sphere* (New York and London: St. Martin's Press and Macmillan, 1999), 93–94.

societies thanked Burke on many occasions for provoking the public discussion that stimulated the growth of the democratic movement.⁴

One of Burke's arguments was that Jacobin theory sought to overturn a political culture based on centuries of experience, custom, subtle adjustments, and practical wisdom. Burke compared a small number of self-interested philosophers to numerous *generations* of political thinkers who had contributed to the "ancient constitution." To counter this argument Thelwall defended the democratic public sphere as a nonviolent space that operated without coercion where ideas, regardless of their origin, acquired or lost legitimacy. Ordinarily Thelwall likes to have it both ways, endorsing both a conflictual public sphere and an ancient constitution that authorizes democracy, but in his two most rigorously logical essays, both responding to Burke, he defends democracy not as a continuation of pre-Norman political values but as an instance of modernity grounded in a theory of labor.

Burke's Wild Rhetoric

The Jacobins discovered themselves in Burke's texts, first in the "swinish multitude" phrase that became a rallying cry for democrats who explored the limits of a new political language free of deference. Also, while Burke aggressively interpreted reality as a surface that concealed depths and complex networks of causality, so Jacobins applied the same techniques to "demystify" aristocratic culture. Burke had discovered the political unconscious. By attacking Jacobinism so ferociously, Burke introduced extremism as a legitimate style and inadvertently sanctioned sensational aspects of popular culture such as Gothic melodrama, sentimental tableaux, and eroticized violence.⁵

Whether his writings and speeches had provoked them into life or not, Burke wanted to close down the emergent democratic spheres of publicity.

---

4. Burke himself takes notice in *Letter to William Elliot* (1797) of the reform societies that have thanked him (EB 8: 30). The Unitarian Society in 1792, for example, gave "Thanks to Mr. Burke, for the important discussions he has provoked." "History of Europe," *Annual Register,* 1792, 34: 369.

5. Andrew McCann illustrates Burke's political use of sentimental conventions in the speeches attacking Lord Hastings in *Cultural Politics in the 1790s*, chap. 2. According to Tom Furniss, Burke "understood the Revolution better than Paine." *Edmund Burke's Aesthetic Ideology: Language, Gender, and Political Economy in Revolution* (Cambridge: Cambridge University Press, 1993), 187. It is possible, however, to appreciate Burke's insightfulness without denigrating Paine's.

Jacobinism

Burke attacked the Foxite Whigs who formed the Friends of the People (11 April 1792) and who had given tacit support to the Society for Constitutional Information. He did this because, even before the London Corresponding Society (LCS) was formed (in January 1792), he feared the power of popular associations, knowing that in France political clubs had given institutional shape to the idea of "popular sovereignty." During the debate on the Quebec Government Bill, Burke's speech of 21 April 1791 calls attention to the "academies of Paris and the clubs of London" (PH 29:365), drawing a parallel between the Jacobin clubs and British associations like the Revolution Society and the Constitutional Society. The aristocratic Friends of the People seemed to imitate the fifty or so French aristocrats who in 25 June 1789 renounced the privileges of the *noblesse* and formed the core of the early revolutionary leadership. Because it was shortly after the formation of the Friends of the People that the government issued its Royal Proclamation against Seditious Writings (21 May), one recent historian, Albert Goodwin, is convinced that the Proclamation was provoked by the Friends of the People, not the LCS and Paine.[6] E. P. Thompson, however, claims that Paine's inexpensive second part of the *Rights of Man* (February 1792) was the main provocation, especially as the LCS and the reorganized Constitutional Society were distributing the essay (MWC 106–7). Regardless of what motivated the government, its repression bore down on Jacobins almost as soon as they became politically active.

Encouraging and justifying the repression consistently, Burke in *Letters on a Regicide Peace* (1796) identifies the "political citizens" and "the British publick" as consisting of about 400,000 people, largely male, of whom about a fifth (or 80,000) he considers "to be pure Jacobins; utterly incapable of amendment; objects of eternal vigilance; and when they break out, of legal constraint." He finds that the radical "minority is great and formidable" and that they have "force" which is "far superior to their numbers" (EB 9:224). Among this 400,000 Burke does not even consider the "tradesmen and mechanics" who comprise the popular associations, which are far beneath his angle of vision. For Burke the political nation is the cultural elite, the social strata from the uppermost levels of the middle class. Burke's sociology seems close to the mark. Patrick Colquhoun's *Treatise on the Resources of*

---

6. Albert Goodwin, *The Friends of Liberty: The English Democratic Movement in the Age of the French Revolution* (Cambridge, Mass.: Harvard University Press, 1979), 207, 213. Many other historians dispute Goodwin on this point. See Gregory Claeys, *Thomas Paine: Social and Political Thought* (Boston: Unwin Hyman, 1989), 75.

the British Empire (1814) discovered an upper class of 512,535, around 4 percent of the overall population.⁷ Burke is worried about the disloyal, dangerous, and talented 20 percent of the elite: "Jacobinism is the revolt of the enterprising talents of a country against it's property" (EB 9:241; *Two Letters on a Regicide Peace* 1796). It is that group of "literary caballers," "intriguing philosophers," "political theologians," and "theological politicians" who seek power (EB 8:61; *Reflections* 1790). As an "enterprising talent" himself, and not a man of property, Burke knew well the group he was opposing.

For Burke the conflict is about not politics alone but cultural power. The example of France illustrated that aristocratic culture could be undermined well before the political structures collapsed. Aspects of the French public sphere—the *salons*, the *Encyclopédie*, Rousseau and the *philosophes*—prepared the way for political upheaval. Those who should be serving the interests of aristocratic society as educators, writers, preachers, theologians, novelists, dramatists, philosophers, and journalists have instead substituted their own selfish interests and allied themselves with the ambitious, landless moneyed interests (EB 8:160; *Reflections* 1790). The "swinish multitude" passage says it succinctly: when "learning" was controlled by the nobility and the church, "Learning paid back what it received to nobility and to priesthood; and paid it with usury, by enlarging their ideas and by furnishing their minds. Happy if they had all continued to know their indissoluble union, and their proper place! Happy if learning, not debauched by ambition, had been satisfied to continue the instructor, and not aspired to be the master! Along with its natural protectors and guardians, learning will be cast into the mire, and trodden down under the hoofs of a swinish multitude" (EB 8:130; *Reflections* 1790). A marvelous error or Freudian slip appears in a passage where Burke attacks Thelwall by saying young gentlemen will prefer the education they receive at "Eaton"—meaning "Eton"—to the learning they can get at Thelwall's lectures (EB 9:163; *Letter to a Noble Lord* 1796). Daniel Isaac Eaton, one of Thelwall's colleagues in the LCS, was a frequently indicted and jailed publisher whose most well-known work was *Politics for the People; or, a Salmagundy for Swine*. Indeed, one can summarize Burke's nightmare: Eaton for Eton.

Burke identifies the swinish instructors who do not know their proper

---

7. The population figures are in Guy Aldred, *Richard Carlile, Agitator: His Life and Times*, 3rd ed. (Glasgow: Strickland Press, 1941), 32.

place with sexual excess, cannibalism, and Judaism. Each signifies a loss of control, and a regression from virtue, moderation, and ultimately, from Christianity. "I am certain," Burke insists, "that the writings of Rousseau lead directly to this kind of shameful evil"—that is, the sexual exploitation of female students by these "debauchers of virgins" (EB 8:316-17; *Letter to a Member of the National Assembly* 1791). Rousseau's novel *Julie*, popular on both sides of the channel, is the proof text for illustrating sexual immorality. The cannibal imagery, which seems now a sign of Burke's loss of rhetorical control, had a factual pretext at the time in the newspaper reports of cannibalism during revolutionary massacres. Burke argues that "the sect of cannibal philosophers of France" and the "cannibal philosophy" itself (EB 9:174-75; *Letter to a Noble Lord* 1796) carried out a cultural desublimation that inverted social hierarchies, with high becoming low, low becoming high. The "cannibal Republick" manifests the vampirish control of Jacobinism, "the evil spirit that possesses the body of France" (EB 9:274, 264; *Two Letters on a Regicide Peace* 1797). He writes that "out of the tomb of the murdered Monarchy in France, has arisen a vast, tremendous, unformed spectre," a "hideous phantom" (EB 9:190-91; *Two Letters* 1797). "By cannibalism, I mean their devouring . . . some part of the bodies of those they have murdered," including drinking blood, all of which was reported in the newspapers (EB 9:245; *Noble Lord* 1796). Factual or fictional, cannibalism is a metaphor for the diabolical incarnation of the philosophical spirit, the transformation of Enlightenment mind into terrorist body; it is the moral extreme limit, just as regicide is the political extreme limit. There is a spectrum of moral weakness displayed by the French revolutionaries, including easy divorce, sexual excess, violence, regicide, parricide, cannibalism; the differences are of degree, not kind. Moreover, the desublimation of desire celebrated by Sensibility, which followed the rejection of traditional modes of deference, sooner or later but inevitably for Burke grows into the most repugnant acts of violence.

Related to the image of cannibalism is Burke's frequent imagery of revolutionary mental disease. "A certain intemperance of intellect is the disease of the time, and the source of all its other diseases" (EB 8:330; *Letter to a Member of the National Assembly* 1791). He assumes that the mind requires repression of the evil instincts if one is to have civilization. "Our physical well-being, our moral worth, our social happiness, our political tranquillity, all depend on that controul of our appetites and passions, which the ancients designed by the cardinal virtue of Temperance" (EB 9:359; *Third Letter on a Regicide Peace* 1797). The revolution has relaxed the emotional restraints on people so that forbidden pleasures are pursued without guilt. "It requires restraint to keep men from falling into that habit" of indulging desires that bring both immediate pleasure and social harm (EB 8:301; *Letter to a Member of the National Assembly* 1791). (As we will see later, the temperance/ intemperance dialectic is an organizing metaphor for Thelwall's political rhetoric.)

The most powerful moral restraint was religion, the weakening of which during the revolution was occasion for Burke's scapegoating of Judaism and Jews. Burke uses antisemitism to link Jews and Jacobins with unscrupulous commercial practices, low social status, and anti-Christian heresy. Iain McCalman's recent article on Burke's antisemitism notes that Lord George Gordon, the most famous convert to Judaism in the eighteenth century, "is the archetypal revolutionary figure who stalks through the pages of the *Reflections.*"[8] Gordon, who singled out Burke as the chief opponent of the militantly anti-Catholic Protestant Association (McCalman 352), employed Radical Dissent's characteristic philosemitic "restorationist" and "conversionist" rhetoric about Jews; Radical Dissent had been responsible for Burke's losing his Bristol seat after 1780. While in prison Gordon associated with known Jacobins like Horne Tooke, Thomas Hardy, and Robert Watson.[9] Encouraging Burke's negative projection, a typical aspect of antisemitism, Burke represses the similarities between himself and Gordon: they were both ethnic and religious outsiders; they were both emotional, sensual, humanitarian, visionary, and extremist (McCalman 367). Antisemitism, which contained and managed sources of personal anxiety for Burke, at the same time yielded ideological dividends in deflecting anti-Catholic prejudice.

It is all too obvious that the attack on Jewish commercialism was ideological: at a time when Britain was borrowing millions of pounds to finance its war debt and developing a huge credit system based on paper money not that different from the French assignats; at a time when Burke himself defended laissez-faire capitalism during a famine year; at a time when even the richest landowners were also capitalists who supported commerce and

---

8. Iain McCalman, "Mad Lord George and Madame La Motte: Riot and Sexuality in the Genesis of Burke's Reflections on the Revolution in France," *Journal of British Studies* 35 (1996): 346; 343–67.

9. The Reverend James Murray, a radical Dissenter who had such an important influence on Thomas Spence, was a staunch member of the Protestant Association in Newcastle.

trade; at a time when Britain was clearly becoming more bourgeois in every conceivable way—Burke demonizes Jewish greed.

Burke's demonized opponents—Fox, Price, Rousseau, philosophes, Gordon, Jews—are Gothic villains in a revolutionary melodrama, figures deriving from popular culture, not the elite culture he tried to defend. Burke's cannibals, Jewish tricksters, seductive tutors, Frankenstein monsters of demonic violence, parricidal children, and sexually promiscuous youth all seem to have stepped out of the cheap urban prints and sensationalist press. There is no arguing with rhetoric as wild as this, the discursive equivalent of the guillotine. Burke's writing turns violently "Jacobin" in its struggle against the Jacobins. Although Burke's efforts strengthened the political repression and cultural reaction, they also strengthened the Jacobin spheres of publicity as well. Symbolic of the unintended consequences that Burke's discourse generated, his *Letter to a Noble Lord* (1796) traces the Duke of Bedford's aristocratic power to its ignoble origins in royal theft, as if Burke were the Jacobin.

Thomas Paine and the Popular Reader

If Burke sought to repress the emergent public sphere, there was one writer who expanded it in such a dramatic way that he restructured literacy in Britain. The popularity of Paine's writing was an embarrassment, an empirical refutation of the loyalist consensus the government desired in its national mobilization against revolutionary France. That Paine himself was outlawed, his writings banned and prosecuted, and his effigy burned illustrated how Jacobin writing was repressed by force rather than reason. The repression, however, was only partially successful, as thousands of Paine's texts were sold in the 1790s, when they were illegal.

To account for the popularity of Paine's writing one must analyze his style. Paine is one of the pioneers in what Olivia Smith has called the "intellectual vernacular" style of writing. Combining vernacular diction and formal syntax, colloquialism and formality, Paine's prose resembles Augustan poetry in its clarity and couplet-like structures more than it does other late-eighteenth century prose. Notes Smith, "To bring formal syntax and vernacular diction together as successfully as Paine does implies that the attributes of syntactical order are inherently compatible with the spoken language, when formal syntax was widely held to distinguish vulgar from refined usage." Bringing aspects of "vulgar" speech to the conventions of polite discourse, Paine also achieves intimacy with his reader by means of "rhetorical questions" and first-person plural gestures of shared knowledge.[10]

To illustrate Paine's style and explore some of its implications, I want to compare the extended metaphor that concludes *The Rights of Man*, Part Two, with a similar extended metaphor in Shelley's "Ode to the West Wind." I also want to describe how Paine's *Letter Addressed to the Addressers* adopts satirical and parodic techniques that become exemplary for Jacobin satire.

To illustrate that the principles of his *Rights of Man* are not "new fangled," he uses "a figure easily understood."

> It is now towards the middle of February. Were I to take a turn in the country, the trees would present a leafless wintery appearance. As people are apt to pluck twigs as they walk along, I perhaps might do the same, and by chance might observe, that a *single bud* on that twig had begun to swell. I should reason very unnaturally, or rather not reason at all, to suppose this was the *only* bud in England which had this appearance. Instead of deciding thus, I should instantly conclude, that the same appearance was beginning, or about to begin, every where; and though the vegetable sleep will continue longer on some trees and plants than on others, and though some of them may not *blossom* for two or three years, all will be in leaf in the summer, except those which are *rotten*. What pace the political summer may keep with the natural, no human foresight can determine. It is, however, not difficult to perceive that the spring is begun.—Thus wishing, as I sincerely do, freedom and happiness to all nations, I close the SECOND PART. (WTP 2:517–18)

James Boulton, who singled out this passage to illustrate Paine's artistry, calls the allegory "as simple as biblical parable" with a clear message that draws upon a universal experience. Paine "has succeeded in detaching himself from his own powerful feelings and has embodied them in a vivid and concrete image which precisely conveys the desired sense of inevitability."[11]

The inevitable growth of spring vegetation surely contrasts with the arbi-

---

10. Olivia Smith, *The Politics of Language 1791–1819* (Oxford: Clarendon Press, 1984), 48–53; the entire second chapter is on Paine, 134–50.

11. James T. Boulton, *The Language of Politics in the Age of Wilkes and Burke* (London and Toronto: Routledge and Kegan Paul, University of Toronto Press, 1963), 137.

trariness suggested in "new fangled," thus countering Burke's accusation that democratic "innovation" is a willful, self-serving strategy for middle-class intellectuals to seize power and violently overturn centuries of "organic" political culture. The natural inevitability of democratic revolution is a "moral" one can draw from this parable, but allegories are notoriously ambiguous. The "single bud" refers to a single individual's democratic commitment, but it also suggests the singularity of first the American and then the French revolutions, something Paine recurrently represents in his essay. The "vegetable sleep" refers then to both individuals and nations. The distinction between "blossom" and "leaf" infers a progressive development toward radical democracy, and the italicized "rotten" infers the forceful abolition of obsolete institutions. Vegetation that is sleeping may, at some point, awaken, but rotten vegetation is already dead. The symbolism here is violent. The essay's conclusion is that England must assemble a political convention voted by the entire population to construct a political constitution to avert a civil war. The organic metaphors—sleeping vegetation and rotten wood—disguise the degree of willful transgression that Paine is recommending.

The allegory's "I" is a casual but objective observer who is doubled as a "single bud," and who has a very personal presence as a well-wisher, a friend that seems to shake the reader's hand at the end of the book. Are the "buds" individuals or are they the *thoughts* of individuals? Or both? In either case, Paine deemphasizes his own role as propagandist because the allegory depicts an impersonal process that runs its course inevitably. No matter what happens, Paine the writer remains as cheerfully congenial as ever. He has called attention to some "natural" truths that rational people will heed, truths Paine himself has not invented. Even the most original aspect of his essay, the taxation and welfare scheme that anticipates the social-democratic welfare state, is so detailed that anyone can check the arithmetic. Paine claims no special knowledge. When the essay refers to Paine himself it does so strategically to stress his independence and impartiality (to contrast Burke's alleged bias as a state pensioner). He uses his own poverty and literary success to illustrate aristocracy's lack of merit (WTP 2:473).

Metaphorical play and allegories are sprinkled throughout *The Rights of Man*. To give one final example, Paine calls a government deprived of "the rights of man" unfit for humans; such an institution is "beastlike," perhaps fit for animals if not people (WTP 2:439–40). He also exploits the animal figure in a later passage where he explains a Swiss "custom" in such a way as to make the political allegory all too obvious. The canton of Berne used to keep at public expense a bear because they believed that without the bear "they should all be undone." After the bear happened to die and was not replaced immediately with a new one, people noticed that the canton prospered just as well without a bear, so "they resolved not to keep any more bears" (WTP 2:447). This allegory, by making monarchy a superstition punctured by "common sense," reinforces the natural, inevitable, nonarbitrary aspects of republican democracy, not the intentions of the allegorist.

Shelley's "Ode to the West Wind," published first in the *Prometheus Unbound* volume,[12] analogizes natural changes and cycles with political revolution, as does Paine's allegory. The fourth and fifth sections of the poem represent the poet in ways that contrast with Paine's self-depiction.[13] Paine's allegorist is cheerful, objective, impartial, and urbane, while Shelley's speaker is tragically conflicted and thwarted, yearning for qualities he lacks, especially the "Uncontrollable." Shelley resolves the speaker's dilemma by means of symbolic violence that transforms allegorist into allegory, prophecy into prophet. Paine's persona in *The Rights of Man* is emphatically like the implied popular reader, but Shelley's persona is emphatically solitary, isolated, detached from ordinary society. He is instead close to the sublime, the inexpressible, the absolute. Paine anxiously downplayed the willful dimension of republican democracy; Shelley's ode dramatizes the conflict between will and nature, desire and natural process. If Paine's allegory is like biblical parable, Shelley's is like some synthesis of Isaiah (the sixth chapter's "coal" suggests "sparks") and Job (the tormented faith and "ashes"). For the authority of his writing Paine relies on the democratic public sphere. Shelley's ode, however, uses a prophetic model of authority that is founded ultimately on the encounter between divinity and prophet. Paine is so wedded to the public sphere that he can justify not replying to various critics of Part One of *The Rights of Man* on the grounds that such criticisms did not sell sufficiently. The public, by opting not to purchase enough copies, had by itself "refuted" unpopular criticisms of Paine (WTP 2:396). Shelley's own position in relation to the public sphere was far more problematic, as his most stylistically popular texts went unpublished or were poorly distributed, and much of his writing is esoteric in the high Romantic style, a deliberate

12. In *Radical Shelley: The Philosophical Anarchism and Utopian Thought of Percy Bysshe Shelley* (Princeton: Princeton University Press, 1982), chap. 5, I show how the volume of *Prometheus Unbound* as a whole functions as a prophetic text.

13. Perhaps the first to call attention to the parallels between Paine's allegory and Shelley's "Ode to the West Wind" was Kenneth Neill Cameron, *The Young Shelley: Genesis of a Radical* (New York: Collier, 1950), 75.

estrangement from the literary market. Although Shelley uses the same naturalistic analogies as Paine, the two writers are differently positioned in regard to the public sphere that shapes their writing decisively. To bolster the authority of his Jacobinism, Shelley appeals to posterity and the ineffable, with which he has a special prophetic relationship; Paine *displays* the grounds of his Jacobin authority by natural analogies as well as pointing to the quantity of his readers. Shelley finds in the Romantic author's prophetic stance a defense against the literary market structurally distorted by repression and inequality, whereas Paine's triumph in the literary market occasioned the repression and cultural offensive that shaped the market in the early nineteenth century. Paine's writing in effect made Shelley's literature inevitable.

Another Paine text that bears comparison with Romantic literature is the remarkable *Letter Addressed to the Addressers on the Late Proclamation* (1792), published while Paine was in France and shortly before the seditious libel trial for Part Two of *The Rights of Man* (WTP 3:45–96). On 21 May 1792 there was a royal proclamation against seditious writings and an indictment of Paine for *The Rights of Man*. The loyalist forces orchestrated 320 (according to Paine's count) loyal "addresses" to the crown affirming the glory of the British Constitution and the wretched evil of seditious blasphemers like Thomas Paine (WTP 3:58). The gloriously unrepentant *Letter* is, if anything, more transgressive than the *Rights of Man*, as the *Letter*'s humor is slashing, its satire uncompromising, and its tone disrespectful and unflappably self-confident. Compared with the hundreds of thousands of copies of his own writings that have sold, he is less than impressed by the far smaller number of people involved in the state-sponsored anti-Jacobin rallies and "addresses." Contemptuous of parliamentary reform, he is convinced that anything short of a "convention" on the French model is inadequate because the present regime has no political legitimacy (WTP 3:80, 94–95). He has no respect whatsoever for the legal case against his writing (WTP 3:65–78).

The *Letter* incorporates a kind of heckling of public speakers that was not uncommon in the oral political culture outside parliament. In this particular satire Paine is mocking Lord Stormont's loyalist speech in parliament, which he reproduces and undermines with bracketed heckling.

> That *we* shall *all* be unanimous in expressing *our* attachment to the constitution of these realms, *I am confident*. It is a subject upon which there can be *no* divided opinion *in this house*. I do not pretend

to be deep read in the knowledge of the Constitution, but *I take upon me* to say, that from the extent of *my* knowledge [*for I have so many thousands a year for nothing*] it appears to *me*, that from the period of the Revolution, for it was by no means created then, it has been, both in *theory* and *practice*, the *wisest* system that ever was formed. I never was [he means he never was *till now*] a dealer in *political cant*. (WTP 3:48)

And so it continues on for many more sentences with sarcastic italicizations and bracketed comments. Merely by repeating Stormont's words with the strategic italics Paine creates parody, destroying the earnest, dignified tonalities of the loyalist address. The first italicized "we" calls attention to the presumption of unanimity that is clearly counterfactual. It also highlights group identities, as Stormont's "we" is hardly the same as the "we" who would read Paine's pamphlet. The first bracketed heckling is especially bold for the represented *thought* of Stormont rather than merely a third-person statement about his being an aristocratic parasite. Representing side by side the words of a Lord and of the "staymaker" Paine is effective social satire. Paine and Stormont are, on the page of this pamphlet if nowhere else, equals. Moreover, the parody and heckling translate into discursive form the abstract concept of a government lacking legitimacy. The antiauthoritarian humor is the style by which delegitimated figures like Lord Stormont are attacked.

Another satirical section exploits the religious piety of loyalist rhetoric by dramatizing a fictional attempt in parliament to suppress a part of the Bible (Book of Samuel) that is hostile to monarchy (WTP 3:50–54). Paine parodies parliamentary style and by reductio ad absurdum exposes the contradictory logic of loyalist discourse, which is skillfully turned against itself. In a comment apropos the suppression of seditious writing, Paine remarks: "It is a dangerous attempt in any government to say to a Nation, '*thou shalt not read*' " (WTP 3:58). Paine's satire irreverently appropriates the voices of political and religious authority, turning one authority against another to counter habits of deference. The mocking, disrespectful tones exorcise hierarchical habits of thinking.

Paine's own authority is the empirically verifiable popularity of his writings. Such a simple fact is easy to pass over. The government replied to Paine's political essays with swift repression, and then with loyalist parades during which Paine's effigy was burned. Meanwhile those hundreds of thousands of contraband copies of Paine's writing were circulating in Britain and Ireland. Burke's authority did not depend on the literary market, where, nevertheless, he prospered: as a member of Parliament he also connected his literary oeuvre to the aristocratic institutions he served. The epistolary form of his essays is Augustan, even if the actual style of those works is Romantic in its digressiveness, metaphorical richness, and rhetorical wildness. Paine, despite his considerable egotism and vanity, was a Jacobin writer, not an author. His works are not just occasional—called into existence by the political occasion—but impersonal in their exploration of objective truths. Although after his death Burke became the prophet against the eighteenth century, he too was largely a writer rather than an author. Retroactively, his writing was turned into literature.[14] Detached from the occasion that gave rise to the texts, his writing came to signify opposition to a general Enlightenment style rather than to discrete opponents. In Wordsworth's blank verse of 1832, Burke's words outlive him to denounce prophetically "against all systems built on abstract rights" so that Burke "with high disdain, / Explod[es] upstart Theory." Under the pressure from Romantic ideology, Paine's writing becomes upstart theory while Burke's becomes literature, attached to ideas "hallowed by time."[15] Thelwall, as we will see, tempers his role as upstart theorist with authority claims linked to nature, so that although he shares ground with Paine he also adopts the prophetic stance when appeals to the literary market alone would be ineffective.

Thelwall's *Sober Reflections*

Burke's *Letter to a Noble Lord* was published 24 February 1796, shortly after the reform movement had failed to prevent the passage of the Two Acts. Thelwall's *Sober Reflections on the Seditious and Inflammatory Letter of the Rt. Hon. Edmund Burke to a Noble Lord*, called by Coleridge Thelwall's *chef d'oeuvre*,[16] effectively defends Jacobin "theory" but does not succeed in

---

14. Alfred Cobban, *Edmund Burke and The Revolt Against the Eighteenth Century: A Study of the Political and Social Thinking of Burke, Wordsworth, Coleridge, and Southey* (London: G. Allen and Unwin, 1929).

15. 1850 *Prelude*, 7: 524, 527–29. Jonathan Wordsworth, M. H. Abrams, and Stephen Gill, eds., *The Prelude 1799, 1805, 1850* (New York: W. W. Norton, 1979).

16. Earl Leslie Griggs, ed., *Collected Letters of Samuel Taylor Coleridge*, 6 vols. (Oxford: Clarendon Press, 1956), 1:221. Griggs misidentifies the reference as *The Rights of Nature*, which is an impossibility because the letter was written 22 June 1796 and *The Rights of*

undermining Burke's overall credibility. Burke's *Letter to Noble Lord* is one of the best things Burke ever wrote, a powerful rhetorical performance that destroys with energy, precision, and thoroughness the Foxite Whig argument that Burke exchanged his political ideology for a generous government pension. Burke illustrates his political consistency and turns the tables on the Duke of Bedford, Burke's principal critic in the House of Lords, by showing that Bedford had inherited his wealth and position, while *he*, Burke, had earned his place and honors. "The Duke of Bedford is the Leviathan among the creatures of the Crown," according to Burke, providing an evocative image that caricaturists adopted readily, portraying Bedford as a swollen whale in satirical prints. "My merits, whatever they are, are original and personal; his are derivative" (EB 8:164–65). Burke assumes the persona of an offended commoner who even plays the Jacobin game of tracing aristocratic wealth to its origins; Bedford's wealth is from the land of an executed traitor confiscated by Henry VIII, and later the first Lord Russell also received confiscated church lands (EB 8:167). Burke cleverly draws the parallel between the arbitrary tyrant Henry and church-destroying French revolutionaries. Movingly representing his reaction to his son's death (EB 8:171), he makes an emotional appeal that secures his position as a credible disputant and injured party. Indeed, by the end of the essay it is Bedford who seems hypocritical, not Burke.

Thelwall's main objective in *Sober Reflections* is not to attack Burke's personal integrity, but insofar as he follows the line of the Foxites, he is no more convincing than they when he denounces Burke's pension. Thelwall attacks the pension as an instance of overall corruption, taking wealth from the working poor and giving it to the privileged and powerful (PEJ 356), but the argument's logic leads one to question any and all pensions, not just Burke's. If Burke's *Letter to a Noble Lord* vindicated Burke's own political integrity and demolished Bedford's, it also tried to read Bedford symptomatically as typical of Jacobinism. Where Burke's essay is weakest, Thelwall's is strongest, defending the intellectual project of Jacobin philosophy. Thelwall defends Jacobin theory by vindicating the democratic public sphere, ascribing violence to tyranny and injustice rather than to the actions of the oppressed, and finally contrasting the "sober" method of philosophy with the intemperate rhetoric of Burke.

Nature was published no earlier than November 1796 in answer to Burke's *Two Letters on a Regicidal Peace*, published 20 October 1796.

Thelwall concedes that the French philosophy that inspired the revolution was flawed. His stance, however, holds that such philosophy failed not because it deviated too much from the norms of aristocratic thinking but because it did not deviate *enough* from such thinking. French ideas were not entirely adequate because the public sphere from which they issued was not sufficiently egalitarian. The aristocratic salons produced a philosophical style marked by "servile effeminacy," "sullen retirement," and "solitary abstraction." In contrast, British democratic ideas are marked by "boldness," "active energy," and "energy of mind" because they are the products of "thronged and promiscuous audiences" and take place "in theatres and halls of assembly" (PEJ 376). The two lattermost phrases within quotations are direct citations from Burke, who characterizes the democratic public sphere as violent. Thelwall turns the tables on Burke by contrasting open political discussion—manly, virtuous, and British—with constrained political speech—effete, aristocratic, and French. Insofar as Burke advocates constraints on political debate, he has placed himself in a "French" position. Drawing upon a durable Francophobic stereotype of effeminacy, Thelwall challenges the anti-Jacobins as unmanly cowards for curbing political debate.

Thelwall uses Burke's *Letter to a Noble Lord* to illustrate the intrinsic rationality of political discussion and to defend not just democratic ideas but the further democratization of the public sphere itself.[17] The "advantages" of Burke's essay, according to Thelwall, "are consequential—certainly not intended; but . . . the mischief is in the thing itself. Mischief and good are merely relative terms; for nothing is exclusively productive either of the one or the other: and with respect to intellectual, or literary exertions, the balance is always eventually, I believe, favourable to the happiness of mankind" (PEJ 335). A text, however "mischievous," causes no permanent harm because, after all, "mankind now read too many books to be permanently injured by any" (PEJ 336). Thelwall defends the process of publicity, inquiry, and debate as inherently rational. To constrain this process is to be

---

17. Kevin Gilmartin's study has a rich appreciation for what he calls the "plebeian counterpublic sphere," to distinguish it from the bourgeois public sphere. *Print Politics: The Press and Radical Opposition in Early Nineteenth-Century England* (Cambridge: Cambridge University Press, 1996), 18. Paul Hamilton illustrates the centrality of the radical public sphere for William Godwin by showing that his *Political Justice* and *Caleb Williams* presuppose the 1790s public sphere (with "unlimited discussion" and the right to "private judgment") before the repression closed it down—and with it, a way of thinking. "Coleridge and Godwin in the 1790s," in Richard Gravil and Molly Lefebure, eds., *The Coleridge Connection: Essays for Thomas McFarland* (Basingstoke: Macmillan Press, 1990), 41–59.

violent and to sustain this process is to promote truth. Any kind of public discourse promotes the social good ultimately: "if he will but write, take whatever side he will, I am sure that truth will be derived from his labours," because any kind of energetic writing will produce reading and interpretation, leading eventually to truthful conclusions. Writing is not controlled by authors but by readers, who in turn are subject to the dictates of a "truth" greater than their individual preferences. Only a mind "considerably warped by the strong bias of interested prejudice" can fail to follow the inevitable drift of public discourse toward "liberty and justice." With their texts writers intend certain effects that are foiled by a social process that produces something quite unlike the original idea. Thelwall's favorite example is Burke's own *Reflections*, which initiated a process that extended "the boundaries of science beyond the narrow pale of opulence" and "carried the invaluable discussion of political principles and civil rights to the shopboard of the artificers, and the cottage of the laborious husbandman" (PEJ 332). Thelwall upholds the democratic public sphere, then, as an instrument of *social* rationality; it is not the product of isolated philosophers spinning out abstract ideas.

Thelwall's model for communicative action is not solitary reflection or parliamentary debate but mass literacy and the political meeting. He provides a theoretical defense of the new social realities symbolized by the huge demonstrations against the Two Acts in late 1795 and the hundreds of thousands who read Paine's *Rights of Man*. By radicalizing the Enlightenment Thelwall transcends the class bias of the bourgeois public sphere and incorporates the lowest social strata of politically insurgent laborers into his public. Moreover, Thelwall does not draw a rigid distinction between speech and writing. The public meeting itself is a rational structure within which effective communicative action takes place. Language is not individualistically defined; rather, language is most truly itself in dialogue, as it passes between people, as writing becomes reading, and as reading becomes many times multiplied and reflected. The "truth" that is in language reveals itself only in social process.

Thelwall's dispute with Godwin illustrates the social basis of Thelwall's language theory. In 1795 Godwin wrote specifically against the LCS in general and Thelwall in particular, claiming that public meetings were dangerous. He explained: "The collecting of immense multitudes of men into one assembly, particularly when there have been no persons of eminence, distinction, and importance in the country, that have mixed with them, and been ready to temper their efforts, is always sufficiently alarming."[18] Alarming, however, is how Thelwall terms Godwin's "cold abstraction and retirement," his *"feebleness of spirit,"* and "solitary vanity." Unwilling to risk the public scrutiny of his "singular speculations" by a popular assembly, Godwin in effect betrays the reform movement and joins its enemies (PEJ 382). (Thelwall ignores unfairly that Godwin *also* argued against passage of the Two Acts.) The democratic public sphere, then, guards against cold abstractions and rationalistic monstrosities. Repression (Burke) and elitist assumptions concerning public rationality (Godwin) actually produce social violence by restraining the only process that can guarantee whether political and social ideas have been adequately tested and probed.

Another way Thelwall counters the charge that Jacobin theory caused violence is to offer an alternative history of the French Revolution. Thelwall's account is similar to but different in important respects from the Girondin narrative already discussed. As long as the revolution was led by philosophers and literary men, it prospered nonviolently. The foreign invasion by the European monarchs, however, introduced something the literati could not control. Only the Mountain was "energetic" enough to mount an adequate defense against the invasion, as the "philosophical" party—the Brissot and Girondin faction—was not ready for action. The September massacres of 1792 were not caused by "cannibal philosophers"; rather, the Duke of Brunswick's manifesto provoked the violence (PEJ 359–62). Thelwall does not endorse revolutionary violence, but he provides a narrative that explains it but does not excuse it: "Inhuman oppression generates inhuman revenge" (PEJ 375). If anything is a quintessential Jacobin narrative, it is that revolutionary violence is caused by tyranny, not anything immanent within the revolutionary project itself. Thelwall, whose perspective here is the standard Jacobin viewpoint, does not think that there was something disturbingly unprecedented about the violence of the French Revolution.

Related to violence is "energy," a common word not just in this essay but in his other 1790s writings. A typical paragraph on the French Revolution in *Sober Reflections* has five uses of energy (or one of its cognates). The "philosophical party" lacks sufficient "energy" for decisive action in the crisis precipitated by the invasion of revolutionary France in 1792; the philosophers

---

18. *Considerations on Lord Grenville's and Mr. Pitt's Bills* (London: Joseph Johnson, 1795), rpt. in Mark Philp, ed., *Political and Philosophical Writings of William Godwin*, 8 vols. (London: William Pickering, 1993), 2: 130. For an illuminating discussion of Godwin's ambivalence over the public sphere, see McCann, *Cultural Politics in the 1790s*, chap. 2.

needed more than "fine-spun theories and speculations" to counter the reactionary violence. Thelwall criticizes the Mountain, "the more energetic party," for "the ferocious barbarity" and "cruelty" by which they abused their power in repelling the invasion. He then contrasts the philosophers, "deficient in the powerful energies of manhood," and the Mountain, "energetic" but "destitute of the humanising temperament of philosophy." (This is one of the earliest versions of the statement so memorably expressed in the first act of Shelley's *Prometheus Unbound*—and rephrased later in Yeats's "The Second Coming"—"The good want power, but to weep barren tears. / The powerful goodness want: worse need for them. / The wise want love, and those who love want wisdom; / And all best things are thus confused to ill.")[19] Finally, he compares the "*imbecility*" of the philosophical party with the "*ferocity*" of the "*energetic party*" (PEJ 361–62). The best things, according to Thelwall, are thus confused to ill, as the energetic Mountain is filled with passionate intensity and the philosophers lack enough conviction to be effective.

While unusual, Thelwall's use of "energy" is not unprecedented. Consider Blake's "energy" in the 1790s: "Energy is the *only* life and is from the Body and Reason is the bound or outward circumference of Energy." Blake concludes the fourth plate of *The Marriage of Heaven and Hell* thus: "Energy is Eternal Delight."[20] William Keach, in a recent essay, suggests that we have neglected to treat seriously Blake's attitude toward violence. Blake seems to have been attracted to the "force" unleashed by the French Revolution, even the Terror. *America* and *Europe*, to name two poems, are quite violent, and we have tended to idealize the violence, ignoring its social reference in the 1790s.[21] Thelwall's "energy," then, seems to be similar to what one finds in Blake's writing: energy signifies the actual power by which unreasonable restrictions on desire will be destroyed.

Two other aspects of *Sober Reflections* illustrate the ostentatious restraint of his reply to Burke. Burke, after all, attacked Thelwall directly in *Letter to a Noble Lord*, to which attack Thelwall refers only twice, once alluding to the "popular schools" denounced by Burke and meaning, of course, the

19. Quoted from Donald H. Reiman and Sharon B. Powers, eds., *Shelley's Poetry and Prose* (New York: W. W. Norton, 1977).
20. From the facsimile reprint of *The Marriage of Heaven and Hell* (Oxford: Oxford University Press, 1975).
21. William Keach, "Blake, Violence, and Visionary Politics," in James A. W. Heffernan, ed., *Representing the French Revolution: Literature, Historiography and Art* (Hanover: University Press of New England, 1992), 24–40.

political lectures delivered at the Beaufort Buildings and at the open-air meetings before the passage of the Two Acts (PEJ 351), and again at the end of the essay in a brief self-justification, which I will soon take up. (A subsequent text by Burke, *Letters on the Regicidal Peace*, which makes no direct reference to Thelwall, provokes a much angrier rhetoric in the first letter of *The Rights of Nature*, as we will see.) In *Sober Reflections* Thelwall is playing cool-headed rationalist against Burke's emotionally unrestrained performance, but the anti-Catholicism and gender symbolism weaken the rationalist logic.[22]

Defensive at being labeled a Jacobin, foreign, and Francophilic, Thelwall fashions himself as a patriotic British Protestant and portrays Burke as a crypto-Catholic whose patriotism is suspect.[23] Burke was attacked his whole career for being a secret Catholic, in part because of his Irish upbringing, including his early education at Catholic schools. Referring to Burke's criticism of Henry VIII's liquidation of the monasteries and religious orders, Thelwall insinuates that Burke, "*the pupil of St. Omer's*," unable to control his "intemperate zeal," harbors a secret fondness for Catholic institutions (PEJ 340). (Was Thelwall aware of the irony that the very term "Jacobin" derived ultimately from a Catholic convent, that the French revolutionaries were repeating the example of Henry VIII with their confiscations? Probably.) When Thelwall identifies the machinery of repression with "Inquisitors," "the "Auto da Fé," and speaks of a new "Inquisition," the allusions are hardly innocent. Their provocative Protestantism emphasizes Burke's supposed Catholicism and hence an un-British anti-Jacobinism (PEJ 347, 358). The irrationality of the anti-Catholicism is disguised behind the myth of Protestant self-control and Catholic emotionalism.

Completing the structure of the argument is Thelwall's presentation of himself as the manly, even chivalrous suitor of a feminized reform— "Reform, like a long-woo'd virgin" (PEJ 347). Burke, as a representative of the aristocracy, is an effeminate pensioner who has prostituted his talent, so that the symbolic logic links Burke with femaleness and prostitution. Comparing his own honest labor as a lecturer with Burke's professional career,

22. The interests of balance require one to point also to Thelwall's strong political support for Catholic Emancipation. Prominent essays in favor of emancipation appear in the *Champion* (11 April 1819; 9 May 1819; 16 May 1819). It is also curious that Thelwall's daughter converted to Catholicism, returning to the faith of Thelwall's grandfather. See *Diary, Reminiscences, and Correspondence of Henry Crabbe Robinson*, 2 vols., ed. Thomas Sadler, 3rd ed. (New York: Macmillan Press, 1872), [diary entry 27 June 1839], 2: 220.

23. Linda Colley's study makes clear the role of Protestantism in constructing British patriotism. *Britons: Forging a Nation 1707–1837* (New Haven: Yale University Press, 1992).

Thelwall turns this against Burke, especially Burke's charge against Thelwall that he was a "pander to avarice and ambition." Just as Burke turned the tables on the Duke of Bedford on the issue of earning rather than merely inheriting wealth, so Thelwall tries to turn the tables on Burke. Despite their obvious differences, there were similarities in their position, as both Burke and Thelwall were skilled orators, men of letters, and politicians who lacked independent wealth and who had to rely on the patronage of others. Burke was possibly irritated by Thelwall's criticisms. In a notebook, Burke ironically laments that he has not been enlightened by the "moral Language of Mr. Thelwall" (EB 9:687).

The passage in which Burke refers to pandering is worth a closer look. Several pages after Burke attacks Thelwall's "vile illiberal school," his "new French academy of the *sans culottes*" (EB 9:163), he focuses on the Duke of Bedford in relation to his ancestors, hoping that the present Duke will be better than the first one, who was guilty of collaborating with the "*levelling tyrant*" Henry VIII (EB 9:167). Noting that some of the subsequent Russells were honorable and virtuous, Burke hopes the present Duke, only thirty years old, will follow in their footsteps:

> Let the Duke of Bedford (I am sure he will) reject with scorn and horror, the counsels of the lecturers, those wicked panders to avarice and ambition, who would tempt him in the troubles of his country, to seek another enormous fortune from the forfeitures of another nobility, and the plunder of another church. Let him (and I trust that yet he will) employ all the energy of his youth, and all the resources of his wealth, to crush rebellious principles which have no foundation in morals, and rebellious movements, that have no provocation in tyranny. (EB 9:169).

The lecturer-pander here exploits the weaknesses of his audience just as a pimp mediates between prostitute and customer. Prostitution, a figure by which Thelwall was attacked in 1803 by Francis Jeffrey, is a recurrent trope for social dependence, ambition, and upward social mobility in Thelwall's own writing, even from his first book of poetry in 1787.[24] The aristocratic

---

24. *Edinburgh Review* 2 (April 1803): 200. In eighteenth-century satire charging one's literary opponents with being "prostitutes" was commonplace, of course. Leigh Hunt in the nineteenth century was associated with prostitution and homosexuality in literary-political attacks. See Kim Wheatley, "The *Blackwood*'s Attacks on Leigh Hunt," *Nineteenth-Century Literature* 47 (1992): 14–17.

convention in satire that dates back to the Restoration and eighteenth century identifies with prostitution certain professional activities—government service and writing especially—deemed essentially commercial and undertaken in bad faith. Those without aristocratic or republican "virtue" and integrity prostitute whatever talent they possess in exchange for wealth.

Thelwall's brief self-defense in *Sober Reflections*, modest when compared to Burke's extended self-justification in *Letter to a Noble Lord*, dwells on the pandering image. Had he been a true pander, a thoroughly unscrupulous go-between for his audience and its desires, Thelwall argues, he would have gotten rich from his lectures. Instead, he derived a small income from a public that paid voluntarily to hear him speak. Burke, on the other hand, enriched himself by speaking against the interests of those whose taxes contributed disproportionately to the pension, a not very honorable reward for a dishonorable labor. If anyone is tainted by the suspicion of pandering, it is Burke, not Thelwall, who sold his services to the aristocracy. Had Thelwall, a universally acknowledged public speaker of great effectiveness, wanted wealth, he would have pursued a career in law, but it was precisely someone from the profession of law who scolded Thelwall, suggesting he should find something better to do than deliver public lectures (PEJ 384). Although I cannot trace the source of that scolding, I presume it was either one of the many judges or prosecutors with whom Thelwall had to deal. Unidentified, this person is attacked by Thelwall—in a parenthesis—for being a *"go-between to male prostitution"* (PEJ 384). Burke is guilty by association in this piece of rhetoric, although he was not the person to whom Thelwall was responding. I presume there was a scandalous episode to which Thelwall is referring, but the unconscious logic suggests that Burke—and people like him (the reference in rhetorical situations like this is irresponsibly slippery)—is not just like a woman and like a prostitute, but is a pander for *male* prostitution. The shameful buying and selling of not just sex but literary discourse is what Burke and Thelwall are discussing here (PEJ 384).[25]

The central focus of *Sober Reflections*, however, is not pandering and sexual innuendo but a defense of Jacobin theory as a product of a radical

25. In the "Prefatory Memoir" to *Poems*, xvii–xviii, and biographical sketch in *Public Characters of 1800–1801* (London: Richard Phillips, 1801): 3: 185, there is an episode of homosexuality represented. An associate of John Impey, the lawyer to whom Thelwall was articled, made a sexual advance that Thelwall "exposed," thus leading to the man's suicide. This episode seems unrelated to the male prostitution evoked against Burke, but it indicates unselfconscious homophobia; Thelwall in neither text expresses any compassion for the unfortunate suicide. For whatever reason the episode is not mentioned in Thelwall's biography.

Enlightenment. Thelwall's analysis of Robespierre illustrates his response to the worst violence of the French Revolution. Contrary to Burke's portrait of the "cannibal philosopher," as though the essence of the Enlightenment were violence itself, Thelwall's Robespierre betrays the radical Enlightenment by hindering discussion and writing. Robespierre did not champion "the cultivation and expansion of intellect" and was in fact Burkean in his "inveterate . . . abhorrence against philosophers and literati." The Reign of Terror was not the triumph and actualization of philosophy but just the opposite: "philosophy was silenced, science was proscribed, and daring speculation soared no more." For Burke and Robespierre the great heresy was "illimitable inquiry," against which both of them struggled (PEJ 368). Inquiry without limits, however, was the revolutionary ideal that Thelwall promoted consistently in the 1790s and somewhat more equivocally later. Such inquiry led him to affirm a public sphere more comprehensive than the bourgeois version, and to practice a form of criticism that anticipates Hegel and Marx in its use of historical dialectic, as "energetic" agents embody a rationality whose logic is historically contingent.

The Rights of Nature

Sober Reflections deflected the Burkean charge that Jacobins were intemperate and unrestrained by reason, but Thelwall relaxes the restraint in his reply to Burke's *Letters on a Regicide Peace*. Burke's essay was published 20 October 1796, and the first part of Thelwall's *The Rights of Nature* is ready at the press, unbelievably, on 5 November, provocatively coincidental with the second anniversary of Thomas Hardy's acquittal in 1794 and of course Guy Fawkes Day, the national day of "deliverance."[26] Accounting for Thelwall's urgency was his belief, perhaps not unreasonable, that he might be either killed by loyalists or imprisoned again, perhaps executed after a trial. Thelwall had been physically attacked several times in 1796 while he was delivering lectures in Lynn, Wisbech, and Yarmouth that were technically

26. It is possible, perhaps even likely, that Thelwall backdated his preface to 5 November for political effect. For five decades the annual dinners celebrated the treason trial acquittals on Guy Fawkes Day, national day of "deliverance." The radical appropriation of nationalist, Protestant, anti-Catholic discourse is worth noting here. For the seventeenth-century discourse on Guy Fawkes Day, see David Cressy, *Bonfires and Bells: National Memory and the Protestant Calendar in Elizabethan and Stuart England* (London: Weidenfeld and Nicolson, 1989).

legal even within the restrictions spelled out in the Two Acts; in each instance the government authorities either sanctioned or permitted the violence against Thelwall or refused to punish his attackers. His pamphlet protesting against his treatment was published at about the same time as Burke's *Letters on a Regicide Peace*.[27] Burke's new essay recommends that the 20 percent of the political public that is "Jacobin" should be repressed forcefully. Thelwall thinks, not entirely without reason, that Burke is calling for the violent suppression of the British Jacobins. Coupled with the actual violence directed against him, Thelwall contends with Burke as if his life depended on it. In *Letter to a Noble Lord* Burke attacked several Jacobins personally, including Thelwall, but in the more recent essay, Burke marks the entire political group for silencing.

The passage that so exercised Thelwall begins by identifying the "British publick," the four hundred thousand "political citizens" with sufficient "leisure" and "means of information" to take part in public discussion. "Of these four hundred thousand political citizens, I look upon one fifth, or about eighty thousand, to be pure Jacobins; utterly incapable of amendment; objects of eternal vigilance; and when they break out, of legal constraint." The Jacobin "minority is great and formidable," with a "force" that is "far superior to their numbers" (EB 9:224). Thelwall's finding "extermination" in Burke's words is not necessarily a product of overreading. *Letters on a Regicide Peace* also asserts that past political societies failing to protect themselves were destroyed (EB 9:192–97), that ordinary repressive measures have been ineffective against the British Jacobins ("Public prosecutions are become little better than schools for treason" [EB 9:198]), and that the conflict with Jacobinism is a contest of violence, not just ideology ("It is with an *armed doctrine*, that we are at war" [EB 9:199]). The words that certainly ring the tocsin of violent repression are these: "pure Jacobins; utterly incapable of amendment." These eighty thousand Jacobins are the demonized physical manifestations of the "cannibal" philosophy destructive of European culture (EB 9:190–91). Apparently alluding to the 1794 treason trials that produced no convictions and that occasioned even greater Jacobin activism, Burke laments that Hardy, Tooke, Thelwall, and their comrades were not found guilty and executed as they should have been. The most visible, prominent, and well known of the eighty thousand British Jacobins,

27. John Thelwall, *An Appeal to Popular Opinion, Against Kidnapping and Murder* (London: J. S. Jordan, 1796). The text is dated 19 October 1796, so it must have been published shortly thereafter.

Thelwall replies to Burke as if this might be his last chance to publish anything. Accordingly, perhaps, *The Rights of Nature* is also Thelwall's best political writing; he has nothing to lose and holds nothing back.

Countering Burke's charges of cannibalism, savagery, and violence, Thelwall points to Burke's own brutality in calling for violence against eighty thousand Jacobins. He defends Jacobinism as a political and cultural initiative that advances civilization to a higher level. Whereas Burke frames his essay as a letter to an aristocrat (a "Member of the Present Parliament"), Thelwall addresses his letter to "the People." (Similarly, the earlier essay, *Sober Reflections*, was addressed to Thelwall's "fellow citizens.") Burke's typical political essays are epistolary. A public letter addressed to a private person from the most privileged class reinforces at a formal level the elitist style and dramatizes the sincerity of the essay, whose addressees have a "name" that is underwritten by property and state power, whereas Thelwall's addressees are the politically disenfranchised. Burke's addressee is a synecdoche for the most privileged layer of the political nation, and Thelwall's is an abstraction for a greatly expanded political nation.

Burke's essay-letters typically meander from topic to topic, as one would in a personal letter that was, according to F. P. Lock, a "conscious rhetorical choice, designed to foster a more intimate relationship with the reader."[28] Thelwall first mirrors Burke's style in the initial "letter," but then structures his own essay more like a treatise in the subsequent three letters, each on a specific topic, all of them part of an extended argument. Referring to Burke derisively as "Mr. B.", Thelwall criticizes the aesthetic eccentricity that characterizes all of Burke's writings except for the systematic essay on the sublime and beautiful. "Tropes, sentiments, and propositions, are every now and then starting up, one knows not why, or whence, or wherefore," writes Thelwall. Then he quotes from memory a couplet from Pope's *Epistle to Dr. Arbuthnot* (171–72): "The things, 'tis true, are costly, rich and rare: / But wonder how the devil they got there!" Thelwall here plays the role of neoclassical upholder of an aesthetic order that Burke violates. "Every metaphor," Thelwall continues, "becomes an allegory; every embellishment a digression; and every digression a voluminous episode. But the reader, who, on this account, should calculate upon the artlessness of Mr. Burke's mind, would do no credit to his penetration." Thelwall then quotes, again from memory,

---

28. F. P. Lock, *Burke's Reflections on the Revolution in France* (Boston: Allen and Unwin, 1985), 63.

Polonius's "If this be madness, there is method in it" (*Hamlet* 2:2). The apparent disorder conceals conscious purpose. "In this excursive frenzy of composition," Thelwall suggests, "there is much deep design and insidious policy."

> He not only writes with a two-fold object—but his objects are in diametrical opposition to each other. It is his intention at once to instruct and to confuse. Even in that small proportion of the people of Britain, whom he calls "the British public," there is a still smaller subdivision (men of complete leisure, and of trained political education) whom he regards as the initiated few, and who, of course, may be expected to catch up, and put together, many of the loose disjointed hints, scattered here and there, with such studied carelessness as to escape the observation of those who "read as they run." Hence, if we want to know the whole meaning; and real object of this master of political controversy, instead of following him through the regular succession of pages and paragraphs, we must seek for the leading traits and positions of his work, and then, putting together the disjointed parts of the syllogism so artfully divided, we must extract the enveloped conclusion for ourselves. (PEJ 395–96)

A guide to Burke's political prose is not needed for the propertied reader who shares Burke's style of discourse, but for the other readers Thelwall provides an aggressive interpretation that reconstructs Burke's "studied carelessness" in order to wrench Burke's writing out of the apparently seamless structure of a sincerely expressive letter and place it instead within the context of rational political debate. Directing his reader to various passages in Burke, Thelwall then describes the meaning thus: Burke is "preparing the minds" of the politically powerful for an additional political repression intending "the utter extermination of every sentiment of reform" (PEJ 396). Thelwall assumes the reader will share his outrage at Burke's comments on the "political nation" that in effect exclude readers like themselves. There is a rough parallel between exclusion by definition—the nature of the public—and exclusion by repression—silencing the inconvenient eighty thousand Jacobins.

Thelwall radically shifts the center of interpretive gravity from its place in Burke's *Letters on a Regicide Peace*. Thelwall's implied reader has little in common with that of Burke. Those critics who find Thelwall's essay an ineffective critique of Burke assume incorrectly that Thelwall is actually interested in refuting Burke's argument *on Burke's terms*, as if both were on the same public stage engaged in a debate.[29] Rather, they occupy very different positions in the political world. Thelwall appeals to his readers as fellow democrats who must protect themselves. In fact Thelwall sent to the LCS twelve copies of the *Rights of Nature* as soon as it was published to be read to the twelve separate sections of the organization.[30] The essay, especially the first letter, was a passionate lecture to his fellow democrats—the radical reading public, not the middle class[31]—on the imminent danger posed by Burke's new call for repression. Indeed, as Günther Lottes points out, Thelwall's lecture style is specifically shaped for the plebeian public sphere.[32] At a practical level, the first letter of *The Rights of Nature* warns his fellow democrats of the new wave of repression and provides some rhetorical ammunition for countering Burke's charges that the British Jacobins are violent and disconnected entirely from the main currents of European civilization. The first letter is a passionate diatribe, an oratorical performance that mirrors while it also criticizes the Burkean wild rhetoric.[33] The other three letters are sober, restrained analyses of the key assumptions in Burke's anti-Jacobin argument, as Thelwall covers rights theory, the theory of property, and the nature of feudalism. (These "letters" by Burke and Thelwall remind us that the letter as a literary form was preeminently political during this period, as Mary Favret has explained in her study.)[34]

In the first letter of *The Rights of Nature* Thelwall cultivates a style and tone that were unlike those of *Sober Reflections* and unlike the subsequent three letters of *The Rights of Nature*. What did he hope to accomplish by

29. A not untypical example is R. B. McDowell, who dismisses Thelwall's criticism as "earnest" but "commonplace," praises Mackintosh's criticism as "intellectually powerful" and "graceful" (EB 9: 11–12). Mackintosh, who was to become a member of Parliament, used the same idiom as did Burke. Thelwall's is a different idiom, but not necessarily less "powerful."

30. Mary Thale, *Selections from the Papers of the London Corresponding Society 1792–1799* (Cambridge: Cambridge University Press, 1983), xxv.

31. Jon Klancher, *The Making of the English Reading Audiences* (Madison: University of Wisconsin Press, 1987).

32. Günther Lottes, *Politische Aufklärung und plebejisches Publikum. Zur Theorie und Praxis des englischen Radikalismus im späten 18. Jahrhundert* (Munich: R. O. Verlag, 1979), 261.

33. For an analysis of "wild rhetoric" that has influenced me, see Henry Golemba, *Thoreau's Wild Rhetoric* (New York: New York University Press, 1990).

34. Mary Favret, *Romantic Correspondence: Women, Politics, and the Fiction of Letters* (Cambridge: Cambridge University Press, 1993).

composing an "intemperate" pamphlet? Burke, however, was the first to canonize rhetorical excess.

Burke's *Reflections on the Revolution in France, Letter to a Noble Lord,* and *Letters on a Regicide Peace* were rhetorically excessive but also normative performances. The convention of addressing a correspondent who shares the gentlemanly code of cultural references, used in all three writings, mitigates the wild rhetoric. The "letter" permits a far looser mode of formal organization than does the treatise or inquiry. There is also the contingency of the extreme provocation to make credible the necessity of loose organization, heated argument, hyperbolic and emotionally agitated diction; the extreme rhetoric mirrors the extremism that called the text into existence in the first place. Burke frames his 1790s political prose as documents called into being by an unprecedented evil—Jacobinism at home and abroad. He must communicate to his readers with the utmost urgency; the ordinary rules of discourse are under suspension; as a writer and speaker he is compelled by necessity. For Burke, Jacobinism disrupts the rules of rhetoric. A degree of strategic lawlessness repels the greater danger of Jacobin lawlessness.

Burke's opponents exploited his rhetorical excesses by developing a discourse cooler than his, more rule-governed, rational, and logical, but doing so also played into Burke's anti-Jacobin argument: that the radicals were cold rationalists detached from the organic processes of history. Where Burke was weakest he was also strongest—defending the French queen, justifying his pension, and attacking the Duke of Bedford, insisting upon war abroad and repression at home to eliminate the evils of Jacobinism—so that citing rational evidence was in some ways beside the point. Even if the queen were not spotless, Burke's defense was chivalrous, and the real point of those purple passages was the affirmation of chivalry that, ironically, scapegoated actual revolutionary women while an idealized one was praised.[35] Even if Burke did not deserve quite so many thousands of pounds, and even if his pension contradicted his earlier support for economic reform of crown patronage, his largess was insignificant in comparison with the Duke of Bedford's monstrous benefits from crown generosity. If Burke were wrong about the nature of Jacobinism, then he must be a warmonger and destroyer of constitutional liberties; if he were correct about Jacobinism, then he is a noble and courageous prophet whose jeremiads might save Britain and

---

35. Julie Carlson, "Impositions of Form: Romantic Antitheatricalism and the Case Against Particular Women," *ELH* 60 (1993): 152–54.

Europe. Accordingly, Burke's flouting of rhetorical decorum does not weaken his writing; it is a sign of his sincerity. Moreover, at the end of his distinguished parliamentary career, Burke was permitted a latitude he exploited to the fullest. He was able to position himself as a Romantic prophet authorized to break the ordinary rules of discourse because of the overwhelmingly powerful evil against which he was fighting.

Feeling perhaps that he had little to lose anyway, Thelwall out-Burked Burke in the first letter of *The Rights of Nature.* Just how egregiously Thelwall violated the rhetorical norms is evident in a review that appeared in a periodical that was favorable to Enlightenment and reform (but not Jacobinism). The attack on Thelwall in the *Monthly Review* is worth a close look for the assumptions that are rarely spelled out clearly and only expressed when they are perceived as having been abandoned. The *Monthly* reviewer's case for Thelwall's "outrageous violation of all" the "rules of literary decorum and propriety" can be summarized thus: Thelwall overreaches himself by pretending to know more about classical culture than he does; in terms of style, he mixes poetic and prosaic diction "promiscuously," and uses terms that in and of themselves are offensive; worst of all, he does not show Burke the respect such a distinguished opponent is due. The *Monthly* reviewer, unconvinced by Thelwall's portraying of Socrates as a sans-culotte philosopher among the laborers, sneers at Thelwall's reliance on translations from the Greek and pounces on what he perceives as an outright error of fact. As if to clinch the demolition of Thelwall's alleged classical learning, the *Monthly* reviewer notes that Thelwall's Socrates is portrayed as if he were the "predecessor and prototype of *Orator Henley!*" (In fact, Thelwall thought highly of Orator Henley, devoting at least one essay to him).[36] The stylistic errors the reviewer belabors are all oratorical qualities that Thelwall's letter quite deliberately uses. Thelwall's lack of deference to Burke goes to the heart of the reviewer's objections:

> The most offensive circumstance belonging to this pamphlet is the petulant scurrility with which the author has treated Mr. Burke.—To protect the glory and fame of great writers from presumptuous and licentious attack is one of the most natural, as well as one of the most pleasing offices of literary criticism. The republic of letters, like every other well-ordered community, has different degrees of established

---

36. John Thelwall, "Orator Henley," *Retrospective Review* 14 (1826): 206–25.

rank and dignity, with a system of manners and rules of politeness corresponding to that variety of rank. Every member of it, however obscure, possesses the most unbounded right to discuss with perfect freedom the opinions and reasoning of every other—but in the exercise of this right, all men are bound to observe the rules of decency. Obscure men owe some deference to established reputation; and men of moderate talents ought to show some reverence for men of superior genius.[37]

The reviewer, ignoring the substance of Thelwall's argument for its style—violently revolutionary—insists that the "well-ordered society" of letters requires a hierarchically sensitive conduct in its pursuit of truth. It is one thing for Burke, as a "great writer" of "established rank and dignity" and as a man of "superior genius," to break the rules. It is quite another thing for Thelwall to write similarly. Here we have an illustration of the disciplining of the reading audience, as readers are differentiated into elite and lesser categories. The *Monthly* reviewer, under pressure, sacrifices the egalitarian ideal of the reader-writer in order to sustain hierarchical distinctions. One sees clearly here how the bourgeois public sphere could be construed to defend social privilege or, as Thelwall did, be construed to defend inquiry without social limitations.

Thelwall's first letter of *The Rights of Nature*, then, alerts his fellow democrats that Burke is leading the political charge against them, and defends philosophically the public sphere, which is the discursive space within which the ideas so offensive to Burke were generated. Thelwall contextualizes Burke's call for repression by locating it in the historic strategy of wealthy elites safeguarding their power by making sure that the people who labor for a living do not acquire a political voice. He points to the socioeconomic structural obstacles to popular Enlightenment in the form of excessive labor and insufficient leisure (PEJ 398). There is a *right* to a standard of living that includes not just a sufficient degree of material comfort but an adequate level, too, of leisure, during which it would be possible to read, reflect, discuss, and write. The "scandalously" low wages necessitate "the unreasonable number of hours" of labor; moreover, the taxes on paper, newspapers, glass, and candles are further "impediments thrown in the way of a cheap, and therefore general, cir-

---

37. *Monthly Review* 21 (1796): 468–72.

culation of knowledge" (PEJ 399). The project of radical Enlightenment necessitates a theory of labor, a topic I will develop separately in this chapter.

Thelwall links together the various aspects of aristocratic privilege. The "hideous accumulation of capital in a few hands" manifests itself politically in the restricted franchise and culturally in classical education. Thelwall denaturalizes all three monopolies with a biological analogy: that all diseases carry within themselves the seeds of their own cure (PEJ 400–401). Because the concentration of wealth has led to rural depopulation and a concomitant increase in manufacturing, laborers are now forced together in numbers far larger than before. Because people are by nature both "social and communicative," they will talk among themselves and diffuse knowledge and promote liberty. "Hence every large workshop and manufactory is a sort of political society, which no act of parliament can silence, and no magistrate disperse." Well before Marx and Habermas, Thelwall points to the emancipatory tension at the center of industrial production between the forces and relations of production.[38]

To illustrate the radicalization of the Enlightenment Thelwall cites Socrates as the "democratical lecturer" who addressed "seditious allegories" to a popular audience, not an elite. This part of the essay particularly offended the *Monthly* reviewer. It dignifies the democratic public sphere both by illustrating its ancient lineage and by removing from aristocratic classical education its moral superiority. Arguing against the conservative Robert Bisset, Thelwall sees Socrates as a victim not of democracy but of oligarchy. By connecting the social relations of factory production to Socratic discourse Thelwall justifies expanding the public sphere and the political nation.

The democratic Socrates is only part of the critique of aristocratic classical culture. Here and in other texts Thelwall ostentatiously and without apology relies on translations, a reliance the *Monthly* reviewer finds culpable. In *Sober Reflections* there are numerous references to Dionysius of Halicarnassus's multivolume *Roman Antiquities*, a translation of which by Edward Spelman (d. 1767) was an important resource for Thelwall's writings

38. An early essay by Habermas deals with the theoretical conundrums of the Marxian theory of production, the tension between the forces and relations of production; hints of his later ideas about communicative action are evident here. "Toward a Reconstruction of Historical Materialism," in Jürgen Habermas, *Communication and the Evolution of Society*, trans. Thomas McCarthy (Boston: Beacon Press, 1979).

in the 1790s. Unlike Blake, who rejects classical learning for biblical prophecy, Thelwall, a fellow "middling-class" professional who was excluded from an elite education where he would have been taught Greek, affirms classical learning mediated by translations. In this regard Thelwall is like Keats, similarly excluded from Oxbridge, equally enthusiastic about translations (remember his sonnet on Chapman's Homer), likewise affronting from a lower-middle-class position the aristocratically inflected classical culture.[39]

Inevitably, with Socrates comes Jesus, as the pairing of the figures was a topos in eighteenth-century writing, extending into the nineteenth century with works such as Shelley's *Triumph of Life* ("the sacred few ... of Athens and Jerusalem").[40] So too Thelwall. He represents Jesus as a democratic reformer and a communist (PEJ 422–23), a provocative way to repel one of the most persistent anti-Jacobin lines of attack, the equation of Jacobinism and atheism. By making Jesus a radical democrat Thelwall challenges the aristocratic appropriation of Christianity, and cleverly parallels Jesus's "democratic" lecturing, harassed by the authorities, with his own difficulties as a political lecturer. "He collected the people together, in great numbers, and lectured them against existing abuses; in the streets, in the wilderness, in the fields, and on the neighbouring hills. The government was alarmed. . . . they set gangs of ruffians upon him, to knock him on the head, with bludgeons and stones." The gangs of ruffians with their bludgeons signify precisely Thelwall's own attackers in 1796. The rhetoric deliberately blurs the differences between Jesus and Joseph Gerrald (and Thelwall), Judas and Burke, the Romans and the Pitt government.

Thelwall, then, portrays both Socrates and Jesus as democratic victims of oligarchy, not unlike himself and the other Jacobins marked out for suppression by Burke. Moreover, he has challenged two pillars of aristocratic culture that legitimize the elite's power, classical education and Christianity. Both Socrates and Jesus supply Thelwall with allegories of political conflict that subvert aristocratic domination with an expanded public sphere animated by the ideal of "illimitable inquiry," and a counterhegemonic culture with Christian and classical affiliations.

---

39. For a discussion of Keats, translation, and class anxiety, see Marjorie Levinson, *The Origins of Keats's Style: A Life of Allegory* (Oxford: Blackwell, 1988).

40. Among the many texts that bring the two together, fairly typical is Joseph Priestley's *Socrates and Jesus Compared* (London: Joseph Johnson, 1803).

Theory of Labor

The three subsequent letters that make up the rest of *The Rights of Nature* assume a very different rhetorical approach. From polemic to treatise, Thelwall's text deconstructs Burke's political theory to provide an alternative that emphasizes especially the roles played by property and labor in civic and political society. Although not a wild rhetoric addressed to a radical audience, the letters' rhetoric mixes polite and popular idioms in a tone that is respectful of Burke. The exposition of ideas is logical and orderly, as in a treatise, but Thelwall employs certain features that mark the text as popular also: each of the three letters is fairly short (and so can be published cheaply); there is no untranslated foreign language and classical sources are cited in their translated editions; there are moments of intimate engagement with the radical reader; the point of view is invariably that of people who labor for a living. To illustrate the latter point, let me quote from a paragraph near the beginning of the fourth letter, on feudalism. After describing the effects of aristocratic monopoly of the land, he insists that there is a minimal standard of material well-being below which working people should never fall: "bread and milk, and meat and beer, and those in full abundance, and warm clothing, and well-covered bed, and a winter's fire, are to be reckoned among the absolute rights of the productive labourer and his family" (PEJ 483–84). I must take issue with one of Olivia Smith's arguments in this context because she claims that Thelwall condescends to his reader, using a different idiom that highlights the inadequacy of the "vulgar" language.[41] The passage I have just quoted has a concrete, even homey ("reckoned") diction, along with a coordinated series of common objects. The typical signs of polite sentences— abstraction, balance, subordination—are absent here. The attention to details like the bed and winter fire betrays an intimate knowledge of laboring-class life. When Thelwall uses abstraction, it is not scientific or objective but frankly partisan.

> Where this distribution [of material goods to laborers at a minimally acceptable level] is neglected, encreased production is but an insulting mockery, and aggravates the evils it should remove. Civil Society, under such circumstances, becomes a grievous yoke; and agricultural science, not a blessing but a curse: for, better is a little that is well dis-

---

41. Smith, *The Politics of Language 1791–1819*, 90. As becomes clear in the next chapter, I make use of Smith for trying to understand Thomas Spence, but on Thelwall we disagree.

tributed, than much that is monopolized and wasted; and small indeed would be the labour, if equally divided, (perhaps not three hours in a day, even under the rudest circumstances of cultivation) that would be necessary to furnish the individual with better subsistence than the labourer now enjoys. (PEJ 484)

Only someone with moral agency can be "insulted," so that the "insulting mockery" of increased production implies a respectful attitude to the laborer. Certain syntactic structures, like the biblical antithesis of bless/curse and the aphoristic "better is a little . . . than much . . ," are marks of a popular style. The criteria for the rationality of increased production are not things like "the wealth of nations" but the moral, physical, and emotional well-being of the worker. Eliminate the "waste and luxury" and then workers would have to labor for only three hours a day, if the labor were equitably distributed. This bold illustration assumes an appreciation for the physical demands of labor, something always repressed in polite discourse.

The Rights of Nature is coherent only because of his theory of labor, something that shapes his other writings as well. The starting point for any discussion of Thelwall and labor has to be Gregory Claeys's pathbreaking essay, "The Origins of the Rights of Labour: Republicanism, Commerce, and the Construction of Modern Social Theory."[42] In his lectures, and especially in *The Rights of Nature*, Thelwall moved decisively away from the anticommercial views expressed in *The Peripatetic* and shared with radicals such as William Godwin. There were four parts to Thelwall's argument, according to Claeys. First, all people had rights to the natural world and had moreover a "reciprocal duty to secure similar rights for others" ("Origins" 267). Second, from these natural rights there comes the right to labor and receive reasonable compensation. Third, in partial compensation for giving up one's access to nature and joining society, one has a "right to the produce of his or her employer proportionate to the profit of the employer. . . . The rights of society were now indexed to the inflation of needs" ("Origins" 269). Finally, instead of a master-servant or market-governed model, Thelwall's model was of a "full partnership" of labor and capital that entailed the assumption of labor's "proportionate" compensation ("Origins" 271–72). Claeys is the first to recognize the significance of Thelwall's contribution to

42. Gregory Claeys, "The Origins of the Rights of Labour: Republicanism, Commerce, and the Construction of Modern Social Theory," *Journal of Modern History* 66 (1994): 249–90. Hereafter "Origins."

radical labor theory. Like Paine, Thelwall argued for a rising standard of living proportionate to the wealth workers actually produced. Implicit here is a defense of collective bargaining and a social wage—that is, cultural benefits such as access to education, art, and leisure. He departs from the logic of the luxury critique that was hostile to commercial civilization, the premises of the moral economy that assumed a fair, stable wage, and the dogma of purely market forces. Thelwall, like Paine, is a prophet of social democracy, a proponent of the kind of "labourist" reforms that have in fact been created by the British labour movement in the last two centuries.

I will illustrate and expand somewhat upon Claeys's main ideas by examining *The Rights of Nature* and some *Tribune* lectures.

In a *Tribune* lecture of April 1795, Thelwall laments workers' falling standard of living, which could be rectified by abolishing "luxury" and equitably sharing the necessary labor. Instead of taking the Godwinian communist approach, however, he makes the normative judgment that a worker should be able to maintain his family "in decency" with eight hours of work daily (PEJ 144). Labor should have but does not presently possess the full legal power to defend its interests by means of its own associations, but employers do in fact associate to keep wages low.[43] Here it is explicit, but throughout Thelwall's writings on labor there is an implicit support for unions and collective bargaining.

During the famine year of 1795 when there were many food riots, Thelwall neither encourages the rioters, like Thomas Spence, nor, like Edmund Burke, encourages private charity while the market works out its ruthless logic. Rather, he identifies the problem as one of artificial scarcity caused by corn laws and especially the inadequate cultivation of the land; he estimates that between one-third and one-half of the cultivable land lies fallow (PEJ 154, 195). Also, farm monopolies, by reducing competition, have increased speculation, driving up food prices and creating scarcity (PEJ 193). Although not absolutely opposed to enclosures in theory, he notes that in practice they have been almost invariably a "calamity" for labor (PEJ 177). Long before Cobbett railed against paper money, Thelwall points to the inflationary effect of the national credit system, which depresses real wages (PEJ 183). Put together, Thelwall's analysis of the artificial scarcity produced by the agricultural capitalism of his time insists that the famine is not an act of nature but a consequence of political decisions; he does not demonize the "middle

---

43. *Tribune* 9 (9 May 1795): 1:201.

men" as villains within the assumptions of traditional moral economy, but rather points outside the "middling classes" to the policies of the landowning oligarchy and its parliament as the true sources of the social misery.

Thelwall's compassion for the immediate suffering of the poor was political, not just humanitarian. One lecture, which seems to have influenced Wordsworth's "Goody Blake and Harry Gill," compares the rich, who plunder entire nations, with "the labouring poor [who] are sometimes guilty of pilfering a stick, or so, from the hedges and fences of their landlords, or perhaps of breaking down a pale or digging up a post for fuel, to warm their shivering hands" (PEJ 292). Using his own research as well as publicly available statistics, he illustrates how the living conditions of labor are far worse than in earlier times (PEJ 278). He justifies the use of labor statistics on the basis of his audience. His earlier audiences were almost exclusively from the LCS, whose largely artisan membership knew from their own lives about their own declining standards of living. His new mixed audiences for the *Tribune* lectures, however, included many from the "middle orders" who lacked first-hand knowledge of conditions for workers, and so needed the information that statistics could provide.[44] Another attempt to undermine the middle-class prejudice against labor is Thelwall's characterization of the workhouse as an immoral prison; his insistence that poor relief is a right, not an act of charity; and that high poor rates are to be blamed not on the poor but on the rich, who segregate themselves into wealthy enclaves to avoid poor rates.[45] The compassion for the poor that Thelwall expresses, then, is not simply humanitarian but politically strategic. He attempts to weaken class prejudice enough to permit a working alliance between labor and the "middle orders." He reminds the middle-class audience more than a few times that it is illusory to think that the poor can be oppressed without the next victims being themselves. He tells his middle-class audience: "unlock the proud portals of your hearts, and let your poor neighbours in. . . . You will no longer think it wise to surrender your own liberties; in order to prevent the common people from enjoying the exercise of theirs."[46] Labor, like the merchant, "will have his proportion of the advantage; eat with more comfort, sleep in a better cabin and be enabled to give his offspring a better education, and a better knowledge of their rights and duties." In short, Thelwall recommends "equal distribution of advantages" accruing from an

44. *Tribune* 31 (30 September 1795): 2:346–49.
45. *Tribune* 31 (30 September 1795): 2:352–55.
46. *Tribune* 46 (9 December 1795): 3:243–44.

expanding commercial society. He does this without, however, mandating equality of property; a "liberal distributive principle" must dictate social policy.[47] Additionally, status-anxious professionals, shopkeepers, and merchants all depend in material ways on laborers.[48] The most forthright appeal to the middle class is a published lecture of 9 November 1795 that was not in *The Tribune* but appeared instead in the LCS publication *The Moral and Political Magazine*. He makes an extended appeal to his middle-class auditors to overcome their class prejudice and join the LCS. In a dramatic move, he invites his audience to join him as he himself is about to walk from the Beaufort Buildings to the place where the LCS is meeting that very evening.[49]

As much as Thelwall appealed to the middle class for an alliance with labor, he hardly championed the rights of bourgeois property. If one can thank commerce for breaking the hold of feudal tyranny, one now has to decry its power to sustain "corruption" (PEJ 291). Under the rule of commerce, according to the *Rights of Nature*, there is neofeudal tyranny: "Property is accumulated in so few hands, and the condition of the labourer has, in consequence, become so abject, that the mass of the people may, in reality, be considered as slaves" (PEJ 482).

Containing his most extensive commentary on labor, *The Rights of Nature* insists that "*every* man, and every *woman*, and every *child*, ought to obtain something more, in the general distribution of the fruits of labour, than food, and rags, and a wretched hammock, with a poor rug to cover it: and that without working twelve or fourteen hours a day, six days out of seven, from six to sixty. They have a claim . . . to some comforts and enjoyments, in addition to the necessaries of life" (PEJ 398–99). Thelwall, anticipating Marx, locates the agency by which labor will be emancipated in labor itself, the human proclivity to communicate: "Hence every large workshop and manufactory is a sort of political society, which no act of parliament can silence, and no magistrate disperse" (PEJ 400). The exploitation of labor will be undermined by the social relations of labor, what Habermas called "communicative action" by which labor finds its "voice" outside established political institutions.

The theory of labor depends on assumptions about nature, one of the most contested words in the eighteenth century. Nature, in the view Thelwall

47. *Tribune* 46 (9 December 1795): 3:247–50.
48. *Tribune* 38 (23 October 1795): 3:99.
49. *Moral and Political Magazine* (December 1796): 290.

derived from writers like Rousseau and poets like Armstrong, is rational in the sense that it seeks a healthy equilibrium that can be disrupted by the interventions of civilization. The *Essay on Human Vitality* and especially the *Peripatetic*, both published in 1793, articulate an Enlightenment naturalism with a Jacobin inflection, or, as he phrases it, "the great code of Reason and Nature" (PEJ 439). Nature is a silent partner of revolutionary reason, an active force independent of human will, a collaborative power upon which political hope can rest. Burke's "nature" is a synonym for social custom (PEJ 405), but Thelwall's is a system of limits, constraints, and energy whose power disrupts oppression and promotes happiness. In the contest between "the energy and enthusiasm of a new conviction" and "the science and mechanism of ancient habits" Thelwall has no doubt on which side nature rests (PEJ 426). By nature labor has a right to discuss politics, and eventually the logical implications of universal suffrage will be translated into institutional realities; eventually the logic of labor's right to a full and satisfying life will also become institutionalized, because that right too is underwritten by nature.

Thelwall expands the Lockean and Smithian notions of the rights of property to include not just *"the fruit of useful industry"* but also *"the means of being usefully industrious"*; these means "are the common right of all" (PEJ 465). One could construe capital investments as useful industry to lend bourgeois property a moral justification, but if everyone has a right to the "means" of being usefully productive, then Thelwall is including something unrelated to bourgeois property, a right to labor, a right to have access to the means of production. This new right is very different from the old right to assistance. Under the moral economy one had a right to public aid during hard times, but under Thelwall's construction one's rights are more extensive than poor relief. For Thelwall labor's social rights undermine the absolute integrity of bourgeois property.

Although labor has a right of access to the means of production, Thelwall does not envision a communist equality of wealth. Such absolute equality, according to him, actually existed prior to feudalism during an early period of agricultural development, but any attempt to return to this primitive communism would be destructive (PEJ 472). After the land has been fully cultivated, then individual rights to landed property cease to remain personal and become wholly conventional. Landed property now rests ultimately on labor, not individual ownership, and the new moral criteria governing landed property are the welfare of the whole, not the rights of possession. The polar star now for the legal status of landed property is the "adequate reward" for labor. If labor finds itself without adequate reward, then the landed property is "the worst of usurpation and plunder" (PEJ 476).

Revising the notion of aristocratic inheritance, Thelwall claims a universal inheritance in the form of a claim to nature's bounty that primitive people had to forsake out of social necessity. In compensation for this universal loss, people have a set of rights, including the right to the "*gratification of the common appetites of Man*" (PEJ 476–77). This right may seem trivial but in fact it implied that workers had a right to have sex and children, something that Malthusian arguments would challenge. Labor also has a right to "*the enjoyment of your rational faculties*" (PEJ 477), an important right whose implications extend to the right to leisure (and limited working hours, decent working conditions), to education, and to cultural expression. The absolute rights of aristocratic property had been long eroded by the bourgeois concept of the labor theory of value, but now Thelwall—and concurrently Paine—weakens the rights of bourgeois property in numerous ways. Setting the stage for politically mediated contests between labor and capital, Thelwall insists that "the labourer has a right to a share of the produce, not merely equal to his support, but, proportionate to the profits of the employer" (PEJ 477). It is not so much that Thelwall anticipates profit-sharing but that he introduces the principle that labor's rights can trump the ownership rights and the profit-seeking of bourgeois property. He is not arguing beyond the parameters of a capitalist society but he is certainly assuming what we would now recognize as welfare state conditions, a market economy heavily leavened by social-democratic institutions. Thelwall does not see the configuration he has sketched as eternal but notes that such a contest of rights is appropriate "in the present state of society" (PEJ 476). Much of *The Rights of Nature* is historical description of how society emerged out of conflict, thus inferring that such class struggle will continue and will shape the future as well.

Although Thelwall does indeed look ahead to what we will be called industrial capitalism, he is acutely aware of the agricultural capitalism that in fact dominated his own society. In one of his most effective rhetorical tours de force, he portrays in the fourth letter of the *Rights of Nature* Burke's organic society based on landed wealth as a morally squalid sequence of conquests, plunders, and murders of the weaker by the stronger (PEJ 487–97). For the wealth created by agricultural labor the desired object should be "*general and impartial distribution*" (PEJ 483), so that the market alone cannot determine the agricultural laborer's standard of living, because the rights of labor, in contradistinction to the rights of landed property, are "absolute" (PEJ 484). Landed wealth dominated not just the agricultural laborer but exploited "their leisure in promoting useful knowledge and liberal science" (PEJ 486). When knowledge becomes "perverted by monopoly," it becomes "evil." Thelwall argues that because the material foundations for knowledge are in fact "labour," there must be universal access to the "advantages" of science and art. Again, Thelwall expands the rights of labor to include cultural rights that are viewed not as luxuries but as essential components of an overall relationship between labor and social power. Despite aristocratic monopoly, it has been from the ranks of the "middle classes" and not from the rich that the most creative thinkers and writers have come (PEJ 487). Thelwall, who takes yet another jab at the Oxbridge cultural elite, also illustrates his theory of history: history is struggle and conflict over power whose structure is shaped by human agency.

The theory of labor that Thelwall developed in the 1790s, then, is complex and undogmatic, anticipating Marxian ideas of industrial production, class struggle, and historical development. He disputes the absolute rationality of market forces but he supports an expanding commercial society within which labor must share a proportion of the wealth, material and cultural, that it creates. Not accepting the Godwinian and Rousseauian arguments of the "luxury" critique of commercial civilization, Thelwall nevertheless highlights the importance of leisure and excessive toil as legitimate political issues. Similarly, he departs from the logic of the moral economy but admits into his analysis moral categories. How exactly workers live, how long they work, how much free time they have, and what opportunities they have for educational development are all proper questions that cannot be answered by pointing simply to the workings of the impersonal market. Just as his expository style brings together popular and polite dimensions, his political strategy is to appeal for a class alliance between the working and the middling classes. The health of an expanding public sphere depends entirely on the success of workers at acquiring a voice and the willingness of middling-class people to hear it without class prejudice.

Conclusion

The asymmetrical "debate" between Burke and Thelwall confirms Gregory Claeys's view that the key issue of the French Revolution debate was "the relationship between economic inequality and social progress, defined in terms of both commerce and manners."[50] Under pressure from Burke's personal attacks, harassed by violent anti-Jacobins on his lecture tour, Thelwall responded with two of his best prose works, stylistically, rhetorically, and substantively. He vigorously defended the democratic public sphere and provided the fledgling democratic culture with important strategies for defending itself, delegitimating the aristocratic culture, and appropriating subversively powerful hegemonic symbols such as rationality, classical culture, and Christianity. By his own example, heroically standing up to Burke and loyalist violence, Thelwall used himself less as a mediator between a realm of truth and his readers who lacked it than as a synecdochic portion of the social whole that he was addressing.

Here is the Jacobin writer who has little use for the role of Romantic author, except that the overall pattern of intemperate rhetorical wildness followed by sober control is a Romantic pattern as well. He practiced a version of what Kevin Gilmartin has aptly named "radical egotism," using his own person for political effect.[51] For the most part Thelwall avoids being victimized by the "dialectic of Enlightenment" that destroys the already existing systems of popular understanding ("superstition" and "prejudice") in order to replace it with an equivocally emancipatory abstract rationality. This is because Thelwall's theory is a product of social rationality—dialogic publicity—underpinned by nature.

A literary Jacobinism without Burke would have been very different indeed. One need only compare the responses to Burke's antidemocratic successor in opposing democratic reforms, Thomas Malthus, to realize how much closer Burke was to the Jacobins than either ever suspected. Malthus shifted the once morally inflected political discourse to pseudoscientific controversies over food and population ratios for a good half century or so. With Burke the political discourse was never scientific; it was ethical, religious, philosophical. Burke inspired Paine and Thelwall to write and think at levels they probably would not have reached otherwise; the stimulus and provocation of his writing enabled an entire artisan and middling-class culture to find a voice and sense of cultural self-confidence in repudiating the "swinish multitude" label.

50. Gregory Claeys, "The French Revolution Debate and British Political Thought," *History of Political Thought* 11 (1990): 61.
51. Gilmartin coins the phrase in relation to the later practices of Cobbett and Wooler, and for all three the "radical egotism" serves the triple purpose of moving the audience from "oral" to "literate" markers of meaning, constituting a form of "recognizable authority," and achieving an "accessible realism." *Print Politics*, 40.

Burke also presented powerful arguments. Different parts of his overall argument were integrated and mirrored in the writing of otherwise strong democrats. Burke exposed Jacobinism's weakest aspects, which the most astute Jacobins also repudiated: the abstract rationalism, the contempt for traditional modes of cultural understanding and expression, abstract individualism, and political violence. Whereas Malthus's ideas sustained a utilitarian social engineering that was hostile to the working class, Burke's ideas led to a Romantic anticapitalism that sometimes was effective in opposing industrial capitalism's worst abuses. Although the British Jacobins demonized Burke, they were perhaps fortunate in having him as their principal opponent.[52]

The public sphere after Burke and Paine includes many new readers brought into a civil discourse that because of repression and loyalist coercion became unfriendly to critical reflection. Caricatured simplifications, paranoid projections, and fierce scapegoating barely restrained by rationalist protocols—all part of the Burkean legacy as well, unfortunately—marked the triumph of anti-Jacobinism that despite itself legitimated aspects of popular culture. There was no denying that the literary market in 1800 was far larger and more politically unpredictable than it had seemed to be in 1789. Although repression had silenced the Jacobin and reform press, outlawed the popular societies, and all but banned dissident political speech of any kind by the late 1790s, the public sphere adapted to the harsh conditions rather than expiring. Jacobins and reformers waited for a more permissive political climate, which did indeed arrive. At one pole a moderate and cautious version of critical reason was expressed in the predominantly Dissenting *Monthly Magazine* (1796) and the Whiggish *Edinburgh Review* (1802), while at another pole Spencean artisans and laborers sustained a radical culture in obscure London taverns. Harsh but inefficient, the repression permitted a

---

52. For the Malthusian legacy, see Gertrude Himmelfarb, *The Idea of Poverty: England in the Early Industrial Age* (New York: Knopf, 1983). For Burke's political legacy, see Alfred Cobban, *Edmund Burke and the Revolt Against the Eighteenth Century*, 2nd ed. (New York: Barnes and Noble, 1961). For Romantic anticapitalism, see the essays by Robert Sayre, Michael Lowy, and Michael Ferber in G. A. Rosso and Daniel P. Watkins, eds., *Spirits of Fire: English Romantic Writers and Contemporary Historical Methods* (Rutherford, N.J.: Fairleigh Dickinson University Press, Associated University Presses, 1990), 23–91. The counter-Enlightenment tradition developed by Isaiah Berlin is in part Burkean; see, for example, his *Against the Current: Essays in the History of Ideas* (London: Hogarth Press, 1979). Burke is still a thinker whose ideas are living. Hans-Georg Gadamer's *Truth and Method* (1960), where Gadamer uses Burke's critique of Enlightenment rationalism, is only one of the most famous examples.

constrained public sphere to function even in the worst of times. The ideological differentiation of the reading public and the disciplining of readers into elite and mass audiences would also be institutionalized to supplement the repression, as Jon Klancher has illustrated.

The middle-class and elite strata of reformers and Jacobins could not sustain their political associations, such as the Constitutional Society (folded by 1795), against the repression as well as the LCS (outlawed in 1799), but their periodicals, such as the *Monthly Magazine*, adapted well to the anti-Jacobin reaction, during which the journal had its greatest moment. A disguised, displaced, and cautious reformism was permitted liberties never granted to plebeian radicalism. The middle-class public sphere also included salon-like gatherings at Horne Tooke's and Joseph Johnson's, literary clubs like the Philomaths, coffeehouses for informal discussion and reading, and celebratory dinners like the one that commemorated the treason trial acquittals, held every year on Guy Fawkes Day from 1795 until 1842.[53] That successful publishers such as the Robinsons subsidized Godwin's research for *Political Justice*, confident they would get a profitable return on a learned treatise devoted to theoretical aspects of Jacobin politics, tells us much about the public sphere in the 1790s, when Godwin's three editions sold four thousand copies.[54] Repression, however, ultimately silenced even the literary public sphere of the middle class: Joseph Johnson, J. S. Jordan, and Benjamin Flower were all imprisoned and heavily fined in 1799–1800, thus attacking the very institutional heart of reform and Jacobin publishing. By also targeting the classical scholar Gilbert Wakefield, who died shortly after his years in jail, the government was signaling to the polite radicals in a not-so-subtle fashion. According to Marilyn Butler, the "government's treatment of Johnson and Wakefield was taken to be unprecedented aggression, the end of the truce against scholars with no defence except pure motives and a small readership."[55] It was not the literary market and rational debate but political repression and organized loyalism that expelled reform from the center of middle-class attention.

53. Thale, ed., *Selections from the Papers of the London Corresponding Society 1792–1799*, xvii. The radical appropriation of nationalist, Protestant, anti-Catholic discourse is worth noting here. For the seventeenth-century discourse on Guy Fawkes Day, see David Cressy, *Bonfires and Bells: National Memory and the Protestant Calendar in Elizabethan and Stuart England* (London: Weidenfeld and Nicolson, 1989).

54. Mark Philp, *Godwin's Political Justice* (London: Duckworth, 1986), 74; Locke, *Fantasy of Reason*, 61.

55. Marilyn Butler, ed., *Burke, Paine, Godwin, and the Revolution Controversy* (Cambridge: Cambridge University Press, 1984), 15.

Jacobinism

The public sphere as a means by which the public would find its "voice" had great appeal to Jacobins like Thelwall. For Jacobins truth emerged in the public sphere or nowhere. As late as 1826, when he was in his sixties, Thelwall waxes lyrical about the Mechanics' Institutes and similar societies as forming the structures by which "mind" triumphs over ignorance. He wants his own *Panoramic Miscellany* to be the "organ of communication between the various Scientific, Literary and Mechanic Institutions," the mediating contact point for the spread of popular knowledge. "By such means, intellect might come to know its strength, and learn to proceed in its benignant work, with the acceleration, and the certainty, that result from union and reciprocation."[56] His monthly periodical, then, would function like a "convention" without incurring explicitly political risks. Popular knowledge for Thelwall was not instead of but always concurrent with politics. When radical politics were too dangerous, popular education was a safe and intrinsically valuable way to cultivate a rationality that would ultimately, if indirectly, effect democratic changes.

56. *The Panoramic Miscellany* 6 (30 June 1826): 716.

part

2

The Voice of the People

> To paint the voice, and fix the fleeting sound.
> —motto for *The Tribune* (1795–96; PEJ 65)
>
> Vox populi vox Dei.
> —*The Natural and Constitutional Right of Britons* (1795)
> and *The Tribune* 18 (PEJ 32; 242)
>
> ... with one congregated voice ...
> —*The Tribune* 17 (PEJ 169)
>
> ... collecting the aggregate voice of the nation ...
> —*The Natural and Constitutional Right of Britons* (PEJ 28)

From Plato to Derrida philosophers have pondered the complexities of representing "voice." For Thelwall and other Jacobins voice was also a practical issue: what procedures will yield something like a popular voice, a voice of the people? Competing systems of representation included the monarchical (the king or queen as representative of the whole nation), the Burkean (the legislator as "virtual" representative of the people), and the constitutionalist (a tripartite structure of monarchy, nobility, and people representing the nation). While Coleridge in *On the Constitution of the Church and State* offers his clerisy as a check against the power of the landed and moneyed interests, Wordsworth developed his influential model of elite literature, distinguishing between the "unthinking" public and the transcendentally constructed "People" whose spirit and knowledge he reveres. The "Deity" inspires the "Vox Populi," but the literary market is utterly unreliable for producing this voice.[1] There were two concurrent developments that responded to the challenge of Jacobin writing: outright repression and autonomous literature. The idea of literature and a cultured elite incorporated and translated some of the key features of democratic ideology, preserving in another form the ideals of equality, communication, and the authority of nature and reason.

I will deal with Thelwall and autonomous literature in Part Three, but in Part Two the focus is on Thelwall's popular poetry and oratory in the 1790s, as well as his oratory from then until the end of his career. As popular poetry and lecturing become closed to him because of repression, he turns to autonomous literature and oratorical theory, speech therapy, elocutionary discourse, and public speaking as a teachable skill. Thelwall never repudiated his 1790s politics, so that the move to literature and elocution was a strategic maneuver to save in some form his political radicalism. As we will see, it was impossible to separate entirely what was a tactical retreat from substantial revision of his ideas, but there is a discernible continuity from the early to the late Thelwall. To give Thelwall's popular poetry a context I have included a section on the LCS poetry in general; included here as well is an excursus on the radical underground, specifically Thomas Spence and Robert Wedderburn, to provide a contrasting example of a path not taken by Thelwall. The path to literature and elocution was undertaken by Thelwall in good faith and was not cowardly; it was an honorable reaction to the threat of imprisonment or worse. Nevertheless, it is instructive to look at Spence and Wedderburn, who represent another approach to the anti-Jacobin triumph.

The public sphere in which Jacobins participated was at no time free from repression. When the LCS was less than six months old the royal proclamation against seditious publications was declared; it was less than a year old when Paine was outlawed. There was no subtle consciousness-distorting trickery, just brute force that the government wielded against popular radicalism. The history of literary Jacobinism is scarred by violence and scapegoating, as the British Jacobins themselves were demonized in literature and punished in reality (executed, jailed, exiled, harassed). George Crabbe's

---

1. William Wordsworth, "Essay, Supplementary to the Preface [1815]," in John O. Hayden, ed., *William Wordsworth: Selected Prose* (Harmondsworth: Penguin, 1988), 412–13.

barely veiled attack on Thelwall, which appeared in the first of his 1812 *Tales*, "The Dumb Orators; or, The Benefit of Society," actually appears about a decade after the most intensive wave of anti-Jacobinism.[2] The poem's central action is the humiliation of the radical Hammond, an obvious figure for Thelwall, by a commonplace Justice of the Peace. The most powerful forces in British society utterly repudiated Jacobinism intellectually and institutionally, suppressing its publications, shutting down its spheres of publicity, and attacking and ridiculing its doctrines. The literary market itself in fact proved to be a revolutionary institution. For many decades thereafter successive ruling elites would prefer an illiterate, poorly educated laboring class to one that might have access to critical ideas.

2. *The Poetical Works of George Crabbe*, ed. A. J. Carlyle and R. M. Carlyle (Oxford: Oxford University Press, 1914), 219–24.

3

Thelwall's Popular Poetry and LCS Culture

The ambiguity of the convention idea—whether to petition or replace parliament—is both legalistic and theoretical. To save their lives in the treason trials, the Jacobins insisted that the conventions about which they spoke were intended merely to educate parliament, but Thomas Paine, writing from France knowing that his *Rights of Man* had been selling in the hundreds of thousands, granted parliament no legitimacy whatsoever and insisted that the "people" had already spoken definitively: a convention would be a timely intervention to install a legitimate government. Paine appealed to the literary market as a representative institution that "spoke" and had a "voice." The difference between the Wordsworth of 1815 and Jacobins like Thelwall who want an expanded public sphere is that Wordsworth insists that an unthinking Public, synonymous with the mass reader, can never achieve a level of understanding equal to that of the transcendental People, but Jacobins believed that popularization, if unfettered by repression and assisted by restructured leisure and labor, could indeed make the reading public truly discriminating and critical. Jacobins too acknowledged the problem of a differentiated reading public, but they aimed at an egalitarian solution, whereas their opponents sought permanently hierarchical distinctions.

Jacobin writing challenged the hierarchical structure of literature. The best achievements of the Jacobins are in forms that have not been ordinarily seen as "literary": radical periodicals, pamphlets, speeches, parodies, songs, manifestos, trial narratives, and other texts usually viewed as subliterary ephemera. Thomas Spence defined "literature" in his dictionary as "learning."[1] Spence's nonexclusive sense of literature was actually the norm before Romantic ideology restricted the normative range of literary expression; the exclusively belletristic sense of "literature" is post-Romantic.[2] The publications of the LCS included songs and popular poetry that mixed oral and print culture, traditional and Enlightenment modes of understanding. On the far left Thomas Spence and Robert Wedderburn produced fascinating texts that mixed Enlightenment rationalism, religious "enthusiasm," and popular culture. For Spence and Wedderburn "voice" emerged only agonistically out of print culture.

The "plebeian" public sphere—"next to, and interlocked with, the hegemonic public sphere"—had been opened up by the seventy or so replies to Burke's *Reflections* and the hundreds of thousands of Paine's readers.[3]

---

1. Thomas Spence, *The Grand Repository of the English Language* (1775) (Menston: Scolar Press, 1969).
2. Discussing the transition to a more exclusive notion of "literature" are the following: Olivia Smith, *The Politics of Language, 1791–1819* (Oxford: Clarendon Press, 1984); Marilyn Butler, *Romantics, Rebels, and Reactionaries: English Literature and Its Background, 1760–1830* (Oxford: Oxford University Press, 1992); and Raymond Williams, *Culture and Society, 1780–1950* (New York: Harper and Row, 1958), esp. the chapter on the Romantic Artist, and *Marxism and Literature* (Oxford: Oxford University Press, 1977), esp. Part 1, Basic Concepts, 11–74.
3. James T. Boulton, *The Language of Politics in the Age of Wilkes and Burke* (New York: Routledge and Kegan Paul, 1963), 75–83. Günther Lottes uses the phrase "plebeijische Öffentlichkeit" in *Politische Aufklärung und plebejisches Publikum. Zur Theorie und Praxis des englishchen Rakikalismus im spatën 18. Jahrhundert* (Munich: R. Oldenbourg Verlag, 1979). Jürgen Habermas, who responds to Lottes's revision of Habermas's pioneering ideas on the "bourgeois" public sphere, concedes that "the exclusion of the culturally and politically mobilized lower strata entails a pluralization of the public sphere in the very process of its emergence. Next to, and interlocked with, the hegemonic public sphere, a plebeian one assumes shape." "Further Reflections on the Public Sphere," in Craig Calhoun, ed., *Habermas and the Public Sphere* (Cambridge, Mass.: MIT Press, 1992), 426.

Burke's "swinish multitude" phrase raised the issue of popular culture in a strikingly provocative way. According to Olivia Smith, "by vividly defining a large part of the population as brutish and inarticulate, Burke provoked them into speech."[4] This "speech" included the LCS and other popular societies that held regular meetings, protest demonstrations, celebratory dinners, sponsored and distributed pamphlets and newspapers, and were the institutional framework for organized and ephemeral forms of self-education and mutual instruction. Religious radicals such as Richard Lee employed an idiom of "enthusiasm" that conflicted at times with the rationalist idioms derived from the Enlightenment, although the two traditions were not utterly incompatible.[5]

The government suppressed even apolitical debating societies with laboring-class and middling-class speakers, despite courageous efforts by Thelwall and others to keep them functioning. According to Thelwall, it was at such debating clubs that he acquired a political education and developed his oratorical skills.[6] For Iain McCalman, the popular debating clubs were the "principal institutional form" of Jacobinism.[7] The short-lived *Politician* (1795) and the financially troubled *Moral and Political Magazine* (1796–97) were LCS publications, but other periodicals only loosely connected to the LCS were much more successful, such as Thelwall's *Tribune* (1795–96), Spence's *Pig's Meat* (1793–96), and Eaton's *Politics for the People* (1793–95) and *The Philanthropist* (1795–96). Although these periodicals did not sell in the huge numbers that Cobbett's *Register* would in 1816, for their time the circulation was substantial, and in fact much larger in actual readership, as a single copy would have many readers. Eaton's *Politics for the People* had five editions by 1795, and Thelwall's *Tribune* had an initial circulation of

---

4. Olivia Smith, *The Politics of Language 1791–1819* (Oxford: Clarendon University Press, 1984), 81. On the "swinish" trope, see Margery Corbett and Ronald Lightblown, *The Comely Frontispiece: The Emblematic Title-Page in England, 1550–1660* (London: Routledge and Kegan Paul, 1979), 59–65; Peter Stallybrass and Allon White, *The Politics and Poetics of Transgression* (Ithaca: Cornell University Press, 1986), 53.

5. Jon Mee, "Apocalypse and Ambivalence: The Politics of Millenarianism in the 1790s," *South Atlantic Quarterly* 95 (1996): 671–97; on Lee 683–87. Mee's book, *Dangerous Enthusiasm: William Blake and the Culture of Radicalism in the 1790s* (Oxford: Clarendon Press, 1992), emphasizes convincingly that "enthusiasm" and "enlightenment" had much in common. See the recent issue of *Huntington Library Quarterly* 60 (1998) devoted to "enthusiasm."

6. "Prefatory Memoir," *Poems*, xix, xxiii–xxv.

7. Iain McCalman, "Ultra-Radicalism and Convivial Debating-Clubs in London, 1795–1838," *English Historical Review* 102 (1987): 309–33.

The Voice of the People

1,250, with a second edition in bound volumes.⁸ The LCS had an activist core of several thousands but could attract to its demonstrations many more thousands.⁹ The government did not outlaw Godwin's *Political Justice* because its high price—£1.16s—would have excluded a popular readership, but in fact some artisans did purchase copies and study the challenging text.¹⁰

Political songs were published as broadsides, distributed widely, and performed at meetings and celebrations. The LCS distributed coins with political symbols, for example to celebrate Eaton's acquittal for publishing Thelwall's "Chaunticlere" allegory about the beheaded gamecock. While it lasted, the artisanal and laboring-class public sphere, which Geoff Eley calls "the founding moment of the nineteenth-century labor movement," sustained a variety of innovative cultural expressions.¹¹ It closed down only because of governmental repression and organized loyalist countermeasures.

Popular political culture depended on literacy and print-culture technology. By the 1790s there was already considerable literacy among the laboring and middling classes due to the Sunday and charity schools, Nonconformist Bible-reading, and a rising standard of living throughout the eighteenth century. Almost 60 percent of all men and 90 percent of all artisans were literate by the end of the eighteenth century.¹² But artisans and tradesmen had little time for reading. John Thelwall was extraordinary in seizing as much time as he could from his duties at work for reading, even to the extent of reading while walking in the streets on business errands. More typical would be his friend and LCS comrade, the shoemaker Thomas Hardy, who restricted his reading mostly to religious and political pamphlets because of his poverty and limited leisure. The overwhelming majority of literate laborers and middling-class people had very little acquaintance with English or European literature,

---

8. "Preface," *The Tribune* (1796), 1: v.

9. Mary Thale, ed., *Selections from the Papers of the London Corresponding Society, 1792–1799* (Cambridge: Cambridge University Press, 1983), xxiv.

10. The cabinet discussed prosecuting *Political Justice* on 25 May 1793. Don Locke, *A Fantasy of Reason: The Life and Thought of William Godwin* (London: Routledge and Kegan Paul, 1980), 60; Albert Goodwin, *The Friends of Liberty: The English Democratic Movement in the Age of the French Revolution* (Cambridge, Mass.: Harvard University Press, 1979), 475, on artisans readings *Political Justice*.

11. Geoff Eley, "Nations, Publics, and Political Cultures: Placing Habermas in the Nineteenth Century," in Calhoun, ed., *Habermas and the Public Sphere*, 329.

12. Alan Richardson, *Literature, Education, and Romanticism: Reading as Social Practice, 1780–1832* (Cambridge: Cambridge University Press, 1994), 45; Lawrence Stone, "Literacy and Education in England, 1640–1900," *Past and Present* 42 (1969): 112.

except for the Bible, and perhaps *Paradise Lost* and *Pilgrim's Progress*. Robert Bloomfield, a shoemaker, came upon Thomson's *Seasons*, Milton's *Paradise Lost*, and various novels only by accident and considerably after he had learned to read fluently. Ann Yearsley, another worker poet, had been familiar with *Paradise Lost* from childhood and was delighted to learn later that Milton had written other poems. The English literary tradition, like political and social power, was something structured to be out of the grasp of most people. Burke's infamous phrase signified a contemptuous rejection of popular literacy that flourished nevertheless.

LCS Poetry

Literary Jacobins and reformers employed a distinctive idiom in part shaped by contemporary events and in part inherited from the previous decades of literary experimentation. The "swinish multitude" statement, the Bastille, a feminized Liberty figure, Liberty trees and loyalist oaks, Enlightenment symbolism (fire, light, sun), and republican nakedness and aristocratic artifice are some of the most common metaphors. The regicide of 1793 and republican ideology in general were expressed symbolically and thematically. Writers also had access to the cultural repertoire of the Enlightenment, especially the work of the three decades or so before 1790 that Marilyn Butler has identified as a time of extraordinarily energetic innovation in all fields, including literature, science, philosophy, theology, and the visual arts. Sensibility, radical Dissent, abolitionism, feminism, and parliamentary reformism all precede 1789. Charlotte Smith's sonnets, Sterne's novels, Mackenzie's *The Man of Feeling*, Rousseauistic educational theories (and Rousseau in translation), empiricist psychology, the Gothic novel, liberal theology, deism, the ballad revival, and antiquarian philology were boldly experimental and antiauthoritarian. The Jacobins and other reformers educated themselves within this Enlightenment culture; they also read the writing of the "country party": Swift, Pope, Johnson, and Gray.[13] John Thelwall wrote a sonnet series while imprisoned for treason that echoed both Milton and Charlotte Smith. Thelwall's antiaristocratic *Peripatetic* borrows from the sentimental tradition of Sterne and Mackenzie. Wollstonecraft refashioned Rousseauistic educational theory and empiricist psychology to condemn the patriarchal miseducation

13. Marilyn Butler has provided the best description of the literary radicalism of 1760–1790 in *Romantics, Rebels, and Reactionaries*, chap. 1.

of women. In their novels Godwin and Wollstonecraft politicized the Gothic villains and victims, and turned the plot of pursuit and escape toward egalitarian social critique. Paine engages Augustan satire in fashioning his plain style, while Godwin's anarchist (mis)reading of Swift's *Gulliver's Travels* leads to the basic argument in *Political Justice*. Wordsworth's revision of the traditional ballad deepened the democratic meanings of the ballad in what Nigel Leask has described as a disguised radicalism—disguising in particular republican agrarianism.[14] One dominant Jacobin strategy was to refashion already existing forms, wrenching the forms askew to permit new kinds of expression.

The literary culture of the LCS included print-culture forms such as periodicals, pamphlets, broadsides, and inexpensive editions of books, but it also included forms of oral and popular textuality: trials and trial transcripts, speeches, toasts, lectures, songs, demonstrations, graffiti, coins, signs, banners, and other publicly symbolic actions. There was indeed a tension between Jacobin and traditional artisan culture. As Günther Lottes has pointed out, Jacobin respectability, self-restraint, and education challenged traditional plebeian culture, but Jacobin periodicals such as *Politics for the People* respectfully accommodated that culture, appealing to traditional plebeian cultural forms to communicate experience.[15] Outright contempt for artisanal culture would merely have mirrored the most vicious class biases, but too much deference to the traditional culture would undermine the rationalistic foundation of Jacobin radicalism. The difficult task was to reach the right balance.

The periodicals associated with the LCS, Eaton's *Politics for the People* and Spence's *Pig's Meat,*, often achieved the desired balance and included in each issue a dimension of popular education and enlightenment, not simply current political news and satire, as Eaton and Spence consciously popularized democratic traditions. Spence's preface explains his purpose clearly: he wants to teach his readers "that their forlorn Condition has not been entirely overlooked and forgotten, nor their just Cause unpleaded, neither by their Maker nor by the best and most enlightened of Men in all ages." By setting side by side extracts from Amos, Luke, Isaiah, Swift, Godwin, Thelwall, Goldsmith, Gray, Shakespeare, Johnson, Algernon Sidney, Paine, Volney,

---

14. Nigel Leask, "Pantisocracy and the Politics of the 'Preface' to *Lyrical Ballads*," in Kelvin Everest and Alison Yarrington, eds., *Reflections of Revolution: Images of Romanticism* (New York: Routledge, 1993), 39–58.
15. Lottes, *Politische Aufklärung und plebejisches Publikum*, 114–33; 253.

"Gregory Grunter," "Porkulus," "a Mechanic," and "Spare-Rib" in issue after issue, Eaton and Spence made available to a popular audience a tradition that had been structured out of their reach. Although both periodicals try to "enlighten" their readers, neither is condescending nor manipulative. Although Spence dominates *Pig's Meat* with his own ideas, especially his plan for land reorganization, Spence's own literary style, which Olivia Smith has called one of the great triumphs of the "intellectual vernacular,"[16] is entertaining and accessible. Moreover, Spence presents his extracts unpedantically, like a passionate amateur scholar who loves the texts and writers he presents to others. Less personal and more clearly a "movement" journal, Eaton's *Politics for the People* also includes letters from LCS members that report and comment on events. The "enlightening" process, then, is not just in one direction, from educated radicals like Godwin and Thelwall to the artisans. One intriguing letter from Edinburgh (March 1794) depicts a struggle between loyalists and Jacobins at the theater, where the band's "God Save the King" was drowned out by the democrats, who practiced a vigorous kind of literary criticism during the staging of *Charles the First:* "The Democratic parts of Cromwell's speeches were received by thundering plaudits, while the pathetic and dignified speeches of Charles were either laughed or hissed."[17] Clapping, hissing, laughing, and keeping absolutely silent were some of the publicly symbolic gestures that Jacobins and reformers also used to express their ideas, even at a loyalist play staged by a loyalist theater. By reporting the episode to the journal—by corresponding—the writer gives it even more effectiveness and power.[18]

Although poetry was not a central feature in either *Politics for the People* or *Pig's Meat*, it was more than a peripheral form of expression. Political songs and satirical allegories could be more symbolically defiant than ordinary political prose. Moreover, at meetings, celebratory dinners, and demonstrations songs played a ritual role, inviting mass participation and gleeful defiance and maintaining morale. Such poetry was designed not to change political perspectives but rather to perform symbolically the ideology already taken for granted. Mark Philp is correct, however, in pointing out that democratic writers played "with ideas and principles, and with their audi-

---

16. *The Politics of Language 1791–1819*, 96–107.
17. *Politics for the People*, 2 vols. (1793–95, rpt. New York: Greenwood, 1968), I:377–79.
18. On the political valence of "correspondence," see Mary Favret, *Romantic Correspondence: Women, Politics, and the Fiction of Letters* (Cambridge: Cambridge University Press, 1993).

ences' intellectual and emotional reflexes," so that although the writing performed an ideology, there was still room for exploration and discovery.[19] Such poetry permitted symbolic triumphs over enemies of reform when real triumphs were more difficult to obtain. I will examine first some songs that display vividly important conventions, then I will turn to Thomas Spence and John Thelwall, who wrote especially effective songs and allegories.

Songs, as opposed to more "literary" forms, depend for their effectiveness on striking contrasts that can be grasped readily. There may be subtle satire in a song but the form itself dictates semantic clarity and repetitive patterns. Some songs are forthrightly aggressive, even symbolically violent, including the use of an apocalyptic-religious symbolism, while others soften their radicalism and affirm a restorative mythology in a constitutionalist idiom whereby democracy is a "return" to an earlier, more egalitarian time.

In the introduction to my anthology *Poetry and Reform*, I identified a recurrent pattern the radical periodical poetry shares with Romantic poetry in general, what I called disguised transgression: the actual degree of innovation is obscured by revising a traditional idiom (PR 26–29). At the level of poetic form there is an attempt to "balance" the customary and novel truths in a way that is homologous with a constitutionalist reform ideology. A song of the 1790s that was composed for a political meeting performs a disguised transgression. "The Genius of France" (PR 43–44), published in the *Morning Chronicle* of 30 November 1792, was described as the "best" song sung at the Southwark Friends of the People meeting and public dinner. Thelwall, a leading figure in the Southwark Friends of the People, possibly wrote the song, which contrasts the evils of the old tyrannical order with the blessings of revolution:

> While France, full of sense and of spirit, pursues
> The cause of the world, with the noblest of views;
> Where tyranny held her unbounded controul,
> Made nature factitious, and fetter'd the soul.
> Let us fill the gay glass, and with rapture advance,
> The soul and the song, to the Genius of France.
>
> See her swains render'd happy—her cities all shine,
> Her hills "laugh and sing" with the gen'rous vine;

---

19. Mark Philp, "The Fragmented Ideology of Reform," in Mark Philp, ed., *The French Revolution and British Popular Politics* (Cambridge: Cambridge University Press, 1991), 70–72.

> Fit emblem of ev'ry true patriot that lives,
> He draws his support, from the embrace that he gives. [10]
> Then hail th' occasion, and boldly advance,
> The glass and the song, to the Genius of France.
>
> See Commerce delighted, extending her arm,
> With virtues, all active, to bless and to charm;
> Where monkery indolent, vicious and blind,
> Laid man all in ruins, and rusted the mind.
> Then lift up the song, and with spirit advance,
> The full-glowing glass to the Genius of France.
>
> See Sages all ardent—see Patriots burn,
> The faith and the moral of nature return; [20]
> While grim superstition retires to her caves,
> And beckons those rebels of nature—the slaves—
> Then Britons join chorus, and nobly advance
> The glass and the song, to the Genius of France. (PR 43–44)

The contrast hinges on two words, "nature" and "soul," as revolution has returned the soul to its natural state of pastoral bliss (st. 2), generous commerce (st. 3), and heroic enlightenment (st. 4). The overall contrast is between pleasure-loving revolution associated with innocent pastoralism, and inward-looking tyranny associated with Gothic secrets and prisons. The song's refrain commands the singers to lift boldly their glasses in tribute to the Genius of France. "Advance" here signifies the hand holding a glass during a toast, and it also connotes a military "advance." "Rapture" (st. 1) suggests Revelation's rapture, hinting at final Judgment and apocalyptic cleansing. "Laugh and sing" (st. 2) echoes Psalm 126 and attaches the Psalmist's joy at being liberated from the Babylonian captivity to pastoral innocence and renovated "shining" cities, as revolutionary *fraternité* bridges the artificial differences between religious and secular, Christian and pagan, rural and urban, English and French. This song, which negates Gothic gloom with pastoral cheer, does not reject religious concepts outright, but realigns them with "nature." The poet stresses the visual dimension by beginning three of the four stanzas with "See." That which is visible, public, open to inspection is natural; only tyrants hide their secrets in dark "caves."[20] The

---

20. On the dimension of the visible in Romanticism, see William Galperin's *The Return of the Visible in British Romanticism* (Baltimore: Johns Hopkins University Press, 1993).

open pastoral plains and the cities of light negate the unilluminated—unenlightened—Gothic enclosures. By redefining nature and spirit/soul, the song recreates symbolically an expansive, cosmopolitan community and discredits the intellectually narrow and culturally repressive xenophobia against which the Jacobins were fighting. This song mitigates its cultural transgression by portraying revolutionary values not as violent iconoclasm but as a nonviolent return to nature. The old regime, not republican democracy, is the source of Gothic violence.

Democratic songs typically assign responsibility for violence to counterrevolutionaries, but sometimes they hint menacingly about retaliation. A 1792 song from the *Manchester Herald*, "The Fire of Liberty" (PR 52–53), employs the constitutionalist idiom of the Norman yoke ("the Norman Conqu'ror") that stifled a "heaven-born" freedom, but it also uses the figure of fire, at once source of light, life-sustaining warmth, and destructive incineration. Fire, an apt metaphor for a movement ambivalent about revolution, could serve equally well as a sign of Enlightenment, illuminating the dark spaces of ignorant superstition, or of revolution, destroying the old so that the new could be born. Another song ambiguously represents violence. Thomas Best (1795; PR 95–96) in Eaton's *Philanthropist* deploys the personification of a female Britannia, a conventional feminized Liberty threatened by male tyrants and defended by male reformers. This pattern of masculine displacement of women reflects male-dominated artisan radicalism.[21] "If Liberty represented woman," writes Joan Landes of the French Marianne that was very similar to the Britannia figure on the other side of the channel, "surely it was as an abstract emblem of male power and authority." The liberty goddess was "chaste, pure, self-sacrificing, and wholly dedicated to the universal aims of the Republic," but this ideological tribute to women was better than the later symbol of the revolution, Hercules, whose displacement of Marianne was misogynistic.[22] In Best's song Britannia laments how England's divinely blessed libertarian tradition of glorious ancestors has been ruined by tyrants. In the final stanza Britannia, in despair, plunges herself into the waves. The poem shifts responsibility for violence entirely onto the

---

21. On the ideological displacements of "masculine" Romanticism, see Anne K. Mellor, *Romanticism and Gender* (London: Routledge, 1993). On women and artisanal and laboring-class radicalism, see Anna Clark, *The Struggle for the Breeches: Gender and the Making of the British Working Class* (Berkeley and Los Angeles: University of California Press, 1995).

22. Joan B. Landes, *Women and the Public Sphere in the Age of the French Revolution* (Ithaca: Cornell University Press, 1988), 161–63.

"great men of state" who have destroyed "Old England" and forced Britannia to suicide.

Some topical songs negotiate violence by turning anticlerical ire toward millennial apocalypse.[23] The fast days, organized by the Church of England, directed prayers and acts of penance toward victory against the French. In *Politics for the People* (1794; PR 88–90) an especially effective satire, "An Hymn for the Fast Day, To Be Sung by The Friends of Mankind," begins with an address to God that includes an apocalyptic level of violent destruction. God is blamed for letting kings, the "scepter'd despots," wreak havoc on the otherwise peaceful world. The first half of the song excoriates the militaristic "Monarchs and Princes," while the second half urges God, in biblical rhetoric, to abolish war by ridding the world of kings; finally, the song concludes with a portrait of the world without war and tyrants. This satirical "Fast Hymn" indeed prays for victory and an end to the war by redefining the terms: kings, not the French, are the enemy; peace is not an insular English patriotism, a "family" with King George at the top of the hierarchy, but "one large family of thine, / As brethren knit in bands divine." The song derives its authority to speak in universal terms—kings in general, not just George—by revising a biblical rhetoric to accommodate republican ideology. Monarchs symbolize the Antichrist of Revelation and the bloodthirsty Moloch of the Hebrew Bible. After the destruction of tyrants—"vultures" and biblical "locusts"—a millennial utopia follows, with a bountiful nature generous to the aged and poor. The song urges God as king to rid the world of kings, and redefines "rights divine" as *popular* sovereignty. "Nature" does not sanction English nationalism and an aristocratic order as in Burke and conservative Romanticism, but a universal egalitarianism that rests on the foundation of a prolific and generous nature. Indeed, reform writers often assume the prophetic stance to discredit injustice.

The popular songs of the early and middle 1790s, then, revised the meaning of crucial hegemonic words and concepts according to a republican ideology in order to reposition *nature* and *soul* from affirming an aristocratic-monarchical culture. Reflecting both a necessity for disguise because of the repression and an ambivalence about revolution, the songs assign responsibil-

---

23. As recent work by Jon Mee and Iain McCalman has shown, the idiom of religious enthusiasm mixed with and existed side by side with more rationalistic discourse within the radical artisan culture. See Mee's study of Blake, *Dangerous Enthusiasm*, and McCalman's "The Infidel as Prophet: William Reid and Blakean Radicalism," in Stephen H. Clark and David Worrall, eds., *Historicizing Blake* (New York: St. Martin's Press, 1994), 24–42.

ity for violence to kings, aristocrats, and the church, while depicting the triumph of a pastoral utopianism, with millennialist accents, over the Gothic darkness. Sung at meetings and demonstrations, these Jacobin poems reinforced solidarity and delegitimated the established culture at the most powerful affective levels of emotional associations; at the same time they enjoyed more freedom from prosecution than other expressions of republican ideology.

Thomas Spence's Songs

Few poets of song were as effective as Thomas Spence in wedding biblical imagery with Jacobin ideology. Spence's "prophetic" use of religious enthusiasm was not opportunistic or cynical, as a few have suggested. I concur with Jon Mee's judgment: "Everything he wrote suggests that he participated in that culture with genuine conviction."[24] Jacobins like Thelwall avoided positive appropriation of biblical imagery and concepts, reflecting the republican deism popularized by Paine's *Age of Reason*, but Spence took another approach. Spence used songs as a principal means of spreading his political ideas. According to Marcus Wood, Spence had "a gift for compact and striking language" and his verse displayed an "impressive variety of metric forms."[25] Whether through the *Song Book* or broadsides sold or distributed in the street or circulated in a tavern as drinking songs, Spence exploited the form with considerable sophistication. As distributor of Cooke's *Pocket Edition of Select British Poets* and author of songs, according to Anne Janowitz, Spence "stands on the cusp of oral and print culture."[26] The government recognized the political song as an effective vehicle for seditious expression. In 1801 a government report on Spence and the Spenceans frequently mentions the "treasonable and seditious" sentiments conveyed in "toasts and songs."[27] Spence popularized a bold plan for land reform that was more revolutionary than mainstream Jacobinism. His songs acquaint his audience with the unfamiliar details of the Spencean plan, but accommodate the audience's presuppositions, using a popular language that collapses the

---

24. Mee, "Apocalypse and Ambivalence," *South Atlantic Quarterly* 95 (1996): 687.
25. Marcus Wood, *Radical Satire and Print Culture 1790–1822* (Oxford: Oxford University Press, 1994), 85.
26. Anne Janowitz, *Lyric and Labour in the Romantic Tradition* (Cambridge: Cambridge University Press 1998), 74–77.
27. "Second Report," PH 35: 1307.

difference between writer and reader.[28] The authority for overturning aristocratic land ownership comes from biblical sources, natural law, popular culture, and the myth of ancient liberty. Spence's songs cite these sources as mutually reinforcing, thus not relying on any single foundational myth: "The Downfall of Feudal Tyranny" (1795; PR 73–75) depicts the Norman conquest as the historic turning point in the fate of English liberty; the "Jubilee Hymn" (1793; PR 63–65) appeals mostly to biblical precedent and natural law; "Burke's Address to the 'Swinish Multitude!' " (1794; PR 69–72) depends largely on popular culture.

P. M. Ashraf perceptively suggests a religious influence on Spence's songwriting from his contacts with radical Dissent in Newcastle-upon-Tyne. Specifically, she cites the Glassites, whose hymn-singing was innovative. "The Glassites introduced a variety of popular verse forms and the more lively metres of secular songs and set them to traditional tunes rather than ecclesiastical music." Consistent with their theology, the hymns of the Glassites were "an affirmation of equality." Although Spence himself was not a Glassite, his brother Jeremiah was a leading figure in the Newcastle congregation, and James Murray, Spence's mentor, was sympathetic to Glassite doctrines.[29] The description of Glas and the Glassites in Eneas Mackenzie's book on Newcastle (1827) reveals that under Jeremiah Spence's leadership the "most complete republican equality exists in their [Glassite] communities."[30] The most radical forms of Dissent anticipate Jacobinism.

Spence's "Jubilee Hymn" (1794; PR 63–65), his most well-known work, advocates radical land reform in a largely religious idiom:

>   1.
>   Hark! how the trumpet's sound*
>   Proclaims the land around
>   The Jubilee!
>   Tells all the poor oppress'd,
>   No more they shall be cess'd,

---

* See Leviticus, Chap. 25.

28. Smith, *The Politics of Language, 1791–1819*, 96–97.

29. P. M. Ashraf, *The Life and Times of Thomas Spence* (Newcastle upon Tyne: Frank Graham, 1983), 104 n.45, 190.

30. Eneas Mackenzie, *A Descriptive and Historical Account of the Town and Country of Newcastle upon Tyne, Including the Borough of Gateshead* (Newcastle upon Tyne: Mackenzie and Dent, 1827), 399.

The Voice of the People

Nor landlords more molest
   Their property.

2.
Rents t'ourselves now we pay,
Dreading no quarter day,
   Fraught with distress.
Welcome that day draws near,
For then our rents we share†,
Earth's rightful lords we are
   Ordain'd for this.

3.
How hath the oppressor ceas'd,‡
And all the world releas'd
   From misery!
The fir-trees all rejoice,
And cedars lift their voice,
Ceas'd now the Feller's noise,
   Long rais'd by thee.

4.
The sceptre now is broke,
Which with continual stroke
   The nations smote!
Hell from beneath doth rise,
To meet thy lofty eyes,
From the most pompous size,
   How brought to nought!

---

†Though the inhabitants in every district or parish in the world have an undoubted right to divide the WHOLE of the rents equally among them, and suffer the state and all public affairs to be supported by taxes as usual; yet from the numerous evils and restraints attending revenue laws, and number of collectors, informers, &c. appendant on the same, it is supposed, they would prefer, that after the whole amount of the rents collected in a parish from every person, according to the full value of the premises which they occupy, so much per pound, according to act of parliament, should be set apart for support of the state instead of all taxes; that another sum should next be deducted for support of the parish establishment, instead of tolls, tythes, rates, cesses, &c. and that after these important matters were provided for, the remainder of the money should be equally divided among all the settled inhabitants, whether poor or rich.

‡Isaiah, Ch. 14.

> 5.
> Since this Jubilee
> Sets all at Liberty
> Let us be glad.
> Behold each man return
> To his possession
> No more like doves to mourn
> By landlords sad! (PR 63–65)

Associating the biblical Jubilee with land reform was not unique with Spence (there are precedents in Moses Lowman and James Harrington),[31] but Spence uniquely popularized the association for the Jacobins. The song's overall logic is apparent in how Spence employs specific biblical passages to develop the concept of the Jubilee, the imagery of the old society's destruction, the imagery of celebration, and the concluding symbol of prophetic fulfillment. From Leviticus 25 Spence derived the Jubilee idea, whereby every fifty years each family recovers whatever land and property it had lost, as the entire society has a year-long sabbath or sabbatical: "The land shall not be sold forever: for the land *is* mine, for ye *are* strangers and sojourners with me" (KJV, 25:23). The land, owned by God, is subject to religious law and morality; private property must give way to a higher authority. The Jubilee trumpet at the song's beginning—citing the biblical verse 9—is like an apocalyptic trumpet that announces the end of time, the Last Judgment, and the New Jerusalem in Revelation. Echoes from Isaiah also contribute to the song's biblical idiom.[32] Spence uses the rhetoric of radical Dissent, the same stream of

---

31. Malcolm Chase, *"The People's Farm": English Radical Agrarianism, 1775–1840* (Oxford: Oxford University Press, 1988), 54–55.

32. From Isaiah 14, written during the Babylonian captivity and prophesying Israel's triumph over Babylon and other enemies, Spence gets the imagery of celebration. The allusions to verses 4–5 and 8–9 are pointedly antimonarchical. Verse 8 reads: "Yea, the fir trees rejoice at thee, *and* the cedars of Lebanon, *saying*, Since thou art laid down, no feller is come up against us." The fir and cedar trees are rejoicing because there are no more tyrants who need palaces constructed with fir and cedar, the most valuable kinds of wood at that time. The innocent trees are no longer cut because the "sceptre" of power (v. 5) has been cut. The lines on hell in the fourth stanza assume Isaiah 14:9: "Hell from beneath is moved for thee to meet *thee* at thy coming: it stirreth up the dead for thee, *even* all the chief ones of the earth; it hath raised up from their thrones all the kings of the nations." In Isaiah, then, Israel's power is so great that even the dead kings from hell come to pay homage. In Spence's stanza 4, the tyrants are "brought to nought" from their previous "pompous" grandeur; now the liberated people are "lofty." So here

cultural meanings that sustained William Blake as well as Christian millenarians such as Richard Brothers and Joanna Southcote.[33]

The full title—"From Spence's Rights of Man. A Song, to be sung at the Commencement of the Millennium, when there shall be neither Lords nor Landlords; but God and Man will be all in all. First printed in the year 1782. Tune—'God Save the King.' "—dramatically contrasts illegitimate power with legitimate by announcing the end of "Lords" and "Landlords." A name for God, "Lord" is embedded in the language of established power, so that Spence connects God and ordinary people by "ordaining" the people as "rightful lords" (st. 2). The tune of "God Save the King" ironizes the downfall of monarchy. The long footnote explaining the reformed parochial system—far longer than the song itself—is clever propaganda, as the song's lyrical and prosaic components reinforce one another. Spence's "parish" is a Jacobinically redefined word that only seems the same as the word used by the state church.

Spence's intimacy with his audience and its everyday life is apparent in the second stanza: "Dreading no quarter day, / Fraught with distress." Quarter days were the four times of the year when taxes and/or rents were due: Lady Day (March 25), Midsummer Day (June 24), Michaelmas Day (September 29), and Christmas Day (December 25), corresponding more or less to the four seasons. Laborers were also hired—or not rehired—on a quarter day. The oppression of the poor is not an abstraction but a felt experience, something he has in common with his audience, not something that is an object of his sympathy.

Another version of the song, not written by Spence but reproduced in the Spencean songbook,[34] is more explicitly millennial. This version of the song—and other songs in the songbook as well—shows how the Spencean movement turned Spence himself into a biblical prophet and how Spence's own songs became occasions for further textual production.

---

is yet another way in which Spence reverses traditional meanings: those who "disobeyed" the rules of deference are now in a position more powerful than the tyrants who have been overthrown, as well as the tyrants of the past and the very system of "divine" punishment. The doves in stanza 5 suggest Noah's dove as one of the symbols of the peace and mercy following the violent flood of judgment. As a sign of finality, the doves "mourn" by the landlords who need comfort, as they have been literally and figuratively dispossessed.

33. For popular millenarianism at this time, see J. F. C. Harrison, *The Second Coming: Popular Millenarianism, 1780–1850* (New Brunswick: Rutgers University Press, 1979). See also Jon Mee's treatment of millenialism in relation to Blake in the 1790s, *Dangerous Enthusiasm*.

34. *Spence's Songs* (London: Seale and Bates, n.d.).

Thelwall's Popular Poetry and LCS Culture

The Jubilee Hymn.
To be Sung an hundred Years hence, or sooner.
Tune "God save the King."

Hark! how the Trumpets sound,
Proclaims the Land around,
    the Jubilee!

Welcome, the day is come,
Blessed Millenium,
That gives to all their Sum,
    of Property.

The Rents of all our Land,
Now they are come to Hand
    make us rejoice;

Each one receives their Share,
Earth's rightful lords we are,
The tuneful Notes prepare,
    lift up the Voice.

Sing to the Lord of Hosts,
And pass around the Toasts,
    to Tommy Spence.

Who through great Peril ran,
Having devis'd this Plan,
The perfect Rights of Man,
    true Common sense.

Now hath the Oppressor ceas'd,
And all the World releas'd,
    from Misery.

From this Time evermore,
Lo! Spence's Plan will pour
Plenty, till it run o'er,
    with Liberty.

This song, which simplifies Spence's own language, creates clear images illustrating the triumph of Spenceanism. Other songs in the Spencean songbook also appropriate the Jubilee. W. Tilly in his "The Spencean Jubilee" writes: "We'll then the grand Millennium see, / So long foretold in Prophecy; / When Nature's God's to reign with us, / And we're to share supernal Bliss." Tilly imitates Spence's own fusion of biblical and Enlightenment rhetoric. Thomas Evans's songs in the songbook are typically religious, as in these lines: "Moses the Prophet of old, / By holy Divine inspiration, / Commanded Land should not be sold, / But equally shar'd by the nation" ("The Spencean System"). Evans treats Spence himself as a divine prophet: "One night on his Bed, / It came into his Head, / While locked up in Shrewsbury Jail; / To send out Field Preachers, / And peaceable Teachers, / With Doctrine that never can fail" ("A Humorous Catalogue of Spence's Songs"). Evans makes Spence a Pauline apostle in the line of the prophets.

Another song, by Thomas Spence himself, is yet another text in which biblical precedent legitimates his land plan. As one of the most effective songs in the songbook, I will quote it in full.

> The Propagation of Spensonianism,
> Written in Shrewsbury Jail in the Year 1801.
>
> Tune—The Lillies of France.
>
> One night as a slumb'ring I lay on my bed,
> A notable Vision came into my Head;
> Methought I saw Numbers forth going to teach,
> And Justice and Peace among mankind to preach,
> Saying, "Men mind your Interest if you've Common sense,
> And hearken to Reason and Friend Thomas Spence.
>
> Tune—Derry Down.
>
> Lo! See but how Eden Spence has set in View,
> And who keeps us from it, he has shewn us too;
> The Cherubim Gentry with their Flaming Sword,
> Encamp right before it all with one Accord.
>
> Thus these Sons of Anak, by Force and by Might,
> Keep our promis'd Land, unto which they've no Right;
> Even Towns which we've builded and fields that we've dress'd,
> While we all like Strangers are quite dispossess'd.

Then hark to this Guide who has spied out the Land,
So plain he instructs you, you must understand;
Take Courage, these Giants we're able to rout,
Their walls must fall down if we give but a shout.

Then rise, take Possession, the whole Human Race,
No wilds we've to traverse we're at home in each Place;
The Cities are ours when we please, where we Live,
And Fields without Purchase we've Nothing to give.

With Sorrow no more then, we'll eat of the ground,
The Curse being removed from all the world round;
The end of Oppression and Lordship being come,
We'll then all rejoice in the bless'd millennium.

No Shame or Reproach can attach to this cause,
In forming Society, by such Just Laws;
All but some vile Judas must wish us Success,
And ages to come our Names they will bless.

Now what is there wanting of you careless Men,
But only your Countenance to us to lend;
The Business is done if you only approve,
And every Obstacle streight will remove.

Tune — The Lillies of France.

    I beheld till these Preachers were well understood
    When the People in all Places arose like a Flood
    All ancient Oppressions were then swept away,
    And Virtue and Freedom for ever did sway.
        Then Men mind your Interest if you've common Sense
        And hearken to Reason and Friend Thomas Spence.

From this song alone we can see that Spence contributed to his own mythmaking as a prophet. The speaker is divinely inspired with a dream while in jail, paralleling the Pauline example, while at the same time invoking both the expulsion from Eden and the conquest of Canaan. The latter is of most consequence in his call to revolution. The third stanza succinctly fuses biblical and revolutionary conquest by invoking emotionally powerful associations, linking British land with the promised land, the British poor with the biblical strangers, and reminding his reader who exactly built the cities and worked the fields. The speaker of the song assumes numerous roles: Pauline apostle, Moses, the righteous spies Caleb and Joshua, and inevitably Jesus, although the latter identification is somewhat tactful (we infer Jesus by means of the Judas reference and the final couplet suggests a messianic role). This and other songs do not generate supernatural expectations because the Spencean millennium depends wholly on human effort; the messianic role is rhetorical and educational, not instrumental.

Another song displays Spence's skill as a literary parodist. In "Burke's Address to the 'Swinish Multitude!'" (1794; PR 69–72) Spence caricatures Burke, mimicking Burke's ideas and language in a grotesquely exaggerated way. Spence parodies Burke's swinish trope and its attendant class attitudes, while focusing principally on issues of taxation in such a way as to raise the question: whose society is this? to whom does Britain belong? Spence's Burke dismisses the democratic reformers as presumptuous overreachers, but in the process of shunting them aside he undermines his own position by acknowledging the high degree of hypocrisy and corruption in the established system of power. The contradiction Spence exploits is that the disenfranchised pay most of the taxes, which are then in turn used as welfare for the rich. Occupying the "Sty of Taxation," the swinish multitude is treated like livestock, but that same multitude also is the source of wealth that a corrupt state steals.

Parodying Burke produces a series of reversals whereby Burke's ostensible meaning is negated by irony. Spence's Burke tells the swine they are far beneath a king, but all that the song associates with monarchy is violence and privilege. The "Constitution" is accordingly demystified in that it is not the Burkean organic state, rooted in centuries of civilized culture, but rather a criminal conspiracy for extracting wealth and labor from the "swine." In biblical tones Spence's Burke tries to awe the "swine" with demonstrations of royal power, but the recital of kingly attributes is ironized by the republican analysis of political oppression through the puns on "Pocket"—suggesting the pocket boroughs—as well as "hanging and curing," referring to capital punishment and achieving resolution to the problems of the poor. Spence undercuts "divine" right when immediately after the word "divine" come the three infinitives describing the royal treatment of the people: to flog them, feed them, and treat them like swine.

Spence's implied author has a pact of ironic complicity with the implied audience, who share the transgression of mocking Burke. By parodying such a powerful opponent, Spence permits his audience to relish the caricatured mimicry. Spence also evokes popular concerns in various parts of the song; for example, the high taxes on glass for windows, which limited the light necessary for reading in laboring-class dwellings, are alluded to thus:

> What know ye of Commons, of KINGS, or of LORDS,
> But what the dim *Light* of TAXATION affords?
> Be contented with that—and no more of your Rout:
> Or a new *Proclamation* shall muzzle your Snout!
>   Get ye down! &c.
> And now for the SUN—or the LIGHT of the DAY!
> "It doth not belong to a PITT?"—You will say.
> I tell you be silent, and hush all your Jars:
> Or he'll charge you a *Farthing* a piece for the Stars
>   Get ye down! &c.

Always ready to exploit a pun, Spence creates a chain of association from the dim light of taxation, to the sun, to the stars, as the repressive "proclamation" becomes figured as a silencing, or rather complete darkening, of popular Enlightenment. To be in the pit of Pitt's repression is to be in the dark and to be located as "low" as possible. The song's last line is: "We'll throw you alive to the HORRIBLE PIT!" As Pitt can no more own the stars than he can the sun, so the exaggeration points to the limits of established power, boosting Jacobin morale. Nature belongs to all, not the few. It is as futile to turn nature into private property for buying and selling as it is to silence and repress the populace.

Spence's songs, then, struggle with the dominant culture at many levels, contesting ownership of prestigious terms such as "nature," "soul," "fathers," "Liberty," and "God," appropriating esteemed discourses such as religion and nationalism, and claiming for itself key topoi: the family, the pastoral, and the apocalypse. Revising a Dissent idiom to sustain a republican ideology, Spence creates songs that are more richly allusive and ironic than the doggerel verse one also finds in the Spencean songbook.

Thelwall's Songs and Allegories, 1793–95

In 1793, trying to circumvent the political repression, Thelwall spoke at a debating club, the Capel Court Society, that ostensibly avoided politics. Thelwall's speech was later printed in the 16 November 1793 issue of Eaton's *Politics for the People*. Thelwall exploits to outrageous effect the allegorical possibilities of beheading an arrogant gamecock. The following month Eaton was indicted for seditious libel, arrested, and kept in jail because he could not pay the two thousand pound bail. He was finally acquitted on 24 February 1794. During the trial the prosecutor made an unintentionally humorous line-by-line interpretation of Thelwall's allegory, so that each time the fable's gamecock was mentioned, he said "meaning our said lord the king." To appreciate more fully the Chaunticlere allegory, it is necessary to recall the context of the fable and the "swinish" popular periodicals.[35]

The animal fable was an established eighteenth-century genre used for political and religious satire, and in pedagogical texts for children.[36] By the 1790s, however, it had declined as a genre until the Jacobins and reformers revived it as a satirical vehicle.[37] Were it not for Burke's infamous "swinish multitude" phrase, the animal fable might not have been exploited as much as it was, but the swinish trope made human/animal analogies prominent.[38] Eaton's *Politics for the People; or, A Salmagundy for Swine*, which drew upon traditional plebeian cultural forms,[39] had ten assorted animal fables — an apt genre for allegorizing social relations and political conflict, especially to reverse the negative associations of the swinish trope. The Aesopian ambiguity of the animal fable was also convenient for circumventing government repression in court, but after the 1790s the swinish metaphor and political animal fables declined, almost disappearing after 1820.

Swine were not the only animal figured in Jacobin writing. Thelwall's

---

35. A version of this section appears in my article "John Thelwall and Popular Jacobin Allegory, 1793–1795," *ELH* 67:4 (2000): 951–71.

36. On the almost uniformly authoritarian children's educational literature, including fairy tales, during the Romantic period, see Richardson, *Literature, Education, and Romanticism*, 109–66.

37. On fables, see Thomas Noel, *Theories of the Fable in the Eighteenth Century* (New York: Columbia University Press, 1975), who shows that fables were an aesthetic instrument for educating the audience, adults and children; Stephen H. Daniel, "Political and Philosophical Uses of Fables in Eighteenth-Century England," *Eighteenth Century, Theory and Interpretation* 23 (1982): 151–71, and Annabel Patterson, *Fables of Power: Aesopian Writing and Political History* (Durham: Duke University Press, 1991), 111–56.

38. Anti-Jacobin poetry also employed the animal fable, playing with variations of "frogs" to satirize the French and rewriting Aesop as well. See some of the fable poems in Betty T. Bennett, *British War Poetry in the Age of Romanticism: 1793–1815* (New York: Garland Press, 1976), 105–7 ("To My Country. The Bees and the Wasps"), 186–89 ("The Depredations of the Rats"), and 341 ("The Frogs and Crane").

39. Lottes, *Politische Aufklärung und plebejisches Publikum*, 253.

"King Chaunticlere; or, The Fate of Tyranny"[40] draws upon the chanticleer from folklore, Chaucer's "Nun's Priest's Tale," and Caxton's "Reynard the Fox." With considerable poetic license, Thelwall portrays his king chaunticlere as an arrogant barnyard tyrant whom he finally beheads; thereafter the beheaded body still moves. He develops extensively two aspects of this narrative, allegorizing the gamecock's regicidal fate, and commenting on the scientific conundrum of a headless body still moving as if alive.

The particular debate topic that gave rise to the "Chaunticlere" fable was whether human nature was motivated most strongly by love of life, liberty, or the opposite sex. The speaker prior to Thelwall argued that self-love was stronger than love of liberty and used the illustrating example of a tortured runaway slave. A runaway slave, having lost his hands and feet as punishment, was further brutalized by being burnt in a frying pan; at which point someone tried to end his suffering by cudgeling him to death, but the slave instinctively protected his head from harm. According to the previous speaker, the slave's protecting himself proved that love of life is stronger than love of liberty. Thelwall leaves unchallenged momentarily the racist and colonialist assumptions of the previous speaker but distinguishes between voluntary and involuntary actions, insisting that the slave was acting out of habit, without thinking, so that he cannot be construed as having consciously *chosen* life over liberty.

One feature of Thelwall's fable is its almost gratuitous analogizing, so that superimposed over a logical argument is a patchwork of digressive comparisons and similes. As Jon Mee points out, allegorical fables like Thelwall's have the linguistic allusiveness—and legal elusiveness—that derives from a "bricoleur" approach to language characteristic of popular radicalism but not of Enlightenment rationalism.[41] After Thelwall mentions the black slave, he develops a parenthetical analogy to "pressgangs," "*slaves of labour*," and "*slaves of war*" (Butler 186). That is, "slavery" is a word that Thelwall detaches from its immediate referent in order to expand the meaning of enslavement beyond the slavery of Africans. He explains the slave's instinctive movement to protect himself in scientific diction that then analogizes

---

40. Reprinted in Marilyn Butler, ed., *Burke, Paine, Godwin, and the Revolution Controversy* (Cambridge: Cambridge University Press, 1984), 185–88, where the piece is under Eaton's name. Hereafter Butler. I do not accept the account in the *Life of John Thelwall* (110) that Eaton significantly revised and made more radical Thelwall's original text, so I am treating the text as Thelwall's, not Eaton's. For the entire account of the "Chaunticlere" episode, see LJT 106–11.

41. " 'Examples of Safe Printing': Censorship and Popular Radical Literature in the 1790s," in Nigel Smith, ed., *Literature and Censorship* (Cambridge: D. S. Brewer, 1993), 81–95.

both the mindless obedience of tyrannized citizens and the grotesque physical movements of the royal "gamecock" after decapitation. His overall argument pivots on the difference between "mental and muscular action": the slave could not rationally *choose* to live rather than die. Analogously, Thelwall points to the absence of moral choice in the political world: "just as men, of base and abject minds, who have been long used to cringe and tremble at the names of kings and lords, for fear they should be clapped up in bastiles, or turned out of their shops, continue to cringe and tremble, when neither shops nor bastiles happen to be present to their imaginations" (Butler 186–87). Threaten the body and the mind follows.

To illustrate his argument he narrates an "anecdote" of a gamecock whose activities resemble those of a tyrannical king. The fable illustrates his argument in two ways. The gamecock had some hectic physical movements immediately after its beheading, thus proving the autonomy of "muscular action." Secondly, Thelwall uses himself to exemplify moral choice because he had been hesitant to get rid of the gamecock even after the evidence was overwhelming that it was ruining the barnyard; he was reluctant to act because of habitual, unreflective, and mechanical behavior. His "aristocratic prejudices" were "hanging about me, from my education, so that I could not help looking, with considerable reverence, upon the majestic decorations of the person of king Chaunticlere—such as his ermine spotted breast, the fine gold trappings about his neck and shoulders, the flowing robe of plumage tucked up at his rump, and above all, that fine ornamented thing upon his head there—(his crown, or *coxcomb*, I believe you call it—however the distinction is not very important)" (Butler 187). By beheading the gamecock, then, he exercises moral choice, overcoming mechanical coercion. In a clever reversal of the previous speaker, Thelwall turns the question into whether one should kill or not kill tyrants.

Thelwall then relates his cooking and eating the gamecock (which was not tasty), and finally returns to the image of the slave in the frying pan over the fire. It would be as absurd to say the beheaded gamecock flapping its wings for the last time signified his belief that life was worth living "even after he had lost his head," as it would be to say a man's life is worth preserving "who is writhing about in *the frying pan of despotism*" (Butler 188). The system of analogy is an odd one: beheaded gamecock (king) and tortured slave (subjects). The purpose of the analogy is to illustrate the argument concerning moral will, but the other argument, that moral choice is possible only by extirpating the habitual fear and awe of "kings and lords," permutates the analogies. The point is made that people, in order to be other than mechanical automatons of habitual determinants, must be tyrannicides.

As soon as Thelwall establishes the allegorical equation of gamecock and monarch, he reinforces the analogy with authority-baiting and disrespectful excess: the decorated "rump" and the "coxcomb." The repression that made political topics forbidden for the London debating societies actually placed a political frame around everything that was expressed, so paradoxically the political meanings were heightened rather than subdued. Illustrating Thelwall's theory of language and its capacity to express more than a single uniform meaning and to subvert authoritarian statements, his allegory operates at several levels simultaneously, each of which is controlled by satirical irony. His allegory permits him a freedom to express regicidal desires that could not be expressed openly in expository prose. The ironic frame turns into humor what would be otherwise not just obviously treasonous but also too bluntly violent for the audience. Irony introduces the disruptive force of playfulness, which increases the range of what could be expressed.

Not surprisingly, Thelwall's fable was prosecuted. Not Thelwall but Daniel Isaac Eaton, who published the fable, was prosecuted, as the British courts concentrated on those who *published* "libels." The transcript of the trial reveals a more complex situation than merely a conflict between a liberty-loving jury and a government eager for repression. The prosecutor Fielding interprets Thelwall's fable as expressing a strong hostility to the English monarchy to as wide an audience as possible. However, he concedes that the *jury* has to decide whether by "gamecock" Thelwall meant King George. Before the 1792 Libel Act juries could decide only whether the libelous material had been published; libel was determined by the government. Therefore, the prosecution had to *convince* the jury that its interpretation of the fable was correct. Fielding admits that the literary meaning is not transparent: "there is a contrivance made use of; it is written in a species of fable; a species of simile or allegory, as it is called, is used to convey those sentiments" (ST 23:1024). The prosecutor urges the jury to remove this "cover" to disclose the intended meaning by reconstructing the author's intention. If the meaning is seditious, then the author must have a seditious character, but these are acts of interpretation that the prosecutor cannot entirely control.

To persuade the jurors, the prosecutor appeals to their fear of revolution, alluding to chaotic violence across the channel, and making an analogy between Eaton's periodical and French violence. Especially damning is the cheapness of *Politics for the People*, which proves that Eaton wants to disturb "the lowest of the people, to excite them to discontents and commotions" (ST 23:1023). Fielding distinguishes between legitimate "free and open discussion" that is protected by the Constitution, and "abusing the liberty of discussion" (1024) by appealing to those "rude and vulgar" readers who are not well "informed" (1023). A rarely challenged assumption at the time was the existence of two kinds of readers, one of which is discriminating, who has at his disposal a body of knowledge that renders judgments reasonable, if not always consistent with orthodoxy. Another kind of reader is utterly passive, someone without a fund of knowledge, vulnerable to manipulation and coercion, whose ignorance can be exploited by clever propagandists. Archibald Macdonald, in the sedition trial for Paine's *Rights of Man*, Part Two, said that the "judicious" reader could refute Paine's spurious democratic ideas "as he went along" because of his prior reading and educated consciousness, but "that part of the public whose minds cannot be supposed to be conversant with subjects of this sort, and who cannot therefore correct as they go along" have "minds perhaps not sufficiently cultivated and habituated to reading," so that they are "ignorant," "credulous," and when politically active, "desperate" (ST 22:381–83). Similarly, in Eaton's trial Fielding posits a potentially violent reader of Thelwall's fable.

Fielding's series of analogies is as follows: French philosopher is to French revolutionaries as Eaton/Thelwall is to English revolutionary mob. Fielding also appeals to the middle-class jury by flattering their business activities (ST 23:1028), criticizing the more extreme reactions to democratic reform and the French Revolution embodied in Burke's phrase, "swinish multitude" (1019–20), and carefully defending freedom of the press and speech (1024). The principal tactic was to scare the jury with fear of revolution. Although repudiating the "swinish" phrase, he portrays Eaton/Thelwall's intentions as animalistic: "ferocious," "savage," "bloody," "cruel," and malevolent (1027–28). The person responsible for the fable is "without feelings of tenderness and compassion," not human but rather "a beast" who could not possibly be "a good father, a good husband, a kind neighbor" (1021–22). As the fable unhinged the usual control over wild analogies, in the wake of Burke's own wild rhetoric, so even the prosecutor finds it necessary to use a wildly metaphorical language, as well as highly speculative surmises.

Gurney defended Eaton by countering the analogies drawn by Fielding. Given an interpretive approach that made analogies too readily, even "Aesop's Fables" would be "the most seditious book that ever was published"; moreover, "scarcely a fable" would not bring "an indictment" if one was intent upon constructing seditious analogies (1038). In fact, Aesopian tales *were* rewritten seditiously in Eaton's journal, something Gurney does not tell the jury. Gurney further asserts that the gamecock cannot be George because the "king of Great Britain has always been denoted by a lion, and the king of France by a cock: the reason of which, I suppose, was, that *gallus*, as you well know [as he well knew they did *not*], is latin for a cock" (1037). Gurney's procedure is fairly simple: as the fable represents tyrants, and as George is not a tyrant but a constitutional monarch, so the fable's gamecock is not George but other monarchs who are tyrannical. Whether by common usage, etymology, or strict definition, the analogy-making capacity of words must be controlled, according to Gurney, who tries to bring language back to a less figurative mode, but he has to rely on specious etymology, another form of metaphorical liberty. He cleverly asks the jury a series of questions, and if the answer to any one of them is no, Eaton must be acquitted. Is the government's interpretation of the fable "the true, the genuine, the necessary sense?" Even if that were the case, is the fable " 'scandalous, malicious, inflammatory, and seditious' "? Finally, Eaton's "motives and intentions" must also be "criminal" (1043). The government, by inflating the importance of the fable, by reproducing the wildly metaphorical language of the fable, made itself vulnerable to a deflating and more sober, strictly literal interpretation.

The judge's address to the jury used language as Gurney did, so that he surely assisted the defense whether that was his intention or not. The jury, according to the judge, must *interpret* the fable:

> A man may use such language, as in the plain terms of it at first may appear to be no libel; but yet, perhaps, by looking into some other expression, or taking the intention of the party in the whole of the book, it will be impossible not to see, that though he uses language that is ironical, yet that you perfectly understand, he means exactly the reverse of what he says; and if from the whole of the work you can collect, and think yourselves bound to collect, reading it fairly, that such was the intention of the party, that will be a libel. (1050)

The defense wanted the jury to read the whole fable, not just the parts extracted by the indictment, and the judge echoed this. The whole must be read to contextualize the parts because the meaning was not transparent. Perhaps, the judge admits, the fable's figurative language conceals a seditious libel, and if such is the case, the jury must be willing to discover it (1050). Understanding the author's intended meaning is the jury's difficult interpretive task.

The government's Fielding was an astute interpreter in at least one way, even though he lost the case: he insisted upon bringing in a wide context by which to understand the meaning of the fable. France, revolution, the cheapness of the periodical, the periodical's provocative title, and so on are all factors we now take for granted as determinants of meaning. His implicit theory of language's metaphoricity was actually not far from Thelwall's own theory of linguistic instability, except that under Thelwall's theory actual regicide could be at most a possible meaning, not necessarily the true meaning that would emerge only after many readings. Gurney's mode of interpretation, while it served the interests of civil liberties, is spurious in one way: the fable makes little sense as a satire on tyrants who live outside Britain's boundaries. The indeterminate aspect is not really whether the allegorical references are British—of course they are—but how exactly to read the tyrannicidal message. From actual regicide to peaceful agitation for reform there is a spectrum of activist politics that the fable could suggest, but the fable does not indicate any single line of real political action. Some kind of action is unquestionably urged, but what exactly it consists of remains unfixed. The tone of Thelwall's allegory is another issue to which neither lawyer pays adequate attention. The phallic puns, the grotesque mangling of the slave, the absurd image of being burned in a frying pan, the gleeful irony all suggest farcical, cartoonish humor, not sober analysis. Indeed, Thelwall later comments that his Chaunticlere story "was told with such an irresistible spirit of humour, that it at once put an end to the argument, and was received with shouts of laughter and applause" (LJT 110). What did that laughter mean? Was it regicidal, if laughter can even be regicidal? Although the prosecution correctly saw Thelwall's allegory as a political action itself and not just the expression of an opinion, he could not convince the jury that the meaning of the action was indisputably seditious. Although the defense won a political victory, it did so on narrow grounds. Had the prosecution not insisted so strenuously that the allegory had to be interpreted as urging real violence against George, if it had argued that the allegory represented *symbolic* violence against established institutions, it might have gotten a conviction.[42]

42. For Mark Philp, the "Chaunticlere" allegory illustrates the experimental, exploratory nature of radical discourse. "The Fragmented Ideology of Reform," in Mark Philp, ed., *The French Revolution and British Popular Politics*, 70–72. According to Jon Mee, Eaton was a

Thelwall's Popular Poetry and LCS Culture

There are hints of regicidal violence at the end of one of the three songs cited by the treason trial prosecutors. Thelwall composed these songs for LCS meetings. The "Sheepsheering Song" concludes its satire of country and city corruption—swindling and confidence games of all sorts—with a direct attack on political corruption (PR 115–18).

> But these are petty sheerers all,
>   And fleece a little flock;
> Behold where *haughty ministers*
>   Fleece the whole nation[']s stock:
> The while *pretended patriots*,
>   A still more venal race,
> With liberty and bawling cant,
>   Would fleece them of their place—
>   When a fleecing they, &c.
>
> But cease ye fleecing *senators*
>   Your country to undo—
> Or know we British *Sans Cullottes*
>   Hereafter may fleece you,
> For well we know if tamely thus
>   We yield our wool like drones
> Ye will not only fleece our backs,
>   By God you'll pick our bones—
>   When a fleecing ye, &c.
>
> Since then, we every rank and state
>   May justly fleecers call,
> And since Corruption's venal pack
>   Would fleece us worse than all,
> May we Oppression's out-stretch'd sheers
>   With dauntless zeal defy,
> Resolv'd fair Freedom's golden fleece
>   To vindicate or die.
>   When a fleecing they do go.
>   (lines 81–108)

---

bricoleur rather than an Enlightenment rationalist, so that the "Chaunticlere" allegory was characteristically allusive and semantically elusive. " 'Examples of Safe Printing,' " in Nigel Smith, ed., *Literature and Censorship*, 81–95.

At the center of social corruption in general is the political fleecing by both the party in power and the opposition. Dismissing the Whigs as fleecers, Thelwall reverses the song's repetitive pattern of passive submission to being fleeced. As the Whigs cannot protect the people, the constitutional system having broken down, the people must protect themselves. The tone shifts in the last three stanzas from ironic humor to earnest declamation, even republican bravado and apocalyptic hints. The figurative logic suggests linkage between shearing and beheading by guillotine. There is no pretense of innocent victimhood, as "we" of "every rank and state" are fleecers of one sort or another, but the song's disenchanted stance makes popular rights that much more compelling as the difference in degree is reinforced by the bone-picking image—suggesting that governmental shearing is of a much more deadly nature than other kinds—and as the "golden fleece" of freedom is one of the very few images of transcendent value in the entire song. To risk death for an ideal, in the context established by the song's meanings, is to be extraordinarily heroic in a world of shearers. Although not elaborated, a system of values counter to shearing is evoked by the "golden fleece"—a fleece not marked by fraud, trickery, and self-interest.

As a song for an audience of mostly urban artisans and middling-class professionals it acquires some additional interest. The ruling class of landowners who would not widen the franchise for the upper ranks of the middle class, much less those lower in the social hierarchy, receive symbolically a thoroughly satisfying fleecing in the song's first half, but their moral status as fleecers is never in question, as their parliamentary representatives are "cut down" in the song's last three stanzas. The song depicts the ruling class, then, as oppressors who are both powerfully evil and helplessly foolish.

Thelwall produced yet another piece of writing out of Eaton's Chaunticlere trial. After being acquitted in his own trial for treason in 1794, Thelwall published in 1795 a satirical ballad entitled *John Gilpin's Ghost; or, The Warning Voice of King Chanticleer*, one of Thelwall's more successful comic poems with a political purpose.[43] The 264-line poem uses the same ballad stanza as William Cowper in his "The Diverting History of John Gilpin," an obvious source for the poem, and makes a satire out of an unpleasant inci-

---

43. *John Gilpin's Ghost; or, The Warning Voice of King Chanticleer; An Historical Ballad: Written Before the Late Trials, and Dedicated to the Treason-Hunters of Oakham* (London: John Thelwall, 1795); rpt. in Donald H. Reiman, ed., *"Ode to Science," "John Gilpin's Ghost," "Poems," "The Trident"* (New York: Garland, 1978).

dent of 1794. As he explains in the preface to the poem, after Eaton had been acquitted of seditious libel,

> I took an opportunity of sending, by a passenger in the *Stamford* stage, a small packet of books to a brother-in-law who resides in *Oakham*, the county-town of *Rutland*, containing, among other articles, some copies of this ludicrous story, and of the still more ludicrous indictment to which it had given birth. But a conspiracy to intercept my papers had been formed by the *great men* of Oakham (particularly Mr. *John Combes*, attorney at law, and agent to Lord *Winchelsea*; the Rev. Mr. *Williams*, who afterwards displayed the critical accuracy of his optics by swearing to my *T*'s and *h*'s, in consequence of having seen me sign my name to the register of my marriage, and Mr. *Apothecary Berry*, who swore he would sell his whole estate but he would hang me!) and these books, by some accident or other (being left at *Biggleswade*, the place where the passengers stop to change coaches) fell into *Combe*'s hand. The *Oakhamites* were in consequence all in a flame. Nightly meetings were held at *"the Crown,"* which is the principal inn at Oakham; the house of my brother-in-law was broke open, and rifled of papers, books, letters, &c. and *lawyer Combes* was posted to London to acquaint the GREAT MAN in DOWNING-STREET with the wonderful discovery. (iv)

Thereafter he composed the ballad, which survived the confiscation of his manuscripts after he was arrested for treason later in 1794. He is publishing the ballad after his own acquittal for treason, just as he wrote the poem initially after Eaton's acquittal for sedition. Indeed, the preface and text of the poem are celebratory, commemorating triumphs over repression. The LCS celebrated by producing medals imprinted with a Chaunticlere image.[44]

The plot of the poem is as follows: The ghost of John Gilpin, a comical character in Cowper's own poem by that name, awakens "Lawyer Combes," the Oakham attorney who seized Thelwall's mail. According to the ghost, Combes is the "son" he sired one drunken night but never owned while alive. In his speech to Combes the ghost urges the lawyer to become a spy and win the government's favor. He singles out a London lecturer—

---

44. Thale, ed., *Selections from the Papers of the London Corresponding Society 1792–1799*, 117 n.50.

Thelwall's own name is coyly withheld—who is teaching the swinish multitude their rights. The ghost transports Combes to Biggleswade, where he seizes Thelwall's mail. Meanwhile the Oakhamite notables, alerted to Combes's discovery of sedition, meet at the Crown. Combes joins them with his prize of Thelwall's papers, when there is a comic reversal: the beheaded gamecock of Thelwall's allegory leaps out of the pages of Eaton's journal and delivers a revolutionary speech, warning the Oakhamites that decapitation is the fate for all those who oppress the swinish multitude.

If the information is correct in the *Life of John Thelwall* (110), that Eaton revised his "Chaunticlere" speech to make it more seditious than it actually was, then it is unaccountable why Thelwall would make no hints whatsoever in the Gilpin satire that Eaton had tampered with his gamecock allegory; moreover, the Gilpin satire emphatically *reinforces* the regicidal meanings of the gamecock's decapitation. One must conclude that the perspective in the *Life of John Thelwall* is not one that Thelwall had in the 1790s.

The poem has three major focuses, a satire on repression and professionals, a protest against the victimization of the poor, and a threat of at least symbolic violence against the oppressors of the poor. Thelwall asserts that anyone who speaks truly about systematic injustice (the rich stealing from the poor with the assistance of middle-class professionals) will be silenced. The poet expects the "pillory" for his "ditty" which will be deemed a *"libel"* because "ev'ry word is true (1:4–8). The satire represents the rich stealing from the poor in terms of taking away bread (1:40), of eating what the workers produce (1:111–12), and of feasting on "others' toil" (2:44). Reinforcing the alimentary symbolism are numerous images of genteel pleasures and even gluttony: the clergyman Williams, "trembling for his tithes," kisses his "buxom maid," and hunts after the mouth-watering game birds (protected by the brutal Game Laws) (2:12–24). The "loaves and fishes" satisfy the Oakham clergy's material appetites only and do not, as Gospel lessons, exercise their spiritual imagination (2:36). The poor endure their oppression because of ideological brainwashing, thanks to the clergy and others who reproduce systematic illusions about the society. "'As all divines agree, / *The Swinish Multitude must crouch / Before the pow'rs that be*' " (2:39–40). The combined efforts of church and state must "awe" the world in order to insure the functioning of the overall system of exploitation (2:49–50). Those in the middle classes who hope to curry favor with the rich and the government can earn money and fame by tormenting truth-speaking radicals

(1:91–96; 1:150–60; 2:31–32). The government inflates the threat of revolution in order to mobilize sentiment against the mildest dissent (1:19–24).

The satire against professionals is relentless. The fourth stanza is a good example:

> And how the Lords of Oakham's town,—
> All men of high degree,
> Apothecaries, men of law,
> And those that 'squires be!—

The first two lines present equivalent abstractions to signify the ruling order of Oakham, but the latter two lines provide the ironic specific identities of the elite, who are hardly aristocrats. Especially clever is the chiasmus of "high degree / Apothecaries" so that the contrast is jarring, especially with the near-rhyme. Professionals fleece and deceive their clients as a matter of course. Night, for example, is described as the hour when "doctors grave,"

> And keen attornies too,
> Their ruin'd clients, in their dreams,
> And murder'd patients view . . .
> (1:45–48)

When lawyer Combes is awakened by the ghost of John Gilpin, he asks who the intruder is:

> "Some client, sure, who gain'd his suit,
>   But died for cost in jail!
>
> "Or some poor famish'd wretch I ween,
>   Compell'd the town to flee,
> Because he could not stand a suit
>   Against my Lord [Winchelsea] and me. . . ."
> (1:56–60)

Lawyers and clergymen in their alliance with the true "lords" of the country exploit, dominate, brainwash, and intimidate the poor. The Gilpin of Cowper's poem was a linen-draper, while Thelwall himself came from a shopkeeper family (a silk-mercer). Here and elsewhere Thelwall's indignation waxes most intensely when the object of his attack is middle-class professionals, especially lawyers.

The protest against the victimization of the poor is mostly indirect and digressive, until the poem's conclusion. The most effective critique of the established order is not by means of the starvation/gluttony contrast but by the humorous play with "crown." The inn at which the Oakhamites meet is the "Crown" where they are said to be defending "the Sign-post" on which is written, of course, "The Crown." A wickedly funny way to mock the Church and King loyalists is to reduce their sacred object of worship to a word, "crown," and then to letters on a sign-post (1:18–20). The Oakhamites worship the "gaudy sign-posts" (1:31) of monarchy and aristocracy. At stake in the war against the radicals is making sure that crown and mitres continue to "swing / At every ale-house door" (2:51–52). In a fiercely anti-Burkean maneuver, Thelwall drains all spiritual meaning whatsoever from the words "state" and "church," stripping them down to mere letters on a commercial sign.

The gamecock's revolutionary speech, which concludes the poem, conflicts with at least one part of the poem, a section that insists the threat from radicals is insignificant (1:19–24). The revolutionary *deus ex machina*—or should we say *gallus ex machina?*—leaps headless from the package stolen by lawyer Combes and foils the Oakhamites' efforts to silence radicalism:

> "Ah, well, ye servile crew, may ye
>   My clarion shrill bewail,
> Whose scream ill-omen'd but forebodes
>   A more disastrous tale.
>
> "My crowing speaks the envious light
>   That soon must clear the sky;
> For *kingcraft's, priestcraft's night* is past,
>   And *Reason's dawn* is nigh.
>
> "In me behold the fate to which
>   All tyranny must bow
> And those who've long oppress'd the poor
>   Shall be as I am now."
>
> (2:81–92)

One way to see these lines is as threatening Jacobin terror, perhaps even the guillotine, to the enemies of the people like those sketched out in the poem, from lords to sycophantic apothecaries, maybe even the king himself. A less anxious reading would stress the Enlightenment symbolism, so that the downfall of tyranny as such and not actual tyrants is only *symbolized* by decapitation. To use decapitation, however, as a symbol at a time when real heads had been severed in France is to play a very high-risk game of taunting the government. Dare the government prosecute Thelwall one more time? Within about two years of the poem's publication Thelwall was forced out of politics anyway, without the government having to go to the expense of trying him in court.

The poem's gleeful and defiant tone suggests a confidence belied by the actual historical events. This poem was occasioned by yet another act of repression, as Thelwall turned into a farcical comedy the seizure of mail he had sent to his brother-in-law. Once again Thelwall has used regicidal beheading to symbolize determined resistance to tyranny, but whether the poem calls for actual regicide or a reign of terror is not certain at all. Rather, Thelwall and the Jacobin movement are celebrating with some bravado their victory, however ephemeral, over a repression that will ultimately prevail. One is reminded of the accuracy of Steven E. Jones's observation, that "satire is produced less in laughter than in violence."[45] An issue of the *Anti-Jacobin Review* for 9 April 1798 contains unambiguous violent threats directed explicitly at Thelwall, hinting not so subtly that his life was in danger.[46] The line between symbolic and real violence was not always strictly maintained, as Thelwall's experiences with violence in 1796–97 indicate only too well.

Conclusion

One kind of fable, then, was indeed tyrannicidal, perhaps even regicidal. Thelwall's exploitation of this dangerous symbolism was not unique in Jacobin poetry. Another such fable, "The Goitre" (1794; PR 79–82), appeared in Eaton's *Politics for the People*. This poem figures the monarchy—and by association, the aristocracy and church—as a diseased tumor or goitre or wen that is sapping the life from the rest of the body politic, thus requiring the "French Surgeon" to "dissever" it. The last stanza urges the "English

---

45. Steven E. Jones, *Shelley's Satire: Violence, Exhortation, and Authority* (DeKalb: Northern Illinois University Press, 1994), 3.
46. George Canning and John Hookham Frere, *Poetry of the Anti-Jacobin* (1799, rpt. New York: Woodstock Books, 1991), 105–7. The threatening lines of poetry are reinforced by an equally violent footnote.

Surgeons" to follow the French example. Of course one could read the violent imagery as a hyperbolic figuration of peaceful reform, but the imagery of cutting in other poems suggests that "the art of lopping" (line 74) was viewed not with horror but with some enthusiasm. The execution of Louis made the imagery of violence prominent in anti-Jacobin satire and propaganda, but the Jacobin movement, at least for a while, played with the language of decapitation. Some regicidal poems play with the symbolism of hair, as the revolutionary style was short, unwigged and unpowdered. W. H. Green's "The Republican Crop" (*The Philanthropist*, 1796; PR 103–4) draws out the analogies between cropping hair and cropping tyrants, the closely cropped Roundheads and the revolutionary French.

Tommy Pindar's "A Tale" (*Politics for the People*, 1794; PR 87–88) depicts two beggars who debate the wisdom of killing their fleas:

> Two beggars seated in a sunny lane,
> Each finding he'd too many to maintain,
> Began to rid them of their retinue,
> As some great folks are sometimes forc'd to do.

The beggars, it is suggested, owe their poverty to the "great folks," whose practice of "economy" during hard times is compared outrageously with the beggars and their body lice. As the rich cut back, so are the poor, but the cutting is figured as literally violent, with the one beggar making the following argument:

> "Shall we," says he, "thus impiously employ
> Our barb'rous hands in shedding insect blood!
> Shall we th' Almighty's creatures thus destroy,
> Created for his pleasure and our good?
> Perhaps to bite us, they're by God appointed,
> And ev'ry louse may be the Lord's anointed;
>   For, this we know,
> That some three dozen centuries ago,
> Their ancestors were sent to plague th' Egyptians,
> Like certain folks of certain high descriptions."
>   (lines 12–21)

Taking Tory nonresistance to absurd extremes, the passive beggar nevertheless evokes rebellious images, the liberation from Egypt, and violence against the Pharaoh. Moreover, he makes the analogy between the plague of the insects and the plague of the English ruling class, coyly referred to as "certain folks of certain high descriptions." The other beggar laughingly replies he will kill the lice that afflict him, regardless of what the other beggar does. The last two lines are characteristically aggressive: "This, please your kingships, is a pretty fable, / You'll understand it—that is, if you're able." The poem does not explicitly equate lice-killing with revolutionary violence but the last two lines suggest, while hinting at the stupidity of the ruling class, no other plausible interpretation.

At the same time that conceptions of aesthetic autonomy were being developed, aesthetic performances such as those we have just looked at—songs and satires utterly dependent on politics—were also being produced. These texts are emphatically popular, not polite, instances of *writing*, rather than author-centered *literature*. Songs were written to be sung—to delight and instruct—at political meetings, and satires were symbolically violent. As legal discourse, the song became an object of contestation over legally permissible political expression. The Chaunticlere allegory as a speech in the public forum was at first a clever circumvention of political repression but became, as part of print culture, a seditious libel that was prosecuted. Although the allegory's violence, however symbolic, was not subtle, its very crudity and broad humor might have persuaded the jury that it was not dangerous. Thelwall's "John Gilpin's Ghost" was in fact more pointedly seditious than the Chaunticlere allegory, but it was also a slightly less popular work in terms of its publication.

The context for the songs, satires, and fables was a plebeian public sphere where radical artisans fused popular and polite forms of expression, both oral and print-centered, that explored the limits of the legally permissible. Thelwall never would have written the Chaunticlere allegory or the Gilpin satire if it were not also for the cultural insurgency of the LCS, the "swinish periodicals," popular education, and courageous defiance of political repression. Poetry such as we have examined in this chapter is part of a cultural insurgency that invites participation, repetition, and public recital, not private reading in solitary silence. Effective texts produce further texts, as Thelwall's speech becomes a published allegory and then a trial transcript and finally yet another poem; Spence's "Jubilee" generates similar prophetic announcements. By recontextualizing and redefining the powerful myths and keywords of the established culture—nature, soul, biblical allusions—the Jacobin writers generated a counterculture able to form its own centers of authority and legitimation.

4

Excursus: Radical Underground: Thomas Spence and Robert Wedderburn

Thomas Spence, republican proponent of the social ownership of the land, was a member of the LCS, a printer, publisher, writer, and popularizer of radical ideas. Scholars have only recently rescued Thomas Spence and the Spencean "underground" from oblivion and condescension.[1] Spence and his followers are important for a number of reasons. Their particular synthesis of religious enthusiasm, Enlightenment rationalism, and plebeian cul-

1. Olivia Smith, *The Politics of Language, 1791–1819* (Oxford: Oxford University Press, 1984), 96–107; Iain McCalman, *Radical Underworld: Prophets, Revolutionaries, and Pornographers in London, 1795–1840* (Cambridge: Cambridge University Press, 1988); Malcolm Chase, *"The People's Farm": English Radical Agrarianism 1775–1840* (Oxford: Clarendon Press, 1988), and *Life and Literary Pursuits of Allen Davenport: With a Further Selection of the Author's Work* (Aldershot and Brookfield: Scolar Press and Ashgate, 1994); David Worrall, *Radical Culture: Discourse, Resistance and Surveillance, 1790–1820* (Detroit: Wayne State University Press, 1992); Anne Janowitz, *Lyric and Labour: In the Romantic Tradition* (Cambridge: Cambridge University Press, 1998).

ture differs from more rationalistic radicalisms, like Paine's, Thelwall's and Godwin's, but it contrasts as well with plebeian traditional culture, which was not nearly as rationalistic as Spenceanism. Thelwall and Spence actually knew one another in the LCS, and both were imprisoned in 1794, but they were not friends. While Thelwall was treated to dinners and tributes after his acquittal in 1794, Spence, who was released from jail without a trial at about the same time, felt neglected.[2] While Thelwall resigned from the LCS and began a series of popular lectures in London in 1795, Spence continued to work within the organization. Although Thelwall makes no mention of Spence in his writing, Spence attacks Thelwall in the title page of *The Meridian Sun of Liberty* (1796), where he inserts a brief satire:

> Let Thelwall and Burke from its splendour retire,
>   A splendour too strong for their eyes;
> Let pedants, and Fools, their Effusions admire,
>   Inrapt in their clouds like flies.
> Shalt Frenzy and Sophistry hope to prevail,
>   When Reason opposes her Weight;
> When the welfare of Millions is hung in the scale,
>   And the balance yet trembles with Fate?

Spence objects to Thelwall's recently published *Sober Reflections* and sarcastically retitles it thus: "Lamentations over the impending Fate of 'the vessel of Hereditary Property.' "[3] The "splendour" to which Spence's poem refers is Spence's plan for parochial ownership and popular control of landed property.

Spence's pique at Thelwall illustrates their ideological and social differences, which make pairing them especially apt. Both men were largely self-taught, but Spence's father was a laborer from Scotland and Thelwall's was a shopkeeper from London; Spence came from radical Dissent, Thelwall from Church of England (with some not-so-distant Catholic connections); Thelwall was London born and bred, Spence from Newcastle. Both writers were shaped decisively by their social situations. Perhaps Spence's—provincial, Dissenting, laboring class—permitted a more uncompromising opposition to the established culture, whereas Thelwall's provided for a broader

---

2. Worrall, *Radical Culture*, 25.
3. A reprint of *The Meridian Sun of Liberty* title page is in the appendix of P. M. Ashraf, *The Life and Times of Thomas Spence* (Newcastle upon Tyne: Frank Graham, 1983).

cultural repertoire. Ideologically, they also staked out different areas. According to Gregory Claeys: "Two roads thus emerged from the utopianism of the 1790s. The first [like Thelwall's] led from a new democratic form of commercial republicanism towards the more welfare-oriented forms of liberal democracy. The second, scouted by Godwin and Spence, pointed towards socialist proposals for a complete community of goods in order to abolish vice and poverty, and to efforts to eliminate political conflict altogether."[4] While Thelwall's ideas anticipate social democracy, Spence's lead to a more radical redistribution of wealth. Thelwall was, to be precise, a moderate radical ambivalent about revolution; Spence was a revolutionary who without hesitation recommended the forceful transfer of power. In terms of their respective literary oeuvres, Spence's largely derives from popular models not far removed from oral culture, whereas Thelwall's is mostly (though not entirely) modeled on polite literature. Spence zealously promoted a phonetic spelling system to make writing and reading more popularly accessible, closer to the popular "voice"; Thelwall displayed on numerous occasions his arduously acquired knowledge of Latin and classical literature.

Writing, language, and culture were central, not peripheral, for the eponymous leader of the agrarian reform movement . Born in 1750 in Newcastle-on-Tyne, one of nineteen children, Spence was the son of his father's second wife, who was a stockinger. His father worked as a netmaker, shoemaker, and vendor of hardware goods. Spence's father, who came to Newcastle from Aberdeen, Scotland, in 1739, taught his children to interpret the Bible while they all worked. "My father used to make my brothers and me read the Bible to him while working in his business and at the end of every chapter encouraged us to give our opinions on what we had just read. By these means I acquired an early habit of reflecting on every occurrence which passed before me as well as on what I read" (PWTS 94).[5] One informing context for Spence's writing, then, is the message of social justice from the Pentateuch, prophets, and New Testament. According to H. T. Dickinson, "Although he later denounced religion as a delusion, Thomas Spence's writings were always replete with Biblical references and shaped by a millennial vision"

---

4. Gregory Claeys, ed., *Utopias of the British Enlightenment* (Cambridge: Cambridge University Press, 1994), xxviii.

5. From *The Important Trial of Thomas Spence* (1803). Thomas Parsinnen, "Thomas Spence and the Origins of English Land Nationalization," *Journal of the History of Ideas* 34 (1973), and Dickinson (vii) identify Spence's father as a follower of the Glassites; only one of Spence's brothers was in fact a Glassite.

(PWTS vii).⁶ Spence as a young man continued to identify himself with radical Dissent, as he became an associate of an "extreme Presbyterian," the Reverend James Murray (1732–82), from 1765 until Murray's death. "Murray taught Thomas Spence to see the stark contrast between Biblical promise and harsh social reality" (PWTS viii). Spence's texts are saturated with biblical references, allusions, influences, and even cadences.

Another of Spence's informing contexts, according to almost all of Spence's commentators, was the provincial radicalism of northeastern England in the period of protests against enclosures, the Wilkes affair, and the American Revolution. The local squires tried to enclose the Newcastle commons but protests, legal and violent, were able to repel these encroachments on ancient rights. This controversy formed the core of Spence's political ideology, as he based his "plan" on parochial ownership of land and sharing of rents, a version of the very idea of a commons, land belonging not to individuals but to the community as a whole. Thomas R. Knox goes so far as to say that Spence's land plan is "little more than the Newcastle Town Moor Act writ large."⁷

Yet another of Spence's informing contexts, according to H. T. Dickinson, was the Enlightenment as it became a part of the self-taught tradition. Reverend Murray had been educated at one of the centers of the Scottish Enlightenment, the University of Edinburgh. Like Derby or Birmingham or Bristol, Newcastle-upon-Tyne had its own version of provincial Enlightenment culture, with a progressive local newspaper and a philosophical society. As Marilyn Butler has observed, for much of the eighteenth century the most innovative intellectual trends came from the provinces, not from London.⁸ Spence had at his disposal a wide range of references, some of which were Locke, Milton, Harrington, Machiavelli, Swift, More, Puffendorf, Newton, Hutcheson, Hartley, and Clarke.

Although his economic-political ideal was agrarian, his cultural ideal was urbane, classical Athens rather than pastoral Arcadia. Accordingly, his peri-

---

6. Biographical information on Spence is culled from Dickinson (vii–xviii) but corrected by the early nineteenth-century sources. That Spence's father was a shoemaker comes from fellow shoemaker Allen Davenport in his *The Life, Writings, and Principles of Thomas Spence* (London: Wakelin, 1836), 1.

7. Thomas R. Knox, "Thomas Spence: The Trumpet of Jubilee," *Past and Present* 76 (1977): 88. An excellent account of the moor controversy is in Ashraf, *The Life and Times of Thomas Spence*, 28–33.

8. Marilyn Butler, *Romantics, Rebels, and Reactionaries* (Oxford: Oxford University Press, 1981), 32–35.

odical *Pig's Meat* provided readers with a wide range of literary extracts, with his own Spencean contributions constituting a small part of the overall total in each issue. In his various portraits of utopia, he does not fail to recommend schools, universities, and theaters as essential for the overall cultural health of the society. For example, in *A Supplement to the History of Robinson Crusoe, Being the History of Crusonia, or Robinson Crusoe's Island* (1782), Spence writes that "every parish has a free-school, with the best of teachers, as also a public library, containing copies and translations of all the best books in the world, so that every one may read and inform himself as far as he pleases" (PWTS 13). Spence's self-taught culture is evident in his mentioning translations and easy access to the *best* books.

Spence promoted his ideas with political activism after he moved in 1792 (or perhaps earlier) from Newcastle-upon-Tyne to London. Spence had actually written what were the centerpieces of his work by the time he arrived in London. The rationale, outline, and even details of the Spencean system were articulated in *The Real Rights of Man* (1775) and *A Supplement to the History of Robinson Crusoe* (1782). His dictionary, with grammar and new phonetic spelling system, was also published fourteen years before the French Revolution.[9] His land plan and linguistic reform, encountering London artisanal radicalism in the 1790s, underwent some changes, but not in basic orientation.

Spence's Prose Writing

One of the most eloquent appreciations of Spence's writing as writing is Olivia Smith's (1984), who finds that Spence employed a literary style that successfully negotiated the difficult relations between writer and popular audience.[10] Spence "does not portray any speakers as having an essentially different language from his own, nor does he portray himself as different from his audience." Using literary traditions known to his audience, he "was not writing in a cultural vacuum" but rather "his millennialism, his chap-books, his songs, his Swiftian, Defoeish, and biblical imagery were literary manifes-

---

9. The land reform system was announced at a lecture on 8 November 1775 at the Newcastle Philosophical Society. Upon publishing the lecture, Spence was expelled from the Society, although the Reverend Murray defended Spence's freedom to publish. Spence's contribution to radical linguistics was entitled *The Grand Repository of the English Language* (Newcastle upon Tyne: T. Saint, 1775). On radical linguistics, see Smith, *The Politics of Language, 1791–1819*.

10. Smith, *The Politics of Language, 1791–1819*, 96–107.

tations of a culture which enabled him to know and to trust his audience" (Smith 107). Accordingly, Spence, like Paine, was able to develop what Smith calls an "intellectual vernacular language," overcoming the dominant dichotomy between "learned" (or "refined") and "vulgar" languages.

The issues of style, cultural authority, and education are closely linked at this time. The intellectual vernacular is shaped by both popular print culture and traditional oral culture. His style is similar to that of James Murray, to whose congregation Spence belonged. In *Sermons to Asses* (1768), which the London radical William Hone reprinted in 1819, Murray uses italics to get the emphatic stresses he would have used in the oral delivery of the sermons. "Heaven sent the light of the *gospel* to *open* the eyes of such *blinded* mortals, that they may *see* their own interest, and *assert* their own privileges."[11] Spence himself did not ordinarily use italics in the way Murray did, but Spence in all his writings fashioned a conversational style. Spence's freedom from the authority exerted by the learned style is so confident in part because his mentor Murray had already cleared the way for him. Murray, trained at Edinburgh University, knew Greek, Latin, and Hebrew, but he avoided a "learned" style. Against the prestige of Latinate abstractions, Murray typically employs an earthy diction: "The poorest man that lives, cannot live without *meat* and *drink, shoes* and *light*—yet he must pay heavy duty [excise taxes] for the *sun that shines in at his window*, for the *beer he drinks*, the *candle he makes use of*, and for the very *shoes upon his feet*" (Murray 49–50). He ridicules the pretensions of the "doctors of divinity" whose learning adds nothing to "true" religion. The "true disciples of Christ" and the most faithful followers of "the christian religion"—always the lower-case "c"—have no use for a classical education. For true "christians" it is completely "unnecessary . . . to be any way learned in the writings of the Greek and Latin fathers."[12] Spence himself at one of his trials echoes almost precisely Murray's kind of populism. Addressing the jury in 1801 Spence says: "And had I been learned, I would perhaps have wrote in Latin, which is an universal language. But knowing but one language, I am obliged like the prophets and great men of antiquity to write in my mother-tongue" (PWTS

11. James Murray, *Sermons to Asses*, 3rd ed. (Philadelphia: John Dunlap, 1769), 16.
12. James Murray, *Sermons to Doctors in Divinity, Being the Second Volume of Sermons to Asses* (Philadelphia: John Dunlap, 1773), 68. In *A Letter from Ralph Hodge, To His Cousin Thomas Bull* (1795), Spence uses the Balaam's ass biblical allusion in ways very similar to Murray in his two volumes of *Sermons to Asses* (PWTS 23). Spence also reprinted some of Murray's work in his *Pig's Meat*, vol. 2.

Excursus: Radical Underground: Spence and Wedderburn

97). The only advantage of writing in Latin is the supposedly larger audience. Elite culture assumed otherwise; Samuel Johnson's dictionary defines "literate" as knowing Greek and Latin. Spence's own dictionary defines "literate" as "learned, skilled in letters" while "illiterate" meant "unlearned." Just how remote from classical assumptions Spence was is indicated by his definition of "tradition": "an oral account of." Oral culture is not for Spence "superstition" over which reason triumphs; rather, oral culture is truthful but by word of mouth, not by print.

Spence utilized a variety of genres whose conventions he manipulated in his prose. Spence sometimes employed an expository "lecture" but more frequently he found other ways to express his agrarianist vision: epistle, dialogue, satire, mock apology, utopian fiction, prophecy, and dream allegory. Some genres are unique to radical politics, such as the arrest narrative, the trial transcript, the courtroom oration, and the model constitution of the new society. Moreover, Spence's thinking was so saturated with literary awareness—landlords as romance giants, utopias from *Robinson Crusoe*—that he drew upon literary categories to read social reality.[13]

One discursive resource Spence exploited was that of "enthusiasm." There is a discernible line of influence from seventeenth-century radical Dissent by way of Murray and the Glassites. Godwin too was influenced by the Glassites (through the Sandemanians) in numerous ways that he then tried strenuously to erase in favor of secular rationalism. Godwin, a Sandemanian until he was twenty-five years old, was influenced by his Sandemanian mentor, Samuel Newton, who had a powerful and permanent influence on his thinking. According to Don Locke, "All these [Sandemanian] doctrines—the superiority of intellect over emotion, the elimination of private property, a complete equality of status, universal agreement arrived at by open debate—would emerge as leading themes in the atheistical *Political Justice*."[14] Spence showed more intellectual maturity, perhaps, by integrating different intel-

---

13. *A Supplement to the History of Robinson Crusoe, Being the History of Crusonia, or Robinson Crusoe's Island* (1782), PWTS 7; in *A Description of Spensonia* (1795), Spence compares landlords to romance giants, PWTS 29. Spence's final work before his death was the periodical *The Giant-Killer*.

14. Don Locke, *A Fantasy of Reason: The Life and Thought of William Godwin* (London and Boston: Routledge and Kegan Paul, 1980), 16–17. Godwin himself was aware of *Political Justice*'s "Sandemanianism," which he eventually repudiated after reading Hume's *Treatise of Human Nature*; see Locke, 142, 144; and "The Principal Revolutions of Opinion," in Mark Philp, ed., *Collected Novels and Memoirs of Williams Godwin*, 8 vols. (London: William Pickering, 1992), 1: 53.

lectual idioms, adding new sources of language and fusing them with the old, rather than violently suppressing the old.

The degree to which Spence's religious idiom is saturated with Old Testament references is one sign of his Dissent ancestry. So Hebraic is Spence's style that even when he quotes the "Golden Rule" he uses not the positive formulations of the New Testament (Matthew 7:12 and Luke 6:31) but the negative constructions of Akiva, Hillel, and Tobit 4:15: "Do not [do] to another what you would not wish done to yourself" (PWTS 59; *Constitution of a Perfect Commonwealth* 1798). Just because Spence never alluded to divine intervention did not mean that his writing used a religious rhetoric cynically.[15]

As a critic of religion who uses religious rhetoric, Spence goes to Blakean lengths to present himself as a prophetic figure. In one of his most ideologically modern works, *The Rights of Infants* (1796; PWTS 46–53), he stages a dialogue between an aristocratic man and a plebeian woman who hardly allows her antagonist to say anything. Indeed, the discursive imbalance, perhaps improbable in the social world, provides a sharp ideological edge to the work. The woman's speech is especially notable for its biblical diction and cadences; one can hear in her voice both a Dissenting preacher and the King James Version of the Bible.

> Hear me! ye oppressors! ye who live sumptuously every day! ye, for whom the sun seems to shine, and the seasons change, ye for whom alone all human and brute creatures toil, sighing, but in vain, for the crumbs which fall from your overcharged tables; ye, for whom alone the heavens drop fatness, and the earth yields her encrease; hearken to me, I say, ye who are not satisfied with usurping all that nature can yield; ye, who are insatiable as the grave; ye who would deprive every heart of joy but your own, I say hearken to me! Your horrid tyranny, your infanticide is at an end! Your grinding the faces of the poor, and your drinking the blood of infants, is at an end! The groans of the prisons, the groans of the camp, and the groans of the cottage,

---

15. Parssinen suggests that Spence uses religion opportunistically, and Chase seems uncertain how to handle the religious rhetoric, at times emphasizing the secular, at other times conceding the importance of religion. Hélène Roger, "A propos de l'utopie et de Thomas Spence," *Caliban* 8 (1972): 71–88, insists that religion, mystifying and counterrevolutionary, was not a positive resource for Spence. Although Ashraf notes extensively the Glassite and Murray influences, her criticism of Thomas Evans for his Christianity implies that Spence was considerably more secular.

Excursus: Radical Underground: Spence and Wedderburn

excited by your infernal policy, are at an end! And behold the whole earth breaks forth into singing at the new creation, at the breaking of the iron rod of aristocratic sway, and at the rising of the everlasting sun of righteousness! (PWTS 50)

Spence's parallelisms, repetitions, biblical metaphors, and quotations all set up the principal ironic twist, which insists that the aristocracy listen to the plebeian speaker who announces the abolition of aristocratic rule. Spence's speaker declares the advent of land reform as the second coming, a "new creation," the "rising of the everlasting sun of righteousness," with an obvious pun on "sun." The aristocratic religion that legitimates aristocratic power and provides imaginary compensation for the laboring classes Spence revalues, revises, and ultimately secularizes as agrarian revolution.

Just as Blake insisted that the Bible was the source of the true sublime, the most exemplary literary text far superior to classical literary models,[16] so does Spence promote Bible reading. A remarkable work, written in London, is the *Pronouncing and Foreigners' Bible*, whose full title I must reproduce:

> containing the Old and New Testament being, not only the properest book for establishing a uniform and permanent manner of speaking, the most sonorous, harmonious and agreeable English and also infinitely perferable to any introductory book hitherto contrived for teaching children or grown persons upon whose mother-tongue it is, *but* is likewise peculiarly calculated to render English universal, for by this book foreigners of any country may be taught to read English much easier than their own respective languages; recommended as the most proper book for Sunday Schools, by T. Spence, Teacher of English, London.[17]

Here we see condensed a number of Spencean preoccupations. He is promoting his phonetic spelling system, by which he hoped to increase plebeian literacy; Bible-reading as cultural empowerment; and the Bible itself as a literary model that blurs the writing/speech distinction. Radical linguistic

---

16. See, for example, the "Preface" to *Milton*. David V. Erdman, ed., *The Complete Poetry and Prose of William Blake*, rev. ed.(New York: Doubleday, 1988), 95.

17. The title is cited in Rudkin, *Thomas Spence and His Connections*, 222. The title page, which I have not seen, is apparently in the Francis Place Collection in the British Library, Add. MSS., 27808. I have yet to locate an actual copy of this work—if one still exists.

theory, according to Olivia Smith, stressed the continuity between speech and writing, with speech dominant, thus providing an alternative to the Johnsonian view of language as principally rooted in classical writing.[18] There is also Spence's Enlightenment trust in the universal capacity to acquire language and become part of a political community. According to Olive Rudkin, Spence's purpose in popularizing the phonetic alphabet was to teach good pronunciation and remove "one of the worst curses of poverty."[19] (Thelwall made a lucrative living teaching "elocution" in the last three decades of his life.) For Malcolm Chase, Spence's ideas for a phonetic alphabet were "an example of the popularization of the Enlightenment *par excellence.*"[20]

Political repression, which affected the LCS and Thelwall as well, shaped Spence's attempts to popularize his ideas. His most famous (but hardly his only) trial was in 1801, which occasioned one of his best works. In London he was arrested on seven separate occasions, being released fairly promptly, or acquitted, five times (6 December 1792; 10 December 1792; arrested January 1793 then acquitted in February 1793; December 1793, arrested and acquitted; in 1798 he was arrested for his suspected role in the United Englishmen group, but he was released shortly afterward without being charged with any crime). In two instances he spent considerable time in jail. On 20 May 1794 he was arrested as part of the repression culminating in the treason trials; he spent seven months in jail before being released. Shortly after the government allowed the suspension of habeas corpus to lapse, he was arrested yet again, this time for publishing one of his most accomplished works, *Restorer of Society to Its Natural State*. Upon being convicted he spent a year in Shrewsbury Gaol, where his health suffered, and he was fined £20 and charged £500 security for good behavior for five years.[21] The repeated acts of repression did not intimidate Spence but inspired him to invent ingenious ways to express his radical vision—chalk graffiti, coins with radical symbols and messages, inexpensive songbooks—and to organize meetings in taverns, or "free and easies," in 1801. By 1807, according to Iain McCalman, the Spencean artisans met every Tuesday night at the Fleece to discuss radical politics, drink ale, and sing radical songs.[22]

18. Smith, *The Politics of Language, 1791–1819*, chap. 4.
19. Rudkin, *Thomas Spence and His Connections*, 28–29.
20. Chase, "The People's Farm," 38.
21. Rudkin, *Thomas Spence and His Connections*, 84. Whether he in fact paid the £500 I have not been able to determine.
22. Iain McCalman describes the free and easies being used for political organizing and for sustaining radical culture at a time of extreme repression. Even though the government had the

Excursus: Radical Underground: Spence and Wedderburn

Before examining the trial and the text that issued from it, I will very briefly discuss an earlier text about political repression. One of his earliest London works, *The Case of Thomas Spence*, shows Spence's characteristic virtues as a writer. Clearly, succinctly, in the plain style, Spence describes how he was arrested, rearrested, and driven from his bookselling stall in 1792. Unable to make a living as a bookseller, he appeals for subscription funds to sustain him financially until he can earn money again. He couches his personal defense using a distancing third-person narrative and in terms of a nationalist argument: the Protestant English legal norms do not permit the kinds of inquisitorial Catholic persecution of opinions from which he has suffered. Aiming for a wide area of agreement with his readers, Spence ignores the specific contents of the text for which he was prosecuted—Paine's *Rights of Man*, Part Two—to emphasize the ancient English liberties trampled by the repression. If one is to be harassed for selling Paine, then one is in effect being punished for making available ideas on government different from the ones upheld by the present administration, so that other authors should be proscribed as well: Swift, Locke, More, Puffendorf. Moreover, he includes in the pamphlet the Duke of Richmond's argument of 1783 for universal suffrage, illustrating the hypocrisy of prosecuting commoners but sparing aristocrats for publishing the same ideas (PWTS 15–21).[23]

Put on trial for publishing *The Restorer of Society to Its Natural State* (1801), Spence defended himself. He made a careful argument in court, reading into the trial transcript the entirety of the indicted text. After a special jury convicted him he had a sentencing hearing at which he protested against the misrepresentations of his ideas and of himself. Addressing the judges who afterward sentenced him to a year in Shrewsbury Gaol, he complained about the way his case had been "so misconstrued, misrepresented, and disguised both by the Attorney General, and the news writers." He continued:

---

power to withhold tavern licenses, it could not suppress tavern radicalism effectively because in London there were so many different places where one could meet; moreover, tavern meetings were not amenable to prosecutions for seditious libel because spies were easy to detect and songs, toasts, and spontaneous speeches were difficult to construe as threats to the State. McCalman, *Radical Underworld*, 1–2, and his article, "Ultra-Radicalism and Convivial Debating-Clubs in London, 1795–1838," *English Historical Review* 102 (1987): 309–33. The government itself recognized the difficulty of suppressing tavern radicalism; see "Second Report," PH 35: 1303, 1307, 1310.

23. Dickinson edits out the Duke of Richmond material; a complete text—Thomas Spence, *The Case of Thomas Spence, Bookseller* (London: Thomas Spence, 1792)—is on microfilm, part of the Eighteenth Century Sources for the Study of English Literature and Culture Series.

> I am held up to the public as a fool or a madman, representing private property both real and personal as intolerable grievances, and which in every parish throughout the kingdom, I would have to belong to the inhabitants of the parish. Whereas I am for giving only the land to the parishes. And again that I likened myself to Moses, the prophets, apostles, &c., than which nothing can be more foolish and libelous, if such a person as I can be libeled. For your Lordships know that I only said that I wrote what I did with as good a conscience, and as much philanthropy as any prophet, apostle, or philosopher that ever existed, and which I made no doubt that your Lordships believe to be true.

He has been treated "either with neglect or with the contempt due to a lunatic" (PWTS 101–2).[24] The exaggerations and misrepresentations of his ideas are due to their association with religious "enthusiasm," the form of Protestant Dissent aligned with the social rebellion of the Puritan Revolution. The government report of 1801, about which Spence complained at his trial, represents Spence and his followers as treasonous levellers, encouraging food riots and welcoming foreign invasion. This same report characterizes them as antinomians: their "religious tenets" are said to "lead (as among the enthusiasts in the reign of Charles the First), to the abrogation of all restraint from temporal authority. The doctrine of an approaching Millenium has found many converts, and is glanced at in some of the publications already noticed" (PH 35:1313). A malevolent press, an anxious government (believing Spence to have been behind the food riots), and an all-but-destroyed reform movement that was not eager to defend someone as radical as Spence all conspired to turn him into someone like Richard Brothers (1757–1824), who was actually in jail at the time as a "mad" prophet. (Nevertheless, the same government report that identified Spence and the "Spensonians" as a politically dangerous group also worried about the "New Jerusalemites" in Yorkshire, followers of Brothers, whose apolitical millennialism still inculcated "an independence of any earthly government" and encouraged seditious reading practices, the "profane perversion of Scriptural Prophecy."[PH 35:1312]) Secular and religious dissidence appeared equally dangerous to the established authorities.

The work for which he was arrested, prosecuted, and imprisoned, and which he read into the court transcript, is *The Restorer of Society to Its Nat-*

---

24. For an excellent commentary on Spence's 1801 trial, see Worrall, *Radical Culture*, 47–53.

ural State (1801; PWTS 69–92), a series of fourteen letters addressed to "Citizen." The title itself reveals its affinity with the constitutionalist ideology of restoration rather than innovation, nature rather than culture, while at the same time setting the stage for seditious transgression. The epistles to "Citizen" do not dwell on the details of the Spencean utopia but on its philosophical implications.[25]

Spence rebuts various objections to his plan, drawing upon resources from Dissent, the Enlightenment, and popular culture. From Dissent he obtains a model of biblical social criticism. Greedy aristocrats are compared with Judas, who betrayed Jesus for money (70, 85–86), and with the Pharaoh of Exodus (72–73); they are contrasted with the righteous Rechabites (Jeremiah 25), who abstained from wine as well as land ownership (85–86). He holds that there is only one legitimate form of land ownership other than the one spelled out by himself, and that is the Mosaic patriarchal system of the ancient Israelites, the inequities of which required a "jubilee" every fifty years to counter monopoly (85). From the Enlightenment he gets a rationalistic model of argument for recommending easy divorce (76), the abolition of monopoly in land ownership (78), and the cultivation of learning, undertaken in an urbane spirit informed by cosmopolitan and international perspectives (82). He defends the importance of intellectual speculation, something popular culture often distrusts. The essay's motto justifies the "bold political innovator" who "leads us beyond the bounds of habit and custom," whose errors are preferable to the stagnation that would result without such troublemakers (69). Spence is not contemptuous of popular culture, however, from which he acquires positive conceptions of popular rights, morality, and moral economy. After addressing objections to his plan, Spence remarks: "there is no end to the stumbling blocks which these aristocrats throw in our way. They cannot bear to see us endeavouring to act for ourselves. They would make us believe that the more they rob us, the better we thrive! That we would rather work for any body than ourselves; and that like stumbling horses we must have riders on our backs to keep our heads up" (72). The popular rhetoric of *us* against *them* dramatizes class conflict, personalizes social oppression, and reinforces solidarity.

In a popular vein, Spence also employs personal stories to illustrate political ideas. For example, he was picking nuts in a wood that turned out to be owned by the Duke of Portland. Refusing to heed the Duke's agent, who

---

25. The writings devoted to the blueprint of the Spencean society include: *The Constitution of Spensonia* (1803), *The Constitution of a Perfect Commonwealth* (1798), *Description of Spensonia* (1795), and *Supplement to the History of Robinson Crusoe* (1775).

wanted Spence to leave the property immediately without the nuts, Spence insisted that the uncultivated wood belonged to everyone, animals and humans alike. He had as much right to the nuts as did the squirrels (79). Spence uses a homespun narrative whose elements were part of everyday living to emphasize that the landowners did not have a moral right to the land. Squirrels should not have more "rights" than people. In another story he ends up advising a guilt-ridden worker who protects a warehouse from food rioters to "keep better company." If he did so, he would not feel guilty (79–80). Spence sees his own land ownership plan as carrying the "moral economy" of the food riots to its logical conclusion.

After serving the year in jail, he published his most rhetorically intriguing work, *The Important Trial of Thomas Spence* (1803; PWTS 92–103), a printed transcript of his trial. Words that he used earlier to address the jury and judge are now addressing readers of the pamphlet. Did he, even when he was in court, know that his words would eventually be turned into print for a radical audience? Without an attorney, facing a hostile judge and "special" jury (that is, one picked to maximize the chances of conviction and minimize the possibility of having a juror sympathetic to radicals), Spence tries to persuade his audience that he does not deserve punishment. Did he perhaps recognize that the judge and jury were hopelessly antagonistic and that his real audience was the radical artisanate outside the courtroom? Perhaps he only wanted to appear to be trying to persuade people he knew were unpersuadable in order to win over *readers* of the trial, once it was over? At any rate, the judge allowed him to read in court the entirety of the *Restorer*, so that although the text was deemed a seditious libel, as a trial transcript it became a legally publishable text. Another rhetorical complication is that *The Important Trial of Thomas Spence* was not sold, like Spence's other works, but was designed as a gift to those who had contributed to a subscription for his financial relief. Such readers would be disposed already to sympathize with Spence, perhaps agree with him; in which case, the goal would have been less persuasion than strengthening the bonds of community. The text, then, seems to have multiple audiences in mind: the jury and judge, the radical artisans Spence wants to lead, and the subscribers who helped Spence and to whom he is indebted. The textual complexity of this work confirms Kevin Gilmartin's observation on radical trials: "even a guilty verdict would not be the last word."[26]

26. Kevin Gilmartin, *Print Politics, the Press and Radical Opposition in Early Nineteenth-Century England* (Cambridge: Cambridge University Press, 1997), 125–26.

Excursus: Radical Underground: Spence and Wedderburn

One difficulty he tries to overcome is his image as a crank or even madman. Would his prison sentence have been longer if he had been perceived as being more mainstream in his political radicalism? Richard Brothers, the self-appointed prophet of the 1790s who wanted to lead the Jews back to Israel, was deemed by the government to be dangerous enough to require imprisonment — but as a madman, not a traitor. There are two ways in which he counters the label of eccentricity: by locating his own political project in terms of both Protestantism and traditional political philosophy. He declares that his land reform plan is merely a refinement of Moses's legislation on property (94). The Bible itself is seditious, according to Spence, if by sedition one means desiring a better, happier, juster world (95). Adopting the tones and cadences of a Dissenting preacher, he urges the court not to be "abettors of oppression" (97). Also, by citing Harrington's trial and discussing Aristotle's relations with Alexander, Thomas More's with Henry VIII, and Machiavelli's with the Medici, Spence expands the frame of references for thinking about repression. If tyrants like Alexander, Henry, and the Medici could tolerate dissident political philosophy that was innovative, then what are we to think of a society protected by the much-praised "constitution" that cannot permit political speculation now?

He is of course trying to have it both ways, as a traditionalist within biblical discourse and a rationalist within philosophy, but he is neither cynical nor opportunistic, as he continues to uphold the ideas he developed earlier in Newcastle. While Thelwall was launching his career as a speech therapist and suspending his political activism, Spence sustained an uncompromising activism for which he paid a high price. Thelwall too published a work by subscription in 1801–2, felt neglected by the reform movement, and made several defenses of his character. Godwin, at this time, after publishing the *Thoughts occasioned by the Perusal of Dr. Parr's Spital Sermon*, was forced to publish under a pseudonym. These were not good days for the Jacobins. Nevertheless, Spence's writing generated a movement that survived repression. The next trial we will look at, in fact, is that of Robert Wedderburn, one of Spence's followers.

The judicial discourse and political repression shaped the poetry and fiction of the 1790s. Godwin's *Caleb Williams* (1794) depicts not only courtroom and jail scenes but the pursuit of an innocent man who is represented to the public as a vicious criminal. Caleb Williams, the educated servant, is punished for seeing through the pretenses of aristocratic power and detecting aristocratic crimes. In the dramatic courtroom scene in Chapter 17 of *Wrongs of Woman*, Mary Wollstonecraft's heroine delivers an eloquent speech only to be deemed an immoral, perhaps "mad" woman by the judge. The inexplicable "crime," extraordinarily harsh "punishment," and never-ending repentance of the Ancient Mariner partake of the judicially punitive atmosphere of the 1790s, as does the victimization of Christabel and the cultural impotence of Bard Bracy. Wordsworth's *The Borderers* has long been viewed as a working through of Jacobin and anti-Jacobin themes under the sign of moral judgment. A section of *The Prelude* that refers to the Reign of Terror and Wordsworth's internalization of Godwinian rationalism owes something as well to the anti-Jacobin terror:

> ... Dragging all precepts, judgments, maxims, creeds,
> Like culprits to the bar; calling the mind,
> Suspiciously, to establish in plain day
> Her titles and her honors, now believing,
> Now disbelieving, endlessly perplexed
> With Impulse, motive, right and wrong, the ground
> Of obligation, what the rule and whence
> The sanction, till, demanding formal *proof*
> And seeking it in every thing, I lost
> All feeling of conviction, and, in fine,
> Sick, wearied out with contrarieties,
> Yielded up moral questions in despair.
> (1850 *Prelude*; 11:294–305).

Constructive treason made treason a *mental* crime. The path from intellectual construction to treasonous, seditious, and blasphemous criminality could be circuitous, indirect, subtle, and complicated. How was it possible to know for certain whether one's thoughts might lead in some way to being labeled criminal? An "overt action" as apparently innocuous as, say, killing a sea bird, might turn out to be exceedingly blameworthy. One's generous impulses might be taken advantage of, as a befriended stranger might turn out to be a spy whose lies become public truth.

Writers like Godwin and Coleridge establish an aesthetic distance from the repression that impacted Spence and his followers more directly. It is nevertheless surprising that even Thomas Evans in 1821 complains that hardly

Excursus: Radical Underground: Spence and Wedderburn

any Spence texts are available in London.[27] At a time when it would have been easy to reprint all of Spence's work, such was not done. Why? I think there are two reasons. One is the Cato Street Conspiracy, upon which I will elaborate in the next chapter. After the 1820 trial and executions, it became risky to be identified closely with Spence and his movement. Spence's own writings, while they do not lead inevitably to something like Cato Street, do not rule out acts of political violence. Spence could not be easily packaged to make his ideas compatible with the moderately constitutionalist tenor of the 1820s. Evans in 1821 and Allen Davenport in 1836 champion Spence but in both cases it is as though it were a resurrection. The second reason for the neglect of Spence's writings is competition from other radicals whose ideas seemed more up to date, less marked by an ethical discourse. Robert Owen, Thomas Hodgskin, William Thompson, and the Ricardian socialists seemed in contrast more scientific, secular, better able to fend off the antisocialist arguments of the Malthusians and other proponents of political economy.

One very curious location for discourse about Spence is in the writing of Robert Southey, who discusses briefly Spence's periodical, *Pig's Meat*, and popular Jacobinism in an 1812 essay directed against Malthus, and who writes extensively about Spence in 1817 after the Spa Fields riots. The 1817 essay is surprisingly sympathetic to Spence, whose plan has truths that are "half understood and misapplied" and accordingly "dangerous." Southey does not dismiss the concept of a community of goods, an idea in many respectable traditions (Cretan, Spartan, Peruvian, Jesuit, primitive Christian, Moravian). Southey even gives a fairly accurate summary of Spence's main ideas, calling Spence himself "poor and despised, but not despicable" but rather "sincere, stoical, persevering, single-minded, and self-approved." Despite all the kind words, Southey still favored legal punishment for Spence. In light of the Spa Fields riots, he regrets Spence was not transported in 1801 rather than given only a one year in prison.[28] Southey finds appealing in Spence's writing the Romantic anticapitalism Southey himself developed, most notably in *Letters from England* (1807) and *Sir Thomas More, or, Colloquies* (1829). As Southey developed ideas to oppose both his former Jacobinism and the ascendant Utilitarian liberalism, he found Spence's ideas

---

27. Thomas Evans, *A Brief Sketch of the Life of Mr. Thomas Spence* (Manchester: T. Evans, 1821), 4.

28. Robert Southey, *Essays, Moral and Political*, 2 vols. (London: John Murray, 1832), 1: 396–412.

useful. As Southey's notice indicates, Spence was not a truly marginal figure, for his rhetorical skills, political integrity, and perceptive criticism of injustice set him apart from the anonymous proponents of eclectic reform.

Robert Wedderburn

I will be looking at only one of the followers of Spence who wrote poetry, Robert Wedderburn.[29] There are references to Wedderburn in Thelwall's *Champion*, but there are other, more compelling reasons to use Wedderburn as a contrastive figure. Thelwall's Jacobin novel, *The Daughter of Adoption*, represents West Indian slavery and the slave rebellion in San Domingo (which I will discuss in Chapter 7), but Wedderburn's work provides an articulate if anguished response to racial oppression that was experienced, not just imagined.[30] Thelwall and Wedderburn were great radical lecturers, both famous for their oratorical skills and ability to compose speeches spontaneously, but Thelwall's orations, as we will see, were anchored by print-culture references and tonalities; Wedderburn's were founded on plebeian and oral culture to such an extent that he was in fact alienated from print culture. Both used their trials and encounters with repression as discursive opportunities, as did other radicals, of course. Thelwall was ambivalent about revolution, even at his most radical period, and after 1800 he steered his politics cautiously away from artisanal activism;[31] Wedderburn was, however, a revolutionary who lived his life in poverty. For social and ideological reasons, Wedderburn makes an illuminating contrast with Thelwall and a look at his work will complement the discussion of Spence.

29. There are also Robert C. Fair, Allen Davenport, and Edward James Blandford, all three of whom are discussed in Janowitz, *Lyric and Labour*. I discuss Fair and Davenport in "Shelley and Radical Artisan Poetry," *Keats-Shelley Journal* 42 (1993): 22–36.

30. We are learning that British Romantic writing was shaped by the experience of racial slavery and imperialism much more than we had thought earlier. Deirdre Coleman, *Coleridge and 'The Friend' (1809–1810)* (Oxford: Clarendon Press, 1988), puts great stress on Coleridge's involvement with Clarkson and the abolitionists. As an indication of this new awareness, see Alan Richardson and Sonia Hofkosh, ed., *Romanticism, Race, and Imperial Culture, 1780–1834* (Bloomington: Indiana University Press, 1997). John Barrell's *The Infection of Thomas DeQuincey: A Psychopathology of Imperialism* (New Haven: Yale University Press, 1991), was an early instance of this awareness.

31. For a concentrated examination of Thelwall's ambivalence about revolution, see my essay, "John Thelwall's Political Ambivalence: Reform and Revolution," in Michael T. Davis, ed., *Radicalism and the Threat of Revolution in Britain, 1789–1848* (New York and London: St. Martin's Press and Macmillan, 2000), 69–83.

Excursus: Radical Underground: Spence and Wedderburn

Iain McCalman has written extensively on Wedderburn, whose writings he has edited.[32] Wedderburn (1771–183?) was a tailor born in Jamaica of a slave mother and Scottish planter father. His antislavery songs compare favorably with those of William Cowper and Amelia Opie, and his speeches and poetry express rarely represented experiences. Wedderburn's experience with violence started at birth, with his mother being sold to a new master while she was pregnant with him, and later being sold to yet another master when he was a young boy, after which he was raised by his grandmother. In Britain he was tried in court on three different occasions and he spent over four years in prison. Violence and his literary creativity are tragically intertwined.

Wedderburn's Poetry

As many as six poems in the journal edited by Wedderburn, the *Forlorn Hope* (which became *Axe Laid to the Root*), appear to have been written by him.[33] In a series of antislavery poems he develops some lyrical possibilities within a genre established by William Cowper's "The Negro's Complaint" (1789)[34] and Amelia Opie's "The Negro Boy's Tale" (1802). Wedderburn's three best abolitionist poems revise conventions sufficiently to achieve a fresh, energetic, and even passionate effect.

"The Negro Boy sold for a Watch" (PR 196) is a monologue that dramatizes in Methodist rhetoric the guilt of a white slave trader. In the last stanza the guilty slave trader, who imagines an accusing God in the biblically familiar wind, thunder, tempest, and lightning, asks God for forgiveness, not the Negro boy or his family. Had he enough moral sensitivity to want forgiveness from the boy and his family, he never would have been a slave trader. One line is not quite what a slave trader would likely say, but its biblical allusion is obvious: "Tho' black, yet comely to their view" (line 8). The Song of

---

32. My discussion of Wedderburn's life derives from McCalman's account in his *The Horrors of Slavery and Other Writings by Robert Wedderburn* (Edinburgh: Edinburgh University Press, 1991)—hereafter HS—and his *Radical Underworld*, chaps. 3 and 7. McCalman's work has been supplemented by David Worrall's *Radical Culture*.

33. In addition to the poems reprinted in *Poetry and Reform*, there is in *Axe Laid to the Root* one poem that seems to be a Wedderburn poem, "The Slaves: An Elegy," 61–62, and another poem, with no title, does not seem to be Wedderburn's but it might be, 62–63.

34. Hardly a marginal influence, Cowper's "The Negro's Complaint" was viewed so positively by the Spencean movement that it was reprinted in their journal, *The Giant-Killer* (6 August 1814): 8. That it was the poem, and not the author, that interested them is indicated perhaps by the *Giant-Killer*'s misspelling Cowper's name as "Cooper."

Song's "I am black, but comely" (1:5) reinforces the poem's overall focus on a racism that finds no legitimating sources in holy writ; it also helps to undermine the black/white dualism that this and Wedderburn's other poems actively subvert. Even a humanitarian poem like Opie's "The Negro Boy's Tale" assumes the ugliness of black skin and finds value instead in the Negro's "soul." There is no evidence Wedderburn read Blake's "Black Boy," but Wedderburn overturns in a Blakean manner the conventional Western evaluations of black and white. Similarly, the poem associates savage brutality with the whites' behavior, while the African is blamelessly innocent.

"The Desponding Negro" (PR 195) represents in a dramatic monologue the tension between the poem's frame situation—the speaker's begging in the street—and the poem's narrative—which explains how he became a beggar. Whereas the previous poem was in iambic tetrameter, this one has mostly anapestic, four-stress lines with pronounced caesuras. (The last poem of Wedderburn's I will discuss has trochaic tetrameter; at the very least, he was a poet who tried different meters.) The four-beat line, as Anne Janowitz points out, is the conventional meter for communitarian poetry, at least that which is modeled after songs.[35] The poet here decides to have his African speaker use standard English rather than some kind of pidgin dialect or transliterated "African" pronunciation, as Wedderburn will use in "The Africans Complaint on board a Slave Ship." The standard diction in "The Desponding Negro" makes dramatic sense, indicating how long he has been in England, and the transliterated pronunciation in the other poem dramatizes the speaker's slighter knowledge of English. The actual narrative is melodramatic: how the speaker was torn from his home, manacled, forced onto a ship from which he tried to escape; a lightning blast blinded him just as he was trying to escape; he was tossed overboard as useless merchandise, and then picked up by a British ship that took him to England. The poem also develops the white/black dualism. The first stanza associates Africa with open space, whereas "dark" is the dungeon of the slave ship. The second stanza's lightning announces with tragic irony the African's blindness and liberation from slavery. The third stanza has an ironic pun:

> The despoiler of man his prospect thus losing
> Of gain by my sale, not a blind bargain chusing,
> As my value compar'd with my keeping was light,
> Had me dash'd overboard in the dead of the night.

---

35. Janowitz, *Lyric and Labour*, chaps. 1 and 2.

Excursus: Radical Underground: Spence and Wedderburn

His value was "light," so he was tossed into the ocean, as if the nocturnal darkness might hide the shameful act. The theme of shame is also reinforced by the eyes of the slave; it is as if the shame of slavery blinded the speaker, who would be spared seeing his enslavement. Shame is experienced always through the eyes. In the next stanza the moonlight creates enough visibility for the British ship to save his life, and in the penultimate stanza, the image of light is figured thus: "And hope's distant glimmering in darkness is lost." The final stanza continues to develop the light/dark imagery:

> But of minds foul and fair, when the judge and the ponderer,
> Shall restore light and rest to the blind and the wanderer,
> The European's deep dye may out-rival the foe,
> And the soul of an Ethiop prove whiter than snow.

When God judges "minds foul and fair"—dark and light—God will restore light to the blind, and the West's guilt and sin, imaged traditionally in Western rhetoric as "blackness," will ironically be more blameworthy, "darker," than that of the despised Africans whose spiritual condition is contrastively white. The principal strategy here is inversion, as the poem reverses the racist logic by means of the imagery, not just by declarative assertion.

The final abolitionist poem I want to look at, "The Africans Complaint on board a Slave Ship" (PR 196–97), borrows from Opie's "The Negro Boy's Tale." Like Opie, Wedderburn employs a transliterated dialect to represent the African's speech; like Opie, he has the African lament his leaving his beloved Africa; like Opie, whose African dies before becoming a working slave, Wedderburn has his African prefer death to enslavement. Opie's poem, however, even though it represents the African's own words, chooses words of a child who is seeking the protection of a white woman, Anna, whose perceptions and words are at least as important as the African boy's. Wedderburn's poem focuses on only the African's consciousness, and the African is a grown man, not a dependent boy. Despite the awkward pidgin transliteration, perhaps an unwise choice dictated by the Opie model, Wedderburn's dramatic monologue presents the reader with a figure whose suffering seems credible; Opie's African boy seems never much more than a well-intended caricature of sentimental conventions.[36]

The speaker's pain is vivid because the poem relies on represented physi-

---

36. Amelia Opie, "The Negro Boy's Tale," in *Poems* (London: Longman and Rees, 1802), 63–79.

cal sensations and the emotional reactions of someone bewildered and desperate. The poem contrasts his African home, now only a pastoral memory he evokes in order to escape his hellish surroundings, and his destination, Gothic confinement. The penultimate stanza compares the loving black arms that used to embrace him with the chains of slavery that now bind him. The poem's last two lines—"When I'm dead they [slavers] cannot hold me, / Soon I'll be in black man land"—do not seem melodramatically exaggerated. Just as he uses dream and memory to escape his condition, so too death provides escape. As a profound repudiation of Opie's apology for the ugly black skin concealing a white soul, Wedderburn's African imagines the postmortal realm as "black man land."

Now I want to look at a poem that might be too polite in style to have been written by Wedderburn, but it deserves to be examined even if Wedderburn did not write it. "An Englishman's Domestic View"—(PR 190–94; published in the 1817 periodical, the *People*, and abridged and reprinted in *Sherwin's Political Register*), was authored by "R.W.", a signature Wedderburn typically used. The short-lived journal *People* (April–July 1817) has a Robert Wedderburn letter (348) and other signs of Spencean participation. The poem's ballad quatrain form—from popular ballads and Methodist hymns—is Wedderburn's favorite form, and the ballad quatrain is unusual for a long meditation poem. The number of references in the poem to slavery, slaves and freemen, chains, enslavement, and other permutations of and allusions to "slave"—fourteen—are astonishingly large in a poem not about slavery as such. There is an untitled poem in Wedderburn's *Axe Laid to the Root* with the same stanza form and many of the same allusions, although lacking the R.W. (PR 196–97).[37] Also, in speeches reported to the Home Office by spies, Wedderburn expresses several key ideas that are in the poem and that seem characteristic of his style of thinking. In a speech of early August 1819 (before Peterloo), a spy records that Wedderburn spoke the following: "After noting the [not legible] persecutions of the Slaves in some of the West Indian Islands he said they fought in some instances, for twenty years for 'Liberty'—

37. The untitled poem in *Axe Laid to the Root* is introduced by "C. T.," who claims the poem was written by the Spencean James Watson for the purposes of leading the Spa Fields rioters, but there is no other evidence Watson wrote this or any other poem. Whoever wrote this poem—if it was not Wedderburn—might also have written the "Domestic View" poem in the *People* by R.W. In a personal communication, David Worrall noted that he believes that Wedderburn is not the author of "Domestic View," that Watson is a more likely candidate.

Excursus: Radical Underground: Spence and Wedderburn

and he then appealed to Britons who boasted such superior feeling & principle whether they were ready to fight now but for a short time for their Liberties."[38] The poem by R.W. is on whether Britons will fight for liberty. The second excerpt from a spy report of 3 November 1819 alludes to paternity, another key theme of the poem: "these Bloody Murdering thieves who could rob us of the Shirt from off our Backs will either be shot or lose their Heads; and to stimulate my sons I take care to show them their degraded situation and call them Cowards!!!"[39] These excerpts illustrate that Wedderburn was very much swayed by arguments based on shame and humiliation, the principal subject of the poem as well as of his autobiographical pamphlet, *The Horrors of Slavery*. If Wedderburn did not author the poem, then the poem's author had to have been someone from that same Spencean milieu and who shared many of Wedderburn's own characteristic concerns.

The poem's first part states the problem that defines the speaker's crisis: he is suffering from a "despair," and his "heart feels th' icy shaft" of some "Demon's touch" leaving him with no remedy, "now no help." Addressing his beloved, the speaker contrasts their former happiness and their present dejection, but the fault rests with neither him nor her; rather, their life together has been diseased by political oppression, particularly the way it has poisoned the speaker's sense of himself. He feels like a slave, not a man who can joyfully bring children into the world. His anger, frustration, humiliation, and powerlessness affect his most private emotions. "And he who weds a maid now woos / Dishonor to his bed" (lines 31–32). He does not want to be a father who by example would have to teach his children submission to the social order (lines 41–44). Indeed, it is better to leave his wife than endure passively the enslaving conditions; disrupting the domestic life shows more "love" than "slaves dare feel" (lines 49–52). (One cannot help noticing how the speaker's deferral of sex for the sake of political honor contrasts dramatically with the sexual stereotypes of "animalistic" poor people.) The poet feels he cannot be a proper father and husband feeling as powerless as he does. The poem's "crisis," then, is powerlessness. Fatherhood is a key symbol mediating the public and private worlds of the speaker.

38. Transcribed by and quoted in Worrall, *Radical Culture*, 132. The term "Peterloo" refers to the following event: on 16 August 1819 at St. Peter's Fields, Manchester, an unarmed crowd of 100,000 laboring-class demonstrators who advocated parliamentary reform were attacked by soldiers, resulting in eleven deaths and hundreds of injuries. The massacre was called "Peterloo" as a sarcastic play on "Waterloo." See E. P. Thompson, MWC 681–91.

39. Transcribed by and quoted in Worrall, *Radical Culture*, 141.

> Fathers! ye gave me blood—not chains,—
> Blood free, thro' ages past;
> And it shall down through freemen's veins,
> Or mine shall be the last!
>
> (lines 45–48)

Although the "fathers" of line 45 are clearly metaphorical, referring to a cultural legacy and not actual progenitors, if R.W. is Wedderburn, then one cannot ignore the circumstances of his own birth, as his own "free" status derived from his father. Also, one can see in this stanza the effects of Jamaican society's relentless emphasis on "blood," although the stanza's "blood" is metaphorical. Another stanza refers to the poet's participation in the war against France (lines 61–64), which is perhaps the heart of the poem because in the war he acted out of loyalty and trust, like Wedderburn, but felt ultimately betrayed. In an allusion to Xerxes, the poet suggests by analogy that England played the role of Persian imperialists, and the Greek heroic role was played by the French, so that while the soldiers were duped into fighting an unjust war, "traitors" at home were robbing "us" (lines 65–68). Treason is another key concept in the poem, its first instance signifying a betrayal of the speaker and those like him. Indeed, one of the distinctive things about this dejection ode is that although it begins in the first-person singular, it shifts to the first-person plural that resolves the poem.

The betrayal of the war is the poem's center, the traumatic event that defines his feeling of enslavement (lines 69–75). A series of violent verbs describes the activities by which the speaker or the people (of which the poet is a part) are oppressed: "*stript*" (line 24), "*poisons*" (line 40), "rob" (line 68), "impell'd" (line 69), "decoy'd" (line 69), "plunder'd" (line 71), "destroy'd" (line 71), and "tore" (line 73). However, the poem's speaker escapes despair first by expressing anger at his victimization, then by putting his victimization in historical context. Viewed historically, his oppression need not be endured passively because of the paternal legacy of freedom passed down through the generations. Although his "heart feels th' icy shaft" of sickly despair (line 13), his "hot blood boils" (line 19) to reflect upon his condition: "Fathers! ye gave me blood—not chains— / Blood free thro' ages past." The heart/blood imagery continues throughout the poem, as blood signifies also the revolutionary violence necessary to maintain liberty ("blood-bought compact"); it symbolizes the covenant between the generations and among the living revolutionaries fighting in the name of liberty ("Let's sign us in our blood," line 136); and it dramatically figures human universality and the sacrifice the speaker is willing to make to maintain the paternal legacy, as the poem concludes:

> His blood for prostrate man he sheds;
> 'Tis shar'd from pole to pole;—
> His spirit thro' the nations spreads,
> And rises with his soul!
> (lines 153–56)

The poem's affirmative conclusion uses a third-person singular pronoun standing for "the Freeman" (line 149) that signifies the speaker and everyone else willing to fight along with him. ("Freeman" has of course an additional connotation for someone from Jamaica.) His personal crisis is resolved only by means of an imagined collective action that is legitimated by a symbolically paternal sanction. The gendered valence of liberty as a paternal legacy has special significance for Wedderburn, whose father was a free white and mother an enslaved black. The betraying oppressors are male, but oppression cannot be overturned except by males, according to the patriarchal logic of the poem. The only things feminine in the poem are his wife, addressed at the poem's beginning, and "England dear" (line 133) of the poem's conclusion. The males, then, are fighting over possession of the women. As the speaker's wife gets replaced by a feminine England, the speaker himself merges his identity into a collectivity, so that both he and his wife are synecdochic parts of a whole. One can view the crisis of the poem schematically as the disruption of the domestic sphere where the man should feel like a master; the domestic sphere's disharmony cannot be repaired from within the sphere itself, but only by making adjustments in the public sphere. Although the female exists at a public level as "nation," it exists always as a symbol for the *effects* of male activity, as something always connected to males by personal pronouns: my, our, your, his, their nation. To contest the power of the oppressor group, the speaker needs someone, a symbolic father, to legitimate his desire for autonomy and control.[40] The paternal legacy is sacred. Invoking Brutus, the speaker gestures

---

40. According to Joan B. Landes, "If Liberty represented woman, surely it was as an abstract emblem of male power and authority." The Liberty goddess was of course patriarchal: "chaste, pure, self-sacrificing, and wholly dedicated to the universal aims of the Republic." When the French Revolution replaced the Liberty goddess with the masculine symbol of Hercules, the replacement was even more misogynistic than the equivocal Marianne icon. *Women and the Public Sphere in the Age of the French Revolution* (Ithaca: Cornell University Press, 1988), 161–63.

toward French revolutionary classicism and its stoic subordination of the personal to the political (lines 125–31). The personal, however, comes right back in the form of a feminine nation, a projection of a desired woman who—so the poet imagines—needs protection. By this point in the poem, the speaker's own suffering has been displaced entirely onto the pain of a feminine nation (lines 137–40). The nation cannot act on her own; she cannot commit violence but can be violated; she suffers without being able to harm anyone else. The poet's crisis as a lover is linked with his crisis as a father, and both crises are resolved only by imagining his successful struggle to stop the suffering of a feminized nation.

The familiar Romantic crisis poem has many varieties, but none follows the pattern of this poem. A weakened private self commences a meditation in which moments of public or collective identification—Wordsworth's "still, sad music of humanity"—punctuate an imagined and remembered engagement with a feminized nature that eventually restores the strength of the private self. The Wordsworthian crisis poem begins and ends with the "I," whereas R.W.'s poem finds resolution only in the first-person plural. Wordsworth's memory is private and personal, but this poet's is social, as he invokes a libertarian past personalized as a paternal gift. In both kinds of poems the poet resolves the crisis by reconciling with a representation of the feminine. The overall meditation empowers the speaker's self and permits the strengthened private self to act more effectively in the public world. Coleridge's dejection poems also conclude with an outward-looking focus for those he loves. Wordsworth's and Shelley's crisis poems leave them as more capable moral agents. Utter escape from the social and moral is a *late* Romantic strategy, not characteristic of the pioneering writers. Nevertheless, the ways in which the poets conceive of a self are distinctive: R.W.'s "I" is never far removed from a "thee" or an "us," but the high Romantic "I" is characteristically individualistic.[41] There is no evidence Wedderburn was familiar with Thelwall's poetry, but the latter's meditation poems deployed, like R.W.'s, the family topos not to affirm individual autonomy but to locate the individual within a community (see Part Three).

---

41. Marlon Ross, writing on women poets contemporaneous with the Romantics, remarks on an identical difference between the two groups: the women poets rarely imagine an utterly isolated self that the Romantics imagine with frequency and enthusiasm. *The Contours of Masculine Desire: Romanticism and the Rise of Women's Poetry* (Oxford: Oxford University Press, 1989). Anne Janowitz recurrently contrasts the communitarian and the individualistic lyric in her reading of Romantic poetry, *Lyric and Labour.*

Excursus: Radical Underground: Spence and Wedderburn

Wedderburn and Oratory

Just as Wedderburn's abolitionist poems dialogically explore different voices, so his oratory is theatrical, a vivid performance of different roles. From McCalman's and Worrall's accounts, his speeches were entertaining, especially when he paired up with Samuel Waddington, a black dwarf known as "Little Waddy." The Black Prince, Wedderburn's nickname, and Little Waddy were well-known London performers at the theater of the radical chapels and debating clubs. At Wedderburn's Hopkins Street Chapel speakers were not even allowed to read speeches; only extempore speeches were permitted. Print culture played a role in the ultra-radical culture, but it was subordinate to the oral culture (HS 23–25). It was difficult to determine with precision the exact nature of irony in Thelwall's Chaunticlere allegory, and it is even more difficult to read the intransigently oral texts of Wedderburn, even the extent to which he was adept in print-culture conventions. During and after his trial and sentencing hearing in 1820 he collaborated with the Spencean lawyer George Cannon, with whom Percy Shelley had dealings in 1815 over the *Theological Inquirer*, but the extent and meaning of the collaboration are ambiguous because Wedderburn had a motive to appear "illiterate" in order to gain sympathy from the jury and judge. Just how illiterate he in fact was and how much the appearance of illiteracy exploited racist stereotypes about black literacy are questions difficult to answer with certainty.

Wedderburn was in jail already when the Peterloo Massacre occurred on 16 August 1819; he was jailed again after the passage of the Six Acts in December. He probably would have joined with his friend Arthur Thistlewood in the Cato Street Conspiracy in February 1820 had he not been in jail. After the Cato Street trials and executions in May, Wedderburn was sentenced to prison for two years.[42] The particular trial we will be examining is his blasphemy trial of 1820. He was in jail between December 1819 and April 1820 (when he was released on bail, shortly before his trial in May). At his own trial he wanted two not necessarily compatible things: to get as light a sentence as possible, and to use the trial for political propaganda. A radical in his late fifties, someone with considerable experience reading the cultural codes, Wedderburn might have played dumb, exploiting the racist predispositions of the court, to provide cover for radical propaganda that he also

42. McCalman, *Underworld*, 51, 134, 137, 139, 151, 191–92; and chap. 3.

wanted to promote. At the trial he presented himself as virtually illiterate, dependent on his lawyer, George Cannon. The judge and jury were inclined to reduce Wedderburn's sentence, but after he presented to the court a long radical speech that had been written out both prosecutor and judge now perceived Wedderburn as unrepentantly seditious and blasphemous. The jury had found him guilty of blasphemy but had recommended mercy in sentencing on account of his lack of "parental care"—an unusual judgment of a man in his fifties (TRW 20). The prosecutor remarked that the jury had recommended leniency only because it thought he was ignorant, but "if he was the author of that paper, which displayed considerable information," he deserved the full weight of legal retribution. In reply Wedderburn said "it was true he could not write, but that he had caused his ideas to be committed to writing by another person." The prosecutor could not recommend mercy because Wedderburn, able to write or not, was a "dangerous" man with "considerable talents, and those too of a popular nature, and calculated to do much mischief amongst the class of people to whom he was in the habit of addressing himself" (HS 139). McCalman blames Cannon as the ventriloquist with Wedderburn as the dummy (HS 28–30), a plausible narrative, but perhaps Wedderburn was not manipulated by Cannon.

At several key points during the trial and sentencing Wedderburn dramatized his alienation from print culture by asking court officials to read his written defenses.[43] At his trial he requested that a court official read a defense that "a gentleman had committed to paper for him" (TRW 8). The phrasing is quite precise; Wedderburn doesn't say that someone else actually wrote the defense, only that someone else committed his defense to writing. Agency for the defense as such is not explicitly claimed by Wedderburn, but the plain sense of his statement is that the "gentleman" who put pen to paper was transcribing *Wedderburn's* ideas. At his sentencing, as I already discussed, Wedderburn says that "he could not write, but that he had caused his ideas to be committed to writing by another person" (HS 139). The provocatively unrepentant defense read at the sentencing destroyed any chances Wedderburn might have had for a light sentence. For taking responsibility for Cannon's own work, Wedderburn increased the severity of his prison sentence.[44] It is possible, however, that Wedderburn acted willfully rather than at the bidding of Cannon.

43. The two texts are a transcript of his 25 February 1820 trial (TRW), and Erasmus Perkins [George Cannon], ed., *The Address of the Rev. R. Wedderburn* (London: T. Davison, 1820), rpt. in HS 131–41, a transcript of his sentencing hearing.

44. McCalman, *Radical Underworld*, 159.

Excursus: Radical Underground: Spence and Wedderburn

When Wedderburn declared in court that "he could not write," he was not speaking the literal truth. We know that he could indeed write.[45] He was saying that he could not write as well as Cannon in the polite language of power that is used within court; he could not write effectively in a scholarly way, or in a way that was fully within the print-culture conventions appropriate in a court where an upper-class English dialect was spoken by judge and prosecutors. Cannon could have been more a *translator* of Wedderburn's oral texts into a print-culture idiom than an author in the ordinary sense. Similarly, when Wedderburn asked someone from the court to read his written defense at his trial, he claimed that he had difficulty reading because of his eyesight, strained by old age and the close work of tailoring for over three decades (TRW 8); at his sentencing he made the same request but omitted the explanation (HS 133). Even if his eyesight were poor, the courtroom theatrics cannot be dismissed, as his request had the result of making himself the mute witness of court officials reading print-culture versions of his ideas that were created within an oral culture. Perhaps Cannon is the subordinate in the collaboration, more in the role of assistant than leader. Although Cannon was Wedderburn's superior within the class hierarchy, Wedderburn was Cannon's superior within the world of London radicalism.

The first pamphlet transcribes Wedderburn's blasphemy trial of 25 February 1820, where a special jury found Wedderburn, a licensed Dissenting minister, guilty of blasphemous libel, contained in a speech he delivered 25 October 1819 at his Hopkins Street Chapel. The government wanted Wedderburn in jail because, according to McCalman, as the most effective Spencean orator in all of London, he regularly attracted an audience of over two hundred people to his twice-weekly lectures. The government's earlier prosecution of Wedderburn for seditious libel failed because Wedderburn convinced a jury that his seemingly seditious language was actually religious

45. His being able to write is obvious in a handwritten letter he sent to Francis Place in 1831 (HS 78). There are some misspellings and the punctuation is erratic, but the letter cannot be construed as the work of someone unable to write. The word "as" is written phonetically as "has." Overall, this note by the sixty-nine-year-old Wedderburn, who was serving a prison sentence of hard labor, suggests someone who is within both oral culture and print culture. Wedderburn would have been encouraged to learn to read and write, at least during the time he was a Methodist as a young man. Further evidence of writing ability would include his religious tract, *The Truth Self-Supported*, published in 1802 (HS 65–77), which is so idiosyncratic stylistically and theologically that one can exclude the possibility of a ghostwriter. McCalman describes the essays in *Axe to the Root* as "a series of oral sermons designed to be read out to semi-literate audiences in alehouses and workshops" (HS 18). McCalman's characterization of Wedderburn's writing style as remarkably oral seems correct.

discourse, the result of his "prophecy and divination" (HS 23). Discovering that London juries were more willing to convict on the charge of blasphemy than sedition, the government indicted Wedderburn again, but waited about three months to put him on trial—two days after the Cato Street arrests.

The second pamphlet transcribes the court proceedings at Wedderburn's sentencing, where the prosecuting attorney and the judge concurred in giving Wedderburn a severe two-year sentence in Dorchester Gaol, despite the jury's recommendation for leniency. The timing of the sentencing, 9 May 1820, is important because it was shortly after Wedderburn's friends had been hanged or transported for their part in the Cato Street Conspiracy. Perhaps Wedderburn knew that even if he had not delivered a provocative speech at his hearing he still would have received a heavy sentence because of the government's zeal to suppress entirely the Spencean movement.

If the Wedderburn pamphlets constitute a single textual event, then one can discern the following structure. At the center is Wedderburn's "blasphemous" speech of 25 October 1819, described almost verbatim by two spies at the trial of 25 February 1820 and commented upon extensively in Wedderburn's defense speeches at the trial and later sentencing. At the trial of 25 February there are two more Wedderburn texts, an extempore speech about his life and a written defense that was read by a court official. At the sentencing of 9 May there were also two texts, a brief extempore speech and a much longer written speech read by a court official; the latter speech was not so much a defense as an act of defiance after the Cato Street executions.

Wedderburn's speech at the Hopkins Street Chapel was a moment in urban radical theater that becomes fixed in the print culture of court proceedings. The two spies must have accurately reconstructed the 25 October speech, because Wedderburn challenges their account only in very minor aspects. One has in the published pamphlet, then, a rare glimpse at radical oral culture translated into print, although it is important to remember that one is missing the live performance, the body language, the facial expressions, the connection with the audience, and modulations of his voice.

The topic for the evening of 25 October at the Hopkins Street Chapel was the following: "Whether the refusal of the Chief-Justice to allow Mr. Carlile to read the bible in his defense, was to be attributed to the sincere respect he had for the sacred writings, or to a fear lest the absurdities it contained should be exposed?" Not surprisingly the evening's speakers, including Wedderburn, argued in favor of the latter hypothesis. The trial of Richard Carlile, an important event for London radicals, resulted in his conviction for blas-

Excursus: Radical Underground: Spence and Wedderburn

phemy and sedition, concluding on October 15, only ten days prior to the Hopkins Street festivities that demonstrated plebeian support for the convicted Carlile before he had been sentenced; the evening's antiauthoritarian speeches illustrated that the radical movement was not cowed into piety or silence by Carlile's disappointing conviction.[46]

Because it provides a rare glimpse of popular oratory and the text is not easily accessible, I reproduce here entirely the trial transcript of the testimony reporting on Wedderburn's speech (TRW 4–6).[47] William Plush had written down what Wedderburn had said on 25 October 1819, and later consulted with another spy, Matthew Mathewson, who attended the lecture (TRW 6–7).

> The subject of the debate was, "Whether the refusal of Chief-Justice Abbott to allow Mr. Carlile to read the bible in his defence was to be attributed to the sincere respect he had for the sacred writings, or to a fear lest the absurdities they contained should be exposed?"
>
> Two persons spoke on the subject before the defendant. Robert Wedderburn then rose; and after complimenting the two speakers who had preceded him, begged leave to call their attention to a few of the absurdities which they had not noticed. He then said, "Christianity, it is true, has been introduced, but it has never been followed; Judge Abbott has no doubt read the bible, and knows pretty well the absurdities it contains.
>
> "Jesus Christ says, 'no man hath ever seen God,' then what a d——d old liar Moses must have been, for he tells us he could run about and see God in every bush. Christ says, no man ever conversed with God, and yet Moses had a long conversation with him; thus, one or the other must be liars.
>
> "Then, there was Balaam's ass, oh! yes, that spoke, and yet they tell us it was God put the words into his mouth; then I suppose God got into the jack-ass.
>
> "Then there is a pretty story they tell us about the witch of Endor. Saul, who had been destroying all the witches as devils, or what not, at last sends for the witch of Endor, to raise up old Samuel, to tell him what he was to do. Now Jesus Christ tells us, that no one can raise the dead but God; then the witch must have the power of God. Then

---

46. For Carlile's trial, see Joel H. Wiener, *Radicalism and Freethought in Nineteenth-Century Britain: The Life of Richard Carlile* (Westport: Greenwood Press, 1983), 44–54.

47. I am supplying the paragraphing.

we are told by the same book, that the souls of the departed either go to heaven or hell; then was Samuel walking about in the matter which composes the earth, or was he gone to heaven or hell? Suppose he was in the earth; then, according to Christ, no one but God, in that case, could raise him; and yet we are told that the witch did raise him. And if in heaven, what power could bring him down? not the power of a witch, who, according to their account, was leagued with devils, and persecuted as such. Oh, how unfortunate for them that the parsons or priests should leave this for us to find out; but as religion is part or parcel of the law of the land, (as our friend says) your fat-gutted parsons, priests, or bishops, would see Jesus Christ d——d, or God Almighty either, rather than give up their twenty or thirty thousand a year, and become poor curates at twenty pounds per annum.

"Jesus Christ, by the new testament, taught the Christian religion; but what did he teach us, what did he say, 'acknowledge no king.' He was a reformer: now every king is a lord. Then he meant, acknowledge no lord, because every king is a lord; every person is the same, that bears the name, as he lords over us, but then he is the Lord's anointed. Jesus Christ says, acknowledge no rabbi, (no priest:) no! he knew their tricks, and says, stand it no longer. Then Jesus Christ says, acknowledge no father; why? because fathers in those days were allowed by law to thrash their sons at any age; the same as is allowed in Russia even to the present day. Times were bad then, and Christ became a radical reformer: now I never could find out where he got his knowledge, but this much I know, by the same book, that he was born of very poor parents, who, like us, felt with him the same as we now feel, and he says, I'll turn Mr. Hunt, and then, when he had that exalted ride on the jack-ass to Jerusalem, the people ran before him, crying out, Hunt for ever! for that was one and the same as crying out, Hosanna, to the son of David! for, as the book tells us, God told David there should never be one of the family wanted to sit on the throne of Israel, till time should be no more; but who heard this besides David?—no one; and yet Jesus Christ says no man hath ever conversed with God: why, then, his grandfather David must be a liar.

"But Christianity consists only in what I told you before: acknowledge no king;—acknowledge no priest:—acknowledge no father: and this, gentlemen, never was practised: for that stupid fellow Paul, his apostle, that he left behind him, taught quite a different thing. *He*

says, pay your tribute money, pay Caesar; but why did he say this?—
Why, because he knew his master had lost his life for saying otherwise; so, thought Paul, I'll tell them to pay their taxes, and then I may go and preach where I like, and what I like, without being afraid of spies, such as Oliver or Reynolds, or such perhaps as are now in this room; for Jesus Christ was betrayed by a spy: he came out, and says, You must not let these people cry out Hosanna; but he was so proud of his ride, he thought he was going to be king of Jerusalem directly, and he said, I must not stop them, for if I do the very stones will cry out: so at last came Mr. Oliver or Mr. Reynolds, and gave him up to Pilate! Thus you see, gentlemen, there never was such a thing as Christianity practised in the world: how unfortunate for them, that after selecting four books out of four and thirty, they should leave so many absurdities for us to find out; and Judge Abbott, knowing them as well as us, thought it would do to have them exposed.

Wedderburn quarrels with the account by the spy only in these matters: not sacred "absurdities" but "supposed absurdities." Also, "Did I not say that Christ taught his disciples, that they should not call or acknowledge *themselves* kings, rabbis, priests, or fathers?" (TRW 6)

The evening's topic invited antireligious polemic to illustrate biblical absurdities, but Wedderburn's speech is less in the spirit of the de-Christianizing campaigns by the French Jacobins and more in the spirit of radical antinomianism. As McCalman explains, Wedderburn typically makes "the bible relevant to the historical and social experience of his audience." He does not debunk the Bible as such but seeks instead to "relocate its magical authority" much as his intellectual mentor Thomas Spence did (HS 26). Biblical contradictions could be used to undermine the overall authority of the Bible, as in deistic polemic, but Wedderburn's strategy is to prove that Christianity has never been put into practice because it is too radical.[48] Wedderburn, whose Bible contains truth and falsehood, plays the truthful parts against the false in order to use divine authority to attack the church and its interpretive traditions that have conspired to hide and mystify the radical ideas of true Christianity. The "fat-gutted parsons" don't want people to read the Bible and discover that Jesus was an antiauthoritarian reformer who urged rebellion against kings, fathers, lords, and priests. He pits the New Tes-

---

48. A Spencean poem in the *Medusa* ([1819], 136), "Man in Prospective," expresses precisely the idea that true Christianity has never been attempted. See PR 240–43.

tament against the Old, but also the New against itself, by criticizing Paul, "that stupid fellow," for making peace with the Romans by turning Christianity into an otherworldly religion; Jesus had been killed for being a rebel so Paul learned that survival meant not being rebellious. In passing, Wedderburn makes numerous allusions to contemporary politics, linking them with biblical history. Jesus's entry into Jerusalem is compared with "Orator" Hunt's triumphant entry into London in mid-September, as the hero of Peterloo was cheered by more than 300,000 people.[49] Judas becomes the spies—Reynolds and Oliver—who betray the radical movement, and Wedderburn acknowledges to his audience that surely there are spies listening this very night, as indeed there were. The end of the speech reiterates the main point, that Christianity has never been practiced. Wedderburn assumes and reinforces social equality with his audience by his idiom, syntax, and use of the first person plural. There is also a millennial note when he links Hunt's triumph to Jesus's entry into Jerusalem; the cross-referencing of different times in the last paragraph approximates the millenarian rhetoric discussed by Walter Benjamin, who writes of privileged moments when "time stands still" to permit the eruption of Messianic time.[50]

To the judge and jury, however, while he has some hope of avoiding legal punishment, he moderates his antinomian radicalism by depicting himself as a victim of slavery and a sincerely religious man in quest of spiritual truths, deploying the sentimental victim narrative and the spiritual autobiography to appeal to the jury. He also, in the extremely able defense of religious freedom and free speech that Wedderburn causes to be read by a court official, appeals to a Protestantism supposedly shared by defendant and jury, judge and prosecutor. At the very end of a restrained argument in favor of toleration that strikes familiar nationalistic anti-Catholic and anti-Islamic chords, Wedderburn finally gets to his own defense. "And where, after all, is my crime?—it consists merely in having spoken in the same plain and homely language which Christ and his disciples uniformly used" (TRW 17). Hoping to tap into the jury's antiaristocratic resentment, he points out something Evangelicals had also long criticized, namely, that the upper classes who were

---

49. Kevin Gilmartin observes that the huge Hunt crowd was an instance of the urban "sublime," difficult to conceptualize or fit into already existing categories. *Print Politics, the Press, and Radical Opposition in Early Nineteenth-Century England*, 131.

50. Benjamin's "Theses on the Philosophy of History" is a good commentary on Spencean radicalism. See Walter Benjamin, *Illuminations*, trans. Harry Zohn, ed. Hannah Arendt (New York: Schocken Books, 1968), 262–63.

Excursus: Radical Underground: Spence and Wedderburn

skeptical and irreligious were never prosecuted for reading "Shaftesbury, Bolingbroke, Tindal, Morgan, Hume, and Gibbon" (TRW 17). He restates more moderately some of the most provocative statements in his Hopkins Street speech, and then reminds the jury that it has the power, under Fox's libel law of 1792, to determine of what blasphemous libel consists (TRW 17–18).

Once he has been convicted, he can publish the transcript and recontextualize yet again his Hopkins Street speech. By adding notes and publishing it cheaply, using the radical booksellers like Richard Carlile's wife and Thomas Davison, Wedderburn ironizes the deferential aspects of his performance at the trial as his speeches become part of radical print culture. Now the gestures of moderation become transparent maneuvers to avoid punishment.

The most dramatic moment at Wedderburn's sentencing hearing in May came when the judge silenced his extempore speech defending himself. Wedderburn had explained that he was skeptical about the witch of Endor episode in the Book of Samuel because his own grandmother, who had raised him, was flogged several times by a white Christian for the crime of witchcraft. He knew for a fact she was not a witch. As he was trying to explain the origin of his skepticism about the episode of Balaam's speaking ass, the judge stopped him, because "the court considered his language was of a nature which they could not tolerate" (HS 132–33). The transcript then reads: "He then said, it might save time and prevent him wounding the ears of the court, if the paper was read that he had in his pocket, which is in the nature of a motion in arrest of judgment" (HS 133). This was doubly ironic because the written speech, while less colloquial than his extempore speeches, surely wounded the ears of the court, quite intentionally so. Moreover, he is able to conceal his own sarcasm by ostensibly deferring to the allegedly superior print culture. The most provocative irony in the written speech is when he tells the court that by suppressing his lecturing activities it has forced him to become a publishing writer, "an author" and "a member of the Republic of Letters." He then calls attention to the antireligious pamphlet addressed to the Archbishop of Canterbury that he recently published (HS 137). The speech drops all the appeals to a British Protestantism and identifies boldly the nature of his religious convictions, his belief in "the simple Deistical and Republican system of Jesus" (HS 138). Knowing that he is not going to get a light sentence, he concludes thus: "as I am so extremely poor that a prison will be a home to me; and as I am so far advanced in life

I shall esteem it an honor to die immured in a Dungeon, for advocating THE CAUSE OF TRUTH, OR RELIGIOUS LIBERTY, AND THE UNIVERSAL RIGHT OF CONSCIENCE" (HS 139). At this point he is not addressing the court but the audience outside the court, the readers of radical print culture.

Wedderburn's speech at his sentencing is not even concerned with the judge and a light sentence. Rather, it speaks to the London radical movement in the wake of the Cato Street executions. He used Cannon's expertise most extensively in the first written speech in February, when he had some hope of swaying the jury. Also at the trial he seems to have manipulated the racist assumptions concerning literacy and blacks when he had some hope of acquittal or a light sentence. As Henry Louis Gates explains in *The Signifying Monkey*, whites did not consider blacks as capable of full literacy, as literacy came to stand for what made Europeans human and Africans less than human.[51] The jury could feel sorry for a poor black who could not write and who did not seem able to read either. When the prosecuting attorney and sentencing judge finally understood the actual degree of literacy possessed by Wedderburn, any moderating sympathy disappeared.

After Wedderburn reached Dorchester Gaol he requested that Carlile teach him to write. Is this another example of Wedderburn playing dumb, trying to exploit racist prejudices? The authorities would have denied a straightforward request to speak with fellow radical Carlile, but if he framed the request as a deferential gesture toward print culture, he might be more successful. Unfortunately for both of them, the prison authorities refused to allow Carlile and Wedderburn to speak to each other.[52]

Conclusion

For Spence and Wedderburn, plebeian oral culture had a conflicted relationship with print culture that was symbolized in Spence's phonetic experiments and Wedderburn's collaboration with Cannon. The relationship was

---

51. Henry Louis Gates, Jr., *The Signifying Monkey: A Theory of African-American Literary Criticism* (Oxford: Oxford University Press, 1988), esp. chap. 4 .
52. Carlile records that while in prison "I was told that Wedderburn was anxious to learn to write." *The Republican* (20 October 1820): 364–65. Wiener, *Radicalism and Freethought in Nineteenth-Century Britain: The Life of Richard Carlile*, 29 n.2; 57. At Dorchester Gaol, where Carlile was not allowed to speak with other prisoners, he tried to get a subscription for Wedderburn, who was treated worse than Carlile. I thank David Worrall for calling these references to my attention.

Excursus: Radical Underground: Spence and Wedderburn

also combative, as *Pig's Meat* embodied Spence's goal of making print-culture rationality available to artisans and laborers, as Wedderburn used print culture to undermine slavery and racism. By inventing different voices in their writing, such as Spence's plebeian woman who silences an aristocratic antagonist, and Wedderburn's slave-trade characters, they undermined the authority of aristocracy and racial slavery. Both illustrate the contemporary relevance of the category "enthusiasm" because of their use of the biblical and prophetic idioms. Because of the land plan and the Spencean scorn for merely political reform, one tends to forget the fully Jacobin origins of the Spenceans in the LCS; even a later Spencean, Robert C. Fair, points back to the birth of his radicalism with his LCS uncle. The emphasis on land, however, one can find in Thelwall's recommendation for cultivating the wastes and breaking up large farms. Despite his rationalism, Godwin was really closer to the Spenceans and their agrarian suspicion of commerce than to Paine and Thelwall, who endorsed commerce (up to a point, of course). The Chartist land plan derives ultimately from Spence's own ideas, so that even after the 1820s the Spenceans entered the mainstream of working-class radicalism. The notion of decentralized political units founded on agrarian production has been important in anarchist thought even into the twentieth century; Gustav Landauer's agrarian socialism and the kibbutz idea are only two examples. While Marxism sometimes has spoken dismissively of the "idiocy of rural life," Spence's urban agrarianism, if one can call it that, has not been easy to dismiss.

Spence and Wedderburn were adept rhetoricians who skillfully developed texts always in the shadow of repression. The range of Spence's writing is truly remarkable, from biblical song to satirical dialogue. From Wedderburn we get some sense of how lively was the plebeian public sphere even as radicals were being put on trial and placed in prison. The abolitionist songs, however well made, are less vivid than the oral performance Wedderburn seems to have delivered consistently at his chapel. With these two writers one can see the power and usefulness of allegory. Rather than being mechanistic and predictable, as Coleridge called it, allegory in fact permits a flexible signification for the writer as bricoleur (as Jon Mee has pointed out). Spence and Wedderburn use borrowed texts and forms that they then turn inside out and against themselves. The allegorical mode also permits spontaneous digressions across different registers, as when Wedderburn passes from Carlile's trial to biblical interpretation to topical political commentary to millennial pronouncement. Spence's biblical allusions evoke popular modes of interpretation that are then recontextualized, made new. A typical allegorical moment is when Wedderburn tried to explain why he disputed the witch of Endor section in Samuel; the narrative about the violence against his grandmother was the new context for that story. Still another context is the judge's silencing of Wedderburn and his having a court official read the deistic critique. This vignette dramatizes the arrogance of power, as his grandmother's and his own victimization are linked together by a biblical passage and legal power.

5

Intemperance, Oratory, and Voicelessness

> I am convinced the *crime* of giving political lectures is in reality my principal offence.
>
> —*The Natural and Constitutional Rights of Britons* (PEJ 57)

Thelwall was an extraordinarily talented lecturer whose oratorical skills even an unsympathetic William Hazlitt praised.[1] Only political repression forced him out of radical politics and into speech lessons, but he was no more cynical about his new career, which sustained him until his death, than were Spence and Wedderburn about religion. Thelwall was genuinely engaged with elocution, speech impediments (having overcome his own), the physiology of speech, and democratic oratory. Nevertheless, repression had something to do with his new career. He went from being the most successful Jacobin orator to the most successful scientific lecturer *about* oratory; he

---

1. Hazlitt has been taken as referring to Thelwall when he writes: "The most dashing orator I ever heard is the flattest writer I ever read. In speaking, he was like a volcano vomiting out *lava;* in writing, he is like a volcano burnt out." William Hazlitt, "Essay XXIV. On the Difference Between Writing and Speaking," *The Plain Speaker*, in P. P. Howe, ed., *Complete Works of William Hazlitt*, 20 vols. (Toronto: J. M. Dent, 1930), 12: 264–65.

taught the techniques that he had in fact used earlier at the Beaufort Buildings, Coachmaker's Hall, Crown and Anchor, and Copenhagen Fields. It goes without saying that the impediments to speech were more than just physiological. His return to political activism and journalism in 1818 is indeed a return of the repressed, but Thelwall the old Jacobin confronted after Waterloo a very different political situation than the 1790s.

Treason Trial and Intemperance

No event better illustrates Thelwall's oratory than his trial for treason.[2] Reading his "Prefatory Memoir" or the *Public Characters* sketch of 1801, one would never guess Thelwall took an active part in his defense, even interrogating witnesses. Only by examining the trial transcript can one appreciate the rhetorical strategies that shape his published defenses, which he could not read in court, especially the *Natural and Constitutional Right of Britons to Annual Parliaments, Universal Suffrage, and the Freedom of Popular Association* (1795; PEJ 3–63). If we understand the trial and his written defense, then we can also understand the ambivalence that motivated some of the most apologetic suggestions in the *Life of John Thelwall*: that his involvement with Jacobinism was mistaken, that he had been disturbed by "intemperate" LCS colleagues, that he planned to quit the LCS at about the time he was arrested for treason, that the popular societies would have melted away had the government left them alone, that the LCS was a cause "which he had begun to deem almost hopeless" in 1794 (LJT 151, 155). The center of this ambivalence is condensed in the word "intemperance," what Thelwall calls in *The Tribune* a "British vice."[3]

Thelwall's treason trial, like the previous trials of Hardy and Tooke, were hermeneutic contests, a conflict of interpretations. Thelwall had to prove that the instances of his "intemperate language" did not signify treason but innocent hyperbole by a nonviolent, constitutionalist reformer. Edmund Burke, no stranger to hyperbolic, intemperate rhetoric, identified intemperance as an especially Jacobin weakness. "A certain intemperance of intellect is the dis-

---

2. A version of this section appears as "The Discourse of Treason, Sedition, and Blasphemy in British Political Trials, 1794–1822," in the *Romanticism and Law* collection edited by Michael Macovski in *Romantic Praxis*, ed. Orrin Wang, at the *Romantic Circles* website (http://www.rc.umd.edu/praxis/).

3. *Tribune* 46 (9 December 1795): 3:258.

ease of the time, and the source of all its other diseases" (EB 8:330; *Letter to a Member of the National Assembly* 1791). The mind must repress evil instincts if one is to have civilization. "Our physical well-being, our moral worth, our social happiness, our political tranquillity, all depend on that controul of our appetites and passions, which the ancients designed by the cardinal virtue of Temperance" (EB 9:359; *Third Letter on a Regicide Peace* 1797). One of those hegemonic concepts difficult to challenge, "temperance" carries the weight of reaction against seventeenth-century enthusiasm and eighteenth-century sensibility. Thelwall does not go as far as Blake, who says of "Prudence" that it is "a rich ugly old maid courted by Incapacity," but he shares with Blake an energetic repudiation of the temperance norm.[4] As a target of government prosecution, however, Thelwall carefully disguises the extent to which he does not accept the normative version of temperance.

The trial transcript and Thelwall's published defense disclose the assumptions governing his oratory and its relation to print culture. Thelwall's theory of creative inspiration entails a necessary moment of "intemperance."[5] In the "Farewel Address" of *The Tribune*, the periodical's final issue, Thelwall explains that he is delaying the publication of his very best and most recent lectures "till leisure and fit opportunity enable me to send them into the world in some convenient form, and in a more correct state." They are his best lectures—his "Philippics"—because "of being delivered on the spur of an awful and momentous crisis," the controversy over the Gagging Acts. The "universal interest and agitation" occasioned an unusually intense "passion" and "more of that fire of expression, and that rapid energy of conception and arrangement, which constitute the soul of oratory" (*Tribune* [1796] 3:322).

Thelwall never delivered a speech of any kind from a written text and relied instead on a few notes to prompt his extemporaneous composition. If the "soul of oratory" is spontaneous energy, why then must he put his recent lectures in a more "convenient" and "correct" form? Presumably he means more than getting the speeches translated from shorthand to ordinary prose. As oratory becomes printed text, it becomes subject to print-culture conventions that require revision, even translation. After his treason trial

4. *The Marriage of Heaven and Hell*, plate 5; David V. Erdman, ed., *The Complete Poetry and Prose of William Blake*, rev. ed. (New York: Doubleday, 1988).
5. An interesting parallel is Jonathan Wooler's practice of spontaneous composition for the *Black Dwarf*, lending his print-culture essays the style of orations. Kevin Gilmartin, *Print Politics, the Press, and Radical Opposition in Early Nineteenth-Century England* (Cambridge: Cambridge University Press, 1997), 72–73.

acquittal Thelwall hired someone to transcribe his speeches in shorthand in part as legal protection and as literary resource for the *Tribune* and other texts. The *Tribune* advertised that the political lectures were taken in shorthand by W. Ramsey and "revised by the Lecturer." He saved all the shorthand transcriptions for possible legal defenses, but he "revised" and "corrected" only his best oral texts (*Tribune* 3:320). Unfortunately we do not have access to Ramsey's transcriptions to see exactly how Thelwall revised, but the printed lectures invariably include moments of "intemperate" expressions that punctuate the oration and that provide occasions for qualification and explanation.

According to Alan Wharam, a lawyer who has studied the trials, the treason charge was not unreasonable. At the heart of the government's case were the political "conventions" called by the Jacobins. Whether "convention" signified a constitutionally protected meeting for petitioning parliament for electoral reform, as the defendants claimed, or an incipient sovereign body designed to *replace* the government, was ambiguous, although much evidence suggested the latter. Had the defendants been charged with only sedition, they surely would have been convicted. The Pitt government, then, was not unreasonable in its prosecution of the Jacobins, whose behavior and words could be construed to infer treasonable actions.[6] Coleridge and Southey, who always ridiculed the Pitt repression as unnecessary, vindicated their youthful radicalism as innocently idealistic rather than seditious. The Pitt government might have been mistaken, but it might have also correctly perceived a potentially revolutionary situation that required intervention.

Inferring treason from words is a cultural topos in the Romantic period. Percy Shelley, upon first learning of the Peterloo Massacre, wrote back to Charles Ollier using the words Shelley had made Beatrice Cenci say after she had been raped by her father: "Something must be done.... What yet I know not" (*Cenci* III.i.87–88).[7] For Beatrice the "something" turns out to be patricide, but what it signified for Shelley is less clear. In the fall of 1819 Shelley wrote of possibly having to return to England for a civil war. To Leigh Hunt he writes: "I suppose we shall soon have to fight in England."[8] Perhaps

---

6. Alan Wharam, *The Treason Trials, 1794* (Leicester: Leicester University Press, 1992).

7. Frederick L. Jones, ed., *The Letters of Percy Bysshe Shelley*, 2 vols. (Oxford: Clarendon Press, 1964), 2: 167.

8. Donald H. Reiman, *Shelley and His Circle, 1773–1822*, 8 vols. (Cambridge, Mass.: Harvard University Press, 1961–86), 5: 1107.

if Shelley, the Hunts, and their friends had in fact collected arms in preparation for a conflict, and if the government had intervened and gathered evidence, Shelley's letters to Ollier and Hunt could have been used as evidence in a treason or sedition trial; Shelley's play, *The Cenci*, could have been used as well. That a canonical Romantic drama could have been a pretext for judicial prosecution indicates how repression and judicial discourse are tangled with literary meanings at this time. The play itself, which has a trial scene, a torture scene, and executions, turns the reader into a jury.

As John Barrell has demonstrated, by the late eighteenth century the crime of treason as defined in the legal precedent of 25 Edward III had been interpreted as primarily a mental act rather than a physical one.[9] As discussed earlier, Chief Justice Eyre defined constructive treason very broadly. Thomas Pfau has commented that Eyre's "extraordinary interpretive latitude" turns mere facts into a concealing "veil" that has to be interpreted.[10] In Eyre's own words: "The entering into Measures which, in the Nature of Things, or in the common Experience of Mankind, do obviously tend to bring the Life of the King into Danger, is also compassing and imagining the Death of the King."[11] Eyre also ruled that nonviolent associations and assemblies advocating parliamentary reform could be treasonous. In fact, almost anything the government did not like could be construed as treasonous. Convictions under constructive treason were not easy, but the concept itself provided an institutional structure for aggressive detection of political dissent.

Because the punishment for treason was execution performed in a ritual manner (drawing, quartering, and so on), juries were more likely to punish political dissenters under a sedition or blasphemy charge. Sedition, a common-law offense, is called by one legal scholar "perhaps the very vaguest of all offences known to the Criminal Law."[12] The traditional definition of sedition focused on the attitude—more or less deferential—

---

9. John Barrell, *The Birth of Pandora and the Division of Knowledge* (Philadelphia: University of Pennsylvania Press, 1992), 122–23, 139. Chapter 6 (119–43) is devoted to the treason trials.

10. Thomas Pfau, "Paranoia Historicized: Legal Fantasy, Social Change, and Satiric Meta-Commentary in the 1794 Treason Trials," in Stephen C. Behrendt, ed., *Romanticism, Radicalism, and the Press* (Detroit: Wayne State University Press, 1997), 38–39.

11. Jack W. Marken and Burton R. Pollin, eds., *Uncollected Writings (1785–1822): Articles in Periodicals and Six Pamphlets. One with Coleridge's Marginalia. By William Godwin* (Gainesville: Scholars' Facsimiles and Reprints, 1968), 134.

12. Edward Jencks, *The Book of English Law* (Boston: Houghton Mifflin, 1929), 116.

toward the sovereign.[13] According to Justice Holt in a ruling of 1704, *any* criticism of the government implied insufficient deference and was therefore seditious (Holdsworth 6:266). Punishment for seditious libel varied greatly in severity, from a few months imprisonment, probationary security, and fines, to transportation and banishment from the realm—the lattermost punishment being an innovation of the Six Acts of 1820. For the period from the French Revolution to the early 1820s, seditious libel prosecutions were extraordinarily numerous. There were more sedition trials in 1792 and 1793 than there had been in the previous eighty-seven years.[14]

Philip Hamburger, in an essay on the seditious libel law, discloses some unintended effects of the legal decisions.[15] The libel law, after prepublication censorship was abandoned in 1696, paradoxically promoted "the art of irony and satire" (Hamburger 738). Moreover, the courts, jealous of their own integrity, did not always do the bidding of the government, and ordinarily followed legal procedures rigorously enough that convictions were not always guaranteed. The hermeneutical rule by which one was to interpret texts was formulated by Justice Holt in 1729: "the understanding given to the writing by all the world" and "such as the generality of readers must take it in, according to the obvious and natural sense of it" (Hamburger 739). Arbitrary interpretation was not permitted. Especially after 1792, when juries first judged whether something was seditious, sedition trials deliberated on "innuendo" and the *shades* of meaning. Satirists like Thelwall in his Chaunticlere allegory were skillful enough to devise ironic texts that frustrated the best efforts of the prosecuting attorneys. The government finally had to rely on the stamp tax to supplement the libel law in its efforts to control the democratic press (Hamburger 751).

To determine whether Thelwall had indeed imagined and compassed the death of the king, the prosecution went to great lengths to find external signs of Thelwall's inner thoughts. Two external signs of Thelwall's political convictions were cited earlier in Hardy's trial, the seditious songs (such as the "Sheepsheering" song) that Thelwall wrote for the LCS and that were widely

---

13. Sir William Holdsworth, *A History of English Law*, 17 vols. (London: Methuen, Sweet and Maxwell, 1966), 8: 338. Hereafter Holdsworth.

14. T. A. Jackson, *Trials of British Freedom* (1940 rpt. New York: Burt Franklin, 1968), 35.

15. Philip Hamburger, "The Development of the Law of Seditious Libel and the Control of the Press," *Stanford Law Review* 37 (1985): 661–765. Hereafter Hamburger. See also Roger B. Manning, "The Origins of the Doctrine of Sedition," *Albion* 12 (1980): 99–121.

distributed and sung, and a seditious comment he made at a tavern after an LCS meeting. According to the spy report, "Mr. Thelwall took a pot of porter and blowing off the head, said—'This is the Way I would serve Kings.'" LCS members challenged this report by recalling the word "Tyrants" rather than "Kings."[16]

Thelwall was troubled by the porter toast, perhaps the most incriminating evidence against him. In the *Natural and Constitutional Right of Britons*, he refers four times to "ridiculous toasts" and over ten different times to "intemperate" expressions in general.[17] As I discussed earlier, Thelwall was not immune from the appeal of regicidal imagery in texts like the Chaunticlere allegory and *John Gilpin's Ghost*. That he made the "ridiculous toast" hardly seems in doubt, although he hints that maybe the spies suggested the toast to him first and he only repeated it, but in either case he spoke it "in the hour of conviviality, without thought or meaning" (PEJ 17).

At the actual trial Thelwall's lawyer Vicary Gibbs concedes that the defendant "was warm tempered" and "sometimes apt to speak his sentiments in stronger terms than his sober judgment would approve" (TJT 39). Thelwall's other lawyer, Thomas Erskine, makes an even more damaging concession, that if Thelwall is guilty of anything it would be at worst "sedition" (TJT 47). Sedition, however, is not treason. The trial transcript and subsequent texts indicate that Thelwall and his lawyers had two different, sometimes conflicting agendas. Thelwall wanted both an acquittal and a vindication of the political movement of which he was a part, but his lawyers wanted only an acquittal. Gibbs and Erskine rest their defense of Thelwall on two things: primarily, the previous acquittals of Hardy and Tooke that destroy the conspiracy case against Thelwall; secondarily, the discrediting of a key prosecution witness, John Taylor, as a bigamist who perjured himself in the past. Especially as half of Thelwall's jurors were also Hardy's, so Thelwall's lawyers argue tenaciously that the third case is just like the other two. In fact, as Marcus Wood points out, the two previous trials were very different, with Thomas Hardy taking a passive role, deferring entirely to his lawyers, while

---

16. Mary Thale, ed., *Selections from the Papers of the London Corresponding Society, 1792–1799* (Cambridge: Cambridge University Press, 1983), 140 n.113. Thelwall complains that "many intemperate expressions sworn to by the spies and informers against Thelwall on Hardy's trial" were fabrications that he could not challenge during his own trial. Had those witnesses testified at Thelwall's own trial, he could have disputed their veracity. Thelwall neglects to mention, however, that half of the jurors for his trial were also on Hardy's and heard the damaging evidence already, so that the government had little to gain by repeating it (LJT 248).

17. PEJ 10, 17, 54, 56 ("ridiculous toasts"); 4, 5, 8, 20, 34, 36, 37, 39, 40, 55, 61 ("intemperance").

Tooke assumed a prominent role, almost as active as that of his own lawyers.[18] Thelwall was not as passive as Hardy or as active as Tooke.

Thelwall additionally elicits from witnesses the information that he spoke in public numerous times against political violence (TJT 35, 37). He is also especially proud of his character witnesses, all four of them from the medical field, whose testimony he reprints in the *Life of John Thelwall* (440–45). He also challenges the integrity of some evidence used against him because when the police seized materials from his house they did not use proper procedures that mandated inspection, cataloguing, and sealing of seized documents (TJT 37). Finally, Thelwall makes sure the jurors learn he was supporting on fifty pounds a year a wife, a mother, and a mentally ill brother (TJT 53). Thelwall's own contributions to his defense are in the areas of ethos and pathos, not political logos. Both Gibbs and Erskine do not seem to take these appeals very seriously, as they rest their case largely on the two prior acquittals.

After the jury deliberated for only seventy minutes Thelwall was acquitted, but his lawyers' defense had little to do with his own actions and words. Thelwall's own ethical and emotional appeals to the jury were marginal to the whole proceeding, which left the political issues undeveloped. He was legally "free" after 5 December 1794, but the cause that he served and the adequacy of his own service were still in question.

The eleventh and twelfth chapters of the *Life of John Thelwall* give a detailed rebuttal of the treason charges. An episode that came out in the trial that was especially difficult to explain was an "intemperate" letter Thelwall had written but had not sent. This letter declares his republican sympathies, supports the Jacobin "Mountain" in Paris, and criticizes America for having "too much veneration for property—too much religion—too much law." He had given vent to his anger because, as he explained, he had just barely escaped yet again from being indicted for political lecturing by the grand jury. At the trial itself and in his print defense there is the apology that "Thelwall was subject to great irritability of temper, a quality which he, in after life, in a considerable degree corrected, and in these moments, for they seldom exceeded a few seconds, of excitement, would say and do things, of which, after a short reflection, he would repent" (LJT 282).

At Thelwall's trial the prosecuting attorneys dramatically highlight the let-

---

18. Marcus Wood, *Radical Satire and Print Culture, 1790–1822* (Oxford: Oxford University Press, 1994), 137.

ter because it was more damaging than even the seditious toast. Whereas one could ascribe a toast to the effects of enthusiasm enhanced by alcohol, a private letter suggests sincere expression of one's thoughts. The *Natural and Constitutional Right of Britons* provides a defense of the letter that was lacking at the trial. He concedes he is, "in private speculations, a *Republican*," but in public he has always maintained that violence cannot enforce private speculations (PEJ 54). He acknowledges that parts of the letter cannot be wholly defended and should instead be extenuated as a result of exasperation. The way he defends the remarks on America is a study in ambiguous phrasing: "I both disavow, and approve it." Because he was writing to someone who "knew my heart" and required "no commentator," he could phrase words elliptically, taking for granted an innocent interpretation. Wrenched out of the context, those same words are politically extreme. He provides a politically moderate interpretation for his words on America (PEJ 55), but this very example reinforces the cogency of what Wharam and Barrell wrote about the treason trials, that the court procedures were applied to discover the meaning of mental operations. Thelwall protests against having "to answer at the bar of the Old Bailey for every intemperate expression" he may utter, or every "crude imagination" he may put on paper (PEJ 55), but oral and written texts are signs of subjective intention, precisely the site for the discourse of treason.

If "intemperance" is a psychological condition which Thelwall has to manage, as Thelwall and his lawyers suggest, "intemperance" is also a feature of his orations. The *Natural and Constitutional Right of Britons* is an "oral" text, not just in style but in origin. The printed text represents the unacted intention to present a defending speech to the jury at his treason trial. Had not Erskine persuaded him otherwise, Thelwall would have delivered a speech from notes, not a prepared text. After his acquittal, he delivered from notes three consecutive lectures that were taken down by shorthand, then ultimately revised for publication. The printed text maintains the fiction of Thelwall's addressing his jury, although in fact he addressed during the three lectures a sympathetic crowd of British reformers and Jacobins (and more than a few spies). The actual readers of the printed text would be neither the jury nor his lecture audiences. The fiction of *speaking* before the *jury* that has the power of life or death over Thelwall makes the heightened rhetoric appropriate. Recurrently punctuating the text are moments of emotional intemperance, usually apostrophes, that then modulate back down to some kind of rational equilibrium. Such is the pattern and structure of the essay.

Similarly, he uses himself to dramatize the compelling case for the radical reforms spelled out in the title, principally by means of refuting the treason charge by redefining treason and rebellion.

There are eight major apostrophes distributed throughout the text, only one of which will I examine in any detail. Near the end of the essay he accumulates numerous examples of the government's exercise of arbitrary power, from suspension of habeas corpus to jury-packing, concluding thus: "was it not time for Britons to rouse from their lethargy, and enter their serious protest against innovations so tyrannical, and encroachments so decisive?" (PEJ 44–45). Precisely at the point he appeals to the audience to take action he heightens the rhetoric even more with the following apostrophe:

> O miserable country, indeed, if thy legislature could meditate so many fatal stabs! and thy sons can be arraigned for treason for crying to the parricides to forbear!
> O miserable country! whose rulers not only demand obedience to their laws, but implicit reverence also to the crude conceptions of their brains—their hints—their threats—their contemplations—the shapeless embrios of their legislative imaginations! (PEJ 45)

Following the whole essay's strategy of refuting the treason charge by redefinition, Thelwall makes the Jacobins themselves the loyal sons victimized by the parricidal traitors of government. Thelwall inverts the treason charges chiastically: from "State charges Thelwall with treason" to "Thelwall charges State with treason." Government—"legislature"—is kept separate from the nation, so that he can demonize his persecutors without seeming to attack the "country." The monarch is subsumed entirely into, but is not identical with, the concept of "country." Inverting the charge of conspiracy, Thelwall makes the government a source of "intemperance," emotional, irrational, extreme, irresponsible, and arbitrary expressions that demand not just obedience but "reverence."

Having demonized his accusers, having used his own intemperate rhetoric to counter the government's intemperance, Thelwall moderates the discourse in the next paragraph, which is a sequence of four rhetorical questions that decompress the concentrated energy of the exclamatory apostrophe; then the "legislature" of the apostrophe is materialized in two subsequent paragraphs on Dundas and Pitt. Finally, a long paragraph redefines the politically explosive concept of "Convention" as "peaceful assemblies of the people for the purposes of political investigation" (PEJ 45–46). The only danger from "Convention" is the prohibition on political meetings, because repression creates conspiracy and violence (PEJ 46).

The rhetorically violent apostrophe, then, punctuates a series of political evils that demand action, but the violence of the apostrophe is followed by a sequence accenting rational analysis and peaceful discussion, not storming the barricades. To use Thelwall's own phrasing, he simultaneously "disavows and approves" his own intemperate rhetoric. Were I to analyze the other apostrophes in the essay, a pattern similar to the one described above would emerge.

In a lecture reprinted in the *Tribune* he refutes and inverts the charges of treason by redefining the concept within a rhetorical pattern punctuated by intemperance ([1795], 1:279–300). The principal argument is that the government itself has treasonously betrayed the nation to the interests of an oligarchy; rebellion is not treasonous but the legitimate process by which to remove usurpers who are indeed treasonous (284). The argument itself, intemperate in its own right, is interrupted by a wonderful moment of intemperance. Playing treason and rebellion against one another, Thelwall used the example of Louis being victimized by his evil and "treasonous" advisers, whose wicked guidance provoked the "rebellion." Precisely after Thelwall says that "I should be almost inclined to say—that they [Louis and his family] deserved the fate which they eventually met" (289), someone from the audience hissed, forcing Thelwall to defend his apparent support for the regicide. He then stresses the evil of the advisers rather than of the king, and apologizes later in the speech for the intemperance of his outraged reaction to the treatment of Joseph Gerrald, who was being transported to Australia for the crime of sedition and to whom he had just bid farewell at Portsmouth: "But let me not lose again the tranquillity of my soul! . . . Let me not, when the sting of indignation and consciousness of injury urges my temper—let me not inflame your minds with similar feelings" (299).

The intemperate/moderate rhythm is not an occasional accident that is different from the ordinary structure of his writing. It *is* the ordinary structure of his writing, as we will see in his later writing and even his nonpolitical writing. He can have his cake and eat it too: he expresses fully his Romantic passion, which then falls under an Enlightenment scrutiny, which is also subject to later Romantic subversion. His dual loyalty to Romanticism and Enlightenment is inscribed in his very style. Similarly, one can see in this pattern the effect of "enthusiasm" on this most secular of radicals, whose style embodies ambivalence over revolution.

Radical Oratory

Thelwall began his career as an orator as a young man, in the 1780s at the Coachmakers' Hall debates (LJT 39–52). When he died at nearly seventy years old, in February 1834, he was, appropriately enough, on yet another lecture tour, this time in the west of England.[19] Between 1792 and 1797 he was the most effective radical orator in Britain. From 1801 until his death he taught oratory, treated speech impediments, and lectured in his capacity as a self-taught professor of language, history, and literature in London and elsewhere on a variety of topics: elocutionary, rhetorical, historical, scientific, and literary. From 1818 to 1822 he became again a political orator in radical Westminster while serving as the editor-owner of the radical-reform *Champion*. He lectured at the London Mechanics Institute in 1833 (LJT 28) and in 1832, in his sixties, he put his oratorical skills at the service of his friend Francis Place and his National Political Union.[20]

Oratory also shaped Thelwall's literary views.[21] In defending Milton's *Paradise Lost* and condemning the "finger-counting monastics" critical of Milton's prosody, he insisted that poetry should imitate speech. Unlike "our *correct* poets" who "anxiously . . . avoid modes of construction and arrangement, which they ought most sedulously to have cultivated," the great Milton writes poetry that possesses "the easy flow of a spontaneous and oratorical utterance" (LHC 164–65). Thelwall appeals to the actual experience of reading the poem out loud for confirmation that it is easy to understand and possesses "that free spontaneous flow of oratorical period."[22] Thel-

---

19. See the obituary notice in the *Gentleman's Magazine* 155 (1834): 548–50.
20. On Thelwall and the National Political Union, see I. J. Prothero, *Artisans and Politics in Early Nineteenth-Century London: John Gast and His Times* (Baton Rouge: Louisiana University Press, 1979), 388 n.41. On an issue central to workers' education, Thelwall criticized sharply the elitist attempts to censor and control the reading material for the Mechanics' Institutes and their libraries. *Monthly Magazine* 60 (August 1825): 19.
21. Walter J. Ong's *Orality and Literacy: The Technology of the Word* (New York: Routledge, 1982) has influenced me greatly in thinking about oral and print cultures, although I realize I have not cited him for any specific idea. He notes the decline of rhetoric since Romanticism (109), a decline challenged recently by Don H. Bialostosky and Lawrence D. Needham, ed., *Rhetorical Traditions and British Romantic Literature* (Bloomington and Indianapolis: Indiana University Press, 1995).
22. John Thelwall, "Mr. Thelwall on Milton," *Monthly Magazine* 22 (1806): 211–13.

wall's concern with the sound, punctuation, and orthography of *Paradise Lost* suggests a familiarity with Capel Lofft's 1793 edition of the poem. Lofft, who took issue with Bentley's editorial procedures, returned to the earliest editions of the poem to retrieve the "original" orthography that had been modernized by Bentley and that was a key to recapturing Milton's authentic "voice." Lofft, a political radical and member of the Constitutional Society, shared Thelwall's literary goal of aligning literature with oratory and countering Augustan "correctness."[23] Thelwall was also convinced that beautiful language had a physical foundation, that natural laws governed the production and reception of sounds. Things "pretty upon paper" may be "revolting to the ear" (LHC 7). Thomas Spence's preference of orality to print culture, especially his efforts in phonetic spelling, was similar to Thelwall's. Not the sight but the sound of words was most meaningful to Spence and Thelwall, both of whom were suspicious of print culture's aristocratic biases.[24]

Thelwall's mode of oratory also reveals his assumptions concerning language. He *always* delivered speeches spontaneously, with the assistance of at most a few written notes (LHC 177, 271). Perhaps Thelwall's preferring Danton to Robespierre might have been because the former spontaneously delivered speeches whereas the latter read rehearsed, written speeches. Well before Wordsworth's *Lyrical Ballads* Preface, Thelwall had developed an orally based literary theory.

One of Thelwall's final reflections on oratory appears in his essay on Orator Henley in the *Retrospective Review* for 1826.[25] In writing about Henley's career, Thelwall unavoidably allegorizes himself. The essay, despite the autobiographical subtext, is without self-pity or sentimental appeal; rather, Thelwall straightforwardly recovers a forgotten innovator in the field of elocution and rhetoric. Unfairly attacked and misrepresented by Pope's *Dunciad*, Henley has not received "justice" from the public for his true "talents" (225). Henley was a courageous pioneer in creating discursive and institutional space for a new kind of popular, largely secular, lecturing in London. That Thelwall too felt neglected and insufficiently appreciated is evident from his

---

23. Capel Lofft, *Paradise Lost. A Poem in Twelve Books. The Author John Milton. Printed from the first and second Editions collated. The original Orthography restored; the Punctuation corrected and extended. With various Readings; and Notes; chiefly Rhythmical* (London: Stockdale, 1792).

24. The emphasis on sound did not lead to a fetishized "correct" pronunciation. Regional accents Thelwall deemed "idiomatic" musical variations, not essential differences (LHC 200).

25. *Retrospective Review* 14 (1826): 206–25.

letters to Francis Place.[26] As Thelwall narrates Henley's life, one can see how the account also applies to Thelwall: Henley's "restless and inquisitive spirit seems to have revolted against established institutions" (208), leading him to leave the church, as Thelwall left law, for the sake of free expression. As Thelwall resigned from the LCS in 1795 to give paid lectures, so Henley avoided identification with any Dissenting religious sect, nor did he form his own sect. He lectured twice a week, like Thelwall in the 1790s, and he "frequently preached upon topics suggested by the transactions of the day" (221). His oratorical style, impassioned and theatrical, is also like Thelwall's, as Henley "committed his sermons to memory, enlivened them with declamation and pathos, and endeavoured to commend their delivery by all the graces of studied action" (210). Henley "from time to time harangued upon the political questions" of the day, outraged the ministry, and was victimized by political repression, as even his "papers" were seized (221). Henley's, unlike Thelwall's, were restored to him eventually (222). Orator Henley's appeals to reason and inquiry offended established authority, so that "Henley experienced the fate of all reformers" (219), a fate Thelwall knew only too well. Thelwall criticizes Henley for some failings, especially his appeals to scriptural authority in argument (224), but otherwise, in the biographical sketch of the neglected victim of political repression, Thelwall also sees himself.

Political Lectures

One cannot separate political message from political repression. All of Thelwall's lectures were shaped to some extent by the experience of repression. When he started his political lecturing for the LCS in November 1793, he intended to raise money for the delegates to the British Convention in Scotland, a convention that was soon dispersed by the authorities, with the leading delegates arrested. Soon, the London mayor and Reeves's loyalist association intervened to stop Thelwall's lectures. According to Thelwall's own account, these biweekly (Wednesday and Friday) lectures charged a low admission fee for "sixty or seventy persons of both sexes," as the audience

---

26. See especially Thelwall's letter to Place of 20 March 1832, in the British Library, BL 65667, Add. 37950 ff. 131–32. He complains that his "sufferings & sacrifices in the Political Cause" and in advancing the "Cause of Educational Science" have not been rewarded or duly acknowledged.

was mostly LCS members and their wives (PL viii). From late 1793 until his arrest in May 1794 Thelwall enjoyed the most democratic audience he would ever have.

These early lectures not only attack the political repression, which the lectures themselves defy, but use the repression as a point of departure to celebrate the cultural activity of artisans: "Mind! mind!—that almost omnipotent faculty of man! superior to the malice of persecution—defies the chains and dungeons of the oppressors" (PL 37). Mind is not individualistic but a product of "*associated intellect*" (PL 40) within the public sphere. Mind too must resist internalizing repression: "For it is better, according to my judgment,—ten times better, to be immured oneself in a Bastille, than to have the Bastille put into one's mouth to lock up one's tongue from all intercourse and communication with one's heart" (PL 38). Andrew McCann comments that the political meeting in and of itself was transgressive and "embodied a kind of public space and interactive practice very different from the practices of culture-consumption that mediated the bourgeois public sphere" and was in fact a basis for an activist "community."[27] Mind cannot be restrained: "when enquiry is once begun who shall determine its boundaries?"[28] Mind too is historical. Thelwall's lectures, as they struggle against repression and raise money for defense funds, are on the history of political repression and resistance to repression in the seventeenth century and the Roman republic. He presents himself as an orator with authority by renouncing—or rather deferring—his private ambition as an author in the "pursuits of taste and literature" for service to the public as an orator—or, in my terminology, a writer (PL 2). Andrew McCann illustrates the way Thelwall's lecture uses "sensibility as an oratorical strategy" by calling attention to literature's limitations and powers and by dramatizing himself as a man of feeling for political effect, exploiting the tension between individualistic sentimentality and communal solidarity.[29] He accrues authority as an orator by renouncing a merely selfish pursuit, and also by acting as the man of feeling whose "sympathy" connects "him with the whole intellectual universe," including "our starving manufacturers" and "widows and orphans" (PL 11, 13). (The very proce-

27. Andrew McCann, "Politico-Sentimentality: John Thelwall, Literary Production and Critique of Capital in the 1790s," *Romanticism* 3 (1997): 42. See also chap. 3 of McCann's *Cultural Politics in the 1790s: Literature, Radicalism and the Public Sphere* (New York and London: St. Martin's Press and Macmillan, 1999).
28. *Political Lectures. No. II. Sketches of the History of the Prosecutions for Political Oppression* (London: John Thelwall, 1794), 23.
29. McCann, "Politico-Sentimentality," *Romanticism* 3 (1997): 35–52.

dure by which he presents his credentials as a radical lecturer—"I look into my own heart, and I believe I know my motives!" [PL 17]—is similar to the prosecutorial measures that will be applied to Thelwall at his treason trial: the court will look into his "heart" to scrutinize his "motives.") Radical oratory theatrically structures subjectivity and represents it dramatically for an audience, thus providing an influential model for textualizing introspection. Because the literature of sensibility emphasizes motive more than action, Thelwall risks emotional self-indulgence by appropriating it for political purposes, but he also restrains a fully developed sentimental performance by pointing, for example, to the need for moderating "the intemperate manner of expression" as well as "violence or intemperance" (PL 14).

The lectures he delivered after his treason trial acquittal were less socially homogeneous and were more of a middle-class character. They were also far larger, as the audience ranged from 480 to 520.[30] In print form he also published some edited lectures in *The Tribune* to both a popular audience that probably could not afford to attend the lectures regularly (a thousand copies at 3d each) and a more elite audience that purchased the deluxe edition (two-hundred-fifty copies at 6d each). Altogether, viewing the biweekly lectures and the published *Tribune*, one notes Thelwall's remarkable popularity at a time of war, food shortages, and political repression. This was Thelwall's great moment in history. His unique talents served him well among the London artisans and middle-class radicals. He was perfectly positioned to address meaningfully readers of Godwin and readers of Paine, LCS artisans and SCI Dissenting intellectuals.

To illustrate the quality of the *Tribune* lectures, I will discuss now three issues of the *Tribune*, one that is a self-conscious defense of Thelwall's lecturing, and two that concentrate on the theater. (In Part Three I will also draw upon *Tribune* material for the "Peripatetic Imagination" and "Against Empire.") Thelwall not only delivered political lectures but reflected on lecturing and the broader phenomenon of cultural creativity.

Clearly a troubling issue Thelwall had to address was his leaving the LCS in early 1795. The treason trial acquittals, although a victory for the popular societies, also occasioned strategic retreats, notably Thomas Hardy's retirement from radical politics. The more elite reform societies like the SCI and Friends of the People folded, leaving the LCS in a more vulnerable situation. Was Thelwall opportunistically abandoning the LCS artisans for an

---

30. "Preface," *Tribune*, vol. 2.

audience with deeper pockets? The fifteenth issue of *The Tribune* addresses this question with frankness. He explains his separation from the LCS as mutually beneficial: the organization will not be responsible for whatever legal difficulties the lectures might entail, and Thelwall will have freedom of thought and expression that active membership would have made impossible. It will be harder to make a conspiracy charge stick if he is not a member of the LCS.

He uses this occasion, however, to launch an unequivocal defense of the LCS and its right to organize openly, even while he discusses his need for making money, for leisure and solitude for thinking and writing, for distance from "party" feeling. He does not take a Godwinian posture, which would pose individualistic reason against social irrationality, but declares that the tension between independent thinking and social conformity is a problem for everyone. Indeed, he typically uses the first-person plural to explain that we must "fortify our minds with virtue, and with principle."[31] Reinforcing the connection between himself and his LCS colleagues, he concludes this issue of the *Tribune* with a reprint of one of the songs cited at his treason trial and sung at earlier LCS meetings. The penultimate stanza of *this* version of "Britain's Glory" refers to the notorious Chaunticlere allegory with these provocative words: "cutting off a *game cock's head*."[32]

Thelwall pushes Enlightenment themes tied to individualism toward a logic of social solidarity. He claims for himself a sphere of discretion for rational reflection, like Godwin, but he attaches it to a project of *social* Enlightenment, an enlightened "congregated voice" (PEJ 228). In another lecture he states: "We live to improve, if we are wise; and if we are virtuous, we live not only to improve ourselves but to improve our fellow beings, by encouraging free and liberal enquiry, and submitting, with candour and sincerity, to their investigation, the sentiments which we believe important to their felicity and virtue" (PEJ 89). The emphasis on sentiment, not just reason, is consistent in statements that link private and public "virtue" (PEJ 101), and that describe an almost mystical unity: "could we persuade mankind to consider the universe, as in reality it is, one continuous system of animated being, and could we persuade the individual to think himself only a part, a portion of that great, and, as far as we can perceive, immortal existence . . . ?" (PEJ 104). Similarly, he speaks of "that great family of human

---

31. *The Tribune* 15 (20 June 1795), 1: 336.
32. Ibid., 340. The version of the song reprinted in the *Life of John Thelwall* does not include these words.

beings every one of which, whatever be his name, his colour, or his country, is the brother of all the rest, and ought to enjoy with them a community of rights and happiness" (PEJ 111).

Also countering individualism is Thelwall's historical awareness, which engages the past as the embodied experience of prior generations, and which militates against melancholy and sensibility (PEJ 107–8). He brings the task of social solidarity from poetry to practical politics by pleading in lecture after lecture for unity between the middle and laboring classes, consciously working against middle-class biases. Typical are the comments that the poor cannot be oppressed without the "middle orders" also feeling the oppression (PEJ 208), and that "those who are now the middling, must soon be the lower orders" because of "oppression" (PEJ 232). But he also opposes popular prejudice, such as the bias of the food rioters against the middling-class food merchants (PEJ 281).

The *Tribune* lectures on the theater, which have as their underlying theme social solidarity, are published in the last two issues of the journal but they were actually delivered to a live audience about a year earlier, in April 1795. Their position as Thelwall's final word enhances their importance. The long delay from oral text to print text illustrates the aesthetic form of drama itself, a form that is performative. Moreover, just as Thelwall's career as a political lecturer began with a renunciation of literary art, so he concludes (at least one phase of) his political career with a lecture on the political meaning of a particular literary art, drama. Additionally, the emphatic references to the classical theater provide an appropriate transition to his new, fully legal—after the Gagging Acts—lecture series on classical history.

Both lectures have an inflammatory title, "The Prostitution of the Public Theatres," with the first one devoted mostly to the Athenian theater and the second one devoted mostly to the English theater.[33] The Athenian theater begins promisingly as the political instruction of a democratic populace in "the general moral of distributive justice" with Aeschylus, Sophocles, and Euripides, but after the Thirty Tyrants, the theater becomes an instrument of oppression, prostituted to arbitrary power. Aristophanes' *The Clouds*, according to Thelwall, reflects the will of the tyrants by ridiculing the "sans culotte" Socrates, the champion of democracy. Socrates is an important figure for Thelwall: he too was a lecturer who brought philosophy to the

---

33. *The Tribune* 48 and 49 (1796): 3: 279–318. The actual lectures were 1 April and 15 April, 1795.

people, who was victimized by political repression, prohibited from lecturing, and brought to trial for a capital offense against the state. That Socrates philosophized out of doors and gave rise to the Peripatetic school of philosophers provokes Thelwall to comment on the union of mind and body that mirrors the social egalitarianism he finds in Athenian culture, where "health and intellect [are] promoted together" and where "oral instruction diffused its animating influence throughout the circle of auditors; and social sympathy went hand in hand with instruction" (3:286–87). As long as democratic structures were maintained, philosophy and theater were cooperatively conducting reliable political education, although he concedes that Athenian philosophy was not as democratic as it could have been, and that the theater was in fact more democratic (3:288–89). After the demise of democratic structures, however, the theater becomes merely a mouthpiece for the tyrants and inculcates the prevailing court opinions.

One of Thelwall's boldest gestures is to draw parallels between himself and Socrates, something he does also in the first "Letter" of *The Rights of Nature* (1796), as I discussed earlier, in Chapter 2. The autodidact son of a shopkeeper appropriates genteel classical culture in an ostentatiously democratic way both in the lecture and the later essay. For example, he relies on translations of Greek texts. For Socrates' trial, he uses an English translation of Moses Mendelssohn's translation, a double distancing from the Greek original, as one outsider borrows from another. In one passage he even brings together Socrates, himself, and the unsuccessful prosecution of the gamecock allegory, comically mixing high and low, classical and contemporary, philosophy and theater (3:296). He turns classical culture inside out: what Oxbridge gentlemen use to validate their authority, Thelwall deconstructs performatively as democratic allegory and seditious satire. Thelwall steals Socrates from Oxbridge and turns him into a martyr who belongs to sans-culotte artisan culture.

Another striking thing about the first lecture is the way Thelwall represents seamlessly the various aspects of cultural creativity as theatrical: philosophy, theater proper, politically motivated trials, political lectures themselves. There being no difference between rhetoric and poetry, each aspect of cultural creativity is an aesthetically framed speech designed to move an audience. Aristophanes' play functions like a state trial in attacking Socrates; both theatrical sites aim to punish Socrates. Similarly, he cites Dryden as a prostituted playwright who sold himself to the same powers that martyred Sidney and Russell. Thelwall highlights the power of ideology without using that word.

The second lecture is mostly about the ideology of the theater in England. His history of the English theater is a narrative of art doing the bidding of power, first ecclesiastical power, then monarchical power, and finally aristocratic power. The secular, even bawdy plays of medieval England could not endure the disapproval of the Church. Thelwall concedes that artists of great power have prostituted their extraordinary talents, have produced great works of art that nevertheless uphold established values. So smothering is the ideological hold on the theater from medieval times through the Restoration that Thelwall depicts the Puritan suppression of the theaters as an *understandable* error. Spenser, Shakespeare, Jonson, Dryden, Otway, are all court poets. Although he does not elaborate on how plays are able to do this, he nevertheless asserts that some plays also subvert court values. He is especially fond of the seditious meanings in Jonson's *Sejanus* (in which he sees the fate of Robespierre played out) and Otway's *Venice Preserved* (which played a role in his own treason trial). Thelwall has his highest hopes for the literary market, an institution that frees artists from prostituting their talent to the state or church. The writer can now appeal directly to the public for support. Thelwall is remarkably negative about the drama of the past and remarkably sanguine about the present and future. He more than anyone knows that the literary market is subject to political repression and other forms of manipulation. In fact, he protests against London's having only two licensed theaters. The success of Paine and Thelwall, not to mention Godwin and the Jacobin novel, is the foundation for the optimism about the literary market in the 1790s. The literary public sphere, until repression and reaction had achieved their goals, sustained a high degree of critical thinking. Also, we have seen again the important metaphor of prostitution, and we will see it yet again in the third part.

Thelwall's Funeral Oration for Hardy

The last instance of radical oratory we will examine here is Thelwall's funeral oration in 1832 for Thomas Hardy, shoemaker, friend, fellow treason-trial defendant, and former LCS colleague.[34] Nearly seventy years old, Thelwall is the only eulogist at Hardy's grave before a crowd of twenty to forty thousand mourners. The funeral of Hardy was a major political event.

---

34. I am relying upon the account in the *Morning Chronicle* reprinted in the *Life of John Thelwall*, Appendix, No. 9, 430–36.

Intemperance, Oratory, and Voicelessness

The fourteen mourning coaches went from Drury Lane to Charing Cross (where a large working-class delegation joined the procession behind the flag of the National Union of the Working Classes), the Strand, Fleet Street, Ludgate Hill, Old Bailey, Newgate Street, St. Martin's, Aldersgate Street, Old Street, City Road (where five thousand people joined the procession), and finally to Bunhill Fields, where Blake and other Dissenters were buried. One would love to know the behind-the-scenes negotiations by a divided reform movement that resulted in Thelwall's being the solitary eulogist. Francis Place's National Political Union, of which Thelwall was a member, was well represented at the head of the procession, but the rival Union led by the Rotunda radicals was immediately behind the carriages. Sir Francis Burdett's carriage, but not Sir Francis himself, was in the procession (Hardy was one of Burdett's pensioners).[35] (Thelwall felt so estranged from Burdett that he wrote to Place in hopes of effecting a reconciliation that does not seem to have taken place.)[36] Orator Hunt's carriage, with Hunt himself inside, was present, however. Only four months earlier during the tumultuous "May days" of the Reform agitation, when working-class support for the Bill was the most militant, Place had orchestrated what amounted to preparations for outright revolution after the House of Lords turned down Lord Grey's Bill, thus blurring the lines between his own "moderate" Union and the Rotunda ultras. In October there was still something of an afterglow following the passage of the Reform Bill in June, but there were tensions that would become open divisions that split the movement. Aristocratic reformers like Hobhouse and Burdett in the first Reform election of 1832 refused to

---

35. Melville Watson Patterson, *Sir Francis Burdett and His Times (1770–1844)*, 2 vols. (London: Macmillan, 1931): 2: 589–90.

36. See the letter from Thelwall to Place, British Library mss. 65666 Add. 37949, ff. 291–92 (28 October 1832). To effect the reconciliation, Thelwall suggested that Burdett chair the upcoming anniversary dinner on 5 November for the treason trial acquittal celebration. According to the *London Times* (6 November 1832), Thelwall made an eloquent tribute to the recently deceased Thomas Hardy at the thirty-eighth anniversary. The article does not mention Sir Francis Burdett who, if he had chaired, would have been mentioned certainly. In Thelwall's speech he notes his own ill health and poverty (too poor to live in London), but focuses mostly on Hardy and urges people to purchase Hardy's recently published book to provide assistance to Hardy's sister. The old editor of the *Black Dwarf*, Jonathan Wooler, made a speech at the meeting in favor of radical reform. Sir Francis, an opponent of universal suffrage, might not have been welcome at this meeting. Earlier in 1832 Thelwall complains to Place of Burdett's neglect, as Burdett would not contribute to a subscription to publish one of Thelwall's projects. Thelwall felt he had a right in his final years to some kind of financial assistance from wealthy reformers. See Thelwall's letter to Place of 20 March 1832, British Library, BL 65667, Add. 37950 ff. 131–32.

endorse the NPU "pledge" composed by Francis Place and designed to pressure candidates (pressure for pledges began in July 1832 and was directed especially against the rate-paying clause in the Bill that excluded all working-class voters). In fact, Place supported a candidate other than Hobhouse, a Colonel Evans who eventually (in 1833) won.[37] After 1832 Burdett drifted toward Toryism, while Hobhouse's opposition to any further parliamentary reform made him unacceptable to both Place and the Rotunda radicals. Rotunda radicals suspected that the Bill was a betrayal of the working class but the full bitterness of the reality of that betrayal would not be felt until later.

Thelwall's formidable rhetorical task was to say something meaningful—as the *only* speaker of the day—to a very large mixed crowd riven by competing ideological commitments. His oration accomplishes four things: he makes a tribute to Hardy's moral courage as the LCS founder and first treason-trial defendant; he monumentalizes both Hardy's acquittal and the political ideals for which he and the LCS struggled; he dramatizes his own—Thelwall's—role in 1794 as the sole surviving treason-trial defendant; finally, he highlights political repression, using Hardy and himself as examples of reformers willing to risk their lives for the cause in order to commemorate Hardy's (and his own) political life as exemplary for future generations of reformers. Thelwall assumes that the 1832 Bill is not the complete realization of reform; accordingly, he gestures to both the Rotunda radicals and the NPU by saying that "as an abstract right—however it might be affected by expediency—no one could deny the abstract justice of Universal Suffrage" (LJT 433). As many expected the new reformed parliament to move quickly toward universal suffrage, these words were commonplace, but they also illustrate the real chasm between those like Burdett and Hobhouse and the proponents of the working-class franchise. For Thelwall the Bill was neither a betrayal nor a fulfillment of Reform ideals but a meaningful, partial step toward democracy. In October 1832 another kind of eulogist might have used this opportunity to declare the Bill as the triumph of Hardy's ideals and the realization of his goals. Thelwall's emphasis could not have been more different. He stresses rather the necessity of struggle, the reality of political repression, the inevitability of deadly contests between power and reformers. One kind of monument that Thelwall presents to the crowd is the twelve

---

37. Graham Wallas, *The Life of Francis Place (1771–1854)*, 3rd ed. (New York: Alfred A. Knopf, 1919), 327.

names of the jurors who acquitted Hardy engraved in gold on a purple tablet. Another kind is the example of Hardy's life, which teaches the perennial lesson of political courage and resistance.

The speech begins with a request for silence, to permit the many thousands to hear Thelwall's words. It is difficult to imagine nowadays an unamplified voice strong enough to reach over twenty thousand auditors, but contemporary reports about Thelwall's powerful voice come from many sources. The first part of the speech, the tribute to Hardy's moral character, plays on and against aristocratic assumptions: "There is a nobility of birth and station—there is a higher nobility of intellect; there is a nobility yet higher, of strong moral principle, which attaching itself to the welfare and happiness of mankind; labours for the general benefit and the promotion of the great interests of the human species" (LJT 431). This concise inversion of the actual class hierarchy redefines a shoemaker's moral deeds as more "noble" than aristocratic lineage and bourgeois accomplishments. Precisely after these words the crowd utters its first exclamation ("hear, hear, hear"). He seals rhetorically the monumentalizing of the twelve jurors' names on the tablet by concentrating invectives against the Pitt government—and all other "corrupt governments" that act similarly, eliciting the second exclamation from the crowd (LJT 433). He then cleverly links the twelve jurors with the twelve defendants. The effect had to have been dramatic, as there was a stark contrast between the twelve jurors who existed only as names on a tablet and the twelve defendants, only one of whom was still alive, the orator himself.

The theme of the solitary survivor he weaves next into a polemic against political repression by telling the story of Burchell, the court official in 1794 who witnessed the government's attempt to pack the treason trial jury. Thelwall uses this other survivor of 1794 to work up the crowd's indignation against unconstitutional tactics by the government; the crowd reacted three separate times. Thelwall saves his most powerful effects for the conclusion, when he makes a transition from the solitary court official whose conscience provoked him to disclose the ugly truth about the government for which he worked to the inevitability of martyrdom. He declares that "no man has a right to agitate the country against the existing government, unless he is resolved to carry his life in his hand, and is ready to lay it down at an instant's warning, rather than apostatize from his principles, or even retire in the hour of peril" (LJT 435). At this point the crowd, according to the *Morning Chronicle* reporter, would have broken out into a loud acclamation were it not "subdued" by the context of the funeral. This is somewhat self-serving, but Thelwall clearly means to use as an object lesson all the defendants who were willing to die, not just himself. To illustrate the meaning of perseverance, he reminds the crowd of his struggles in 1796–97 during his provincial lecture tour, the "seven times" he avoided violent attacks against his person. Although he petitioned parliament through the offices of Burdett to stop these attacks, the government responded by rewarding one of his tormentors, Captain Roberts, with a promotion (LJT 435–36). The aristocratic government was "determined, at whatever cost, to put a stop to the spirit of reform . . . [it was] resolved to drown the voice of reason in a torrent of blood" (LJT 436). Hardy, Thelwall, and the LCS, then, created a "voice" that was always in danger of being silenced and that had finally effected a partial reform forty years later.

The final emphasis of his speech is on struggle and conflict, persevering against the threat of violence, resisting the temptation of apostasy and retreat. Thelwall could have adopted the tones of congratulatory triumph in October 1832, but chose instead to monumentalize the kind of resistance the Chartists would be soon putting into practice. It is fortunate that Thelwall did not adopt the tones of self-pity that he sometimes used in letters to his friend Place. Rather, Thelwall rose to the occasion and made a speech worthy of Thomas Hardy, himself, and the experiences of the LCS.

Voicelessness

The danger to which Thelwall's funeral oration for Hardy alluded was voicelessness, the condition of wanting to speak but not being able to do so. Voicelessness is also the effect of a degraded public sphere, the debilitation of structures—press, education, meetings, lectures, pamphlets, leisure, associations, protests, petitions—by which an insurgent group might find its voice and articulate its ideas. There is also the voicelessness of those with speech impediments, which affliction Thelwall studied and treated with much effectiveness. He went from being the most famous political lecturer in Britain to the most famous professor of elocution and speech therapy. The political repression drove him to study and earn a living from the techniques of speaking. It is striking that he found such success in his new profession. At his London Institute, which was at once a residential and day school as well as a clinic, he taught and treated adults and children for very lucrative fees. By 1813 he was prosperous enough to have a library stocked with close to four thousand volumes.[38] He had achieved middle-class social status because of his Institute, sending his sons to Cambridge, and earning enough money to be able to purchase the reform newspaper, *The Champion*, in 1818. One might wonder how helping young vicars, barristers, and MPs to hone their public speaking skills promoted democratic political ideals. Had Thelwall concluded his career with the Institute he would not be as interesting a man as he was. He instead launched into still another career as a public radical at age fifty-four and found himself nearing sixty years of age and facing the prospects of imprisonment yet again for political transgressions.

The Technology of Voice

Thelwall's ideas on oratory have not been given the attention they deserve. His writing on prosody, or "rhythmus," as Thelwall called it, occasioned an expert on the history of English prosody, Thomas Stewart Osmond, to exclaim "how much there is to admire in Thelwall's work."[39] Following the ideas of Joshua Steele, the pioneering prosodist of the eighteenth century, Thelwall rejected the Augustan correctness of syllabic meter for a Romantically organic sense of accentual meter. Every sentence, verse or prose, he noted, has its own "rhythmus."[40] Thelwall has a prominent place in modern histories of the elocutionary movement;[41] for F. W. Haberman, Thelwall "was the outstanding speech therapist and the foremost lecturer and teacher of elocution in his day."[42]

The political repression he struggled against in the 1790s can be renamed as a speech impediment or the condition of speechlessness, two problems Thelwall approached after 1801 as a speech therapist and scientist of lan-

---

38. John Thelwall, *Plan and Object of Mr. Thelwall's Institute* (London: J. McCreery, 1813), 10. The *Plan and Object* lists prices; residential school fees ranged from 200 to 300 guineas per annum. Treatment for a single speech impediment was 5 guineas.

39. T. S. Osmond, *English Metrists: Being a Sketch of English Prosodical Criticism from Elizabethan Times to the Present Day* (1921; New York: Phaeton Press, 1968), 128.

40. Osmond, *English Metrists*, 91.

41. Robin Thelwall, "The Phonetic Theory of John Thelwall (1764–1834)," in Eugénie J. A. Henderson and R. E. Asher, eds., *Towards a History of Phonetics* (Edinburgh: Edinburgh University Press, 1981), 188–89.

42. F. W. Haberman, "John Thelwall: His Life, His School and His Theory of Elocution," in Raymond F. Hawes, ed., *Historical Studies of Rhetoric and Rhetoricians* (Ithaca: Cornell University Press, 1961), 197. The original article appeared in *Quarterly Journal of Speech* 33 (1947): 292–98.

The Voice of the People

guage. Several political cartoons at the time symbolize the political repression with an image of a man's lips shackled shut.[43] Living out at a literal level the very rhythm of his rhetoric, Thelwall after 1801 avoided legal difficulties and loyalist violence. Early in the *Letter to Henry Cline* he refers to the rhetoric of intemperance: "The excentric fire of youth hurried me away to other [nonscientific] topics; with an impetuosity, which maturer judgement may regret, though integrity cannot repent of the principle." Scientific study gave way to "the more ardent rays of popular enthusiasm" (LHC 2) and "popular" politics, to which of course he would return a decade later, eventually getting arrested for seditious libel at the behest of the Constitutional Society, the so-called Bridge-Street Gang of right-wing activists. Thelwall was again "intemperate." The ultimate danger of being intemperate was to be deprived entirely of speech, a voice, and public language.

A text published five years before the *Letter to Henry Cline* makes an important transition from political to "elocutionary" discourse. The *Trident of Albion* is not a political recantation, even though it features prominently several tributes to Lord Nelson.[44] Thelwall steers the popular nationalist sentiment in favor of Nelson and against Napoleon away from aristocratic and royalist ideology by framing the war against France as a traditional English battle against foreign invasion, thus tapping into the constitutionalist idiom of Saxon democracy and the Norman yoke. Thelwall's explanation and defense of elocution's importance in this work, moreover, describe the apparently apolitical oratorical science as covertly Jacobin. He holds that elocution, the science and art of speaking publicly, is a universally teachable skill (T 10). Accessible to all, elocution performs a fusion of print and oral culture (T 4) while at the same time turning the act of "reading" into a social practice primarily oral, social, and popular rather than visual, individualistic, and private (T 42). Thelwall envisions not just political speeches but an oral transmission of important texts, public readings as regular social events. Also anti-elitist is Thelwall's repudiation of the ineffability topos, as he proclaims that "still does the voice of Nature cry within us, to give latitude to this artless language" (T 21). One can learn to express the full range of one's own

---

43. See, for example, the print entitled "A Free Born Englishman!" from 1819 in the British Museum (catalogue number B. M. 13287) that is reprinted in Michael Wynn Jones, *The Cartoon History of Britain* (New York: Macmillan, 1971), 123.

44. *The Trident of Albion, An Epic Effusion; And an Oration on the Influence of Elocution on Martial Enthusiasm; with an Address to the Shade of Nelson* (Liverpool: G. F. Harris, 1805). Hereafter T.

emotions. The best of Athenian classical culture is not only teachable to all but is also something that can be appropriated now and turned to practical use. Suggesting that Liverpool could be another Athens, Thelwall tries to harness the patriotism evoked by Nelson's death to a democratic renewal sparked by a popularized classical oratory (T 45–46). Even when condemning Napoleon, Thelwall criticizes him from the left by citing Bonaparte's victimization of Toussaint, the Jacobin leader of the slave revolt in San Domingo (T 34). Another consequence of the Enlightenment universalism, however, appears in the summary of his proposed twenty-fourth lecture, where he will speak on: "Provincialisms, Vulgarisms, Cockneyisms, Hibernianisms, Scotticisms" (T 64). Thelwall could envision a city-state that would remain within the paradigm of universal reason, but local, regional, and class varieties of the English language seemed to be simply "error" rather than difference.

The *Trident of Albion* claims that Thelwall has "neither taste nor leisure for political disquisition" (vi), but the essay is marked everywhere by politics. Similarly, *Letter to Henry Cline* adopts an apolitical scientific stance only to retain political allegory.

His writing about oratory, speech impediments, and language in the *Letter to Henry Cline*, although not ostensibly political, allegorizes Jacobinism in much the same way that Blake, Wordsworth, and Coleridge also allegorized politics in their ostensibly apolitical writing. The *Anti-Jacobin Review*, however, did not detect any Jacobinism in its review of the *Letter to Henry Cline*; rather, it used the instance of *Henry Cline* and other elocutionary works to announce that Thelwall was now a loyal Briton whose opposition to France had proved his worthiness. This exempted him from being scapegoated as an evil Jacobin. The discussion of his elocutionary works was sympathetic.[45] The *Monthly Review* applauds Thelwall's turn from radical politics to "useful" intellectual labors, but criticizes nervously the actual content of the elocutionary writings and warns Thelwall not to "materialize the operations of the human mind."[46] The moderately liberal *Monthly* reviewer is not nearly as convinced as the *Anti-Jacobin* reviewer that Thelwall is no longer dangerous.

Cline, a friend from 1788 who testified at Thelwall's treason trial, Horne Tooke's physician, was a prominent medical professor, one of the many

---

45. *Anti-Jacobin Review* 40 (1811): 298–304.
46. *Monthly Review* 70 (1813): 293–305.

medical professionals on the political left. Addressing a letter to Cline was not an ideologically neutral act because Cline's political sympathies were well known. The very loose structure of a letter permits Thelwall to wander from topic to topic in the "eccentric" style of the earlier *Peripatetic*. Moreover, after the letter proper he has an "appendix" almost as lengthy as the letter itself into which he places miscellaneous essays. By reproducing some of the Table of Contents I can show that the sequence of ideas is neither entirely arbitrary nor logically overdetermined.

> *Union of Physiological and Elocutionary Science, p. 1. Temporary aberration from Scientific pursuits, 2. Uses of retirement, 3. Discovery of the Physical principle of rhythmus (Milton and Dryden), 4. Numbers of the Paradise Lost, 8. Application of the Discovery to treatment of Impediments—Harmony of utterance and composition—Oratorical utterance—Health, &c. 9. Case of three brothers in Brecknock, with enunciative Impediments, 11. Treatment and Cure, 13. Causes of delay in more extensive application of the principle, 14. First Idea of a Scientific Course of Lectures on Elocution, 15.*

Classifying these different topics, one finds philosophical science, personal narrative, literary criticism, elocution, and the case study. Under one of these five rubrics goes almost everything in the *Letter to Henry Cline*. The exact sequence of any one of these topics is not always predictable. The actual letter to Cline is roughly chronological, as it traces the development of Thelwall's ideas as they grew, step by step. Another epistle by a Romantic poet addressed to a good friend written about the same time focused on the growth of the poet's mind: Wordsworth's *Prelude* also has a miscellaneous quality.

Thelwall insists that both poetic harmony and speech defects are physiological, that natural laws govern poetry as much as stuttering, lisping, and speechlessness. Poetic taste and elocutionary clarity are not mysterious accidents but objects of scientific study that are subject to improvement. Running through the *Letter to Henry Cline* is a strong conviction that the disorders and diseases of human utterances are correctable. The "omnipotency of mental energy" applies only to poetry and speech (LHC 33), but one can hear in the scientific enthusiasm the political Jacobinism that has had to go underground and express itself disguisedly.

A literary form shaped by Thelwall is the case history. The first case history establishes a recurrent pattern where he seemed to stumble into a situation that at first seemed utterly obscure only to yield later to Thelwall's expert analysis and treatment. "The two brothers from Brecknock" could be the title. "A hatter, in Brecknock, into whose shop I had occasion to go, having heard that I had been an orator, and probably believing (for such was the superstition of that enlightened neighbourhood) that I was a bit of a conjuror, also,—thought me a proper person, to whom to prefer his piteous complaint, of an affliction that visited his family. 'He had two as fine boys as ever eyes were clapped on; but their mouths were not made like other people's mouths: they could not speak.'" One appreciates the tension between Thelwall and the Welsh hatter whose own idiom is represented vividly in the quoted sentences, especially the "clapped on" verb. Britain's greatest radical orator who is unable to make political speeches finds his vocation in curing those who "could not speak."

The speechlessness is caused somewhat by neglected bad teeth but mostly by "habit and inattention." By "setting them to read, and marking the elements in which they were most defective, I soon perceived—that the whole chaos of their speech (for such it very nearly was) consisted in the absolute deficiency of one elementary sound, and the imperfection and confused misapplication of two or three more." He prescribes a simple, repetitive regimen suited to the abilities of the boys and within a short time the two brothers from Brecknock can speak (LHC 11–13). Thelwall's procedure is not mysterious. He examines all the organs that produce human sound, listens to the sounds produced, knows the mechanical prerequisites for the production of each sound, and invents exercises that produce the desired sounds. He breaks down a complex whole into its parts, ignores extraneous distractions, and creates solutions that are simple and quick.

Not all Thelwall's cases yielded happy results as easily as his first case, but most of the case histories follow the same pattern. A young woman from Edinburgh whose "face would become blackened, the eyes convulsed, and whole frame agitated to the most distressing extent imaginable" becomes, after a dozen Thelwall lessons, a fluent speaker (LHC 63–64).

Some of the causes operating through the physiological are "moral" or "intellectual."

> It is curious, also, to observe the various and even contradictory circumstances (all connected with the passions and operations of the mind) under which these convulsive actions [speech disorders],

occasionally, take place. I have known some gentlemen whose impediments almost entirely disappeared in the presence of gay assemblages and female society; some, who could never get out a syllable, if there were a beautiful woman in company. Some have but little difficulty except in the presence of strangers;—others are never so seriously affected as before their own parents, or the persons under whose authority they are placed. (LHC 68–69)

Although he is willing to use whatever purely physical remedies that might work, he observes that "no treatment merely physical . . . ever produces any thing more than temporary relief: for medicine was never yet radical in the removal of diseases of the mind. The imagination, the judgement, and the passions, require other physicians than the pupils of Galen and Hippocrates" (LHC 70). Thelwall, like Freud, is a keen observer of symptoms that he cautiously and skeptically subjects to the rigors of understanding. The political allegory works here too as well, as Thelwall points to "radical" causes of some diseases that cannot be cured by superficial treatments guided by superficial knowledge.

Another consequence of his professional work was to devote much time, attention, and intellectual passion to the disabled, like the blind boy whose speechlessness Thelwall cured (LHC 86–98), or the poor man speechless from epilepsy (a disease Thelwall's own brother had) (LHC 99–101), or other speechless beings who are described as "idiots" until Thelwall develops an effective therapy. He folds into his account several letters and case histories of John Gough (1757–1825) of Kendal, a blind speech therapist who is in effect Thelwall's collaborator, his Fliess or Breuer (although Thelwall's collaboration was much less troubled than those of Freud).[47] Gough coins a beautiful phrase that captures the spirit of their project of helping those with impaired speech: "mutilated talents" (LHC 121). The apparent mutes and "idiots" are invariably capable of full utterance if one only discovers the path to the center of their neglected powers. The political allegory here is also obvious. Speechlessness is typically a consequence of neglect that reformed and rational education ameliorates. As a therapist Thelwall scorns any versions of paternalistic dependence and fashions therapeutic strategies that permit as much independence as possible. There were several cases where the

---

47. Thelwall made original discoveries on the role of the larynx in the production of sound. See Robin Thelwall, "The Phonetic Theory of John Thelwall (1764–1834)," in Henderson and Asher, ed., *Towards a History of Phonetics*, 188–89.

well-meaning but debilitating efforts of a loving parent to help his or her child prompted Thelwall's stern remedy for correction. He prescribed that the diseased or disabled person "do every thing for herself, that she could possibly do" (LHC 137).

Thelwall's affinity with the language-impaired—he lisped when he was young—is similar to the poet John Clare's affinity with animals. It is evident in his case histories that he has an empathetic identification with those he helps, but that the sympathy does not interfere with effective treatment. Each successful case is another allegorical illustration of self-improvement and the rational application of knowledge.

Voicelessness: The Second Silencing of Thelwall

Thelwall, who used the pages of his *Champion* to promote radical reform in 1818–21, abandoned the newspaper precisely at the point the Constitutional Association—the "Bridge-Street Gang"—instigated a seditious libel indictment to court. Thelwall's case was never brought to trial, perhaps only because he disengaged himself from the newspaper. A revealing episode in the history of the *Champion* is Thelwall's writing on the Cato Street Conspiracy, the attempted coup by a group of Spenceans who were manipulated by government agents. What Thelwall wrote in the *Champion* about the Cato Street Conspiracy might have decisively aroused "Dr. Slop"—John Stoddart (1773–1856) of the *New Times*—to call for Thelwall's prosecution and the closing down of the newspaper he edited, perhaps the first important move against Thelwall that led eventually to his arrest. The *New Times* played a key role in setting up the Cato Street rebels because it printed a false notice of a cabinet dinner, where the rebels planned to assassinate the government ministers.

The story of Cato Street can be told briefly: With the most experienced Spenceans in jail (Dr. Watson and Wedderburn) or estranged from the movement (Evans), leadership passed temporarily to notoriously belligerent and impulsive Arthur Thistlewood, a veteran of the Spa Fields riot, the 1817 treason trial, and a year in jail for having challenged Sidmouth to a duel. A significant minority of the radical movement after Peterloo was willing to take up arms against what it deemed a murderous and illegitimate government. Just how large this group was or how widespread the revulsion against the government is very difficult to determine, but it is indisputable that in

Scotland, Yorkshire, and London some radicals did indeed take part in "risings." It is also not in dispute that government spies acted as *agents provocateurs*. Whether Thistlewood and his colleagues would have gone as far as they did, without the assistance and encouragement of the spies, toward actually trying to assassinate the cabinet is not at all certain. The spies encouraged the conspiracy to become far more serious than it would have otherwise.[48] As the government knew all along what the conspirators were going to do, it was an easy matter to catch them long before they tried to attack the ministers. One of the arresting police agents was killed during the raid, but the authorities seized or later captured the principal agents of the Cato Street Conspiracy in late February of 1820. After a perfunctory trial, five of them—Thistlewood, Ings, Tidd, Brunt, and Davidson—were hanged as traitors, and others were transported.

The lead article in the *Champion* for 26 February was on Lovel's recent assassination of the Duke of Berri, an unpopular member of the French royal family. Thelwall phrases his condemnation of the assassination thus: if Berri's assassination was bad, Peterloo was worse. Moreover, the murder of the duke is symptomatic of "ultra-royalist" evil, in which England too is complicit. Political violence, however unjustifiable, is symptomatic of social injustice. "There is no safety for princes, or for governments, but in their respect for the principles of liberty, or in the affections and veneration of their people" (129).

Even without Cato Street Thelwall's lead article was bold. It occurred, after all, after the Six Acts, when many prominent reformers—Henry Hunt, Francis Burdett, John Hobhouse, Richard Carlile, and Thomas J. Wooler—were indicted, jailed, or on trial. The year 1820 (the Six Acts) was looking like a repetition of 1795 (the Gagging Acts). Cato Street and the immediate prospect of new treason trials evoked for Thelwall the year 1794, the date of his own treason trial. That he realized his danger as soon as he heard the news is evident from the two postscripts he added to the Duke of Berri article. The first postscript conforms to a familiar Thelwall pattern of rhetorical equivocation, nervously condemning the attempted assassination as

---

48. Still a useful source that contains the newspaper reports, the trial transcripts, and other materials is George Theodore Wilkinson, *An Authentic History of the Cato-Street Conspiracy* (London: Thomas Kelly, 1820; rpt. New York: Arno Press, 1972). Thompson's MWC, 700–706, and Iorwerth Prothero, *Artisans and Politics in Early Nineteenth-Century London: John Gast and His Times*, 127–31, and Worrall, *Radical Culture*, 187–200 are all excellent on the Conspiracy.

"horrible and detestable" but refusing to retract a word of his Berri essay; he even reiterates his main point that political violence comes from injustice. The second postscript displays more composure, as he identifies Thistlewood as a notorious figure in radical London well known for his irrational politics. From the very first report on Cato Street Thelwall urges a cautious skepticism toward the government charges because he suspects the foul work of spies and *agents provocateurs*. He even inserts a remarkable anonymous report that turns out to be very reliable, pointing out the involvement of spies and the government's prior knowledge of the rebels' activities. I suspect the author was probably George Cullen, a Spencean who was formerly with the LCS and was friendly with both Thelwall and Thomas Hardy.[49] "May not the moment for the detection or development of the plot (whatever it was) have been thus critically determined upon for a grand theatrical effect? — as a dashing, electioneering maneuvre? — or for the sake of its bearing, in the sway of passion and sympathy, upon some approaching trials? — As the popgun plot was so opportunely promulgated on the very eve of the important State Trials of 1794!" (131).

Thelwall does not waver from the approach he takes initially. First, he condemns political assassination but encourages his readers to be skeptical of the government and its use of spies and agents. Next, he does not let his readers forget Peterloo, the 1794 State Trials, or the true origins of political violence. Cato Street not only brings Thelwall back in memory to his own 1794 but also threatens to become for him the first few steps leading to yet another confrontation with the repressive power of the state. It surely was no accident that in March right after Cato Street the *New Times* launches its campaign to shut down the *Champion* and punish Thelwall.[50] At a political dinner in the Crown and Anchor Tavern attended by over six hundred people, after a highly stylized procession through London by the radical heroes Burdett and Hobhouse, Thelwall makes one of the speeches. His theme is liberty of the press, and he cites the dangers, from outright hanging to transportation, for exercising what should be a constitutional right.[51]

However fearful of prosecution, Thelwall acted boldly, provocatively addressing two lead-article "letters" to the Lord Chief Justice Abbott, the principal magistrate for the Cato Street trials, immediately before and even

---

49. J. Ann Hone discusses Cullen briefly in *For the Cause of Truth: Radicalism in London 1796–1821* (Oxford: Clarendon Press, 1982), 228.
50. See the *Champion* (25 March 1820): 196–97.
51. *Champion* (8 April 1820): 230–31.

during the trials. The "intemperate" gesture is his addressing Abbott in a tone that assumes equality; it almost does not matter that Thelwall's rhetoric is otherwise respectful toward the judge. Thelwall reminds the chief justice of the basic rights that the defendants possess simply by being citizens, and lectures him on "the legal and constitutional Antiquities of our country" and the legal wisdom of "our venerable ancestors" ([22 April 1820]: 257). He also alludes to the government's use of spies and agents without discussing them directly—which would be illegal under Abbott's ruling not to discuss the trial in print until the trials were completed—by returning to 1794 and describing the activities of spies in great detail (258–59). The most important feature of the letter is the tone of absolute moral disapproval of spies and *agents provocateurs*. Thelwall wanted to influence the outcome of a trial whose verdict was doubted by almost no one from the time the men were arrested. To realize just how provocative Thelwall himself was by writing in this vein one must remember that the nonradical press simply portrayed the Cato Street revolutionaries as subhuman monsters—atheists and deists—who deserved the worst kind of punishment.[52] The conservative *Courier* attacked the *Morning Chronicle* for being insufficiently harsh toward the conspirators, and the *Times*, even before the trial and presentation of evidence, called for a "purification of society" and speedy punishment of the conspirators (3 March 1820). In the second letter Thelwall continues to scold the Chief Justice for prohibiting any publications about the trial until the trials are completed ([29 April 1820]: 273–74). That these letters did not lead to Thelwall's prosecution suggests Abbott chose to ignore them.

After the Cato Street convictions Thelwall is legally permitted to comment directly on the case in the weekly editorial essay, called "The Mirror of the Week." The strongest criticism of the government comes in the summary of Thistlewood's case. Thelwall portrays Thistlewood as far more humane than the spy Edwards, who orchestrated the plot for the government: Thistlewood refuses to blow up the House of Parliament as Edwards suggests because in the explosion innocent people would have died; he also refuses Edwards's suggestion that they attack the party given by the Spanish Ambassador because women present might be harmed. That the government immorally employed spies reflects the moral tone of the society after Peterloo, an event that has degraded the popular morality to the extent that now

---

52. Wilkinson in his *An Authentic History of the Cato-Street Conspiracy* consistently stresses the irreligious character of the conspirators and assumes that only those who were not Christians could have acted as they did.

assassination is an openly discussed political option (as it was not before Peterloo); Peterloo has "metamorphosed poor starving wretches from sufferers into fiends: not many, however, we trust, into such fiends as these" ([29 April 1820]: 280–81). After the executions of the five men on 1 May, Thelwall displays more sympathy toward them than the "fiend" imagery would suggest possible, but the brief comparison of Thistlewood and Edwards already humanizes the former while it demonizes the latter. The government is the truly fiendish party.

Even the hostile accounts of the executions leave a favorable portrait of the Cato Street rebels, who showed strength, courage, and passionate feelings for their families as they faced death.[53] Thelwall wants his readers to contrast the punishment of these five men with the complete exoneration of the men responsible for Peterloo. Instead of joining the chorus of moral condemnation of the rebels, he directs his moral outrage at the government. An apostrophe early in the essay calls attention to the Manchester magistrates, yeomanry, and government ministers who perpetrated and sanctioned Peterloo, a greater crime than the spy-engendered plot ([7 May 1820]: 292). He develops further his idea about popular morality being corrupted by Peterloo. "The bruising matches of the street vulgar have had always a sort of chivalrous honour and generosity in them"—even during the Gordon Riots of 1780, when "not an assassination was perpetrated." If the popular morality has become bloodier, the government is mostly to blame (293).

About a year later, almost to the day, Thelwall found himself arrested and jailed overnight. Charles Murray of the ultra-loyalist Constitutional Society brought an *ex officio* information for seditious libel against the *Champion*'s editor, specifically for an editorial essay on Burdett and Peterloo that was actually an arbitrarily chosen text, neither more nor less seditious than Thelwall's other editorials (*Champion* [5 May 1821]: 274–77). For two months afterward the *Champion* attacked Murray and the "Bridge-Street Gang," as well as "Dr. Slop" (John Stoddart), who ran the *New Times*. These were perilous times for radical journalists. Jonathan Wooler of the *Black Dwarf* was sentenced to fifteen months in Warwick jail in the same month (June) in which John Hunt of the *Examiner* went on trial for a libel against the House of Commons. The Queen Caroline affair provided some protective cover for radical agitation, but not everyone was as successful in avoiding

---

53. Even in Wilkinson's book the conspirators in their final days are portrayed fairly sympathetically.

legal punishment as William Hone, whose satires with Cruikshank's prints were spectacularly popular in 1820.[54]

Thelwall's day in court took place in December, almost half a year after the initial arrest. The government intimidated the radical press, not simply by jailing and prosecuting editors; the very *threat* of being called to trial while a charge of seditious libel was over an editor's head was sufficiently damaging in itself. The jury that had been impaneled for Thelwall's trial, it turned out, had been "tainted" by the presence of members of the same Constitutional Association that had brought the information against Thelwall. The judge for Thelwall's case was none other than the same justice Abbott who presided over the Cato Street trials, who passed the sentence on Wedderburn, and who was the addressee of his two *Champion* letters to the chief justice in April 1820. So damaging was the *prospect* of being convicted for libel that Thelwall came close to permitting a trial to go forward even with Constitutional Associators on the jury, because "nothing could be so ruinous to me, as to have a prosecution of this kind suspended over my head, from term to term, in this manner." Thelwall finally agreed with his lawyer not to be tried by the tainted jury, but he could be tried later (*Champion* [15 December 1821]: 797–98).

He never was tried for the libel, but he evidently disengaged himself from the *Champion* after December 1821. The *Champion* that was published in the first half of 1822 has few signs of Thelwall's active participation, even if he still technically owned the newspaper. Conviction for seditious libel under the Six Acts could mean "banishment," like the fate of Joseph Gerrald, whom he lamented in the *Tribune* lecture in 1795. A logical inference is that he left the *Champion* and radical journalism out of fear of being convicted of seditious libel. He escaped being tried for libel thanks to a technicality.

Conclusion

Thelwall's own career continued for more than a decade after the Cato Street Conspiracy, but his reaction to it illustrated that he had not lost his political courage. He was driven out of radical activism by political repres-

---

54. The Whigs and the reform movement, including Thelwall, defended Queen Caroline when the new king, George IV, tried to divorce in 1820. See Thomas Laqueur, "The Queen Caroline Affair: Politics as Art in the Reign of George IV," *Journal of Modern History* 54 (1982): 417–66.

sion once again, this time leaving the field of battle probably a little sooner than he would have twenty-some years earlier. Once again he retreated strategically and found other openings within the public sphere for his writing and speaking. His own radicalism was not identical with that of Spence and the Spenceans, who embody for Thelwall as did no other group the appeal and danger of "intemperance." Spence assumed the norms of popular culture as instinctively as Thelwall accepted the norms of Enlightenment culture. Spence would never write of people like the Cato Street radicals as "fiends" because he knew them so intimately; he could never create the distance from them that Thelwall readily achieves. On the other hand, Spence never enjoyed the large audiences that Thelwall had for most of his career. Spence paid a price for his particular kind of politics. Each radical has his characteristic strengths and weaknesses, which derive from the hard choices each had to make.

Thelwall's reaction to Cato Street illustrates also that the boundaries between the ultra-radicals and more moderate radicals were not impermeable. Thelwall reported sympathetically on the acquittal of Samuel Waddington, "Little Waddy," Robert Wedderburn's friend and Allen Davenport's colleague in the Spencean movement (*Champion* [23 September 1820]: 617). Five months after the Cato Street executions Thelwall still taunts the government with "intemperate" assertions that the magistrates behind Peterloo are more morally culpable than Thistlewood (*Champion* [21 October 1820]: 690). The *Champion* ([13 May 1820]: 314) also records Robert Wedderburn's sentencing somewhat laconically, in a brief report that includes a wonderful detail: "a person who happened to smile at the repetition of one of the offending [blasphemous] passages was ordered to quit the Court." That person could have been Thelwall. Even if Thelwall were not the offending party, his report was provocative. By inserting the detail without critical comment, a pointed comment is made.[55] There are times when a smile alone can be the voice of resistance.

Oratory for Thelwall was always a democratic instrument. Unlike privately read literature, oratory entails a live audience that constrains and inspires the orator, spontaneous composition, and a thicket of legal prescriptions. His great moment on the historical stage in the 1790s depended on the plebeian and middling-class public sphere, within which oral and

---

55. Another sign that the boundaries between "respectable" and ultra-radical politics were not absolute is that Francis Place helped Thomas Evans, Jr., get the editorship for the *Manchester Observer* in early 1820.

print-culture conventions mixed. His phonocentric emphasis did not lead to author-centered and individualistic literature, as a Derridean would expect, but rather to audience-centered writing and intertextuality. Phonocentric writing, unlike correct Augustan literature, came from the body, the same body that labored, congregated in groups, and was subject to intemperate impulses. The characteristic genre for such writing was the seditious allegory, the ambiguous expression shadowed by repression. Such allegories make use of whatever is conveniently at hand; topoi are recontextualized and invite further textual production rather than semantic closure.

part

3

Jacobin Allegory

Jacobin allegory is vividly illustrated by one of the charges against Thelwall at his treason trial, his behavior at Covent Garden during a performance of Otway's *Venice Preserved*. He led a round of vigorous applause after the Pierre-Jaffeir dialogue early in Act One, where the conspirators speak lines that were construed, because of the applause, to have immediate political reference. The applause would have stopped the play temporarily at the end of Pierre's speech:

> We've neither safety, unity, nor peace;
> The foundation's lost of common good.
> Justice is lame, as well as blind, amongst us;
> The laws (corrupted to the ends that make 'em)
> Serve but for instruments of some new tyranny,
> That every day starts up t' enslave us deeper.

The intervention of Thelwall's applause at such an early part of the play recontextualizes the entire drama. After two more nights of similarly political applause at the same lines, the play was "shelved." Thelwall remarks that the play, although intended to "pay court" to Charles the Second and satirize the Shaftesbury conspiracy, "was, at this time, converted into a provocative, not an antidote to jacobinism, and the following year, during the discussion of the 'Convention' bills, was played nightly, at Covent-garden Theatre, to thronged houses, who loudly applauded its popular sentences" (LJT 286). By recontextualization Thelwall inverts the meaning of the Otway play. Oral and print texts that do not have absolutely fixed meanings are available for political contention and power struggle, as repression both exerts constraints on literary expression and provides opportunities for it. The Covent Garden episode exemplifies allegory on the reception side of reading, an act of aggressive interpretation. Not all examples of political allegory are as transparent as that. Introduce the imminent danger of legal prosecution, complicate the expression with outright ambivalence, and a text's allegory could be only faintly detectable — real but heavily censored.

Thelwall wrote both kinds of allegory, as we have seen, using conventional symbols in his "Chaunticlere" lecture and "Sheepsheering" song, but deploying ambiguous rhetoric in essays such as *Letter to Henry Cline*. The works we will examine in this part of the study are allegorical of the writer's relation to place, both geographical and social. The title of one of his greatest works, *The Peripatetic*, evokes Hellenic philosophers discoursing out of doors; the novel itself reinforces and expands those associations to include the poet as wanderer, gypsy as vagrant, poet as vagrant, poet as gypsy, writer as sociological observer and political critic, poet as eccentric — wandering out of an established center. The phrase "pedestrian writing" now connotes imprecisely phrased and casually pondered work, but in the early nineteenth century it signifies a writer walking over land populated by the disenfranchised, breaking free from the restrictions of established genres and commonplace perceptions, allowing for and welcoming spontaneity and unforeseen experiences, testing ideas with personal observations, conversing with strangers, learning more about the world as it actually is and not as it has been represented. Just as the fictional Sylvanus Theophrastus and his friends make "eccentric excursions" outside London, the actual Thelwall made numerous pedestrian journeys, to which he alludes in his political lectures and essays.

One relation of writer to place is national identity. As we have seen, during his battles over treason and sedition he aligned himself with a native strain of political heroes (Hampden, Sidney, Milton) and traditions (Saxon democracy, English liberties). His Enlightenment rationalism, the basis of his opposition to empire, countered the dominant ethnocentric Englishness and Protestantism. In a number of works Thelwall opposed empire and imperialism as he tried to retain a nationalism without conquest. His second novel

(1801) forthrightly attacks West Indian imperialism, while his *Poems, Chiefly Written in Retirement* (1801) undermines imperialism more indirectly and aslant by staging a complex decentering of British identity that mirrors his own Welsh "exile" from London politics. In his epic *The Hope of Albion* he goes back to the Saxon king Edwin to explore the mythical transition from paganism to Christianity, and in his lyrical drama on King Arthur he chooses a Welsh locale for a clash between Briton and Saxon that allegorizes the "Norman yoke" myth. At the heart of both works is the search for compromise between the competing ideals of national peacefulness and national resistance to foreign conquest. Thelwall's own ancestors—Saxons who settled in Wales to escape the Normans; Catholics who only in the eighteenth century became Protestant—suggest the instability of national identity.

One last relation of writer to place is social class and status. From his earliest poetry to his most mature essay Thelwall never forgot his origins in the "shopocracy" as the son of a silk mercer and several times apprenticed member of the "middling class." Ambitious for the highest achievements in writing, Thelwall faced the same kinds of anxieties that afflicted other middling-class writers such as Keats and Blake. To write for money had long been established as honorable by Pope and Johnson, but Thelwall's early writing is filled with allusions to prostitution and social climbing, the very things Francis Jeffrey would later find Thelwall guilty of. In numerous narratives, allegorized and undisguised as well, Thelwall told the story of his highest ambition thwarted by fate. These "Thelwall the Obscure" narratives—in essays, fiction, drama, poetry, memoirs—lack the gloomy pathos of Hardy's novel, as Thelwall records numerous triumphs as well, but they similarly locate the source of greatest frustration in powers outside his own control. Whether they are self-serving and self-pitying rationalizations or lucid moments of self-awareness, Thelwall's autobiographies are socially typical. Shopkeepers like Thelwall step out of their assigned role when they write serious poetry and reflect critically on national politics. Whereas writing was one of several options for a young Wordsworth, Coleridge, Byron, and Shelley, Thelwall had to struggle for a writerly identity, just as did Blake, Keats, and Clare.

6

The Peripatetic Imagination

Thelwall's political lecturing was always linked with walking. In a *Tribune* speech of 1795 he reports that "I have been rambling, according to my wonted practice, in the true democratic way, on foot, from village to village, from pleasant hill to barren heath, recreating my mind with the beauties, and with the deformities of nature" (PEJ 151). He defends in another speech his "democratic excursions" on foot to learn about the "intermediate and lower orders" in the Isle of Wight, Portsmouth, Gosport, and Chicester. At the last place the dangers of pedestrian travel were forced upon him, as he just barely avoided a kidnapping attempt.[1] Such risks must be taken for the sake of truth because even "topographers" are subject to the influence of "power and privilege" and can misrepresent their landscapes (*PEJ* 250). Among Thelwall's writings there are three topographical works we will examine, the

1. *Tribune* 24 (4 September 1795): 2: 186-90.

novel *The Peripatetic* (1793) and two essays published in the *Monthly Magazine* (1797–1801). These illustrate his project of truthfully representing people within a place, a project that is complicated by his own position as observer and participant. As he imagines himself and his characters in a landscape, he inevitably brings in his own class position, social anxieties, and political agenda.

Eccentric Muse

The *Peripatetic* is a self-conscious work with extensive genre-mixing and digressive structure within Sternean sentimental conventions.[2] Like the *Lyrical Ballads*, the *Peripatetic* announces itself as an "experiment" without "the refuge of a single precedent, behind which its irregularities may be sheltered" (P 1:v). The genre mixing is its distinctive quality: it is constituted by "the novel, the sentimental journal, and the miscellaneous collection of essays and poetical effusions" (P 1:vi). Such mixing is governed by the attempt to reflect the processes of thinking and feeling, or the "association of ideas" (P 1:23). (Coleridge and Wordsworth, with a similarly empiricist interest in Hartleyan association, also tried to represent primary mental processes). The novel's various appropriations of classical culture, from the Latin inscriptions to the Latinate character names and the evocation of the Greek school of philosophy, are both within and outside of the idiom of genteel Enlightenment culture. The novel's classicism is so slanted democratically that it loses much of

2. Unfortunately I was not able to make use of Judith Thompson's new edition of *The Peripatetic* (Detroit: Wayne State University Press, 2001), but her essay on *The Peripatetic* is in print: " 'A Voice in the Representation': John Thelwall and the Enfranchisement of Literature," in Tilottama Rajan and Julia M. Wright, eds., *Romanticism, History, and the Possibilities of Genre* (Cambridge: Cambridge University Press, 1998), 122–48. The third chapter of Grumbling's dissertation "John Thelwall: Romantick and Revolutionist" discusses the influence of Sterne and other writers on the *Peripatetic*. The reception of the *Peripatetic* was generally favorable. The politically conservative *Critical Review* [12 (1794): 32–36] disapproved as not "decent" some of the political ideas, but otherwise the reviewer has some praise for Thelwall's novel, noting that it contained "many strong truths" and fairly good poetry. The more politically liberal *Analytical Review* [21 (1795): 556–60] and *New Annual Register* [15 (1794): 248] were also favorable. The *Analytical* reviewer did not think the novelist was an "original genius" and was additionally bothered by the novel's carelessness, but the unusual form of the novel was deemed merely Sternean. The *New Annual* reviewer praised the "easy and familiar style" that the novel shared with Sterne's *Sentimental Journey;* he or she also admired the "amusing and entertaining" novel for its "many sensible and just observations, intermingled with the excentricities of a lively imagination."

its exclusively polite quality and is not far from the unmistakably popular—and biblical—idiom of Spence and Blake. "The actual revolutionary theme which dominates *The Peripatetic*," according to Vernon O. Grumbling, "is democracy."³ Its ambiguous status as both popular and polite is embodied materially in its very publication. In the 1790s, at the height of Thelwall's political fame, the three-volume *Peripatetic* was sold by the Jacobin booksellers—Eaton, Symonds, Ridgway—for nine shillings. This was surely not cheap (about half the weekly wage of a laborer at the time), but it was not as expensive as Godwin's *Political Justice* (£1 16s).⁴

The *Peripatetic*'s treatment of the gypsies reflects the tension between popular and polite styles. The novel's gypsies represent a metaphorical mirroring of the poet's own eccentric, wandering, homeless, restless energy, which feels confined within any domestic space (or genre); but later in the novel, the gypsies are a metaphorical mirroring of the idle aristocracy and its immoral theft of the wealth created by the industrious classes; at yet another point, they symbolize a stubborn and inexplicable timelessness that resists the Enlightenment hypothesis on the power of environment; at yet another point they constitute a social heterogeneity like that found in a Walter Scott novel, valuable especially for its difference; and finally, in a section on the king of the gypsies, they are used to parody the larger society in an almost comic version of monarchy.⁵ None of these imaginative renderings is definitive or ultimately ironizing. All are subsumed in a sprawling narrative of stylized eccentricity, whose proximate model could be Laurence Sterne. According to Gary Harrison, the gypsies, a staple of the "picturesque," represent for Wordsworth "an underclass in a state of war against the property holders," just as they do for Thelwall.⁶ David Simpson shows, in relation to Wordsworth, how the gypsies operated in the popular imagination to signify "at once thieves and vagrants but also lovers of freedom and independence," as well as "seducers and libertines . . . [and] uncomplicated and guilt-free sexuality."⁷ Wordsworth's treatment of gypsies is as ambivalent as Thelwall's. For both poets the gypsies represent a transgressive desire that marks in its

---

3. "John Thelwall: Romantick and Revolutionist" (Ph.D. diss., University of New Hampshire, 1977), 111.
4. Peter H. Marshall, *William Godwin* (New Haven: Yale University Press, 1984), 121.
5. P 2: 41–48, 70–74, 81–82, 84–87, 115–30.
6. Gary Harrison, *Wordsworth's Vagrant Muse: Poetry, Poverty and Power* (Detroit: Wayne State University Press, 1994), 103.
7. David Simpson, "Figuring Class, Sex, and Gender: What Is the Subject of Wordsworth's 'Gipsies'?" *South Atlantic Quarterly* 88 (1989): 545.

repressions, inhibitions, and displacements the characteristic direction of Romanticism. What it means to be a poet in a distinctively Romantic way is connected with the figure of the gypsies for both Wordsworth and Thelwall.[8]

The reader of Thelwall's *Peripatetic* becomes educated in the art of making analogies. The gypsies are like X, Y, Z, and so on, but our perception of the particular object—the gypsies—is not clarified but complicated by multiple associations. The analogy-making brings the reader to perceive the gypsies in a way contrary to the Enlightenment goal of refined precision. Thelwall's writing acknowledges the explosive metaphoricity of language in relation to objects that Byron would exploit so unrestrainedly in *Don Juan*. In the *Peripatetic*, objects point to others as the numerous lyrical and subjective "effusions" are consistently expanded or ironically deflated by social-political commentary, urbane dialogue, and neoclassical imitation.

The sentimental tale of Belmour and Sophia, a revolutionary translation of *Romeo and Juliet*, which threads its way through the novel from beginning to end, is the overdetermined narrative of love frustrated and betrayed by mercenary fathers. (The equally conventional Julia and Vaudracour story in the 1805 *Prelude* is yet another version, but Thelwall's, unlike Wordsworth's, ends happily.) By 1793 this fiction, already a transparent political allegory of the *ancien régime*'s repressive power, provides a minimal kind of recurrent pattern and coherent structure upon which the Sternean associations can have free play. It also sustains a Romantic character type, the melancholic or suicide, whose literary manifestations include Werther, Coleridge's "dejected" persona, the ancient mariner, Wordsworth's poet-figure in "Resolution and Independence," the numerous Byronic solitaries, and Shelley's Maniac in *Julian and Maddalo* (one of the characters in the *Peripatetic* is named Julian). Each of Belmour's periodic returns in the novel unsettles any kind of intellectual complacency that might have been achieved. The novel's dialogic structure forces the reader continually to attend to the social world, as the stylized character names and sentimental conventions effectively defamiliarize the London suburbs and their suffering inhabitants.

There seems to be little question that Wordsworth's *Excursion* is modeled after the *Peripatetic*. Wordsworth borrowed Thelwall's pedestrian encounters, stylized dialogues, staged revelations, sociopolitical and philosophical decla-

---

8. Anne Janowitz in an MLA Convention paper of 1997 locates John Clare's poems on gypsies within a Romanticist framework of individualism and communitarianism.

mations.⁹ Thelwall, still a radical in 1814 when *The Excursion* was published, enthusiastically praised a poem that was notable for its repudiation of radical politics. Surely Henry Crabbe Robinson was not the only one at the time to have noticed that Wordsworth took many things from Thelwall "without acknowledgment."¹⁰ Thelwall himself did not complain publicly.

The *Peripatetic* has other characteristics that we might call Wordsworthian. In short, Thelwall was a major influence on Wordsworth. Thelwall's "Wordsworthian" memory is evident in one episode where the poet records an incident from early childhood, "my sixth, or seventh year" (P 1:78–81).¹¹ Upon a vacation trip to Margate he loses himself in contemplation looking from the pier, deep in thought and silence, apart from the others, who are discussing conventional topics like "the decay of trade and the balance of power." First, his meditation blocks out everything else. "And so riveted was my attention by the majestic scene, that, while gazing on its beauties, I suffered the hours of refreshment to pass over me without regard, and the spreading orbit of the sun to decline below the horizon, without reflecting how I was to return to my friends." Second, the scene from the pier becomes something other than a picturesque moment by slipping over into the sublime, as occurs in Wordsworth's childhood memories as well. At sunset "the ebbing tide still riveted my enchanted ear, and the veil of darkness was almost closed over the face of heaven when (after a long and anxious search) I was discovered in this situation, hanging, in sweet enthusiasm, over the artificial precipice, and listening to the dashing surge." Simultaneously he is found by those who love him and he discovers himself in the estrangement from those he loves. On the border between safety and danger, he hangs "in sweet enthusiasm."

The significance of the memory is also Wordsworthian. His solitary "enthusiasm" is the occasion for his being labeled an "idiot," someone out-

---

9. On Thelwall's influencing Wordsworth's *Excursion*, see Grumbling, "John Thelwall: Romantick and Revolutionist," 229, 235–43. Carl Woodring sees the *Excursion*'s Solitary as not just Fawcett but also Thelwall. *Politics in English Romantic Poetry* (Cambridge, Mass.: Harvard University Press, 1970), 134. Thompson also sees the Solitary as Thelwall in the Welsh "retirement" (*MWC*, 176). For another angle on the Wordsworth-Thelwall relationship, see David Simpson, "Public Virtues, Private Vices: Reading Between the Lines of Wordsworth's 'Anecdote for Fathers,' " in David Simpson, *Subject to History: Ideology, Class, Gender* (Ithaca: Cornell University Press, 1991), 163–90 (Thelwall material, 172–90).

10. Robinson, *Diary, Reminiscences, and Correspondence of Henry Crabbe Robinson*, 2 vols., ed. Sadler, diary entry of 12 February 1815; 1: 248.

11. Grumbling discusses Thelwall's prefiguring of Wordsworthian memory in "John Thelwall: Romantick and Revolutionist," 230.

side the community, but the experience, a "spot of time" in the Wordsworthian sense, also anchored his identity and connected him with a world wider than his friends and family. The word "idiot" is interesting for Wordsworth's poem "The Idiot Boy" and Thelwall's exploration of idiocy from a scientific perspective in the *Letter to Henry Cline*. Both Wordsworth and Thelwall see various figures of the Other—gypsies, idiots—not as picturesque color enhancing an otherwise drab landscape but as sublime mirrorings of themselves.[12] Another point has to be made in this context. Thelwall's representation of subjective moments of acute self-consciousness does not entail solipsism. Karl Kroeber phrases it nicely: the "intensely individual experience" represented by Romantic writers is actually "a means for improving or enhancing community."[13] There is nevertheless a difference in emphasis between Thelwall's and Wordsworth's depictions of memory. Thelwall's are in a sprawling, multivoiced novel whose social meanings are prominent, whereas Wordsworth's representations of memory are emphatically private in *The Prelude*, the great epic of individualism.

The entire novel is a defense and performance of "eccentricity," a pedestrian excursion literally and figuratively, a meandering from a center. As in the "glad preamble" of the *Prelude*, in which Wordsworth feels he can travel anywhere and be equally blessed, so in the *Peripatetic* the poet assumes that wherever he walks will provide philosophical inspiration equal to that which animated the greatest philosophers of the past. Thelwall writes, in lines that prefigure "Tintern Abbey":

> These fields, these hedge-rows, and this simple turf,
> Shall form my Academus: through this vale,
> (Ye hallow'd manes of the boasts of Greece!)
> Thro' this low vale will I suppose ye walk'd
> Pouring divine instruction, or, reclin'd
> Upon these verdant hillocks, musing deep,
> The silent energy of soul collected,
> And soar'd, on Contemplation's awful wing,
> Into the highest heaven.
>
> (P 1:10)

---

12. Thelwall did not especially like Wordsworth's "Idiot Boy," despite the ideological affinities. See Burton R. Pollin and Redmond Burke, "John Thelwall's Marginalia in a Copy of Coleridge's *Biographia Literaria*," *Bulletin of the New York Public Library* 74 (1970): 86.

13. Karl Kroeber, *British Romantic Art* (Berkeley and Los Angeles: University of California Press), 93.

The blank verse, the demonstrative pronouns, and the inspiration of a "common" nature for philosophical truths are typical of the poetry in the *Peripatetic*, whose Wordsworthian qualities are too pervasive to document exhaustively. An early instance of what Celeste Langan has called "Romantic vagrancy," Thelwall's novel achieves coherence by means of association of ideas provoked by the chance encounters and the accidents of pedestrian travel.[14] As in Wordsworth, Thelwall finds the center in the margins. The gypsies; the drunken poor; old farmers; the mad, the foolish, and the eccentric provide truths inaccessible in any other way. Through these marginal figures "nature" speaks truths that are unknown in the artificial idioms of polite society.[15] However, Wordsworth did not just borrow certain features from Thelwall. He intensively enhanced the individualistic aspects and muted the communitarian ones, to use the categories employed by Anne Janowitz to characterize the dialogue that *is* Romanticism.

Numerous sentimental vignettes in the *Peripatetic* both criticize and use sensibility to make political observations. One poem, "Daughters of Albion's gay enlighten'd hour!", foregrounds bird-catchers to protest acts of immoral consumerism, such as eating slavery-tainted sugar. Middle-class "taste," especially that of women, dramatizes the tension between aesthetic pleasure and ethics, but the fundamental issue is commerce itself—"thou doubtful, and thou partial good!" that permits "a few" to "fatten... upon the toils of all" (P 1:35–36). The female consumer is also a figure for the reader, as literature too falls under suspicion as an exploitative luxury. To counter readers' passivity Thelwall ironizes the poems with antiphonal prose episodes that are in turn ironized, as the novel's structure is digressive, jumping from the present to something similar in the past and then returning again to the present. The reader, who is constructed as an antibourgeois, is educated into perceiving the immorality of merely passive enjoyment and embracing the sublimer pleasures of nonlinear narrative and ironic lyricism. Caged

14. Celeste Langan, *Romantic Vagrancy: Wordsworth and the Simulation of Freedom* (Cambridge: Cambridge University Press, 1995). Although her study does not deal with Thelwall, its development of the trope and social practice of walking is central to Thelwall.

15. The "Wordsworthian" *Peripatetic* is perhaps an apt occasion to discuss Thelwall's other connections with the younger poet. One of Thelwall's *Champion* poems is a compassionate and remarkably Wordsworthian "Sabbath Meditation" in blank verse that focuses on a poor woman in London ([8 July 1820]: 447). The "Sylvanus; or, the Pupil of the Groves" is another Wordsworthian piece, revised from 1793, which constitutes a modest poetic autobiography. Its first installment appears in the *Champion* (9 September 1820): 590–91, and it is reprinted in full in the *Poetical Recreations of the "Champion" and his Literary Correspondents* (London: Champion Press, 1822), 77–83. Donald H. Reiman edited the facsimile reprint (New York: Garland, 1978).

songbirds and sugared tea are no more innocent than other practices corrupted by social luxury.

An episode that seems to have disturbed Coleridge,[16] "Midnight Ramble," describes a solitary walk of six miles by Sylvanus Theophrastus, who hopes for a view of moonlight over the Thames but gets instead the sunrise. Anticipating a pattern in *The Prelude*—willful deeds disappoint but the providentially unexpected experience is even better—the speaker uses the encounter with the landscape to criticize the authoritarian religious instruction of youth and describes his own loss of childhood faith and his acquisition of a mature secular faith in "universal benevolence," "Sensibility," "Justice," and "mercy." Like Shelley in "Hymn to Intellectual Beauty," Thelwall here politicizes the concept of a "natural" religion. Unlike Godwin, however, the influence of whose ideas are evident throughout the *Peripatetic*, Thelwall's natural religion is marked by the style of "enthusiasm," not rationalism. One poem, "Still as the young Enthusiast I pursue," celebrates without embarrassment an emotional exuberance closer in style to Methodism than to Voltairean rationalism (P 1:99–100). In yet another instance of secularizing a religious dimension, the speaker seeks a contract with the reader to his "confessor" so that he can "give a copy of my own eccentricities to the World" even at the risk of appearing vain and egotistical (P 1:103).

Landscape in the *Peripatetic* is historical, not just natural. As Judith Thompson has observed, Thelwall's characters follow "the Thames, the main artery of Britain's commercial empire and the old Roman road from London to Dover, which is also the route of Chaucer's Canterbury pilgrims, leading back through the heartland of British society and literature."[17] As Theophrastus, Ambulator, and Belmour (who anticipate another trio, Shelley's Julian, Maddalo, and the Maniac) walk through Dartford, they recall the place where Wat Tyler's revolt began, then criticize Hume's account, and finally defend the recent execution of King Louis (P 2:24–28). Similarly,

---

16. Coleridge criticized Thelwall specifically for the idea of authoritarian religious instruction in a letter to Hugh J. Rose (19 November 1818). Earl Leslie Griggs, ed., *Collected Letters of Samuel Taylor Coleridge*, 6 vols. (Oxford: Clarendon Press, 1959), 4: 879–80; although the letter does not mention *The Peripatetic*, one assumes that this was the original source. In Coleridge's letters to Thelwall himself he did indeed attack his friend's attitude toward Christianity. See especially the letter of 17 December 1796, Griggs, ed., *Collected Letters of Samuel Taylor Coleridge*, 1: 279–85.

17. Thompson, "'A Voice in the Representation': John Thelwall and the Enfranchisement of Literature," in Rajan and Wright, ed., *Romanticism, History, and the Possibilities of Genre*, 138.

when they reach the Crag River, where Hengist the Saxon defeated the Britons, they declaim against the ill effects of mercenary troops and apply the historical lesson to the recent republican defeat of the mercenary Swiss Guards (P 2:5–7). Connecting disparate times and places, the Crag River and the Tuileries, Hengist and the Swiss Guards, ancient British and modern French history, the *Peripatetic* interprets social reality aggressively, moving recurrently from nature to history to politics and back again. That the mercenary Saxons turned against and conquered their nominal employers is a topos that Thelwall uses to justify the French republicans, even to the extent of preferring Marat and revolutionary terror to the worse evils of despotism (P 2:9–11).

The education of the reader and the instability of the narrative entail moments of literary criticism throughout the novel. It is as if Thelwall incorporates his "preface" into his experimental "lyrical ballads." The comments on Milton and Charlotte Smith are part of his argument in favor of an alternative canon. Like other Romantics, Thelwall read *Paradise Lost* in the Blakean "satanic" way. Thelwall believes that Prometheus "suggested to our own Milton the first idea of that portrait, which he has painted at large, with so much terrible sublimity, in his infernal monarch—the chief of the fallen angels" (P 2:213). Shelley in his *Prometheus Unbound* would remythologize both Milton's Satan and Aeschylus's Prometheus in the spirit of Thelwall's comments. The spirit of those comments is Romantic in the specific sense that Milton is being made part of a national canon, including also Shakespeare, Dryden, and Charlotte Smith, and deemphasizing Pope. Pope's poetry is not without value, according to Thelwall, but it is a lesser kind; Pope is "a very pretty poet" with a "fine sense" and a "correct judgment," but Dryden has sublime "enthusiasm," "fire," and "stately majesty," along with "simplicity of diction" and "forcible tenderness of sentiment and expression."[18] The greatest poets with their "daring flights of high enthusiasm" are superior to the "correct" poets (P 3:32–33).

The defense of Charlotte Smith's sonnets in the *Peripatetic* and in an essay in the *Universal Magazine* directly challenges aesthetic categories that he deconstructs as social and political power. Thelwall's characters praise the elegiac sonnets of Smith, which other critics have condemned as "illegiti-

---

18. That Pope's poetry was misread in the process of the eighteenth-century construction of a Romantic/Augustan antithesis has been argued persuasively by Robert Griffin in *Wordsworth's Pope: A Study in Literary Historiography* (Cambridge: Cambridge University Press, 1995).

mate." Ambulator labels Smith's violation of poetic decorum as a "glorious crime" that "burst the unnatural fetters of arbitrary authority, and exert[ed] the free-born energies of the soul" (P 1:123). The most valuable sonnets are those using blank verse or elegiac stanzas, as the "legitimate" sonnet is deemed hopelessly artificial (P 1:125). The *Universal Magazine* essay is even bolder because Thelwall elevates Smith's sonnets above those of Milton. The political rhetoric in the aesthetic discussion is unmistakable, as Thelwall protests against the "pedantic prejudices in favour of the models of established writers, by which the wings of aspiring genius are shackled," and continues thus: "The prerogative of name triumphs over the natural distinctions of merit; improvement is decried as heretical innovation; and, in the court of Parnassus, as in those of law, *to be right*, in opposition to precedent, is frequently *to be wrong*." The positive qualities Thelwall finds in Smith's sonnets are nervous energy and sublimity. According to Thelwall her "*illegitimate* sonnets (for the spiritual court of criticism has thought proper to bastardise them) display a more touching melancholy, a more poetical simplicity, nay I will venture to say, a greater vigour and correctness of genius, than any other English poems that I have ever seen, under the same denomination; and I certainly do not mean to except the sonnets of Milton." Smith's much-maligned use of other poets' lines in her sonnets is turned into a display of her "liberality of mind." Scorning the distinctions between the sublime (Miltonic) and domestic (Smithian) sonnet, rejecting with sarcasm any unironic use of the adjectives "legitimate" and "illegitimate" applicable to sonnets, Thelwall compares two sonnets on the nightingale by Milton and Smith to *Smith's* advantage.

By defending Charlotte Smith's sonnets at the expense of Milton's, Thelwall gives a democratic edge to the literary criticism. A recent critic, Daniel Robinson, reminds us that during the eighteenth century the Miltonic and Petrarchan sonnet forms were deemed of a higher order than the English or Shakespearean ones favored by Charlotte Smith and Thelwall.[19] Just as *Paradise Lost* became "holy writ" by the end of the seventeenth century,[20] so did Milton's sonnets assume monumental cultural authority, which Romantic

19. Daniel Robinson, "Reviving the Sonnet: Women Romantic Poets and the Sonnet Claim," *European Romantic Review* 6 (1995): 98–127.
20. On *Paradise Lost* becoming "holy writ," see Marcus Walsh, "Bentley Our Contemporary," in Ian Small and Marcus Walsh, eds., *The Theory and Practice of Text-Editing* (Cambridge: Cambridge University Press, 1991), 179.

poets sometimes challenged. Thelwall insists that Smith's sonnets are inferior to those of Milton only if one imposes an arbitrary system of prescription on the sonnet, using Milton's sonnets as the model for the "legitimate" sonnet. Using the criteria of "imagery," "harmony," and aesthetic intensity—"nervousness," "feeling," and "sentiment"—he finds Smith's sonnets better than Milton's. In the process of defending Smith, Thelwall uses politically loaded words: phrases and arguments against precedent, prescription, and arbitrary authority. Defending Smith's elegiac sonnet form, which deviates from the Miltonic model, Thelwall comments that the "time is coming, I hope, when we shall estimate things, not by their titles, but their merits." Although Milton is "without rival" in the epic genre, Charlotte Smith dominates the sonnet.[21]

Thelwall's peripatetic muse wears the red liberty cap as it inspires antiauthoritarian genre mixing and an enthusiastic style that is digressive, metaphorical, dialogic, and ironic. Although genre mixing puts forward the author's presence as the individuating force disrupting communally agreed-upon genres, Thelwall's *Peripatetic* is so stylized that the author's presence is also dispersed rather than concentrated. Landscape is a site for historical and political reflection, not just private self-discovery. As an experiment, the novel coaxes its readers, rather than shocking them, into recognizing the pleasures of a new canon. The readers who give up the old pleasures for the new find delight in organic form, the association of ideas, the unexpected turn, ethical rigor, historical reflection, and private intensity. Also, with matter-of-fact bluntness, the *Peripatetic* enacts a popularization of classical, aristocratic, and high bourgeois culture five years before the *Lyrical Ballads*. The novel is more socially centered writing than the than author-centered literature, but literature as such is engaged, cited, revised, ironized and imitated.[22]

21. J.T., "An Essay on the English Sonnet; illustrated by a Comparison between the Sonnets of Milton and those of Charlotte Smith," *Universal Magazine* (December 1792): 408–14. I assume that J.T. is Thelwall because we know he wrote for the *Universal Magazine* in that period, that he thought highly of Smith and used her "elegiac" sonnet style, and that the argument and language are similar to what one finds in *The Peripatetic* where there is an explicit defense of Smith's sonnets paralleling the argument in the *Universal Magazine* essay (1: 122–25).

22. See also the contrast drawn by Anne Janowitz between Thelwall's "interventionist" (LCS songs) and "representational" (1801 blank-verse lyrics) poetics. *Lyric and Labour in the Romantic Tradition* (Cambridge: Cambridge University Press, 1998), 89. The dichotomy she draws roughly corresponds to my writing/literature distinction. Writing that is "representational" can also have, as I argue, an "interventionist" dimension by means of allegory and other systems of symbolic meaning.

Nature and Anti-Jacobinism

Thelwall challenged anti-Jacobinism in two topographical essays that appeared in the *Monthly Magazine* between 1798 and 1801, during the period of Thelwall's political disengagement.[23] The *Monthly Magazine*, established in 1796, was, according to Jon Klancher, "the first organ of a newly self-conscious English middle-class reading audience."[24] Largely Dissenting, the *Monthly Magazine* published some writing that was Jacobin but overall its political ideology was more moderate and its politics far more prudent than was typical for literary Jacobinism. The locodescriptive and walking tour essays in the *Monthly Magazine* represent a "nature" marked everywhere by political hope and anxiety. E. P. Thompson characterized Thelwall's "Pedestrian Excursion" as "unremarkable," dismissing it as merely "conventional rehearsals of the 'romantic and picturesque.'"[25] I find this essay and Thelwall's essay on the Wye valley much more distinctive than that.[26] "The Phenomena of the Wye, during the Winter of 1797–98," an essay interesting in its own right, contrasts with how Wordsworth wrote about the Wye in "Tintern Abbey." Indeed, several months after this essay was published in May, 1798, the Wordsworths made their historic visit to Tintern Abbey; shortly after that, in early August, the Wordsworths, accompanied this time by Coleridge, visited Llyswen farm. The sociological reports on the living conditions of the poor in the "Pedestrian Excursion" anticipate similar writings by Cobbett.[27] The land Thelwall traverses and the journey he makes are sites for sociological, cultural, and political-economic reflection. The aesthetic moments of picturesque and sublime picture-painting within the conventions of the guidebooks are infrequent and somewhat

23. A version of this part of the chapter appeared as "Jacobin Romanticism: John Thelwall's 'Wye' Essay and 'Pedestrian Excursion' (1797–1801)," in Peter Kitson, ed., *Placing and Displacing Romanticism* (Aldershot: Ashgate Press, 2001).
24. *The Making of English Reading Audiences, 1790–1832* (Madison: University of Wisconsin Press, 1987), 41.
25. Thompson, "Hunting the Jacobin Fox," *Past and Present* 142 (1994): 105; TR, 175.
26. John Thelwall, "The Phenomena of the Wye, During the Winter of 1797–98," *Monthly Magazine* 5 (May 1798), 343–46; "A Pedestrian Excursion Through Several Parts of England and Wales During the Summer of 1797 ," *Monthly Magazine* 8 (August 1799), 532–33; 8 (September 1799), 616–19; 8 (November 1799), 783–85; 8 (January 1800), 966–67; 9 (February 1800), 16–18; 9 (April 1800), 228–31; 11 (March 1801), 123–25; 12 (September 1801), 103–6; 12 (October 1801), 198–200; 12 (November 1801), 305–8.
27. Grumbling notes the parallels between Cobbett and Thelwall, "John Thelwall: Romantick and Revolutionist," 104.

unconventional.[28] Whereas Thompson was disturbed by what he considered Thelwall's class bias, I find the most disturbing subtext of the essays to be the fear of violence and the concomitant sense of powerlessness.

Thelwall was forced to retire from politics in the summer of 1797 because of the violent attacks against him. As he would later explain in the pages of the *Champion:* "He never did desert the public—the public deserted him. He was left alone, as it were, in the field—abandoned by timid friends, and surrounded by sanguinary enemies. . . . [It was necessary to take] a temporary retreat to silence and obscurity" in order to save his life (6 June 1819: 351–52). An alternative that Thelwall deemed unthinkable but one that was taken by a large number of 1790s radicals was anti-Jacobin apostasy. Political recantation, which would have stopped the violent harassment, might have been an lucrative career move. As he began his walking tour from Derby, unable to work as a provincial journalist— he had just been fired after only two weeks as editor of the Derby *Courier*—he sought a way to support his family; he could no longer lecture in public.[29] After a very happy ten-day visit with Coleridge and the Wordsworths, he stayed with several other friends in nearby Gloucestershire, then he rented a farm in Llyswen, Brecknockshire. His first choice for a residence had been Nether Stowey, which, however, could not accommodate the most infamous "acquitted felon" in Britain (William Windham's phrase for the 1794 treason trial suspects). Thelwall's letter to his wife and the blank verse poem "Lines written at Bridgewater" express vividly how much Thelwall wanted to settle near the Coleridges and

---

28. Nevertheless, the essays have an undeniable "picturesque" dimension. The Wye essay explicitly cites the precedent of William Gilpin, and the "Pedestrian Excursion" refers to Thomas Gray's guidebook, *The Traveller's Companion, In a Tour Through England and Wales; Containing a Catalogue of the Antiquities, Houses, Parks, Plantations, Scenes, and Situations, in England and Wales, Arranged According to the Alphabetical Order of the Several Counties, a Catalogue, County by County, of Interesting Places to Visit. A New Edition* (London: G. Kearsley, 1800). As the edition I looked at was a "new" edition, Thelwall's copy in 1797 would have been an earlier one. The edition I saw was pocket size.

29. The fullest, most recent treatment of the violent attacks on Thelwall in 1796–97 is by E. P. Thompson, "Hunting the Jacobin Fox," *Past and Present* 142 (1994): 94–140; TR, 156–220. Thelwall himself wrote about the experiences extensively, both at the time they happened and later. *An Appeal to Popular Opinion Against Kidnapping and Murder, Including a Narrative of the Late Atrocious Proceedings at Yarmouth*, 2nd ed. (London: J. S. Jordan, 1796). In the *Champion* (24 Oct. 1819: 670–71), Thelwall describes a hitherto unrecorded episode of violence against himself at Stockport in 1797.

Wordsworths.[30] Meanwhile, government spies had taken notice of Coleridge's friends, and spies sent several reports to the Home Office.[31] Because of Thelwall's presence, however brief, the Wordsworths lost their lease to the Alfoxden cottage. Thelwall's renting the Welsh farm signified his inability to continue any longer as a political activist. Like the republican regicide Henry Marten, who was imprisoned after the Restoration in Chepstow Castle on the Wye, Thelwall at Llyswyn farm on the Wye in 1798 was also a monument to the failure of revolution, as Nicholas Roe has pointed out in relation to "Tintern Abbey."[32]

Broken up into ten separate pieces in the *Monthly Magazine*, and published between August 1799 and November 1801, the "Pedestrian Excursion" makes no mention of Thelwall's experiences with repression, the violent encounters with anti-Jacobins, almost being kidnapped at Yarmouth by sailors, and the spies who shadowed him wherever he went. Richard Phillips the publisher and John Aikin the editor might not have published the essay if it had included yet another "appeal" to the public by Thelwall on the repression that victimized him. The *Monthly Magazine*, formed in the wake of the repressive Two Acts, purchased its freedom to publish by practicing rigorous self-censorship. Only at the very end of the essay does Thelwall become self-reflective. Even here, he continues to refrain from providing specific complaints: "*Saturday* 15, my companion [J. Wimpory, shoemaker][33] took his farewell of me, directing his course homeward in the Southampton stage; and shortly after I took my farewell of Bath, thenceforward to pursue my way with solitary step—far from each endearing intercourse—seeking from without for the happiness that was not within, and exclaiming, every time that the smoke of the lone cottage from some sequestered dingle chanced to rise upon my view—'When—when shall I be the peaceful lord of such a mansion, and repose me again in obscurity!' " (12 [Nov. 1801]: 308).

30. The 14 July 1797 letter is transcribed by Grumbling, "John Thelwall: Romantick and Revolutionist," 215.
31. See the account in Nicholas Roe's *Wordsworth and Coleridge: The Radical Years* (Oxford: Oxford University Press, 1988), 248–62, and his "Coleridge and John Thelwall: The Road to Nether Stowey," in Richard Gravil and Molly Lefebure, eds., *The Coleridge Connection: Essays for Thomas McFarland* (London: Macmillan, 1990), 60–80.
32. Nicholas Roe, *Politics of Nature: Wordsworth and Some Contemporaries* (Basingstoke: Macmillan, 1992), 130.
33. Wimpory was identified by E. P. Thompson in "Hunting the Jacobin Fox," *Past and Present* 142 (1994): 107 n. 54; *TR*, 208 n. 54.

Thelwall dramatizes here a solitary pathos, some of which Coleridge seems to have borrowed in his 1802 "Dejection" ode (the lines "seeking from without for the happiness that was not within" are too distinctive to be coincidental). The "Pedestrian Excursion" is, in the tradition of William Gilpin, public travel literature that excludes merely personal commentary, not the more privately inflected "sentimental journey" after Sterne and Rousseau. Thelwall's earlier *Peripatetic* was a more Sternean lyrical "journey," in which the journalist's own thoughts and associations took precedence over external events.[34] Were the "Pedestrian Excursion" to continue after the last paragraph, it would have to be modulated to the new lyrical, self-conscious inwardness. The lyrical turn in the essay's conclusion disturbingly punctuates the whole previous essay, undermining its status as reportage. What he cannot discuss directly—the public violence against him, his sense of being abandoned—nevertheless affects the essay in numerous ways.

Prior to the abrupt and surprising conclusion of the essay, it conforms roughly to the form of a travel journal. Although parts of the essay do indeed rehearse the conventions of the picturesque genteel tour, as Thompson observes, Thelwall also works against those conventions in certain ways. The walking tour itself, although it became thoroughly respectable in the Victorian period, still had democratic associations, as the preferred means of travel was by coach and horseback.[35] When the essay describes some inns as more pleasant and generous than others, it is shifting the emphasis from the tourist sights, always Gilpin's focus, to the walk.

A subtle revision of picturesque conventions occurs when he is directed to a beautiful view, not by Gilpin or Gray, but by an old peasant near East Knoyle. The description and meditation, perhaps because of the unusually spontaneous circumstances of finding the view, show Thelwall at his descriptive best.

> From the summit, thus pointed out to us, we commanded one of the most pleasing views I had ever seen. Hills and vallies, rich, fertile, and

---

34. William Gilpin, *Observations on the River Wye*, intro. Jonathan Wordsworth (1782; rpt. New York: Woodstock Books, 1991).
35. See Roe, *Politics of Nature*, 127–29, Anne Wallace, *Walking, Literature, and English Culture: The Origins and Uses of Peripatetic in the Nineteenth Century* (Oxford: Clarendon Press, 1993), and Jeffrey C. Robinson, *The Walk: Notes on a Romantic Image* (Norman: University of Oklahoma Press, 1989), chaps. 5 and 6 especially.

variegated, were seen finely interspersed with woodlands and cottages, and here and there some prouder mansions; while other hills, dimly descried through the mists, bounded the prospect and mingled with the horizon. Beautiful slopes and dells and climes, cloathed with fern and coppice, formed the rough foreground of the picture; and the sky, cloudy, but rather wild and sublime than monotonous, formed a *sombre* but not unsuitable accompaniment; while a shower of rain gave additional freshness to all the nearer objects, and deepened the emerald tint of the short close turf we trod. Anon the moving curtains of the sky were rent, and the beams of the sun, breaking through the interstices of dark clouds, brightly illuminated the distant western hills, whose mitigated splendours, seen through the misty veil of an intervening shower, gave a finishing tho' transient beauty to the whole. (11 [March 1801]: 104)

The description never emphasizes any special receptivity that Thelwall uniquely possesses, and escapes to some extent the static and painterly qualities of the picturesque tradition. Although he does indeed "compose" a picturesque view with foreground and horizon, his language does not strain to get remarkable effects. The description pays more attention to general shapes and configurations than details. Thelwall does not pretend he can capture fully the beauty of the scene, but he accepts the more modest task of representation without drawing upon the topos of linguistic ineffability.[36] Although he calls this "the most pleasing view" he had ever witnessed in his life, he strikes here the same comfortable tone he adopts in his blank-verse meditations, as his nature description partakes somewhat of the qualities of the conversation poem. It is difficult to imagine Wordsworth, Coleridge, or Shelley letting an opportunity like this slip without making post-rhapsodic commentary on nature, imagination, theology, philosophy, and so on. This restraint, which we find also in Dorothy Wordsworth's landscape descriptions, corresponds to Thelwall's overall treatment of landscape and aesthetics: picturesque beauty, however pleasurable, is not permitted to displace the social labor and political conflicts that also are part of the land's meaning. By

---

36. For the ineffability topos as being consistent with the Romantic ideology, see Anne Janowitz, *England's Ruins: Poetic Purpose and the National Landscape* (Oxford: Basil Blackwell, 1990), 15. A key text for understanding Romantic landscape is of course John Barrell's *The Idea of Landscape and the Sense of Place, 1730–1840: An Approach to the Poetry of John Clare* (Cambridge: Cambridge University Press, 1972).

not representing his private reactions to beauty except in a general way, he suggests that receptivity to beauty is not an aristocratic privilege, and that it derives neither from birth nor from special spiritual election. Commenting on what he calls "evocative poetry," Arnold D. Harvey captures succinctly what these scene-painting passages achieve: "They evoked not an unrepeatable moment of awareness but rather a mood which all readers might experience; their appeal was not to each of their readers' sense of his [or her] own uniqueness, but rather to their shared fund of memories and perceptions."[37]

That the "Pedestrian Excursion" does not have many "views" like this is one of the essay's distinctive features. Even this example of the "picturesque" is not author-centered literature but socially centered writing. Although Thelwall does not attack the conventions of the picturesque tour directly, he nibbles away at some of its assumptions. Thelwall's response to the classical statuary in Wilton House is an even clearer example of his unconventional tourism, as he uses the occasion to evoke classical republicanism, defend tyrannicides like Brutus, and praise the uncompromising Socrates at the expense of the time-serving Seneca (9 [Feb. 1800]: 17).

The essay's most distinctive feature is its sociological focus. The sociological observations predate Cobbett's by several decades, and in some respects are superior to Cobbett's: Thelwall dramatizes himself far less, generates far fewer simplistic myths about an imaginary past, provides more information about the lives of the rural poor, and does not scapegoat Jews and Quakers. Thelwall's evaluation of the overall quality of life is more reliable than Cobbett's quirky perceptions. When Thelwall reaches a village, he records how well the laborers seem to be doing in the following categories: the fertility of the land on which they work, their physical appearance, the condition of the children, their wages, their dwellings, their factory work hours, their degree of literary education, and their overall cultural state. He notes whether the poor have a cow or access to the commons. The overall effect of his reports is extraordinarily gloomy, because most of the laborers seem to be ignorant, overworked, listless, in poor health, with their standard of living declining. Moreover, the children of the poor are exploited in factories and deprived of both an education and freedom to play. The recurrent theme of his sociological reports is that "monopoly" is reducing the number of farmers, increasing the size of farms, and wrecking a previous

---

37. Arnold D. Harvey, *English Poetry in a Changing Society, 1780–1825* (New York: St. Martin's Press, 1980), 34.

rural economy that seemed to work well. Moreover, he notes with much concern the spread of the factory system, which concentrates workers into unhealthy dwellings especially harmful to children. We find here a practical application of his labor theory worked out in *The Tribune* and *The Rights of Nature*.

Indeed, he saves his most concentrated ire for child labor in factories. As someone who did not have much playtime in his own childhood, Thelwall sees child's play as one of the "rights" of humanity. He protests the unequal distribution of leisure and labor: while squires frolic, children toil. At the Overton silk mill, for example, he reports that most of the workers are children, "from 5 years of age to 14 or 15. They have 1s. per week during the first year they are employed, and an addition of 3d. per week every year that they continue at this employment. The hours are from 6 in the morning to 7 or 8 at night" (8 [Nov. 1799]: 784). He compares the factory to a prison that produces, finally, female prostitutes and male soldiers and sailors (8 [Nov. 1799]: 785). At the Quidhampton woolen mill children start work as young as five. These are the years when these children should instead be "stretching their wanton limbs in noisy gambols over the green" (8 [Jan. 1800]: 967). At the Froome cloth mill the children work fourteen hours a day, earning between 1s. 6d. and 2s. 6d. per week (12 [Oct. 1801]: 199).

As an urban intellectual, Thelwall also pays attention to the literacy and cultural quality of each place he visits, noting the presence, and more often absence, of libraries, reading rooms, and book shops. His lament for the low cultural level of every place he visits is sometimes connected with a protest against the new stamp tax, which discouraged popular literacy, but Thelwall also criticizes the people's lack of intellectual initiative. One disappointment Thelwall records is the meager amount of conversation he was able to elicit from those he met. Cobbett's *Rural Rides* is spiced with narratives by laborers and farmers in their own words. Militating against any frank interchange between Thelwall and the people he met would be his own identity as a notorious radical. Yet another factor would be the recent naval mutinies and the fear of invasion from France. It is not surprising that he found few laborers willing to talk to him extensively.

His meeting with one literate laborer ("he read *several* newspapers") occasions a lament for the low cultural level of the poor, who, even if educated, have very limited horizons. "Unfortunately, however, we could no way turn his conversation into the channel we desired. He talked of nothing but Parker and the delegates, of war and of parties. In short, he was too full of liquor and *temporary politics*, to furnish any information on the subject of *political economy*" (8 [Sept. 1799]: 619). If Thelwall identified himself, as one imagines he must have, then one understands the reluctance to talk with this "acquitted felon" shadowed by spies. The anxiety, fear, and anger Thelwall might have experienced at various times during his journey go unreported, but perhaps one can find something of his frustration displaced in his commenting on the invariably obtuse state in which he finds working people. Thelwall's distinction between temporary and more enduring politics is curious, because although he always, even at the peak of his political career as a radical orator, took a philosophical view of politics, he also had no trouble making meaningful the newsworthy minutiae and ephemera of political discourse. Thelwall, like most intellectuals, could not accept political and philosophical differences at face value from laborers who had to be seen as being culturally deprived, "hopelessly surrounded by a sort of intellectual desert," "driven into habits of intemperance to supply the deficiency of external stimuli" (8 [Sept. 1799]: 619). After all, Thelwall had paid a high price for being a "tribune" for such people. Now that he was being forced to retire as tribune, he devalues the prose of politics while taking away with him, as compensation for a real loss, the poetry, the truly enduring ideas.

There is a detail in Thelwall's report on the workers that cannot be passed over, and that is the reference to Parker and his "delegates." On the day after Thelwall began his journey, Richard Parker (1767–97; *DNB*) was hanged for his leadership of the Nore mutiny, which had begun on May 10. Would there be anyone in Britain who would not have wanted to talk about this remarkable rebellion? Thelwall makes it seem that the laborer was interested in mere trivia. Unfortunately we have no account of the laborer's comments or Thelwall's response. In actual context, talking about "political economy" would have been escapist. Something else might be at work here, namely, Thelwall's own desire to separate himself from political activism, at least in writing. There was much speculation at the time about the mutineers' revolutionary motives, so that it would not have been impossible for Thelwall to have gotten reimprisoned on some imagined link between himself and the naval mutinies.[38] In addition, in the final years of the London Corresponding Society's existence, from 1797 to 1799 when it was outlawed altogether, the group moved toward plotting violence with the United

---

38. Prior to the Nore, there was another serious mutiny at Spithead; see E. P. Thompson, MWC, 167–68. See also Arnold Schmidt, "Alienation and Displacement: Wordsworth and the Naval Mutinies of 1797," *Nineteenth-Century Contexts* 17 (1993): 204–13.

Irishmen. What better way to illustrate how utterly free he was from anything resembling violent conspiracies against the government than to express bored disdain for discussions with laborers about the naval mutinies?

Thelwall was impatient with other poor people he met. Near Murrel Green he meets an old thresher whose "rustic humour" is amusing, but when Thelwall presses him for sociological information—wages, living conditions, and so on—he is silent. Thelwall then complains about the general English reluctance to discuss important issues that affect them, and he insists that this reluctance is a major obstacle to "improving" overall conditions (8 [Sept. 1799]: 619). If anyone should understand the power of repression and social intimidation to affect one's willingness to speak frankly, it should have been Thelwall. At Fonthill, for example, when he calls the people "immersed in the most stupid ignorance, and scarcely competent either to the answering or the comprehending of the most simple question" (11 [March 1801]: 124), he is forgetting his more rational analyses of why people are so uncommunicative. His particular blindness, I believe, is only partially class prejudice, as Thompson thought. It is mostly self-deception: Thelwall cannot fully acknowledge the extent to which the government and the ascendant aristocracy had criminalized both him and his political ideas. Rather than face his own powerlessness, he blames the poor for being powerless. Thelwall's travel essay, then, is a remarkable if also flawed document, one of the finer achievements of British Jacobin prose, at least as energetic and intellectually rigorous as anything Cobbett wrote later. The principal limitation of the essay is its inability to reflect critically upon Thelwall's role as London intellectual victimized by repression.

The second, much shorter essay, "Phenomena of the Wye," has the concentrated effect of a prose poem. While paying homage to Gilpin in the first paragraph, and noting how "an excursion on the Wye has become an essential part of the education, as it were, of all who aspire to the reputation of elegance, taste, and fashion" (5 [May 1798]: 343), Thelwall develops unfamiliar aspects of the familiar: how the Wye's beauties at night, in winter, and during the spring floods provide an allegorical narrative of natural and social meanings.

Here is Thelwall describing the Wye on an especially dark night when almost nothing can be seen:

> The night was dark and comfortless—no moon, no star in the firmament; and the atmosphere was so thick with vapours and descending

showers, that even the course of the river was scarcely discernible. In short, nothing was visible but a sky of most sullen grey, and one vast sable mass of surrounding mountain, skirting on either side the sinuous valley, and prescribing in every direction the bounds of vision. Never before was I so deeply impressed with the power of mere outline. Here were no diversities of tint, no varied masses of light and shadows: the whole picture consisted of one bold, unbroken, but eternally diversifying line, and two broad masses of modified shade—'No light, but rather darkness visible;' and yet the eye was feasted, and the imagination was filled with mingled impressions of sublimity and beauty. (344)

If the Wye is beautiful even in winter, without vegetation, then it could be beautiful still at night; by logical extension, its beauties could be experienced mostly within the imagination, with only a few visual hints. The kind of picture he is painting here is remote from the picturesque views at the time. It is not something that could be captured in a Claude glass or within the parameters of a frame. Like the view from the hilltop offered by the peasant guide in the previous essay, this particular view requires the presence of the living body situated in time; it is not an experience that can be captured fully in any aesthetic medium. Writing can *represent* it to some extent.

As political allegory, the well-known Milton line from *Paradise Lost* (1:63) leads us to the blinded Milton, blind but living on after a failed revolution, blind but with a lucid intelligence and imagination; we are also led to Satan, expelled and exiled, after having fought the good fight. This section of Thelwall's essay has none of the self-pity that he could have drawn from Milton. Within the darkness visible Thelwall, the defeated rebel, gains strength and power from the elemental nature that ought to be frightening but is not, ought to be enfeebling and symbolic of loss and death, but is not.

The essay also stresses the winter landscape. Thelwall portrays the naked beauty that the vegetation conceals, as he establishes both nakedness and underlying structure as allegorical elements. In James Thomson's "Winter," for example, the poet counters the overwhelmingly morbid associations of that season, but Thelwall's affirmation of winter is even more unequivocal. "To know how to cloath her [nature] to the best advantage, we must strip her naked" (343). The French revolutionary style in clothing, which the British democrats imitated, was the more "natural" style that followed the body's contours. The usually prudish Wordsworth uses the word "naked" in his poetry to signify only the most emotionally intense moments. From the nakedness of nature Thelwall turns to abstract nakedness—"nakedness itself is but beauty without a veil"—to human nakedness, "the perfection of the human form," and "the sublime of human nature" (344). By humanizing the sublime of winter, by transforming the absence of vegetation into a metaphor for nakedness, Thelwall avoids making his aesthetic appreciation into just another pictorial commodity. Aesthetic values for Thelwall are ordinarily attached to social values. The winter landscape is in fact better than the lush summer's—"more permanent" and with "a superior charm" (344).

Even the spring flood becomes a social allegory, as the extraordinarily harsh flood of 1795, which he himself did not witness but did hear about, is described with its own "sublimity" and "terrors," as "rails, land-marks, trees innumerable, and even sheep and cattle, were borne down by the rapid torrents from the mountains, or whirled away from the meadows and low lands by the infuriated course of the river; whole plantations were shattered, and several bridges were entirely swept away" (345). The spring flood that he is imagining is called a "universal deluge." Thelwall is representing natural violence with the same rhetoric used at the time for political violence (and used also in Milton's "fiery deluge" in the "darkness visible" passage). Everything falls victim to the universal deluge, to the overwhelming sublimity of a powerful force that sweeps all before it. The very geography is transformed, as the familiar guideposts and human constructions within nature are swept away, forcing people to start over. The parallels here with social revolution as Thelwall and other intellectuals experienced the 1790s are obvious. Thelwall's angle on this destructiveness is not elegiac, as one might have expected, but just the opposite: he is affirmative, as the violent flood actually assists poor people, giving them free firewood and fertilizing silt for their crops (346). Indeed, "the ravages they [the floods] commit are more than compensated by the good which they distribute" (345). The "nature" in this passage, according to Nicholas Roe, does not produce Romantic ideology but instead expresses purely "revolutionary force that works to expose . . . [social] misery and inequality."[39]

The wintry nakedness provides an apt symbol for Thelwall's own ruined political efforts, for the "fruitless" efforts of the revolutionaries. In this context, his defense of the underlying strength and beauty of nature, which he links to human nature, is a defense of his own philosophical assumptions

39. Roe, *Politics of Nature*, 136.

concerning the overall rationality of nature and the improvability of humanity. That is, humans are not monsters; winter is not a graveyard; the absence of greenery does not mean the absence of meaning and purpose.

Conclusion

These topographical works begin and end in hope, but the final hope is austere. Considering the apostasy and recantation of other 1790s radicals, one notes the courage of austerity. As landscape embodies nature, national history, private history, and labor, these works have philosophical, political, personal, and economic meaning for Thelwall. Placed side by side, they make up a kind of *Prelude*, with the *Peripatetic*'s enthusiastic revolutionary hope and the *Monthly Magazine* essays' retreat, retirement, and hopeful endurance. Wordsworth and Coleridge, of course, went in other directions from those taken by Thelwall here. Inserting Thelwall's own revolutionary experience into the more familiar trajectories of disenchantment and disillusionment provides at the very least a contrasting example. His Jacobin allegories undermine aristocratic culture at the level of literary form in an enthusiastic style, however secularized.

The displacement and ambiguity at the center of Jacobinism are especially evident in the landscape writing, which finally is quite different from the work in this genre of Coleridge and Wordsworth. The younger poets insert a unique self into a "realist" nature, and these reciprocally reflect each other. Coleridge's stormy sky or Wordsworth's naked wall is symbolic in the way of Goethe, but also allegorical of a private inwardness whose details are elided. We later readers allegorically supply the Sara Hutchinson, the truly stormy object of desire, and the Oedipal guilt that is written on the naked wall. Romantic symbolism tries to limit the allusiveness of words, but we can violate them with allegorical interpretation. Thelwall, however, scorning the topos of ineffability, goes to unusual lengths in enhancing the allusiveness of his writing. Figurative desire is always externalized, rarely symbolized: Belmour's erotic and neurotic obsessions are stylized, made typical and culturally resonant. Sylvanus Theophrastus's late-night communions with nature might reflect Thelwall's own inwardness, but the character's name is so improbable according to "realistic" criteria that the reader thinks less of the author and more of pastoral conventions. Thelwall's depiction is startling because the stylized representation is superimposed on the London suburbs of 1792. We are aware in new ways of both the stylized depiction and the realistic setting, as the reciprocal interaction leads ultimately to social meanings, not private ones. Similarly, Thelwall's topographical writing portrays a landscape already inscribed with meanings that he tries to uncover. When meaning cannot be had, this muteness allegorizes his own speechlessness because of political repression. Wordsworth's most vivid landscapes—the Alps in Book Five of *The Prelude*—allegorize timeless processes that Thelwall historicizes—the flooded Wye valley, the naked winter woods.

Against Empire

Alan Richardson and Sonia Hofkosh, in introducing a collection of essays on Romanticism and imperialism, remind us that the non-Western world has been typically an object available for use by the Western writer. Moreover, we Romanticists forget, if we ever knew, the extent of the British empire during the Romantic period: by 1820 a full quarter of the entire world population was under British rule.[1] Like other things that might have earlier seemed tangential to the central topics of Romanticism, imperialism has forced itself into our awareness. We would expect the Jacobin Thelwall to oppose the slave trade and slavery itself, which of course he did, but it is surprising to see how important anti-imperialistic themes are in his writing. His opposition to empire was clear: "it would be a happy thing for the universe in general, and for Britain in particular, if there were no such a thing as a colony or depend-

---

1. Alan Richardson and Sonia Hofkosh, eds., *Romanticism, Race, and Imperial Culture, 1780–1834* (Bloomington and Indianapolis: Indiana University Press, 1996), 3.

ency in the political system of the universe" (PEJ 294). His *Tribune* lectures are sprinkled with comments against empire and slavery; his first novel protests against slavery-tainted sugar; his second novel opposes West Indian slavery; his 1801 volume of *Poems* is structured around the idea of empire; and his later journalism protests regularly against antisemitic oppression, including the Hep-Hep riots in Germany and discrimination against the Jews in general.[2] For Thelwall imperialism and racism contradicted the Enlightenment ideal of a universal humanity within which Africans, West Indian slaves, Scottish, Irish, and English were all one "brethren" (PEJ 242–43).

Imperialism was the commercial spirit at its worst. In *Democracy Vindicated* Thelwall criticizes empire thus: "The system of enslaving different and detached countries by what is called commercial colonization (that is to say, murdering one-half of the people, and reducing the other half to bondage, that the victor may monopolize the plunder of the country) was left to modern invention."[3] His Saxon ancestors who fled the Norman invasion for Wales remind him of a historical pattern of conquest, domination, and resistance. In two poems he restructures national myths, to accommodate a critique of imperialism but also to incorporate the realities of ethnic and religious mixing. As we saw in Chapter 5, his tribute to the naval hero Nelson tried to turn nationalist sentiment away from triumphalist militarism.

It is not as though Thelwall were entirely exemplary in his views. He was not. He made a few nasty comments about Jews;[4] exploited anti-Catholic prejudice, as we saw in Chapter 2; and made some equivocations in his

---

2. The *Champion* sympathetically records Zionist ideals on 3 January 1819 (9), and reports compassionately on the victimization of German Jews on 17 January 1819 (37–38), and on 10 October 1819 (640).

3. *Democracy Vindicated* is Thelwall's version of Walter Moyle's *An Essay Upon the Constitution of the Roman Government*, which is reprinted with most of Thelwall's notes of commentary, including the one on imperialism, Caroline Robbins, ed., *Two English Republican Tracts* (Cambridge: Cambridge University Press, 1969), 251. For a discussion of *Democracy Vindicated* see my "John Thelwall and the Revolution of 1649," in Nigel Smith and Timothy Morton, eds., *From Revolution to Revolution: Liberty's Journey, 1650–1830* (Cambridge: Cambridge University Press, 2000).

4. In the *Champion* (17 December 1820): 824–25, Thelwall allows his defense of Queen Caroline to digress into an attack on the Stock Exchange "Jews," but this antisemitic comment is rare; more typical is a straightforward criticism of the Frankfurt Rothschilds for loaning money to Austria but without antisemitic comment in the *Champion* (17 March 1821): 171. Although there is a snide comment about Jewish religious observances in the *Monthly Magazine* ([25 September 1825], 139), more typical is the praise of the Talmudic tales translated by Hyman Hurwitz in the *Panoramic Miscellany* (31 January 1826), 90–91.

Against Empire

account of the slave rebellion in San Domingo. Overall, however, he is usually on the side of the angels, so to speak. This is to his credit; he also provides an example by which one can contrast the deeds and words of others when we put attitudes about empire in context. We will examine three separate texts that express and reflect anti-imperialist themes, the 1792 historical opera *The Incas;* the 1801 Jacobin novel *The Daughter of Adoption;* and the 1801 volume of poetry *Poems, Chiefly Written in Retirement.*

Thelwall's Phantom Opera:
"No! no! no Jacobins here, all Loyal, all Loyal."⁵

We know little about *The Incas; or, The Peruvian Virgin.* There is a manuscript copy of the play in the British Library in Thelwall's hand, but the "Historical Opera" was neither produced on stage nor published in full.⁶ According to Allardyce Nicoll, Thelwall submitted the play to Covent Garden's Thomas Harris, who produced in December 1792 not *The Incas* but a play very close to it, Thomas Morton's popular *Columbus,* which Thelwall insisted was plagiarized from him.⁷ Thomas Morton, one of whose plays introduced Mrs. Grundy to the world, made his theatrical name with *Columbus,* according to Joseph Donohue. Alternately amusing and sentimental, this melodrama (written shortly before such a genre actually existed) was a well-written play that appealed to audiences in part through the very attractive character Harry Herbert, the Englishman, "stage surrogate for the audience."⁸ Harry Herbert, however, is similar to two of Thelwall's characters, the heroic Faukland and the Falstaffian Pedrillo. According to the *Biographia Dramatica,* the early nineteenth-century source for Nicoll's information, rumor at the time "insinuated" that Morton plagiarized from Thelwall. While *Columbus* was on stage *The Incas* was being advertised, a specimen of which was published in a peri-

---

5. From a 1799 satirical print against Sheridan's *Pizarro;* quoted by Joseph W. Donohue, Jr., *Dramatic Character in the English Romantic Age* (Princeton: Princeton University Press, 1970), 136.
6. BL add. mss. 38622. The handwriting is the same as in Thelwall's letters.
7. Allardyce Nicoll, *A History of Late Eighteenth Century Drama, 1750–1800* (Cambridge: Cambridge University Press, 1927), 101.
8. Joseph Donohue, *Theatre in the Age of Kean* (Oxford: Basil Blackwell, 1975), 90–92.

odical of 1792.⁹ There is no comment on this episode in any Thelwall text I have seen, but there are letters related to the theater, one of which is to Henry Harris, Thomas Harris's son.¹⁰ Given the time of this episode—the very end of 1792, when Thelwall was a radical activist, a member of the Southwark Friends of the People but not yet the LCS—one speculates that Thelwall's protests were limited by his activism and perhaps his hope of not alienating Harris. Perhaps Harris or Morton paid Thelwall a small fee, but Thelwall had to have been irritated by the success of Morton's play and was perhaps chagrined by the later success of Sheridan's *Pizarro*, yet another South American play similar to Thelwall's.

If Morton plagiarized from Thelwall, he also made important alterations. Morton's opening scene—the religious ceremony worshipping the sun—is from Thelwall or Thelwall's own source, Marmontel.¹¹ In either case there is a superficial alteration from Incan to Aztec sun worship, and an overall geographical shift from Peru to Mexico. Morton inserts a nationalistic Briton—Harry Herbert—into the cast of Spanish and American characters just as Thelwall does, but Morton's Briton is ostentatiously English while Thelwall's Falkland is a cosmopolitan citizen of the world. At the center of Morton's play is a love conflict (Cora's love for Alonzo is vexed by Cora's having already been dedicated to the sun god). Their love threatens to bring down the punishment of death on both of them, but at the play's end the ancient customs are adjusted to produce a comic resolution. In Thelwall's play the love conflict is similar, in that Faulkland falls in love also with a native American whom he wants to marry but cannot. In his play the cause of the separation was a prior betrothal he made, not out of love but out of duty. In both plays the protagonists and their lovers have the obstacle of a prior commitment. Both plays criticize the Spanish brutality against the native Americans that is hypocritically justified by Christianity. Both plays use the norm of "nature" primarily against European civilization but also against Ameri-

9. Harris was co-owner and manager of Covent Garden from 1767 until his death in 1820. Philip H. Highfill, Jr., Kalman A. Burnin, and Edward A. Langhans, *A Biographical Dictionary of Actors, Actresses, Musicians, Dancers, Managers and Other Stage Personnel in London, 1660–1800*, 16 vols. (Carbondale: Southern Illinois University Press, 1973–91), 7: 137–39. David Erskine Baker, Isaac Reed, and Stephen Jones, *Biographia Dramatica*, 2 vols. (London: Longman, Hurst, Rees, Orme, et al., 1812), 2:322.

10. In the letter to Henry Harris, British Library Add. mss. 27,925, f. 56 (18 November 1817), Thelwall proposes an idea he had discussed earlier with the actor Edmund Kean about producing Shakespeare's *Richard the Third*.

11. *Les Incas, ou La Destruction de l'Empire du Pérou* in *Oeuvres Complètes de [Jean François] Marmontel*, 7 vols. (Paris: Imprimier-Libraire, 1819–20), 3:2.

can superstition. Both plays have comic subplots that derive ultimately from Shakespeare.

Morton's play deviates from those of his models, Thelwall and Marmontel, especially ideologically. A major plot line develops around the mutiny against Columbus led by the villain Roldan. The nationalistic Harry Herbert sides with Columbus to allegorize Britain's siding with Louis XVI. Also, Morton balances Enlightenment criticism of "unnatural" Western customs with harsh criticism of Aztec human sacrifice and the virgin cult to soften the anti-imperialistic tone considerably.

There is nothing comparable in *The Incas*, where the defeat of the Spaniards by the Americans is represented as a completely unmixed blessing. The Spanish hostage, Elvira, is well treated, emancipated after the last battle, and conspires with the villain, Masseru, to corrupt Incan institutions and frame the hero Faulkland with the accusation of blasphemy against the sun deity. Although a native Incan plots to trap Faulkland by manipulating religious rituals, the play represents these actions as corrupt deviations from the norm. In fact, the English hero, who also goes by the name of Sidney (and Sydney), evokes the seventeenth-century martyr to Stuart absolutism. In addition, the chief priest's son, Rocca, is in fact an "enlightener," as he promotes liberal ideals like tolerance and forgiveness (3:5). The very center of the play's action is the conspiracy against and testing of Faulkland. The conspiracy fails because of Rocca's armed intervention—an allegory of the recent republican triumph over Louis' soldiers at the Tuileries—and Myrrha's exposure of the conspiracy to the high priest. These events in the play are designed to evoke the British political repression, which by late 1792 included the criminalizing of *The Rights of Man*, outlawing Paine, and organizing burnings of Paine's effigy and writings. Faulkland's stoic endurance, from his unhesitating loyalty to his prior commitment to the unworthy Elvira to his calm resignation before the executioner's fire, resonates with classical republicanism, which was modeled after Brutus and Cicero, the figures appropriated by the French revolutionaries. Insofar as the play is nationalistic at all, it celebrates British republicanism.

The play's ideology is closer to the spirit of Diderot's *Supplement to Bougainville's Voyage* than of James Mill's treatise on India. In this regard Thelwall is more faithful to the Marmontel model than Morton. Although Morton lifts from Marmontel the entire Alonzo and Cora story with few alterations, he omits the numerous Enlightenment dialogues that show the Incas questioning their own idolatry. Marmontel's Alonzo, like Thelwall's

Faulkland, is an enlightener, but Morton's Alonzo is strictly a character of romantic comedy. Marmontel's Incan king declares that "la raison" is superior to "la loi," as he thanks Alonzo who "nous détrompe, nous éclaire, et nous fait révoquer une loi inhumaine."[12] The difference between persuading a less technologically developed people and conquering them is not absolute, as power attaches itself to persuasion, but neither Marmontel nor Thelwall justifies conquest in the name of progress.

Thelwall and Morton also appropriate Shakespearean "low" comedy in different ways. Morton's Harry Herbert is the plain-speaking Englishman who flirts with the bawdy Nesti, an American as feisty as her suitor. They fall in love. The parallel romance of Cora and Alonzo in Thelwall is pitched at a more ethereal level. Harry's skeptical irony is directed against both idealistic rhetoric and middle-class professionals like lawyers and doctors; plain speaking punctures the illusions of both. Because Harry comes to represent the English-speaking audience, yet another victim of plain speaking's power is Enlightenment idealism, universalism, and naturalism, which are now associated with the revolution across the channel. Plain speaking in Thelwall's play is identified with the Falstaffian Pedrillo, who is Faulkland's battle-avoiding servant. Pedrillo, who tells lies, runs away from danger, flirts with and chases the elusive Gulira, contrasts starkly with Faulkland, his master, who always tells the truth, faces every difficulty openly, and wins the heart of the chief priest's daughter, Myrrha. Thelwall plays Pedrillo for laughs too, as he gets many crowd-pleasing lines, but they are not nationalistic, as are those of Harry Herbert. Morton's Harry truly deflates the pretensions of other characters associated with false, idealistic rhetoric; Thelwall's Pedrillo is mostly a butt of humor, a coward whose rationalizations only superficially remind us of Falstaff.

As Faulkland awaits execution (3:4), the play becomes revolutionary allegory, not just an anti-imperialist tale. Faulkland/Sidney, unafraid of death, prepares himself to face the end after he has, like Socrates, refused the offer of escape. When Rocca tries to persuade Faulkland to take flight, the dialogue draws upon the topos of revolution or reform as Rocca's impatience— "I see an unfortunate friend struggling with the wave and shall I reflect whether I am to wet my garments in saving him"—counters Faulkland's caution—"Rocca thy words are wild. Thou dost not meditate any act of violence[?] [I]s this the doctrine thy friend hath taught thee[?]" (3:4). When

---

12. Marmontel, *Les Incas*, 3:2, 493.

Rocca intervenes to save Faulkland from the pyre, the allegory is French and contemporary. The defenders of the established order speak accusingly to Rocca and his men: "How here [at the holy altar] shall force avail!" But Rocca and his followers reply: "Here Justice shall prevail" (3:7). Justice drives out custom at the most holy site of the culture. Moreover, as the denouement unfolds, it turns out that Masseru had corrupted the holy institutions and had created only the illusion that the sun divinity had spoken against Faulkland. The discovery and exposure of holy fraud are very much part of the French revolutionary culture. A further political point is made when Masseru is pardoned rather than executed, an allusion to the debate over Louis' fate, not executed until January 1793. It is also politically resonant that Faulkland's alleged crime is blasphemy, in fact one of the favorite charges leveled against British radicals. Faulkland as an enlightener labels the prophetic process by which divinity supposedly speaks to the priest "superstitious" and "madness" (2:5), but he does not mock the Incan religion openly.

It is unfortunate that Thelwall's play was not produced. As a three-act opera it could have been staged at one of the "illegitimate" theaters if the patent houses turned it down. That Harris preferred a nationalistic play with an American theme like Morton's to a revolutionary, Enlightenment play like Thelwall's is not surprising in late 1792 as the government was moving quickly toward declaring war against France and domestic radicals. Morton's *Columbus* was popular but few plays rivaled the popularity of Sheridan's *Pizarro*, an event of 1799 that had to have troubled Thelwall, although I have not seen any text that addresses the issue—except perhaps indirectly, in his 1801 anti-imperialist novel that we will look at shortly. Before that, however, it is useful to examine Sheridan's play.

In late 1795 Sheridan, along with Fox, worked with Thelwall and the LCS in trying to defeat the Gagging Bill. Sheridan with the other Foxites boycotted parliament in 1797 to protest against the continued war and neglect of domestic reform. But in 1799 Sheridan writes and produces *Pizarro*, what Joseph Donohue has called "a famous piece of loyalist propaganda" that allegorizes the conquistador as Napoleon, the Spaniards as French, and the peace-loving native Americans as Britons.[13] Sheridan's model was Kotzebue, not Thelwall, but Sheridan's play shares many qualities with Thelwall's. Ideologically, however, they could not have been more different.

---

13. Donohue, *Dramatic Character in the English Romantic Age*, 137–39.

Pizarro was seen as a loyalist play whose appeal was patriotic, above party politics, whereas *The Incas* cannot be construed even after its initial 1792 time frame as anything other than a Jacobin play. Although some on the left attacked *Pizarro*'s opportunistic loyalism, and some on the right found heresy lurking between the lines, these criticisms were beside the point of wide public enthusiasm for a patriotic play that remained in the Drury Lane Theatre repertoire for over sixty years.[14] Precisely when Thelwall himself was in Wales, in exile, driven out of public life, with the LCS outlawed altogether, Sheridan was welcoming the king to his private box to witness the popular loyalist performance.

Thelwall's Abolitionist Novel

Under the pseudonym John Beaufort, a name that barely concealed that Thelwall had delivered his lectures at the Beaufort Buildings only five years earlier, the four-volume *The Daughter of Adoption* was published by the radical publisher Richard Phillips in 1801, providing the Thelwall family in Wales with some much-needed cash. The novel, betraying the effects of hasty composition (see the account in the "Prefatory Memoir" [*Poems* xlv–xlvi]), needed both pruning and considerable revision to bring out its strongest qualities. Nevertheless, however imperfect, *The Daughter of Adoption: A Tale of Modern Times* distinctively contributes to the genre of the Jacobin novel at a time when loyalist fictions were more lucrative.[15]

It is necessary to sketch in the West Indian background, especially the rebellion of San Domingo. At the beginning of the slave revolt in San Domingo (1791), Britain had almost a half million slaves in the West Indies. In 1793 the French freed the slaves of San Domingo and in 1794 slavery was abolished in the French empire. Britain sent a military expedition to the West Indies to suppress rebellions in its own islands and to seize whatever territory it could, including San Domingo (Britain captured Port au Prince in June of 1794). There were slave rebellions in British islands like Grenada, St. Vincent, and St. Lucia; in Jamaica, the largest British holding, there was a maroon war. The West Indian expeditionary force failed to seize San Domingo, which it left

---

14. Cecil Price, ed., *The Dramatic Works of Richard Brinsley Sheridan*, 2 vols. (Oxford: Clarendon Press, 1973), 2: 629–35.

15. John Beaufort [John Thelwall], *The Daughter of Adoption: A Tale of Modern Times*, 4 vols. (London: Richard Phillips, 1801). There is no modern reprint of this important novel.

in 1798, and incurred huge casualties. According to historian David Geggus, "over half of the troops sent out to the West Indies died there."[16] France failed to reconquer what was called Haiti but it succeeded in capturing and killing the leader of the revolt, Toussaint L'Ouverture.

Thelwall's novel pivots around the West Indian setting of the 1790s. Its main character, Henry Montfort, by the end of four volumes finally marries the radical feminist Seraphina, the daughter of adoption referred to in the title. The would-be happy couple has a complicated set of obstacles to overcome, most of which derive ultimately from the conventions of Gothic Romance and sentimental fiction: uncertain and concealed origins of both Henry and Seraphina; various conspiracies and plots by villains to separate the two lovers; a kidnapping and near rape; the threat of coerced, mercenary marriages; an evil, violent patriarch who is an authoritarian father and philandering husband. Spliced onto the Gothic and sentimental conventions are recognizably Jacobin elements. About a third of the novel takes place in the West Indies, in San Domingo, during a sympathetically portrayed slave rebellion. The novel's heroine and moral compass, Seraphina, is a Creole who has received an education from her adopted father in the New Philosophy of liberty, equality, and women's rights. Her lucid judgments correct the errant ways of Henry Montfort, whose character has been flawed by aristocratic and masculine privilege. Henry's (ostensible but it turns out not biological) mother, Amelia, had tried to provide her son with a morally exemplary upbringing, which Seraphina reinforces later. Forthrightly abolitionist and anti-imperialist, critical of marriage and gender inequality, the novel also supplies radical criticism of a favorite Jacobin target, the education of the young.

Seraphina illustrates the Jacobin truism that education is more powerful than hereditary structures, because her biological mother, Morton, and biological father, Montfort, are utterly unlike her. Rather, she takes after her adopted father, the philosophical and benevolent Parkinson, a kind of Godwinian figure, an ex-clergyman as was Godwin. (The name Parkinson echoes the LCS writer and physician James Parkinson [1755–1824], who described the nerve disease that was named after him.) Seraphina was raised within a utopian enclave, separated from the "corrupting" influences of the planters and their slaves, so that her character becomes a trope for

16. David Geggus, "The Anglo-French Conflict in the Caribbean in the 1790s," in Colin Jones, ed., *Britain and Revolutionary France: Conflict, Subversion, and Propaganda* (Exeter: University of Exeter, 1983), 35.

"natural innocence," as well as the New Philosophy of her stepfather. Indeed, the very idea of a utopian enclave here seems to be a nostalgic imagining of what might have been if Thelwall had been able to join the Nether Stowey circle in 1797. Nether Stowey is evoked explicitly in an episode where, in the midst of beautiful Caribbean scenery, Henry exclaims to his friend Edmonds, " 'What a scene, and what an hour . . . to hatch treason in!' " Edmonds replies: " 'What a scene, and what an hour . . . to make one forget that treason was ever necessary in the world!" (Vol. 1, Book 3, Chap. 2, p. 283). This passage *à clef* repeats a conversation among Thelwall, Coleridge, and Wordsworth at Nether Stowey that was recorded later in Coleridge's *Table Talk* for 27 July 1830.[17] Parkinson's "exile" from the planter society allegorizes Thelwall's own exile in Wales.

The novel's treatment of sexuality and marriage is also Jacobin in its criticism of mercenary marriages and the sexual exploitation of women, and its celebration of sexual love among equals. The sexually predatory Montfort is a Gothic villain who corrupts and then kills in a duel the man who turns out to be Henry's biological father. (There is a seduction episode with Henry and a farmer's daughter that I will discuss in the next chapter.) Seduction and sexual exploitation are commonplace symptoms of class and gender inequality exemplified in Henry's own temptation as a seducer; such narratives are sociopolitical as well as moral.

The Wollstonecraft influence is evident in the novel's treatment of loveless, mercenary marriages, Amelia's and then her friend Louisa's. Louisa, widowed after a year, would lose her inheritance if she should remarry, but she falls in love with and marries Captain Bowbridge, the eventual victim in a duel with Montfort. It turns out that Bowbridge and Louisa are Henry Montfort's biological parents: after Amelia's child by Montfort died at birth, she secretly "adopted" her friend's baby after both mother and father had died. The love between Amelia and Louisa repeats the female friendship represented in Wollstonecraft's *Mary*, and Louisa's pursuit of love after a loveless marriage repeats the pattern in Wollstonecraft's *Maria*. One of the novel's boldest moves repeats a controversial episode recorded in William Godwin's *Memoirs* of his wife (1798): Wollstonecraft's unmarried sexual relationships with Gilbert Imlay and then Godwin. Not only do Seraphina and Henry Montfort make love without being married, but Seraphina also

---

17. Peter Kitson, "Coleridge's Anecdote of John Thelwall," *Notes and Queries*, n.s., 32:3 (September 1985): 345. Hartley N. Coleridge, ed., *Specimens of the Table Talk of Samuel Taylor Coleridge* (Oxford: Oxford University Press, 1917), 122.

justifies the sexual conduct as proper because her love for Henry is sanctioned by nature (Vol. 2, Book 5, Chap. 2, p. 163). After discovering that marrying Henry would result in his being disinherited, the pregnant Seraphina refuses to marry him; moreover, she does not care about the social opprobrium placed on her as an unwed mother. She wants Henry to be faithful to her, but doubts that marriage alone would guarantee his fidelity (Vol. 2, Book 6, Chap. 3). After the death of her child, Seraphina still rebuffs Henry's marriage proposal because he refuses to live a virtuous life. Until he undergoes "reform" and gives up the corruptions of aristocratic living, she will not marry him (Vol. 3, Book 7, Chap. 1). Even when she entertains the possibility of marriage, she speaks as a utilitarian, noting that she might be more useful to society were she married (Vol. 3, Book 7, Chap. 2, p. 59), in much the same way that Godwin and Wollstonecraft justified their own marriage. Near the end of the novel, Seraphina again sets the terms for their possible marriage as honest poverty, because genteel luxury makes virtuous living impossible; Seraphina insists that Henry work for a living, and that their marriage be completely egalitarian (Vol. 4, Book 10, Chap. 3). When Godwin and Wollstonecraft were being scapegoated as evil Jacobins, especially for their sexual morality, Thelwall's novel appropriates positively their most uncompromising ideas.

The novel is also strongly Jacobin in its treatment of the San Domingo slave rebellion at a time when the slave trade in Britain and slavery itself in the British empire were flourishing. In Henry Montfort's shocking introduction to West Indian slave society, he discovers the physical brutality against slaves, the sexual exploitation of especially "mulatto" women, and the incongruity of gentleman planters who treat other gentlemen politely but who are utterly barbaric to slaves (Vol. 1, Book 3, Chap. 1). Although the novel represents realistically the slave violence against Europeans during the rebellion, the moral onus for the violence is with the planters and Europeans. Discourse about the slave rebellion also refers to the revolution in France. Parkinson takes the "Godwinian" line against revolution and for gradual change, but Edmonds undercuts Parkinson with observations that the planters are not likely to "reform" a system that provides them with so much profit (Vol. 2, Book 4, Chap. 1, pp. 6–7). Parkinson seems to get the better of Edmonds, however, when he disputes the latter's suggestion that the rebellion would be less violent if the leaders were wiser (Vol. 2, Chap. 1, p. 17). When Henry and his friends are caught in a battle between planters and slaves, they side with the planters, but when they witness the sickening brutality of the planters against the slaves, they regret their partisanship (Vol. 2, Book 4, Chap. 1, p. 28). Two comments, one by Edmunds and the other by Henry, capture their position vividly: "it were better to die than live to see these horrors" (p. 33), and "the oppressions of these tyrants have rendered their slaves too vile for liberty, though yet not so vile as themselves" (p. 38). Seraphina echoes their views: "The atrocities of the revolted slaves, can never reconcile me to the tyranny that made them so atrocious!" (Vol. 2, Book 5, Chap. 1, p. 124). Commenting on the San Domingo rebellion in *The Rights of Nature*, Thelwall anticipates Seraphina's observation: "the master who falls by the bondsman's hand, is the victim of his own barbarity" (PEJ 408).

The novel attacks slavery itself more forthrightly than it does racial coding and stratification, which Thelwall did indeed attack in other writings. For example, a *Tribune* lecture unsettles racist assumptions when Thelwall speaks sarcastically of "the divine right of our white complexions," as if whiteness gave title to ownership of black people. In this same lecture he compares British laborers with West Indian slaves, not in order to denigrate the sufferings of the latter, as Thomas Carlyle would later do, but in order to draw out common traits to protest against injustice.[18] Thelwall's novel addresses racism implicitly, however, when it vindicates the "Creole" Seraphina and shows at least one virtuous slave. (The racial coding of "Creole" seems to be that "whiteness" is compromised by the "blackness" of being a native on an "uncivilized" island; Seraphina "transcends" her Creole origins but Morton her mother does not.) The conclusion of the novel only mildly disrupts the racist categories, because the utopian community formed around Seraphina and Henry in north Yorkshire is all-white and socially homogenous. Nevertheless, in its context, *The Daughter of Adoption* challenges the anti-Jacobin cultural reaction at fundamental and subsidiary levels.

The Welsh Connection

When Thelwall settled on a small farm in Llyswen, Brecknockshire, Wales, in 1797, after he no longer could sustain a public role as lecturer and jour-

---

18. *Tribune* (27 February 1795): 2: 150–58.

nalist because of the political repression, he was in fact returning to a nation where his ancestors had lived for many years. Moreover, he used his stay in Wales (1797–1801) to allegorize resistance to imperial conquest. According to the biography published by his wife, Thelwall's ancestors were Saxons who settled in North Wales to escape the Norman conquest (LJT 1). This account mirrors exactly what Thelwall wrote in his 1801 "Prefatory Memoir" (*Poems* ii). An additional detail in the biography places Thelwall's particular branch of the family in the "counties of Cheshire and Lancashire, where in the reign of Henry IV., [the Thelwalls] had a castle, which they defended to the last extremity against the famous chieftain Owen Glendower" (LJT 1). Owen Glendower (1348–1415), who led the last Welsh rebellion against English domination, was omitted in 1801 because it contradicted the anti-imperialistic theme Thelwall reinforced throughout the entire volume, memoir and poetry. According to a modern source, Thelwall's family came from Plas y War, Denbighshire.[19] The Denbighshire Thelwalls practiced "extensive intermarriage," according to other modern sources.[20] Thelwall's ethnic background, then, was both Saxon and Welsh, so that when he settled in Llyswen he was, in some sense, returning to his roots.

Connected with the Welsh roots is a political antiquarianism that was especially appealing in 1801 when Thelwall was refashioning his image as a radical in retirement at a dangerous time of political repression. The Saxons for Thelwall were both democratic pioneers and imperialistic invaders and conquerors. Although the antiquarian question of the democratic status of the Saxons seems to be only marginally relevant to actual politics, in fact antiquarianism was one of the areas where late eighteenth- and early nineteenth-century opponents and proponents fought out their ideas. Janice Lee in a recent article shows how Obadiah Hulme's claim in 1771 for a Saxon origin to radical reform—universal suffrage and annual parliaments—provided a traditionalist foundation for democratic argument independent of the rationalistic basis used by Paine and Godwin. So seriously was Hulme's argument considered that the *Anti-Jacobin Review* in 1798 directed an important counterattack against Saxon democracy. Appeals to the ancient Saxon

---

19. Meic Stephens, ed., *The Oxford Companion to the Literature of Wales* (Oxford: Oxford University Press, 1986), 575.
20. Glanmor Williams, *Recovery, Reorientation and Reformation: Wales c. 1415–1642* (Oxford: Clarendon and University of Wales Press, 1987), 95; R. R. Davies, *Conquest, Coexistence, and Change: Wales 1063–1415* (Oxford: Clarendon and University of Wales Press, 1987), 422.

constitution by the reform movement started to decline only in the 1820s.[21] The Norman Yoke myth goes back to the seventeenth century.[22]

Thelwall was not alone in linking his radicalism to Wales and the Saxons. Alan Liu has shown how Wordsworth, when he was closest to his Jacobin ideas, associated Wales with threatening violence. While he was visiting with his Cambridge friend Robert Jones in 1791 (or 1793), Wordsworth had a memorable encounter with an angry, perhaps intoxicated Welsh priest who, offended by Wordsworth's insensitive comment about the Welsh language, threatened Wordsworth with a knife. Liu links the threatened violence against the "vile Saxon" Wordsworth with the legend of the "treason of the long knives" when Hengist and the Saxons betrayed and slaughtered the Welsh.[23] This particular cluster—Hengist, Saxons, Welsh—appears in one of the major works of Thelwall's 1801 volume of poetry, *The Fairy on the Lake*, a lyrical drama whose villain is none other than Hengist's daughter, Rowenna. In Thelwall's play the Saxons are in fact the conquering imperialists against whom Arthur and the native Britons—that is, the Welsh—fight.

Poems, Chiefly Written in Retirement is structured around Wales, the nation that gave his ancestors asylum. First, although the protagonist of his epic poem, *The Hope of Albion*, is Edwin of Northumbria, the first English king to convert to Christianity, the connection with Wales is in Edwin's defeat by the Welsh king Cadwallon, the last Welsh monarch to rule over all of the Britons.[24] More striking, however, is the frontispiece entitled "Cerrig-Enion." This print shows a stone memorial marker at whose base is sitting a woman bent over in apparent grief. On the left foreground is a short tree whose full branches draw one's attention to the center of the picture, an image of sunlight behind a cloudy sky. The quotation beneath the picture is from Thelwall's poem, Effusion 10, "Cerrig-Enion": "Why on the moul'-dring tomb of other times / Sits the lorn wanderer." The "lorn wanderer" is Thelwall's wife, who is lamenting the recent death of their daughter Maria, and "Einion" is probably a Welsh chieftain, Einion Glyd, lord Elvel, the

---

21. Janice Lee, "Political Antiquarianism Unmasked: The Conservative Attack on the Myth of the Ancient Constitution," *Bulletin of the Institute of Historical Research* 55 (1982): 166–79.

22. R. B. Seaberg, "The Norman Conquest and the Common Law: The Levellers and the Argument from Continuity," *Historical Journal* 24 (1981): 791–806.

23. Alan Liu, "Wordsworth and Subversion, 1793–1804: Trying Cultural Criticism," *Yale Journal of Criticism* 2 (1989): 55–100.

24. John Davies, *A History of Wales* (London: Penguin, 1990), 62–63; Joseph P. Clancy, *The Earliest Welsh Poetry* (London: Macmillan, 1970), 204—confuses Cadwaladr, Cadwallon's son, for Cadwallon.

friend and assistant of Giraldus Cambrensis, killed by the Normans in 1177.[25] Aside from the local accident of Einion's tomb being in the neighborhood to provide an apt symbol for mourning, Einion's being a Welsh leader and intellectual slain by the Normans enhanced Thelwall's identification. Young leaders with intellectual training who died before they were able to complete their careers parallel Thelwall's self-pitying image of himself driven into exile. The Welsh connection provides more than a bathetic background for Thelwall's self-regard because it also socializes his victimization. The Pitt government in its repressiveness reveals its Norman legacy of imperial conquest. An antiquarian focus is especially helpful during this period of loyalist fervor, as native English Edwin and native Welsh Einion take historical precedence over the latecoming Normans. When direct political discourse is blocked from expression, the more indirect and allegorical discourse of antiquarianism is both legally safer and open to mythographic revision. Even in his literary history we see the antiquarian praise for the peaceful literature of the poetic Saxons contrasted with criticism of the militaristic culture of the bellicose Normans.[26]

The most unforgettable poems in the volume are the ten blank-verse effusions on the sudden death of his first child, Maria. These painful poems, a ten-part lamentation, are *in place of* an elegy as he cannot take advantage of the expressive possibilities of that form; the very evasion of the poetic form is a Romantic sign that the grief is too recent to avail itself of that tradition. Like the poem to his son Hampden, these assume a stance of helplessness before hostile powers. Resolutely secular, these raw feelings of loss and grief are not channeled into the comforting forms of public elegy, but Thelwall finds his own community of suffering, his wife and several unnamed friends. By the last poem he writes of "our Maria," not just "my Maria," as he finds in the tomb of the Welsh hero Einion a fit symbol for his own grief. Einion's political significance as a fellow victim of "Norman" repression is important, but so too is the tomb's proximity to where Maria died and to where, more important, he finds his grieving wife. The poem's speaker relieves his grief by imagining other forms of loss and suffering that might have caused his wife to grieve at Einion's tomb, turning the tableau of his wife at the tomb into a

25. For shedding light on this mystery I thank Damian Walford Davies (University of Wales, Aberystwyth) who found the information in Edwin Poole, *The Illustrated History and Biography of Brecknockshire* (Brecknock, 1886), 180. I also wish to thank Peter Kitson (University of Wales, Bangor) for providing me with helpful information. See also William Owen, *The Cambrian Biography* (1803; repr.New York: Garland, 1979), 108.

26. *Champion* (24 January 1819): 64.

figure for "ruins." Haunting the scene is the image of a solitary "felon Kite" that awaits yet another death for scavenging. The kite assumes allegorical meaning—the natural forces that took their daughter away—but the poem does not go any further into metaphysical criticism of nature à la Thomas Hardy. Rather, the poem's latter half focuses on Einion and his wife. Thelwall appropriates Einion's symbolism—political virtue defeated but honored—to make sense of his own political suffering, to which has been added the tragic loss of a child. Einion symbolizes hope because the tomb itself testifies to enduring political resistance. Hope is evident too in "Nature's glories" that illustrate life's power over death. As a "budding flower" that has been "cropp'd," and as "mournful music," Maria survives. We see by the last effusion that Thelwall is finally able to use the traditional consolations offered by the elegy. In this final effusion the grief is socialized as "our sighs," connected with the genre of the elegy and not dependent wholly on personal "effusions." His grief is now rooted in a place that honors political virtue. From the first effusion, addressed to Joseph Gerrald,[27] to the last one citing Einion, Thelwall mourns a double loss, his daughter and his political hopes. His poetic mourning seems to have worked through his grief rather than merely have acted it out repetitively as Einion and nature symbolize continuity and survival after trauma.[28]

The centerpiece poem of the 1801 collection, the Arthurian lyrical drama, *The Fairy of the Lake*, shares with the personal lyrics the same Welsh locale. Vortigern's castle, Gwertheyrnion, was actually "situated among the fastnesses of Plynlinmon, near the source of the Wye," but Thelwall moved it to "the Beacons of Brecknock (Farinioch)" (*Poems* 205). This act of poetic freedom reinforces the identification of Arthur and Thelwall—and Einion. Arthur's defeat of Rowenna, the Saxon sorceress, daughter of Hengist who betrayed the Welsh—"the treason of the long knives"—wife of Vortigern, the most hated of kings in Welsh legend and history, and the burning of Vortigern's castle represent a victory of the native Celts over the invading imperialists. Thelwall appropriates this cultural capital by means of an allegory whereby Arthur's victory—only made possible by the intervention of the Lady of the Lake—figures

---

27. Andrew McCann has identified the poem's "J____ G_____" as Joseph Gerrald; *Cultural Politics in the 1790s: Literature, Radicalism and the Public Sphere* (New York and London: St. Martin's Press and Macmillan, 1999), 105.

28. Dominick LaCapra has been applying the Freudian concepts of mourning, repetition, working-through, and acting out to cultural studies and history. See his *History, Theory, Trauma: Representing the Holocaust* (Ithaca: Cornell University Press, 1994).

Against Empire

the workings of history at important transitional junctures. Arthur, like Einion, evokes the topos of winning by losing: Celtic Christianity's triumph over Saxon paganism is only one of the moral victories Arthur's ultimate defeat by the Saxons symbolizes. Similarly, Einion's fall at the hands of the Normans becomes a moral victory by being memorialized and sustained throughout the generations as a symbol of anti-imperialist resistance.

The Fairy of the Lake, modeled on Dryden's popular Arthurian play, "shares," according to Roger Simpson, the "stage tradition of spectacular transformations and of burning towers."[29] The play focuses on the destruction of one order and the emergence of another, with the most powerful force being represented as a feminine entity very much like the Romantic Muse or Nature so common in Thelwall's other poetry. The nationalistic poem is experimental and, at a structural level, perhaps too "Jacobin" in its celebration of the overthrow of old authority to appeal to a conservative public.[30] The play depicts the Saxon Queen Rowenna, who is in love with Arthur and who plots the death of her husband, Vortigern. By marrying Arthur she can unite the Saxons and Celts, thus ending their warfare. Vortigern's incestuous passion is for his daughter Guenever, the object of Arthur's desire. A sorceress, Rowenna has less success with her magic than the more powerful Fairy of the Lake, with whose assistance Arthur attacks Rowenna's castle after Vortigern is poisoned. Rowenna dies in the flames (a detail Scott used in Ivanhoe for the death of the Saxon Ulrica). The play concludes with Arthur's coronation celebrated by the chief of the Welsh bards, Taliessin.

This is Thelwall's version of the fall of empire, the master-theme of Romantic literature, according to Marilyn Butler.[31] Arthur is not especially

---

29. Roger Simpson, *Camelot Regained: The Arthurian Revival and Tennyson 1800–1849* (Cambridge: D. S. Brewer, 1990), 128. The *Peripatetic* comments on Arthur as a topic for epic treatment less worthy than Alfred (3: 48). Dryden's play being the primary model for *The Fairy of the Lake* acquires credibility when one recalls the whole chapter in the *Peripatetic* devoted to praising Dryden's work and fixing the English literary canon with the triad of Shakespeare, Milton, and Dryden. P 3:24–33.

30. Grumbling reads the political allegory of *The Fairy of the Lake* as a warning against England's alliance with counterrevolutionary Austria and Prussia. See "John Thelwall: Romantic and Revolutionist," 183. See also James Douglas Merriman, *The Flower of Kings: A Study of the Arthurian Legend in England Between 1485 and 1835* (Lawrence: University Press of Kansas, 1973), 137–39; Roger Simpson, *Camelot Regained*, 128, 175–76, and 236; Alan Lupack, ed., *Arthurian Drama: An Anthology* (New York: Garland, 1991), xvi–xvii.

31. "The Political Narratives of Romantic Poetry and Criticism," in Kenneth R. Johnston, Gilbert Chaitin, Karen Hanson, and Herbert Marks, eds., *Romantic Revolutions: Criticism and Theory* (Bloomington and Indianapolis: Indiana University Press, 1990), 133–57.

heroic, because magical forces that operate independently of his will are far more powerful than he. According to Alan Lupack, Thelwall's is the *only* Arthurian play that does not portray Arthur heroically, as *The Fairy of the Lake* subverts the heroic ideal itself.[32] Out of frustration Arthur peevishly tosses away his weapons. Matching Arthur with the Falstaffian Tristram provides comic relief and diminishes Arthur's dramatic stature. The truly potent forces in the play are the two females, Rowenna and the Fairy of the Lake, who represent not individual women but political and natural energies that shape history. Higher than Arthur, in fact, is the bard Taliessin, who correctly mediates and interprets the world-historical spirit (one might contrast Taliessin here to Coleridge's Bard Bracy's visionary impotence in *Christabel*). Remarkably, the supersession of Saxon paganism is not emphatically Christian. Thelwall the naturalist withholds the naming of the Christian triumph by turning the play's final lines into a epithalamion for Arthur and Guenever, prefiguring Shelley's fourth act of *Prometheus Unbound*, which celebrates the marriage of Prometheus and Asia.[33] Indeed, there is a not-so-subtle mocking of the trinity, with recurrent references to the paganistic love of "three," "a favourite number . . . among you Scandinavians"—three witches, three fates, and so on (3:2). Moreover, Arthur criticizes Rowenna's religion as an "idolatrous faith" that has repressed "the chaste affinities that link / The social frame of Nature" (2:4). The implication is that Christianity here is not the telos of history but the historically specific expression of natural religion that supersedes the historically obsolete paganism, an earlier but cruder expression of natural religion. Thelwall's version of transcendence, then, is entirely historical, almost Hegelian.

One should not exaggerate Arthur's lack of heroism. He resists the trickery of Rowenna; he is true to Guenever; he is horrified by and rejects what he perceives as the immorality of Rowenna and Vortigern—their acts of murder, incest, treason. The play strengthens these themes by linking Rowenna with Lady Macbeth. Arthur's lack of military success does not disqualify him for moral leadership. He and his bard have correctly interpreted the spirit of history—symbolized by the Fairy of the Lake—which acts on their side.

---

32. Lupack, ed., *Arthurian Drama*, xvi–xvii.
33. Donald H. Reiman's suggestion in the introduction to the 1978 Garland reprint of the 1801 *Poems* that the play influenced Shelley's *Prometheus Unbound* seems precisely on target. Roger Simpson has drawn attention in *Camelot Regained* to the play's masquelike qualities (236), and the *Peripatetic*'s (2: 49) defense of Arthur as a subject for poetic representation and its regret that Dryden did not complete an Arthurian epic (240–41).

Arthur's diminished heroism, if one can call it that, consists in remaining available to the forces of history that make his "self" as such utterly contingent. Here is an instance of hero and divinity that is modeled very differently from what we see in Homer and Vergil. Arthur's actions are not just aided or supplemented by the supernatural power; his actions express the essence of that supernatural power—essence being understood as historically contingent, and not timeless.

Thelwall makes another turn to history in *The Hope of Albion*. I have already suggested a Welsh connection between the epic fragments on Edwin of Northumbria and the theme of anti-imperialism by way of Cadwallon. Given Thelwall's ambition, a national epic was inevitable. Stuart Curran has remarked upon the "proliferation of epics" during the Romantic period inspired by nationalist anxiety over invasion from France, the Milton revival, and Hayley's influential *Essay on Epic Poetry* (1782), which promoted a national epic celebrating "British Freedom."[34] Following the work of David Quint, Alan Richardson has remarked on the generic ties of epic to empire that go back to Vergil's *Aeneid*.[35] According to Richardson, opposition to empire in epics and other genres was "a legitimate if decidedly minority position" taken by poets like Blake, Helen Maria Williams, Landor, Campbell, James Montgomery, and Samuel Rogers. They "assail[ed] empire in the years between the American Revolution and Waterloo." The Spanish conquest of the indigenous Americans had "long served the purposes of English nationalist and anti-Catholic propaganda,"[36] as we have seen already with Thelwall's *Incas*. Thelwall's own *The Hope of Albion* shows the influence of Milton and Hayley but not Francophobia. The historical legend for his epic is a curious choice, the seventh-century English king Edwin, "the exiled prince of Deïria, and consequent establishment of English liberty, and [of] the Christian faith" (*Poems* 177). According to David Hume's history, one of Thelwall's acknowledged sources, the brutal king of Bernicia, Adelfrid, expelled his wife's infant brother, Edwin, out of fear of being challenged for power. About Edwin's disinheritance, an anti-imperialist theme with personal resonance for Thelwall, as we will see later in the "Prefatory Memoir,"

---

34. Stuart Curran, *Poetic Form and British Romanticism* (New York: Oxford University Press, 1986), 158–61.

35. David Quint, *Epic and Empire: Politics and Generic Form from Virgil to Milton* (Princeton: Princeton University Press, 1993). Alan Richardson, "Epic Ambivalence: Imperial Politics and Romantic Deflection in Williams's *Peru* and Landor's *Gebir*," in Alan Richardson and Sonia Hofkosh, eds., *Romanticism, Race, and Imperial Culture, 1780–1834*, 270–71.

36. Richardson, "Epic Ambivalence," 268, 265, 267.

Hume writes that Edwin, "unjustly dispossessed of the crown of Deiri," was forced to wander "from place to place in continual danger from the attempts of Adelfrid" until he received protection from Redwald, the East Anglian king. Even in East Anglia he was threatened, but Hume has Edwin make a stand: "it were better to die, than prolong a life so much exposed to the persecutions of his powerful rival." His nemesis Adelfrid is finally and suddenly killed when Edwin's protector Redwald launches a surprise attack. Thereafter Edwin is a popular king who married a Christian, permitted religious freedom, converted to Christianity "after a serious and long inquiry," insured everyone's personal safety, instituted a period of peace, and ruled with fairness. His happy reign ended with his death in battle at the age of forty-eight. After Edwin came more years of brutal power struggles within the Heptarchy and a return to paganism.[37]

The ideological and personal motives behind the choice of Edwin are numerous. Edwin was renowned not for military prowess but for his ability as a peaceful, tolerant, just leader. As a young exile and wanderer, persecuted by a violent tyrant, Edwin resembles Thelwall himself, finding protection in Wales from loyalist gangs and government agents. The way Edwin converts to Christianity—after lengthy research—makes the king more a figure of Enlightenment rationalism than Anglican orthodoxy. From dispossession and exile to triumphant restoration Thelwall concisely symbolizes his own hopes for the democratic movement. *The Hope of Albion* was to cover primarily the two-week period when Adelfrid was overthrown, Edwin elected as king, and the temple of Woden "cleansed" of idols.[38] Within the two-week time frame, the epic was to have numerous flashbacks to Edwin's childhood. Like *The Fairy of the Lake*, the epic concentrated on a moment of historical transition roughly parallel to Thelwall's revolutionary epoch. The poem, not finished in 1801, was apparently completed in 1815, according to Henry Crabbe Robinson, but never published in its entirety.[39]

---

37. David Hume, *History of England*, 6 vols. (Boston: Little Brown, 1854), 1: 33–37. The Edwin material is also in Milton's history, a source one imagines Thelwall would not have neglected. Milton has a few poetic anecdotes lacking in Hume that Thelwall would have been negligent not to have used. *The Complete Prose Works of John Milton*, 8 vols., ed. Don M. Wolfe (New Haven: Yale University Press, 1971), 5: part 1, 197–205.

38. See the description of the poem in the *Champion* of 29 September 1821 in the "Renovator," reprinted in *The Poetical Recreations of "The Champion"* (London: Champion Press, 1822), 235–36.

39. Robinson, *Diary, Reminiscences, and Correspondence of Henry Crabbe Robinson*, 2 vols., ed. Sadler [diary entry 12 February 1815], 1:248.

The portions of the poem that were published indicate clearly two of Thelwall's interests, the solitary exile who becomes a wise leader, and the religious transformation from a violently coercive paganism to a more humane Christianity. The brutality of Adelfrid and the Heptarchy in general was reflected in the society's religious worship that Thelwall contextualizes in relation to the Enlightenment syncretic mythography that so preoccupied Blake and Shelley. The Saxon Woden, for example, is made parallel with Moloch, Mars, and Baal (*Poems* 186–87). "Pagan Superstition" is then "homicidal worship" (189–90). The peaceful Edwin was to find his way to Christianity as the most appropriate religious equivalent of his own secular morality. One fragment of his epic published in the *Monthly Magazine* (October 1825), entitled "Superstition," contrasts unnatural and violent superstitious idolatry that places "a demon on the throne of God" with "Reason! thou, / Whose genuine inspiration in our hearts / Makes revelation of the sole true faith— / Whose attribute is pure philanthropy, / Unlimited by sect, or rank, or tribe, / Tint of a skin, or colour of creed" (239). The direction this fragment takes suggests a line of development somewhere between Shelley's *Queen Mab* and *Prometheus Unbound*.

As a democratic hero Edwin is less laden with legendary and historical material than either Arthur or Alfred and thus permits even more latitude for imaginative elaboration. Edwin mediates between the old and the new to provide a transition to the new epoch required by the spirit of history. As in *Fairy of the Lake*, Christianity is presented as historically contingent and not timeless, a relative expression of nature's religion, not an absolute. As allegory, Edwin represents the peaceful arts of more civilized social harmony in contrast with war, conquest, and brutal self-interest. The samples of the poem that were published in *Poems* and later in the *Champion* and *Monthly Magazine* were promising, so that if it were finished, as Robinson claimed, it is unfortunate Thelwall never published the entire poem. It is surely possible that Thelwall's completed epic remained in manuscript form and was unfortunately lost after his death. The huge cache of Thelwall manuscripts, once owned by Charles Cestre, that were lost in the twentieth century might have included such a work. Here we have yet another symbol of dispossession, unfulfilled promise, and thwarted ambition.

The poems in the 1801 volume are indeed unlike the LCS songs and satires he wrote in the 1790s, but they do not purchase their Romanticism at the expense of politics. These poems protest repression, thematize anti-imperialism, allegorize the aristocratic oligarchy as invading Normans, reconfigure republicanism with less stoic familial themes, and revise nationalistic myths democratically. Whereas Coleridge and Wordsworth developed the conversational blank-verse poem for private themes that nevertheless expressed public meanings, Thelwall's conversational poems are also a continuation of his overall project of fitting orality into print-culture conventions. The volume is closer to author-centered Romantic literature than anything he had written previously because of the long "Prefatory Memoir" that makes Thelwall's own identity such a prominent focus. Nevertheless, the volume's sociopolitical meanings ultimately overwhelm the psychological.

Was Thelwall a good poet?[40] In 1838 William Wordsworth, not known for flattering other people's poetry insincerely, had no apparent reasons to exaggerate when he told the widow Cecil Boyle Thelwall that "Mr. Coleridge and I were of opinion that the modulations of his [Thelwall's] blank verse were superior to those of most writers in that metre."[41] For the characteristically stingy Wordsworth, his comments on Thelwall are high praise. Even earlier, in 1817, writing to Haydon, Wordsworth praised Thelwall's "harmonious blank verse, a metre which he wrote well for he has a good ear."[42] Also very telling is the exchange of letters between Coleridge and Thelwall in the 1790s on poetry. Coleridge usually takes Thelwall's advice in revising the lines Thelwall finds wanting. The tone of the correspondence is appropriate for an exchange of views by two practicing poets who respect one another's work. Coleridge assumes a condescending stance only later, after political differences have vexed the relationship beyond repair.[43]

---

40. Reiman, "Introduction" to *Ode to Science*, v–x, suggests Thelwall's very best work compares well with the best poetry of the more famous Romantics, and he wrote numerous good poems and many more interesting and promising poems that initiated experiments the more famous Romantic poets exploited successfully. Grumbling's "John Thelwall: Romantic and Revolutionist," esp. chaps. 3–5, has the most extensive work on Thelwall's literature that anyone has written.

41. Alan G. Hill, ed., *Letters of William and Dorothy Wordsworth, 2nd edition, The Later Years. Part 3, 1835–1839*, 7 vols. (Oxford: Clarendon Press, 1982), 6: 641.

42. Mary Moorman and Alan G. Hill, eds., *Letters of William and Dorothy Wordsworth: The Middle Years. Part 2. 1812–1820* (Oxford: Clarendon Press, 1970), 3:361.

43. For the Thelwall-Coleridge relationship see Nicholas Roe, *Wordsworth and Coleridge: The Radical Years* (Oxford: Clarendon Press, 1988), 248–62, and "Coleridge and Thelwall: The Road to Nether Stowy," in Richard Gravil and Molly Lefebure, eds., *The Coleridge Connection: Essays for Thomas McFarland* (Basingstoke: Macmillan, 1990), 60–80. See also Judith Thompson, "An Autumnal Blast," *Studies in Romanticism* 36 (1997): 427–56; Grumbling, "John Thelwall: Romantick and Revolutionist," 188–224; Warren Gibbs, "An Unpublished Letter from John Thelwall to S. T. Coleridge," *Modern Language Review* 25 (1930): 85–90, and Burton R. Pollin and Redmond Burke, "John Thelwall's Marginalia in a Copy of Coleridge's *Biographia Literaria*," *Bulletin of the New York Public Library* 74 (1970): 73–94.

Conclusion

While Thelwall was fashioning himself as a radical in retirement, a farmer of a thirty-five acre farm, he was also maintaining an intense correspondence with radical friends such as Thomas Hardy[44] and occasionally attracting the attention of spies. Several Home Office reports link Thelwall to the riots of Merthyr Tydfil as well as regular attendance at meetings of "Jacobins" in Hereford.[45] Thelwall visited Merthyr Tydfil "during the rioting of September 1800" and "attended meetings of workmen" there; he was in fact present at the food riot of 20 September 1800 which lowered the price of food that had nearly doubled in a year. Although the rioters did not harm anyone seriously, the authorities hanged two men and transported one man for life.[46] What exactly Thelwall was doing is impossible to know. In numerous *Tribune* lectures he had spoken against food riots and it is unlikely that he had changed his mind. Did he see the Welsh rioters as imperial victims, somehow different from English rioters? As we have discovered more of his activities after his 1797 "retirement" we know they involved more than just milking cows.

The issue of self-fashioning I will defer briefly until the next chapter. Here, I want to note the different protagonists of his anti-imperialistic works: Faulkland/Sidney, the English Ché Guevara, fighting for the Incas and against the conquistadors; Seraphina, the Creole feminist and revolutionary; Arthur and Edwin, who mediate the historical spirit and translate it into social reality. The lattermost example suggests liberal imperialism except for the fact that they are native Britons who explicitly distance themselves from militarism and imperial conquest. If a commitment to Enlightenment rationalism and naturalism necessarily entails ties to imperialism, then Thelwall is a liberal imperialist who accepted the goals of Western domination but repudiated the means—military conquest. Does in fact Enlightenment lead to empire? Thelwall did not think so, as he distinguished between persuasion and domination.[47]

---

44. For the Hardy and other letters at the time, see especially P. J. Corfield and Chris Evans, "John Thelwall in Wales: New Documentary Evidence," *Bulletin of the Institute of Historical Research* 59 (1986): 231–39. Damian Walford Davies is at work on an edition of Thelwall's letters.

45. David J. V. Jones, *Before Rebecca: Popular Protests in Wales 1793–1835* (London: Allen Lane, 1973), 27–28.

46. Jones, *Before Rebecca*, 73, 135, 206–20, 19.

47. The issue of Enlightenment and its legacy is too complex to explore here; I will return to it in the concluding chapter. See a contemporary exploration of the issue in James Schmidt, ed., *What Is Enlightenment? Eighteenth-Century Answers and Twentieth-Century Questions* (Berkeley and Los Angeles: University of California Press, 1996).

Jacobin Allegory

Like Blake, Thelwall was a "prophet against empire" who revised national myths in mythographic poems. More historical than Blake, Thelwall's writing against empire has an Oothoon-like Seraphina and a Los-like Edwin, but Faukland, Einion, Arthur, and the Fairy of the Lake reveal what is distinctively Thelwallian: the spirit of history speaks (or is made to speak) in a way Hegel would understand and Blake would deem idolatrous. Blake seeks to return imaginatively to an absolute that Thelwall relativizes as the spirit of history. Thelwall's historicism aligns him on the left with Shelley and on the right—or center—with Coleridge. The center of his opposition to empire was not a conviction that individual cultures should develop only according to their own organic logic, as the Romantic conservatives believed (Burke, Herder, Wordsworth); rather, empire—with racism and antisemitism—contradicted the procedural rationalism of the Enlightenment ideals that grounded his historicism. Thelwall has no use for the noble savage myth because he is committed instead to dialogue, argument, persuasion, and public reason. His Incas have distinctively American qualities but they also allegorize contemporary European events; his Seraphina, despite her protected upbringing, is a European feminist, not a naive innocent; his Edwin embraces Christianity but only from rationalistic inquiry, not emotional conversion. Thelwall's is a procedural not a dogmatic rationalism; he upholds the process of debate that is unconstrained within a public sphere. His images of utopian retreat represent strategic moves to save public rationality, rather than to constitute a new Romantic subjectivity that repudiates politics and history.

8

Autobiographies

There is hardly a Thelwall text that is not in some way also autobiographical, from his self-references in political lectures to forms of identification with historical and fictional characters. Thelwall's earliest poetry published as a young man supplied readers with versions of his "life," both disguised as allegory and presented directly. His Jacobin lectures contained narratives about himself because his political role as democratic "tribune" required self-representation, just as at his treason trial he had to defend his "character." When, in 1801, he offered to the public a volume of poetry, he had to provide also an autobiographical preface to counter the anti-Jacobin representations of his life. To write with the cultural authority of a poet, he had to create a "life" sufficiently representative for his audience, just as Wordsworth did in *The Prelude*. His final work, the *Life of John Thelwall* published by his wife after his death and ostensibly "written" by her but constructed almost entirely by Thelwall himself, appropriately concludes a writing career intersected at almost every point with autobiography.

The present chapter is mostly on the 1801 "Memoir" in part because it is a crucial transitional text from the Jacobin 1790s. The "Memoir" has patterns that one finds in other Thelwall works both before and after 1801. Thelwall found already available for use and revision the cultural narratives about the self-taught intellectual, middling-class writer, and radical politician that he shaped into a "life," a story in which the truth of the self is represented. Pressures on Thelwall's writing necessitated his representing a self in writing. The actual narratives of individuation have a structure and logic that tell us much not just about Thelwall but about middling-class writers, anxieties about writing, and the tension between solidarity and social advancement.

Narrating a Life: Writing as an Anti-anti-Jacobin

In 1801 three different Jacobins vindicated themselves in public, defending not so much their political ideas as their moral status. The 1801 version of Thelwall's autobiography (as the "Prefatory Memoir" in *Poems*)[1] shares qualities with both Godwin's 1801 apologia, *Thoughts occasioned by the perusal of Dr. Parr's Spital Sermon*, and Thomas Spence's self-defense at his trial in 1801. In the first chapter we already saw how Coleridge began in 1800 to define Jacobinism by providing narratives that would discern the past in terms of a new agenda. Anti-Jacobinism made autobiography one of the most urgent genres for Jacobins, in order to repel false representations and clear a space for public expression.

Thomas Spence at his sentencing hearing countered the various misrepresentations of his words in order to establish moral agency. Spence's disclosing at his trial the detail about his father and the critical reading of the Bible, as I described in Chapter 4, provides a moral context for Spence's politics. He is telling the public: I am used to question authority and to search for truth fearlessly because my father raised me that way. He also tries to resist the caricatured portrait of him by the government and the newspapers,

---

1. I have reworked and revised an earlier treatment of the "Prefatory Memoir" that appeared as "The Rhetoric and Context of John Thelwall's 'Memoir,'" in G. A. Rosso and Daniel P. Watkins, eds., *Spirits of Fire: English Romantic Writers and Contemporary Historical Methods* (Rutherford, N.J.: Fairleigh Dickinson University Press and Associated University Press, 1990), 112–30.

but not by retracting his radical ideas (PWTS 92–103). To counter his caricature as a mad enthusiast completely outside the boundaries of legitimate political debate, he strenuously defends the political and moral nature of his ideas. The autobiographical detail about the Bible is just one of many strategies Spence employs to assert a "life" that is morally responsible.

William Godwin's response to Parr, of which Coleridge thought very highly,[2] subverts the anti-Jacobin attacks by recontextualizing a "story" that was familiar. Godwin reestablishes moral agency by artfully reframing the story of British Jacobinism. Godwin had been attacked by so many for so long (from about 1797) that he had become for the polite reading public the demonized synecdoche for the entire Jacobin complex, British and French. Godwin's rebuttal follows several strategies: he turns the charge of Jacobin violence and authoritarianism against the anti-Jacobins, he historicizes anti-Jacobinism while he explains his consistency and the nuanced revision of his ideas, and he illustrates the nature of his philosophy performatively by distinguishing between rational and irrational criticism.

The anti-Jacobins are violently authoritarian: they gang up on Godwin, do not allow him to respond, and vilify his motives rather than challenging ideas and arguments. James Mackintosh's lectures, which were unpublished, thus not permitting any response by Godwin, were as abusive as anything Robespierre did to incite popular violence against his intended victims; the lectures criminalized philosophical differences in ways reminiscent of the "Dominican" inquisition. (Godwin's "Dominican" usage evoked the ecclesiatical roots of the word "Jacobin"). Also, being attacked not by name but periphrastically, Godwin was dehumanized further. Had people left Mackintosh's lectures to attack Godwin physically, they would have acted within the spirit of those lectures. This, too, from a former political ally and supporter of the French Revolution![3]

---

2. Coleridge writes in the margins of his own copy of Godwin's text that the essay reflects "great honour on Godwin's Head and Heart" and Coleridge regrets he spoke "unkindly of such a man." Quoted in Peter H. Marshall, *William Godwin* (New Haven: Yale University Press, 1984), 229. A cryptic formula in Coleridge's notebook for January 1800 reads as follows: "Mackintosh?+?Godwin?=?Godwin?+?Thelwall." *The Notebooks of Samuel Taylor Coleridge, 1794–1804*, 4 vols., ed. Kathleen Coburn (Princeton: Princeton University Press, 1957), 1: 637. My decoding: as Godwin attacked Thelwall in 1795, so Mackintosh is now attacking Godwin.

3. William Godwin, *Thoughts occasioned by the perusal of Dr. Parr's Spital Sermon* (London: G. G. and J. Robinson, 1801), in Mark Philp, ed., *Political and Philosophical Writings of William Godwin: Political Writings*, 7 vols. (London: William Pickering, 1993), 2: 173–76.

Jacobin Allegory

The historical narrative constructs a steady Godwin whose praise for the French Revolution was always qualified by condemnation of coercion. Early in the French Revolution the most excited partisans blamed Godwin for being lukewarm; later, the same people condemned Godwin as a monster for still maintaining a political creed no longer in fashion. What caused this "apostasy"? When people turned most strongly against the French Revolution and the British Jacobins in mid-1797, the revolution in France was actually more moderate than it had been earlier, when it was far more popular. Godwin suggests, then, that the anti-Jacobins are superficial, emotionally volatile, and philosophically shallow (166–70).

He concedes he has changed his thinking somewhat, notably on the matter of the emotions, what he calls elsewhere the "Sandemanianism" of *Political Justice*, but otherwise he stands by his treatise. If one is willing fearlessly to subject received political opinions to the rigorous criteria of rational justice, then something like *Political Justice* will be the result. Even the Sandemanian error of omitting a role for the emotions was not malicious; rather, it was motivated, like the rest of the treatise, by a desire to pursue the truth, wherever that might lead ("enquiry was the pilot who might be expected to steer me in the haven of truth"[171]).

While Mackintosh and Parr leveled calumnies at Godwin, Malthus's essay on population was an earnest challenge to Godwin's actual ideas. Taking Malthus seriously, Godwin makes the effort to answer his objections to *Political Justice* (194–206). Even if the rebuttal of Malthus is somewhat tedious, Godwin has at least illustrated by example the difference between defamation and argument. Like Spence, Godwin writes himself into a space where he has moral agency and is no longer a demonized creature.

If it is clear from the government reports of 1801 that Spence was the proverbially dangerous popular radical, and from the massive attacks in the polite literature that Godwin was the proverbially despicable polite radical, what then was Thelwall's status? By the time he retired from active politics in mid-1797—Thelwall's calendar parallels Godwin's in this regard—he was the most notorious Jacobin lecturer and political activist, occupying an especially dangerous place between the polite world of Godwin and the popular world of Spence. The "Prefatory Memoir" to his volume of poetry has one very difficult task: it must persuade the reader, more polite than popular, to suspend preconceptions and entertain the possibility that a Jacobin could produce valuable writing that was not necessarily "Jacobin." Thelwall does not renounce Jacobinism; he declines only to promote it actively. Can such

Autobiographies

a person publish polite writing that a middle-class reading public would want to purchase? Can an unrepentant Jacobin write texts that are not "Jacobin" also?

A hostile landlord and the disastrous harvest of 1800 ended John Thelwall's three and one-half years as a farmer on this thirty-five acres in Llyswen, Brecknockshire, a remote Welsh village. He could have found another farm, but he decided instead to reactivate his career as a public writer with *Poems, Chiefly Written in Retirement*.[4] Earlier in 1801 the publisher Richard Phillips had paid him desperately needed cash for the novel *The Daughter of Adoption* by "John Beaufort."[5] With the 1801 *Poems* he reduced the risk of publishing in his own name by relying on subscription rather than the anonymous market. If he wrote about politics he risked the public scorn to which Godwin was responding, and probably also political repression (Jacobins far more moderate than he, such as Gilbert Wakefield, Joseph Johnson, and Benjamin Flower, were being prosecuted and imprisoned). Thelwall refused to recant his radicalism, but he wanted to make a living as an intellectual. He was dependent on a public that now was largely anti-Jacobin.

Thelwall himself captures his situation in 1801 in a letter to fellow radical Joseph Strutt of Derby, to whom he writes that he is still an "old republican" but that his radicalism is "smothered in silence, except when with a chosen few" (PJC 239). The Miltonic echo of the "chosen few" from *Paradise Lost* evokes another revolutionary poet required to displace symbolically the radical politics he cannot openly avow. Thelwall, however, hardly retreated completely from politics, even at the most reactionary moments of the political repression. While in Wales he was in contact with the radical poet and scholar Iolo Morganwg, and he was somehow involved in the Merthyr Tydfil riot of September 1800. Another detail of his life absent from the "Memoir" is that during his Welsh exile he corresponded extensively with political colleagues and friends; according to one spy's report Thelwall sent and received between twelve and twenty letters *per day* (PJC 236–37). When did he have time to do farm labor? The "Memoir" protests against the government's interference with his mail even during his Welsh exile, but he

---

4. Another reprint of this work, along with several others by Thelwall, has been issued by Garland, with an introduction by Donald H. Reiman, in *Ode to Science, John Gilpin's Ghost, Poems, The Trident of Albion* (New York: Garland, 1978). The third edition (1802) includes some new material in the "Prefatory Memoir."

5. According to a note in the third edition of the "Prefatory Memoir" (1802), Thelwall insists he had no responsibility in making up the John Beaufort pseudonym (xliv).

fails to explain that many of his correspondents were fellow radicals. Correspondence itself had long been radicalized (note well, the London *Corresponding* Society).

The 1801 *Poems* is Thelwall's attempt to rehabilitate his status as a public intellectual. The "Prefatory Memoir" and the volume that houses it are structured like a sentimental narrative in which the hero is an innocent victim of injustice. The book sold very well (1,500 copies by subscription in the first edition, and there were two more editions). He used the book's favorable reception to become a self-nominated professor of elocution, lecturing around England and Scotland, finally settling in London in 1806 after he had succeeded in Liverpool and elsewhere. His elocution and speech therapy business eventually prospered enough so that in 1818 he was able to buy the moderately reformist *Champion* and turn it into a radical-reform periodical while he also participated in London reform politics at public meetings. The *Poems* succeeded because thereafter he was able to publish in his own name and make a living as an intellectual.

When he retired from active politics in mid-1797, he did so because he had little choice.⁶ Especially suspect to his polite readership in 1801 was his having lectured to the "lower orders" in 1792–97; such lecturing violated one of the most fiercely maintained assumptions of the established literary culture, namely, the dichotomy between the "judicious" and the "uneducated" reader (which we saw illustrated in Chapter 3's discussion of the "Chaunticlere" trial).⁷ Near the end of the "Memoir," Thelwall complains

---

6. For Thelwall's political career in the 1790s, see Vernon O. Grumbling, "John Thelwall: Romantick and Revolutionist" (Ph.D. diss., University of New Hampshire, 1977), chaps. 1 and 2; and especially E. P. Thompson's MWC, esp. 156–60; "Disenchantment or Default? A Lay Sermon," in *Power and Consciousness*, ed. Conor Cruise O'Brien and William Dean Vanech (London and New York: University of London Press and New York University Press, 1969), 156–62; and finally "Hunting the Jacobin Fox," *Past and Present* 142 (1994): 94–140 (rpt. in TR 156–220).

7. The former was educated enough to read subversive texts without danger because his or her learning permitted him or her to interpret and discriminate. The latter, however, was like an empty vessel that a subversive text filled without any act of interpretation; this passive reader, then, was unable to make proper use of such a text and would turn against established authorities if exposed to it. For example, in the sedition trial for Paine's *The Rights of Man*, Part 2, attorney general Archibald Macdonald prosecuted the case only because Part 2 was published in a cheap edition and distributed so widely among poor people. The "judicious reader" could "refute" Paine "as he went along," but the text was placed in the hands of those incapable of interpretation, "that part of the public whose minds cannot be supposed to be conversant with subjects of this sort, and who cannot therefore correct as they go along." These passive readers have "minds perhaps not sufficiently cultivated and habituated to reading," so that they are "ignorant," "credulous," and, when politicized, "desperate" (383). Thelwall was worse than Paine in one respect: one did not even have to read his words but only listen to them. Quoted in ST 22: 381.

that "he has to encounter prejudice and hostility in those classes of society, who alone can be expected to have a taste for such [poetic] compositions, or to give them extensive encouragement" (xliii). Although this seems to be a version of the judicious/uneducated reader dichotomy, it reflects the economic reality of the poetry business: the book-buying public was socially different from the public that attended his political lectures. Nevertheless, one kind of poetry Thelwall writes presupposes not just the money to buy books but also the leisure to read them according to certain literary conventions. The other kind of poetry, the popular poetry he wrote for the LCS, has a different audience, but that radical public cannot be reached through ordinary publication in 1801. Although he does not accept the judicious/uneducated dichotomy, which he attacks directly in one section of the "Memoir," he has to depend on a reading public that does accept it.

The timing of his public reappearance does not seem accidental. Thelwall's retirement from and return to public life roughly coincides with the activity of the Foxite Whigs. On 26 May 1797, Grey's motion for parliamentary reform was overwhelmingly defeated, leading the Foxite Whigs to secede from Parliament and retire to their country estates. The historian J. Ann Hone points out that one could view the Foxite secession from parliament as a prelude to rebellion, not an act of stoically endured defeat; Fox and his group were very close to leaders of the United Irishmen, for example.[8] If one could view the Foxites this way, then one understands why the government kept its eye on Thelwall at this time.[9] On 4 February 1800, Fox returned to Parliament, and a year later Pitt resigned; moreover, peace negotiations that would result in the treaty of Amiens in March 1802 were under way in 1801. (We have already seen in Chapter 7 that Sheridan made his rapprochement with loyalism in 1799.) That Thelwall's political retirement (even the choice of a rural retreat is Whiggish, except that Thelwall actually performed physical labor, something the Whig magnates would never have contemplated) and reentry into public life coincided with the moves of the Foxite Whigs probably indicates the degree to which, consciously or unconsciously, his decisions were influenced by the most liberal wing of a social group to which he did

---

8. J. Ann Hone, *For the Cause of Truth: Radicalism in London 1796–1821* (Oxford: Clarendon Press, 1982), 44.

9. Hone records a spy report of July 1801 (*For the Cause of Truth*, 103), and Roger Wells found Home Office documents relating to government suspicions that Thelwall might have been involved in the naval mutinies of 1797, precisely at the time of his "retirement." *Insurrection: The British Experience 1795–1803* (Gloucester: Alan Sutton, 1983), 92.

not belong.[10] The "Memoir," however, portrays a chain of disasters that forced Thelwall to reenter public life in order to take care of his family. (Paul Magnuson has shown recently how Coleridge in 1798 countered anti-Jacobin representations by publishing poems that highlighted his pious domesticity.)[11]

The parallel with Fox raises the issue of social class and politics. During his most radical period (1792–97), Thelwall was an intellectual leader for educated artisans and the "middling classes." The specific social group from which he came, with which he identified, and to whom he spoke in most of his lectures was "the second and third rate class of tradesmen," those of the "middling classes" who were between laborers and the middle class (LJT 21). According to a historian of the period, "There was often no great gap between journeyman and small master or shopkeeper, tradesman, self-employed engraver, printer, apothecary, teacher, journalist, surgeon or Dissenting clergyman."[12] This social group filled the ranks of the LCS, which was influential with the urban poor and which, according to one of its famous members, Francis Place, was just as valuable for social and edu-

---

10. Vernon O. Grumbling, in "John Thelwall: Romantick and Revolutionist," disputes the emphasis Charles Cestre's *John Thelwall, A Pioneer of Democracy in England* (London: Swann Sonnenschein, 1906) places on the Whig influence on Thelwall's political thought, which, according to Grumbling, was also influenced by Toryism, which provided "a concern for economic and human ties as well as simply political ones" (84). Grumbling also sees Thelwall's political ideology as closer to socialism than to free-market liberalism (99). Iain Hampsher-Monk, Geoffrey Gallop, and Gregory Claeys have written recently on Thelwall's political philosophy. Hampsher-Monk, influenced by Pocock, sees Thelwall as a natural rights theorist, not a utilitarian like Godwin. "John Thelwall and the Eighteenth-Century Radical Response to Political Economy," *Historical Journal* 34 (1991): 1–20. Gallop sees Thelwall as a theoretical republican and a practical reformer, strategically steering between a too-moderate reformism and a feared violent revolution. "Ideology and the English Jacobins: The Case of John Thelwall," *Enlightenment and Dissent* 5 (1986): 3–20. Claeys, who stresses Thelwall's civic humanism and republicanism, also links these to a theory of natural rights and a prototypical social-democratic radicalism that promotes an egalitarian redistribution of wealth, leisure, and cultural opportunities. See his introduction to PEJ, xiii–lvi; and his "The Origins of the Rights of Labor: Republicanism, Commerce, and the Construction of Modern Social Theory in Britain, 1796–1805," *Journal of Modern History* 66 (1994): 263–74. Günther Lottes shows how Thelwall's political theory plays between the poles of country-party and natural rights philosophy. *Politische Aufklärung und plebejisches Publikum: Zur Theorie und Praxis des englischen Rakicalismus im spatën 18. Jahrhundert* (Munich: R. Oldenbourg Verlag, 1979), 267–99.

11. Paul Magnuson, *Reading Public Romanticism* (Princeton: Princeton University Press, 1998), chap. 3.

12. I. J. Prothero, *Artisans and Politics in Early Nineteenth-Century London: John Gast and His Times* (Baton Rouge: Louisiana State University Press, 1979), 20.

cational reasons as political ones. Many former LCS members became "respectable" and prosperous businessmen, just as Place and Thelwall (lifelong friends), had done, and they assisted one another in ways typical for union members but not for competing businessmen.[13] Nevertheless, because the middling class was not powerful enough to contest for power on its own, it sought alliances with either the middle class or the working class.

Thelwall, who came to intellectual maturity long before the anti-Jacobin cultural reaction, never abandoned the Enlightenment assumptions he had acquired in his youth. He tried to make these assumptions fit new circumstances, but he did not, like Coleridge, articulate a new synthesis. Thelwall's literary Romanticism was largely unmarked by counter-Enlightenment concepts or by disillusionment with the French Revolution. In a letter to Thomas Hardy of 12 December 1805 he expresses disgust with Napoleon, whose tyrannical behavior "has destroyed, perhaps for ever, all my glorious speculations of the improvability of man, & blasted the best hopes of Europe." E. P. Thompson sees this letter as a recantation, but afterward Thelwall still advocated universal suffrage and even, according to Henry Crabbe Robinson, strongly supported Napoleon. Thompson interprets Thelwall's "disillusionment" as a result of having placed too much political hope in a foreign power; Thelwall's focus should have been the British working class. The letter of 1805 to Hardy expresses rather Thelwall's *moment* of disillusionment, from which he obviously recovers.[14] His comments on Napoleon in his later journalism are usually praise that is qualified, similar to how Byron represented Bonaparte. The following statement is typical: "In the very vices and tyranny of Napoleon, there was a grandeur of soul, a magnificence of conception, a potency of execution, which made some atonement for his oppressions" (*Champion* [30 January 1820]: 65).

---

13. Mary Thale, ed., *The Autobiography of Francis Place, 1771–1854* (Cambridge: Cambridge University Press, 1972), 198–200.

14. Thompson, "Hunting the Jacobin Fox," *Past and Present* 142 (1994): 138; TR 202–3. The Hardy letter is in Edgell Rickword, "Thelwall and Hardy," *Times Literary Supplement* (19 June 1953): 402. Evidence that Thelwall's political despair was momentary rather than definitive comes from Henry Crabbe Robinson, who reports in his diary for June 30, 1815, that when Napoleon was defeated at Waterloo Thelwall was one of the very few people he knew that still sympathized in some degree with Bonaparte. Thomas Sadler, ed., *Diary, Reminiscences, and Correspondence of Henry Crabbe Robinson*, 2 vols. (1872 rpt. New York: AMS Press, 1967), 1:257.

Vindicating a Moral Character

The "Memoir"'s first task is to inoculate the implied reader against the virus of radicalism by circumscribing what is meant by "politics." Thelwall "is desirous that the politician should be forgotten; and that, till the prejudices of party shall subside into the candour of unimpassioned appreciation, he should henceforth be known and noticed (as here he is introduced) only as a candidate for poetical and moral reputation" (*Poems* ii). Using the third person adds objective credibility to the "Memoir," especially because he also notes that he is merely expanding the article on himself in Phillips's *Public Characters*, as if someone other than himself had written it.[15] That "poetical" is linked so closely with "moral" is no accident. The kind of autobiographical and sentimental literature he is offering to the public makes the author's morality an issue. Separating the moral from the political would not be an easy task; for one thing, Thelwall had written and spoken frequently against the separation. Indeed, one mark of the Jacobin ideology on both sides of the channel was to insist upon politics as an extension of ethics and to judge politicians by a very stringent moral code.

As a democratic "tribune," appealing to a different audience, Thelwall also had to establish his moral identity. Early in one particular speech, he makes an ethical appeal: "I have renounced myself those pursuits of taste and literature to which, from my boyish days, I have been so fondly devoted, as to sacrifice to them the flattering prospects of affluence and worldly ambition, which a lucrative profession presented before me; and have devoted myself, whole and entire, to the service of the public . . . whose happiness alone I look forward to as my dearest, and my ultimate reward" (PL 2).[16] Just as the Romantic bard must renounce worldly ambition, so the tribune must also prove his disinterestedness—in this case, by renouncing his role as poet! Whether in politics or literature, the intellectual asserts his autonomy and the special qualities that separate him from those

---

15. Almost all of the information and most of the wording in the *Public Characters* sketch are contained in the "Memoir," which, however, is approximately eight times longer. It seems likely that Thelwall himself composed the *Public Characters* sketch that contains, apparently, not a single error of fact. *Public Characters of 1800–1801* (London: Richard Phillips, 1801), 3:177–93.

16. The central text for Thelwall's own version of the bardic myth was James Beattie's *The Minstrel*, which, according to the *Peripatetic*, was the poem in which he discovered his identity as a poet: "I traced in the youthful manners and dispositions of Edwin, the faithful delineation of my boyish years; and beheld, as in a mirror, the reflection of those features that so evidently marked my own eccentric mind" (1:97).

he serves. In the "Preface" to *The Tribune*, Thelwall claims his "higher motives" in publishing his lectures; higher, that is, than fame or profit.[17] Indeed, he claims he is sacrificing both fame and profit by conducting and then publishing his lectures, but he is willing to undergo the sacrifice for the sake of "the oppressed and industrious orders of society" (*Tribune* 1:vii). In fact, even before the 1795 lectures, as I have already noted, he effaced himself and added to his authority as a tribune by resigning from the LCS. After many months of lecturing in 1795, he writes of having "sold myself to the public," of no longer having personal interests: "I am no longer my own property" (*Tribune* 3:2). As tribune, he becomes subject to the conventions of that role, which require a disinterested motive in politically educating his immediate audience and representing their interests. These conventions, which reassure the audience and provide a norm by which tribunes are judged, obscure the tribune's *own* interests, material and otherwise, which no human being can ever fully repress.

The literary and the political were a troublesome pairing throughout his entire career, a vivid dramatization of which appears in the *Life of John Thelwall*. The biographer provides a novelistic glimpse of Thelwall's thinking at the very moment when the jury was deliberating on his guilt or innocence at the 1794 treason trial: "he could not help contrasting his present situation with that which he might have occupied, had he continued in the literary career which he had found so consonant to his tastes and so flattering to his worldly prospects. This [the literary career] had held forth to him personal safety, wealth, distinction, honour, and reputation." But then he recalls his motives for political activism: he brings to mind "the thousands of the labouring classes of his fellow countrymen bowed to the earth by the weight of oppressive taxation, which deprived them of the commonest necessaries of life" (LJT 256). Thelwall's *Letter to Henry Cline* distinguishes between the scientific career he began in the early 1790s and the political career that supplanted it by means of the "excentric fire of youth" that fueled his "popular enthusiasm." Suggesting that there was no discernible line between "science" and "politics," Thelwall omits from this characterization that he was expelled from the medical society in 1793 because of an aggressively materialistic lecture he had delivered. After he was forced to close his radical-reform newspaper, the *Champion*, in 1822, he published an ostentatiously apolitical *Poetical Recreations of the 'Champion' and his Literary Corre-*

17. *The Tribune* (1795), 1:vi.

spondents that pulled out of the periodical the "literary" pieces, which were immune from prosecution.[18]

To return to the "Memoir," after reassuring his readers that they will not have to confront his politics, he writes about his ancestors, grandfather and father, highlighting the "respectable" aspects of his family and describing how three generations of Thelwall sons are defrauded of a rightful patrimony. Thelwall thus becomes a representative political figure synecdochically enacting the constitutionalist mythology that portrays Britons as having been robbed of their democratic rights by usurpers (the Normans, the Stuarts, the boroughmongers of Old Corruption). His grandfather Walter (a Catholic) was cheated of his rightful property because as a naval surgeon he treated not just the British but the Spanish (Catholics) as well, thus committing an unforgivable political misdeed that disqualified him from laying "claim to the inheritance of his fathers" (*Poems* iii). This is the stuff of sentimental fiction, whether true or not: an act of "benevolence" leads melodramatically to punishment. It is also political myth, as the theme of disinheritance appears in many Romantic texts. From the myth of Saxon liberty being taken away by the Normans to Scott's theme of the "disinherited" in *Ivanhoe*, Romantic writers dramatized the process whereby one's rightful place in the world had been wrested away by an unjust patriarchal authority.

The treasured patrimony also eludes Thelwall's father due to the "selfish apathy of certain relations" (iii). Whatever property Walter had accumulated was squandered in his grandmother's second marriage. His father, a London silk mercer who died when Thelwall was ten years old, is idealized, while his older brother assumes the role of tyrant.[19] His father "formed great expectations" of his son John, hoping to make him "an historical painter" (vii), but this plan was undermined after his father's death by the family's failure to follow the father's will in selling the silk shop. Instead, they continued the business and Thelwall was forced "against his own inclination, and in violent opposition to every indication of his mind" to work "behind the shop counter" until he was sixteen, after which he was apprenticed to a London tailor. Before being apprenticed, he tried to become a painting student but "the mistaken economy of his mother made the premium and expences an insurmountable bar." Had the family followed the paternal will by selling the

---

18. John Thelwall, *Poetical Recreations of the "Champion" and his Literary Correspondents* (London: Champion Press, 1822). Donald H. Reiman edited the facsimile reprint (New York: Garland, 1978).

19. See LJT 11 for the brother's physical abuse of Thelwall.

business, John would have had enough money to pay "a painter of some eminence" for instruction. He next tried unsuccessfully to apprentice himself to the theater (viii).

The ever-elusive patrimony and Thelwall's intellectual ambitions are structurally homologous with constitutionalist ideology, which assumes a democratic constitution that has been fraudulently betrayed by a self-aggrandizing aristocracy. By following his own desire for intellectual distinction, he is in fact fulfilling the true wishes of the absent and now powerless father; he has formed an alliance with his dead father against the various tyrants who try to coerce Thelwall away from his true identity. The Oedipal story acquires some new dimensions in the biography of Thelwall published after his death, where we learn that Thelwall's brother and *mother* physically abused him until he was eighteen years old (LJT 11), and that he had an intensely ambivalent relationship with Horne Tooke (LJT 346–54). Tooke was a painfully inadequate patron and father-figure who disapproved of Thelwall's marrying Susan Vellum, urged him to give up radical politics after the treason trials, and who did not provide an iota of assistance to Thelwall when he was most needy and desperate (1797–1801).

His schooling was, without exception, miserable except for what must have been a remarkable three months when he was taught by a clergyman named Harvey (tributes to whom are in his 1787, 1793, and 1801 poetry). Harvey's libertarian teaching methods, which included being friendly, informal, encouraging, and allowing a degree of student initiative, "sowed" in Thelwall's mind "the seeds of literary ambition" (vi). Thelwall's political lectures adopt Harvey's pedagogic style: conversational, dialogic, informal, personal, encouraging initiative on the part of his audience. Much of his poetry, too, represents an amiable persona. In describing both his father and Harvey, the "Memoir" notices as most endearing those qualities not traditionally masculine, especially for the middling class: his father was "mild and gentle" and "the enemy of no human being" (iv); Harvey was a "conversational champion," "remarkably lax" in discipline. The qualities of his ideal males are congruent with Thelwall's own sickliness and "want of figure" (viii). Physical weakness as a sign of spiritual strength was a sentimental convention. Whether the young John had read sentimental fiction as a sickly youth hardly matters; he would have been acquainted with the sentimental conventions in some way. Those conventions, a version of which gave rise to the bardic myth, gave Thelwall a way to articulate his unhappiness with middling-class life. Indeed, disease seems to be a sign of intellectual "election," as his physical incapacity disqualifies him for the allegedly strenuous rigors of commercial activity.

Except for Harvey, Thelwall was primarily self-taught, learning the most when stealing some moments for reading books from the hours of labor. One of the things he shared with the audience for his political lectures and with fellow LCS "citizens" was the pride of the autodidact. It is perhaps difficult for us now to understand the prejudice against the self-taught, but one gets a vivid specimen of this prejudice from Thomas Noon Talfourd in his biography of Lamb. Talfourd, who contributed essays and poetry to *The Champion* and who, like Lamb, knew and liked Thelwall, writes:

> Like all men who have been chiefly self-taught, he [Thelwall] sometimes presented common-places as original discoveries, with an air which strangers mistook for quackery; but they were unjust; to the speaker these were the product of his own meditation, though familiar to many, and not rarely possessed the charm of originality in their freshness. Lamb at least, felt that it was good, among other companions of richer and more comprehensive intelligence, to have one friend who was undisturbed by misgiving either for himself or his cause; who enunciated wild paradox and worn-out common-place with equal confidence; and who was ready to sacrifice ease, fortune, fame—everything but speech, and, if it had been possible, even *that*—to the cause of truth or friendship.[20]

This comic portrait has little to do with Thelwall as he actually was, but the stereotype of the autodidact without a classical education proves irresistible for Talfourd.

Although Thelwall became moderately wealthy in the 1810s from his elocution business, he nevertheless identified with artisans and laborers. Two of his longest friendships were with Thomas Hardy and Francis Place, both self-taught artisans from the LCS. Thelwall mixed easily with more genteel intellectuals, but he felt closest to those who did not attend Oxbridge. There is a tribute to Thomas Hardy in one of the earliest of Thelwall's issues of *The Champion*. He publishes a philological discovery that Hardy has made and then cites Hardy as an example of what a "plain and simple man" from a "humble station" may make of himself; such a man contributes to the liter-

---

20. Thomas Noon Talfourd, *Memoirs of Charles Lamb*, ed. Percy Fitzgerald (Philadelphia: J. B. Lippincott, 1892), 179.

ature "which was once confined, and which the oppressor would wish to confine again, to the privileged circle of the expensively educated few" (*Champion* [27 December 1818]: 823). In the "Memoir" he articulates the social class identification he experienced as a young apprentice, when he found that the men from a slightly lower social stratum than his own were more intellectually congenial than the shopkeepers with whom he had grown up. He makes a sociological observation to emphasize the point:

> The manufacturing and working classes . . . are much better informed than the thriving shopkeepers. . . . The former have their common hive, as it were, to which each brings his stock, however small, of intellectual attainment, where it grows by copartnership, and is enjoyed in common; while the other secluded, for so many hours of the day, from all conversation, but what relates to the mere object of barter, toils, insulated, like the *Solitary Bee*, storing up his profits in his particular cell. (*Poems* x)

Vindicating the social group for which and with which he worked as "tribune," he also idealizes the journeymen and artisans by highlighting their desire for knowledge. He gives to the shopkeepers the stereotypical qualities associated with laborers, intellectual dullness and "low" pleasures ("the pipe, the bottle, or the bowl"). He also undermines the dichotomy between the judicious and the uneducated reader by showing that formal education is not a prerequisite for intellectual culture.

In the account of the year and a half he was a tailor's apprentice—as Francis Place also had been—he associates his literary ambition with his physical illnesses. When he was too sick to work he could read "at his mother's country house" (xiii). His particular ailments were asthma and "inflammations of the lungs," both of which could represent his repressed desire for literary fame as an actor or poet speaking a language that transcends commerce. Work literally made him sick, which in turn permitted him to fulfill his desire for literature. Being too sensitive for the business world was already a cliché in Thelwall's time, as novels and poems portrayed gentlemen too exquisitely receptive to fare well in the hard, greedy world (Mackenzie's *The Man of Feeling* [1787] is a good example of this; the hero literally dies because of his sensitivity). The Romantic myth of the poet, including a sickly, alienated childhood, is governed ultimately by sentimental conventions that established a huge gap between literary and material-economic realities.[21] An additional lure of a literary career was that the profession of writing was one of the very few careers truly open to all talents; one could rise upon one's own efforts in literature, whereas similar efforts in most other fields open to someone like Thelwall could never entirely circumvent the obstacles of class.[22]

The "Memoir" then relates Thelwall's brief career in law after his master-tailor canceled his indentures. Thelwall's three and a half years as a law apprentice culminated in a complete revulsion against the profession. His "objections to the profession itself were radical and insurmountable," because as a lawyer he could not "give unreserved utterance to the existing convictions of his heart" (xvii). Both the "Memoir" and the biographical sketch in *Public Characters* highlight an episode of attempted homosexual seduction by a lawyer who worked with John Impey, to whom Thelwall was articled. The lawyer committed suicide after Thelwall "exposed his infamy" (xviii).[23] The only hint that Thelwall might have felt anything but righteous contempt for the unfortunate man is contained in his 1793 novel, where the character Wentworth exclaims:

> *Reason is not sole Arbiter in the human mind.* Imagination has also a considerable share in the enjoyment and perturbations of the soul: nor will her vivid impressions always submit to the cool and regular deductions of Philosophy. For my own part, I confess no circumstance of my life ever disturbed my tranquillity so long, as having been the innocent cause of a fellow-creature committing the crime of suicide. — *Innocent?* — I was something more than innocent; for in yielding to the honest indignation of my heart, and exposing the horrid vices of a wretch who had endeavoured to seduce me to a participation of his guilt, I acted according to the dictates of my conscience, and believed myself to be discharging a duty to society. And yet, when the intelligence was brought me, that, to escape from the public infamy I had brought upon him, he had put a period to his existence,

21. All the Romantic poets tell some version of the unhappy, traumatized childhood narrative. See Donald H. Reiman's reflections on this and other psychological aspects of Romanticism in his *Intervals of Inspiration: The Skeptical Tradition and the Psychology of Romanticism* (Greenwood, Fla.: Pennkevill, 1988).

22. It is remarkable that in Raymond Williams's account of the social origins of English writers from the Tudor to the Modernist periods there are so many below the professional and gentry-aristocratic class. *The Long Revolution* (Harmondsworth: Penguin, 1961), 254–70.

23. *Public Characters* 3:185.

Autobiographies

I felt a thrilling horror creep through every vein; and scarcely could I close my eyes again for many months, without having my imagination haunted with mangled corses, graves, and charnel-houses, and all the dreadful phantoms of a distempered brain. (P 3:120–21)

Thelwall does not develop the anxiety he felt at the time in the two straightforward autobiographical texts (and the episode is left out entirely of the *Life of John Thelwall*), but in a fiction he gives it some expression. Unselfconscious homophobia leads "Wentworth" to insist upon his "innocence" — sexual and moral — and to justify his deed by reference to social necessity. Even the guilt is stylized as Gothic horror. He *yielded* not to sexual temptation but to "honest indignation." He is betrayed by his "imagination" that disturbs the "tranquillity" he should have had, according to his rational judgment. One does not know the circumstances but one imagines a simple "no, thank you" would have been enough, unless of course the lawyer was putting extraordinary pressures on Thelwall.

I believe that another episode connected with his law apprenticeship is a version of the same narrative. This episode appears in the *Life of John Thelwall* but not the "Memoir" or *Public Characters* sketch. His master sent him on an errand to Norwood, a London suburb, to serve a writ. He enjoyed the several hours' walk through the various "beauties of nature," which helped put him in a frame of mind that resisted completing his task. Nevertheless, he went to the house, where he received generous hospitality from the wife, whose husband would be returning home shortly. Thelwall dropped not-so-subtle hints about the purpose of his visit, so that when he returned later the man was nowhere to be found. Thelwall thought that he had fulfilled the letter of his duty to the law, but also the spirit of his morality, which did not want to see a man in debtor's prison (LJT 24–26). Thelwall uses this episode to illustrate his unsuitability for the legal profession. He is here duplicitous for a cause higher than the mere law, but in the previous episode the mere law is higher than any possible extenuating circumstances. Both episodes vindicate his moral rectitude. Other versions of the writ-serving episode suggest that the account in the *Life of John Thelwall* is perhaps not completely truthful.

His 1793 novel has Sylvanus Theophrastus try to serve a writ on a man in Norwood — the very same place. In this version the family's generosity is again emphasized, but a new element is introduced. In addition to a dutiful wife there is a beautiful, innocent daughter, Anna, to whom our hero is much attracted (P 1:110–16). The novelistic version contrasts the "dissimulation" the Thelwall-figure cannot avoid practicing and the "artlessness" of the desirable Anna. The full extent of the guilt the actual episode provoked is suggested by yet another version of the writ-serving that appeared in his 1801 novel. The Thelwall figure is Henry Montfort, a fifteen-year-old who, with a group of other drunken Etonians, vandalizes a farmer's henhouse. The farmer is further victimized by the landlord and his agents and lawyers, all of whom conspire to pressure farmer Wilson to sell his land. As in the typical Jacobin novel, Thelwall draws much attention to the class injustice against the Wilsons. Henry, trying to help the Wilsons pay their debts, acquires surreptitiously the necessary fifty pounds. When Henry tries to deliver the money to farmer Wilson, the farmer is not at home. It is Wilson's beautiful, emphatically "innocent" sixteen-year-old daughter Mary who is the grateful recipient. Henry falls in love with her and, the novel makes quite clear, he would have succeeded in seducing her if the school vacation and Henry's vigilant mother had not intervened.[24]

The *Daughter of Adoption* version, then, casts the Thelwall figure in a more unflattering and more explicitly sexual light than the other versions. He is the seducer, not the object of seduction, but he saves the family from debt (in all versions he acts heroically in some way toward the indebted family). The 1801 novel version sexualizes the power of class and money, providing an inverted rendering of the lawyer's attempted seduction of the younger, dependent, weaker Thelwall. The inversion and idealization ironically produce what would have been appropriate in the first place but was absent there: guilt.

Law, then, represents for Thelwall's autobiography a duplicity that amounts to a speech impediment. As he phrases it in the "Memoir," "Prone and habituated, upon every subject, to give unreserved utterance to the existing convictions of his heart, he looked forward, with indignation, to the prospect of letting out his hand, or his voice, to venal pleading" (*Poems* xvii). He did not want to "prostitute" himself. Now perhaps the strange cluster of associations in Thelwall's counterattack on Burke, which I discussed in Chapter 2, becomes a little less enigmatic. The line between selling his language and his body is uncertain for Thelwall. Even the words just quoted from the "Memoir" equivocate between body and mind: "his hand, or his voice." The lovely Mary Wilson and Anna of the two novelistic versions are

---

24. *The Daughter of Adoption*, 4 vols. (London: Richard Phillips, 1801), 1: bk. 2, chap. 1–3.

Autobiographies

linked to prostitution by virtue of the culturally axiomatic progression from seduced innocent to corrupt prostitute.

There was only one profession that promised free expression of one's inner being, the free use of one's own words, the unprostituted public use of language. Or so it seemed to Thelwall at age twenty-two in 1786, now free of his law indentures, who began his career "as a literary adventurer." He published by subscription *Poems on Various Subjects* in 1787, which was noted favorably by the *Critical Review* and which led to his meeting new people and forming "truly valuable friendships" (xix). In his early years as a literary intellectual toiling on "Grub Street," he lived in Lambeth with his mother and ailing brother, earned around fifty pounds a year, edited the *Imperial and Biographical Magazine*, wrote for other periodicals such as the *Universal Magazine*, and was engaged as a teacher. By 1791, his prospects were good enough—two to three hundred pounds a year from various sources—to marry and move to a more prosperous neighborhood, where he expanded his intellectual contacts. In the narrative of his early years as a literary intellectual, Thelwall's success is recurrently sabotaged by forces out of his control. For example, his proud success at Guy's Hospital and the Physical Society, where as a member he delivered several lectures, culminated with his expulsion from the Society because of political prejudice (xxii–xxiii). His lectures, which argued that mental "phenomena" could be "explained upon principles *purely* Physical," were not quite as innocent as he claims. In 1793 materialistic ideas, even in a medical treatise, were "Jacobin."[25]

A similar narrative accompanies his prospects as a dramatist. Thomas Holcroft, so impressed by the 1793 *Peripatetic*, urged Thelwall to write for the London theater, where Holcroft was a prominent playwright (xxi). (That Thelwall neglects to mention at all his 1792 *Incas* in this context is further evidence of how heavily censored the "Memoir" is.) According to the "Memoir," after the treason trials (Holcroft was indicted too), Thelwall could have enjoyed great literary success, but instead he sacrificed his literary prospects for politics (xxix). As he complains in 1801, he is excluded from the literary institution for which he seems most suited—apparently the theater (xliii). The London theaters were indeed sensitive to political heresy,

---

25. *An Essay Towards a Definition of Animal Vitality* (London: John Thelwall, 1793). For the medical context of the 1790s and the early nineteenth century, see Owsei Temkin, "Basic Science, Medicine, and the Romantic Era," *Bulletin of the History of Medicine* 37 (1963): 97–129; Hermione de Almeida, *Romantic Medicine and John Keats* (Oxford: Oxford University Press, 1991); Nicholas Roe, *John Keats and the Culture of Dissent* (Oxford: Clarendon Press, 1997).

eventually driving Holcroft from the stage, but the "Memoir" makes it appear as if Thelwall's theatrical career were prevented from prospering solely as an individual instance of prejudice, a personal attack, as if it had happened to a hero in a sentimental novel. Rhetorically, the victimized individual is more appealing than a victimized ideology and political movement.

In the "Memoir" he cannot avoid discussing his political career. First, he portrays his acquisition of democratic "principles" as an organic, natural process produced by following the dictates of his reason and "heart." He receives from politics, however, only "anxieties and misfortunes" (xxiii). He makes it seem as if his democratic ideology happened *to* him, so that any sort of blame would be beside the point. Second, his political narrative emphasizes civil liberties, political procedures (rather than ideas), and ordinary fairness. His entry into politics, for example, was precipitated by his outraged reaction to the rigging of the Westminster election in 1790, and his earliest political awareness was acquired by participating in a debating society that had no political agenda. He persuaded the debating society to concentrate solely on history and politics, but ultimately he was excluded from the Coachmakers' Hall for political reasons. In fact, he began his career as a political lecturer only after the government repression had made "apolitical" debates impossible (xxv–xxvi).

Thelwall's account of becoming a tribune omits from the narrative many Jacobin details that might have disturbed his readers. By late 1792 or early 1793, the political situation was so highly charged and polarized that democratic ideas could not be debated in a gentlemanly manner. Thelwall's lectures were bold political actions, not exercises in abstract civil liberties, as his audience swelled from a lowly sixty at a Compton Street newspaper room to an impressive 750 at the Beaufort Buildings (xxvi). What was politically terrifying to anti-Jacobins—democratic orators lecturing to large audiences of the "uneducated"—the "Memoir" turns into a story of entrepreneurial success, adherence to abstract rights, and personal courage. The "Memoir" does not assert untruths but leaves out the raw, passionate political conflict of that time.

One way Thelwall represents the most significant event in his political life—his seven weeks at Newgate Prison, five months in solitary confinement in the Tower, the treason trial—is to protest against the seizure and loss of his literary manuscripts, books, engravings, and notes that were unrelated to politics. He transforms this episode into an allegory directly related to the "Memoir"'s purpose of vindicating his own literary reputation: "in the fiercest warfare of opinion, the Temple of the Muses should still be sacred: confiscation should not extend to intellect and the arts: there should be no war against the mind" (xxvii–xxviii). Of all the things he could have depicted, he highlights the loss of his literary manuscripts. Of the trial itself, he discreetly refers the reader to his lawyers' speeches in court, especially those of the famous Erskine (xxviii–xxix). He mentions but does not quote from the long speech Erskine would not allow Thelwall to deliver to the jury, *The Natural and Constitutional Right of Britons* (1795). The only representation of his experiences he selects for mention is the 1795 *Poems written in close confinement in the Tower and Newgate*, "the first published attempts . . . at correct composition" (xxix). In deferring to his lawyers' representations and accenting the literary correctness of his prison poetry, Thelwall again downplays his activism. He omits whatever would weaken the case for his being a harmless political victim: his active participation in his own defense, as well as the LCS songs, satires, and toasts.

After leaving prison Thelwall resumed his lecturing activities, publishing his lectures in *The Tribune*. As a tribune and writer, he was supposed to represent the "people" and its interests, but as a writer of the "Memoir" he constructs a sentimental performance, an appeal to the reader for tolerance on the basis of feeling and sensibility. A tolerant reader might forgive the Jacobinism and grant Thelwall the authority to represent the culture's aspirations. Thelwall, however, is not willing to recant his political ideas, something that probably disqualifies him from getting elected as bard by the polite reading public. Both Wordsworth and Coleridge understood that a poetry with any chance of representing the British culture's inner convictions had to be counterrevolutionary. Wordsworth's 1814 *Excursion* and Coleridge's political journalism announced their recantation of radical politics. Thelwall never wrote the recantation piece that was prerequisite for becoming a writer in the mainstream culture. The "Memoir" was written instead of such a piece.

The "Memoir" is a sentimental narrative of someone who ultimately becomes a "man of feeling" and literary intellectual; the unfeeling world drives the hero into exile where he is still hounded by persecutors; additionally, he is a victim of bad luck (the unfortunate 1800 harvest) and loses his firstborn child, his beloved daughter, to a fatal illness; driven to desperation, he is forced to leave his isolated farm and settles in what he calls a safer, more civilized town (apparently Hereford), even if his notoriety ruins any chance for a social life, which he sorely misses. If the reader accepts the narrative and all its conventions, Thelwall would at least lose his pariah status and could contend openly for the highest literary honors. However deferential he is to his audience, Thelwall withholds the narrative of recantation.

Writer as Prostitute

Even a hostile reviewer of Thelwall's *Poems*, Francis Jeffrey, had some favorable words for the "Effusions," the private lyrics in the 1801 *Poems*. The literary public could grant Thelwall authority to represent his *own* feelings but not society's broader cultural concerns. One way to escape the logic of the sentimental narrative is to impugn Thelwall's character, to interpret the "growth" of his mind not as a tragedy of repression but as a sentimental farce of presumptuous arrogance. Francis Jeffrey does precisely this in his review of the 1801 volume in the *Edinburgh Review*.[26] "In every page of this extraordinary Memoir," Jeffrey writes, "we discover traces of that impatience of honest industry, that presumptuous vanity, and precarious principle, that have thrown so many adventurers upon the world, and drawn so many females from their plain work and embroidery, to delight the public by their beauty in the streets, and their novels in the circulating library" (Jeffrey 200). Even a moderately liberal Whig periodical now takes for granted anti-Jacobinism: whatever political reforms might be desirable, "Jacobin" equality must be ruthlessly beaten down. The analogy between Thelwall and a streetwalking, novel-writing woman suggests that both are guilty of disturbing a natural order in which women perform menial tasks and men from the "middling classes" stay behind the shop counter; also, Jeffrey contrasts a legitimate literary culture unconnected with buying and selling with a presumptuous democratic culture marked by the most immoral kind of economic exchange, prostitution. The prostitution cluster of images and ideas is reminiscent of the Burke-Thelwall exchange of insults in 1796 (discussed in Chapter 2). (One liability of the bardic myth of literature's unworldly origins is that it is not dissimilar to the reactionary idea that only leisured "gentlemen" can create and properly judge literature; Jeffrey employs this idea with great zeal.) Yet he also draws another implicit comparison: for just as the British Jacobins upset the natural political order by promoting social equality, so various literary pretenders from the lower classes try to gain recogni-

26. Francis Jeffrey, *Edinburgh Review* 2 (1803): 197–202.

tion as serious writers, upsetting the literary order. Jeffrey groups Thelwall with ploughboys, carpenters, hairdressers, valets, waiters, shoemakers, and tailors, all of whom have tried to acquire literary "distinction" (197). Robert Bloomfield, who was both a "ploughboy" and a "shoemaker," was a spectacular poetic success (he also attended the debates at the Coachmakers' Hall where Thelwall received such an important education).[27] There were other poets, not nearly as successful, from the "lower orders": Joseph Blackett, Kirke White, and Ann Yearsley, to name three. Jeffrey represents them all as social bounders who try to avoid the hard work that destiny has allotted them.

The Thelwall-Jeffrey controversy did not end with the review. Shortly after the review, Thelwall's Edinburgh lecture on elocution was disrupted by hecklers who were orchestrated, according to Thelwall, by Jeffrey (also in attendance). Thelwall published an attack on Jeffrey, then Jeffrey (or a very close friend) attacked Thelwall anonymously, and finally Thelwall wrote a reply to this.[28] Thelwall's pamphlets protest against his difficulties in making a living because in Edinburgh he could neither lecture nor sell any literature. If his career as elocution professor was to be subject to the same persecution as his political career, he could not live as an intellectual. Jeffrey's hostility, however, was actually moderate compared to the anti-Jacobin diatribes typical of an earlier period. The anonymous pamphlet replying to Thelwall is marked by a sneering contempt for Thelwall and his unforgivable but no longer dangerous politics. Jeffrey finds especially offensive Thelwall's portrait of himself as an emergent literary intellectual. According to Jeffrey's pamphlet, Thelwall is lazy, lacks integrity, and sells himself to anyone who will buy; he has "broken his indentures to three regular professions, purely because he had an 'abhorrence' of 'trade,' and 'a distaste for drudgery;' and who has since lived as an Itinerant Lecturer on Politics, History, and Elocution."[29] The adjective "itinerant" resonates for Thelwall because as a poet he

---

27. In Capel Lofft's Preface to *The Farmer's Boy* (1800), there is a brief portrait of Robert Bloomfield's life in which the Coachmakers' Hall debates are discussed. See Robert Bloomfield, *Collected Poems (1800–1822)*, ed. Jonathan N. Lawson (Gainesville: Scholars' Facsimiles and Reprints, 1971).

28. John Thelwall, *A Letter to Francis Jeffray [sic], Esq., On Certain Calumnies and Misrepresentations in the Edinburgh Review* (Edinburgh: Thelwall, 1804); Anon., *Observations on Mr. Thelwall's Letter to the Editor of the Edinburgh Review* (Edinburgh: D. Willison, 1804); John Thelwall, *Mr. Thelwall's Reply to Observations on Mr. Thelwall's Letter to The Editor of the Edinburgh Review* (Glasgow: W. Lang, 1804).

29. *Observations on Mr. Thelwall's Letter*, 13.

portrays himself as a "peripatetic," an imaginative wanderer who could not follow a regular course but rather experienced nature and other people intuitively; moreover, he took pride in writing verse that wandered away from the established rules. Also, his literal wandering from place to place was dictated by political repression and persecution. Jeffrey's use of "itinerant," however, evokes dangerous vagrants, beggars, rabble-rousing democratic orators, and religiously suspect Dissenting preachers, as well as peddlers, gypsies, and others without a fixed place or station. Especially in the *Peripatetic*, there are recurrent representations of various "itinerants," including vagrants, beggars, peddlers, gypsies, and even the unconfined insane, with all of whom the wandering and "eccentric" poet feels an affinity. The novel's narrator, Sylvanus Theophrastus, is especially drawn to gypsies, who perform no productive labor but who enjoy "savage liberty" and who are remarkable for "their eternal propensity for conversations" (P 1:47), thus suggesting parallels between the "eccentric" poet and the gypsies.

Both men won the debate but in different ways: Thelwall's defenses of himself were successful enough to permit his elocution business to flourish, but Jeffrey's attacks were consonant enough with public feeling that Thelwall's *literary* career was not nearly as successful as Thelwall wanted it to be.[30] Moreover, Jeffrey's attack and Thelwall's reception in Edinburgh served as a warning that Thelwall hardly needed: if he was tempted to inject radical politics into his elocution business, he would be punished without mercy.

Jeffrey was attacking self-taught writers in general by attacking Thelwall. It is perhaps useful to look back at the very beginning of Thelwall's career as a poet to see how the poetry worked through the problem of courting a polite audience with ambitious poetry that was packaged as the product of a self-taught, humble poet. In the "Apology" to the *Poems on Various Subjects* (1787) Thelwall concedes his lack of a classical education and university training, but pleads that he is utterly sincere and incorruptibly virtuous.[31] The real extent of his learning—he read Vergil and Horace in the original language—did not appear in the "Apology." As many "uneducated" writers of the past had done and would do in the future, Thelwall based his literary authority on feeling rather than thought. The lack of an aristocratic education becomes, under the sign of "nature" and "artlessness," a positive force

---

30. According to Thompson, the witty Jeffrey won the debate easily, as Thelwall was too self-pitying to launch a convincing defense of himself. "Hunting the Jacobin Fox," *Past and Present* 142 (1994): 120–21; TR 188–90.

31. *Poems on Various Subjects*, 2 vols. (London: John Denis, 1787). Hereafter PVS.

in the production of poetry, because in the Romantic system of values set up by the *Poems on Various Subjects* artfulness is a chief sin. Insincere artifice, the doubleness of linguistic expression that does not match subjective intention, is the principal force of evil in poem after poem. Of his Muse Thelwall says that she "may sometimes glow with the ardour of a lover" but "she will never be found to burn with the impure fires of a courtezan" (PVS 1:vii). Although eager to please the public and win fame, the poet will not sell himself or write *only* to please and win fame.

Traditionally the muse is the inspirational force that the poet obeys, worships, and is guided by, but Thelwall merges the identities of poet and muse. The muse becomes a feminized figure of Thelwall's poetic ambition. (Compare the way Jeffrey, who had not read these poems, will draw the analogy between the autodidact Thelwall and female prostitutes.) The figure's gender and the prostitute analogy are no accidents. As a self-educated male writer he is on the same cultural level as a woman writer, both lacking the cultural credentials to write with the fullest authority.[32] Thelwall is also distinguishing himself from those self-educated writers, ordinarily women, who published their work unabashedly for the sake of money. A Romantic system of values deriving from feeling, genius, and imagination permits him to contest for the culture's highest literary honors even without a classical education.

The courtesan image, while signifying the mercenary writer, emphatically calls attention to the writer's dependent situation. How are genius, profound feeling, and Shakespearean imagination recognized? Only by those cultural authorities who can endorse the genuine existence of such high aesthetic values. These classically educated cultural authorities are the credentialed arbiters of poetry. One can compare the young Thelwall with the young Lord Byron. After Byron's first volume of poems was attacked by some reviewers, Byron retaliated with a fully developed satire that positioned him as an equal among his critics. Thelwall, by virtue of his cultural position, cannot write a satire like *English Bards and Scotch Reviewers*. When attacked, Thelwall is permitted to represent the integrity of his character, but he is not well positioned to rebut his critics on matters of taste. Another possibility, the one chosen by the "self-taught" William Blake and Thomas

---

32. Brian Maidment has explained and justified his use of the phrase "self-educated poets" in his *The Poorhouse Fugitives: Self-Taught Poets and Poetry in Victorian Britain* (New York: Carcanet, 1987). Marlon Ross has written about the women poets contemporaneous with the Romantic poets in his *The Contours of Masculine Desire: Romanticism and the Rise of Women's Poetry* (Oxford: Oxford University Press, 1989).

Spence, was to reject root and branch the cultural system of literary values for their own biblically inspired visions, and to take the route of "enthusiasm." Indeed, Thelwall himself took that route with his LCS satires and songs.

The courtesan image suggests too the possibility of a poet's creating something that might appeal to readers but which would be merely artifice, something not reflecting the poet's subjectivity. Who would know the difference except the poet himself? Since the poet's only grounds for acceptance and fame are untutored genius, natural feeling, and authentically imagined perceptions, he has to protect those originating sources from suspicion, but the courtesan image acknowledges the uncertain status of the self-educated writer's words.

The poems themselves connect poetry and sex to allegorize social ambition. Most of the poems in the volume are ballads, modeled after Percy's *Reliques*, on the traditional ballad themes of ill-fated love, especially love being ruined by social ambition. The excessive desire for social advancement by one of the lovers or the parents of one of the lovers is the typical obstacle to the happy resolution of the love story. In each poem true love triumphs in the end, even if the lovers die, because in some manner the illusory quality of social gain and the more enduring power of love are demonstrated. (The ballads in Percy's *Reliques* are not so idealistic or single-mindedly concerned with social mobility.) The social ambition theme allegorizes Thelwall's own anxiety as a self-educated poet whose success would necessarily catapult him out of his own social class.

The poet's anxiety as poet is expressed through the theme of seduction. Indeed, the book's longest poem, "The Seducer; or, Damon and Amanda," treats seduction as a major social problem. The "Prefatory Essay" to the poem identifies the "vice" of seduction "superior in turpitude to that of murder" (PVS 1:101). As a sign of an alarming increase in promiscuity, Thelwall's seducer exploits innocence and travesties love; his actions lead inevitably to prostitution and crime. Speaking insincere words of love is analogous to a poet's own insincerity, symbolized in the muse-as-courtesan metaphor. In the poem Damon seduces and abandons Amanda, feels guilty, and tries to reconcile with her, but Amanda, distraught over Damon's betrayal, has gone mad. In typical ballad fashion, after Amanda dies so does the repentant Damon, who realizes too late he cannot live without his beloved (PVS 1:109–80)

Seduction is also a figure for the duplicity of words. In "The Seducer" the victim is not only the betrayed and maddened Amanda but the seducer himself, Damon, who belatedly understands himself. His duplicitous words to win access to Amanda's body were in fact sincere, although he thought at first he did not truly love her. If Thelwall's poetry, to follow the lesson of language's duplicity, were to win favor, how would he know whether his muse were virtuous or insincere? If he is dependent on the cultural authorities for the validation of his poetry, how can he know that they have treated his writing properly, in treating him like an ardent lover rather than a dissembling courtesan? If he knew how to win literary fame but held back because such writing did not reflect his deepest feelings, would he actually forsake such fame? Also, how could he ever know what the cultural authorities would think if, by definition, he were outside their mode of perception, not qualified to make a reliable judgment? That is, if he knew how to acquire literary fame by dissembling, such a knowledge presupposes a degree of cultural literacy he allegedly cannot have. Finally, is the anxiety over seduction an anxiety over being a seducer or being the seduced?

These questions can be answered to some extent by looking at one of the most self-revealing poems, "Elegy VIII. The Execration" (PVS 2:106–9). Seduction exists here as the experience by which Thelwall became a poet rather than the practitioner of some "low mechanic art" (line 8). He is not the seducer but the seduced. The poem's meaning emerges primarily through two pairs of parallel binary figures: low/high and animal/spirit. The poem, an elaborate vindication of the high and spiritual at the expense of the low and animalistic, develops the conceit of the poet's complaining about his being a poet rather than a dull, insensible, brutish illiterate. The complaint seems almost tongue-in-cheek because the spiritual life is expressed in the language of "low" bodily pleasures; he does not seem to be sacrificing anything. The muse, for example, is figured as a sirenlike woman whose charms he cannot resist and by whose power he is "undone" (line 4). He loves "Science" with a "wild, enthusiast ardour" (lines 5–6), "throbs" with pity (line 16), "glows" with refinement (line 16), and experiences youthful solitude as "bliss" (line 18). Forsaking the low pleasures of the "grov'ling, sensual brute" (line 56), he pursues the more uncertain joys of literary fame. That the low and animalistic have a class-determined meaning is explicit, as the "low mechanic art" of some trade or business is exchanged for the high, imaginative, and spiritual art of poetry. (According to the "Memoir," Thelwall indeed viewed the money-making activities available to someone like himself, from running a shop to working at law, as antithetical to his literary aspirations). As the external world contracts in importance, the internal world expands; he literally gives birth to his inner self—"I nurs'd the embrio fire" (line 29).

As "refinement" is a process without end, as his inner self requires perpetual tending, as literary fame is something he can strive for but not necessarily acquire, he has indeed exchanged a more defined, measurable, tangible, and controllable world for a world that is indefinite, inconstant, spiritual, and unpredictable. The poem, then, is about transcending particular class restrictions, but it also describes what it feels like to pursue a literary life. Imagining literary failure but hoping for success, he chooses spiritual unhappiness over brutish sensations. The last stanza is the only place in the poem where Thelwall modulates from the first-person singular to the plural, as he makes his own experience into a synecdochic sign for the aspirations of an entire culture struggling against the low and animalistic:

> And sure the keener feelings we possess,
>   The more of Science does the bosom fire;
> We bear resemblance to the brutes the less,
>   And tow'ring rise in dignity the high'r.

Before the cultural battle over the swinish multitude, this poem's revulsion toward the low and animalistic indicates just how raw the cultural nerve was that Burke's phrase inflamed.

Thelwall avoided the worst effects of the cultural system that defined the self-taught poet. According to Alan Richardson, "the 'uneducated' poet represented . . . the last vestige of the system of literary patronage otherwise outmoded by an increasingly market-oriented publishing system."[33] About the subscription system under which Thelwall's 1787 volume was published, Richardson comments that subscription is middle-class patronage that "functioned to guarantee political quiescence as well as personal 'gratitude,' and lapses (or perceived lapses) in either could end a poet's career," as happened with Thomas Dermody and Robert Bloomfield. Such a system infantilized plebeian poets.[34] Thelwall avoided such a fate in 1787 because the poetry itself represented at a symbolic level the writer's own anxiety about losing independence to a patron and writing only for money. Later, of course, his political radicalism was something patrons could no longer control, so that

---

33. Alan Richardson, *Literature, Education, and Romanticism: Reading as Social Practice, 1780–1832* (Cambridge: Cambridge University Press, 1994), 248.

34. Richardson, *Literature, Education, and Romanticism*, 249–50.

his 1801 subscription was a genuine negotiation between a needy writer and a skeptical public.

Conclusion

Thelwall's becoming an elocution and speech entrepreneur was hardly arbitrary. He went from democratic tribune speaking on politics to lecturing on classical history, which ended with his forced political retirement. After a long public silence because of political repression, he lectures on the *process* of lecturing; all political content has been omitted and what remains is pure technique. Although his elocution writings are largely apolitical—or political in an allegorical way—they are also entirely within Enlightenment assumptions: he draws upon his medical materialism to reduce speech problems to their purely physical operations; he asserts that anyone, regardless of birth, can become an effective public speaker; he emphasizes the importance of public speaking in a vital political culture. Moreover, he injects into even his elocution training radical politics somewhat disguised. Although Thelwall's London Institute excluded "subjects of religious controversy and party politics," it focused on "history" in decidedly republican and democratic ways by making the pupils research Saxon democracy, the ancient constitution before the Normans, the origins of feudalism, and the reign of Alfred (LHC 262–64). Thelwall allowed the students themselves to connect the dots from ancient English history to contemporary politics. It seems, however, that market considerations worked against the Institution's democratic tendencies. By 1813 Thelwall was so successful that his library had between three and four thousand volumes, he lived in a spacious mansion (even though the rooms were used also to house students), and he had been able to send his son to Cambridge.[35] In 1818 he could *buy* an established newspaper and run it in the way he wanted.

Although Thelwall bristled at Jeffrey's calling him a prostitute, he did indeed turn to elocution to provide for his family. He had acted upon a suggestion by a Quaker friend from Manchester in 1801 to take up lecturing on elocution to earn money (LHC 15–16). He was hardly naive about the cultural cash nexus, as is evident in his political lectures. In Volume 2 of the *Tri-*

---

35. The information is contained in John Thelwall, *Plan and Objects of Mr. Thelwall's Institution* (London: McCreery, 1813).

bune, he attacks the power of wealth to determine the ideological meanings of literary culture, showing that literary representation is also tied to power:

> These privileged classes though not themselves very famous for works of genius, have, in a considerable degree held not only the sword but the pen. For money will make the pen to go as well as the mare: nay, power and patronage will command it without the assistance of money and therefore it is, that more than one half of the romances which are sent into the world under the denomination of histories, political surveys, views of society and *morals*, topographical descriptions, and the like, are stuffed with nothing but servile adulations and time-serving misrepresentations, to gloss over the conduct and characters of the higher, and calumnious abuse and false descriptions of the lower orders—calculated to steel the hearts of the readers against them. (PEJ 250)

In another passage, he further develops the theme: "The powerful orders have the opportunity of painting the common people in whatever light it suits them; and to the disgrace of literature it has hardly ever happened that any man of considerable talents has had the disinterestedness and independence of mind to enlist himself in the service of the latter" (PEJ 251). Power is not exerted just by government and wealth but also through literary culture. These passages also illustrate the extent to which they bear the weight of the culture they are protesting against: "direct" literary democracy is not considered because the writer is located between the "people" and the literary public; the "people" cannot represent themselves. The literary tribune, unlike the aristocratic writer, *accurately* represents the interests of those who cannot represent themselves, but here one finds that Thelwall endorses what is really a version of Burkean thought, a "virtual" literary democracy.

The "Memoir" employed sentimental conventions to enable Thelwall to gain the "voice" he had lost in 1797. To some extent he regained that voice, but what he had lost was considerable. Between 1793 and 1797 he appealed to two audiences within a vigorous public sphere. Thelwall directed both "correct" compositions like the *Poems Written in Confinement* and popular works like the "Chaunticlere" and "John Gilpin" satires to a large reading public that had made him a successful writer and lecturer. The audiences were distinct, but that distinction could be blurred, as he sought to counter class prejudice. By 1801 his plebeian audience was gone: the booksellers, the printers, the periodicals, the lecture venues, the network of connections within the LCS—now outlawed—were no longer available. The middle-class audience, which was available but anti-Jacobin and loyalist, maintained some faint contact with its former radicalism by purchasing three editions of the 1801-2 *Poems*. It was really the *Edinburgh Review*, which began publishing in 1802, that captured the ideological moment for the middle class as the unrepentant old "Jack" could not hope to do. Jeffrey, Brougham, and the other liberal intellectuals who wrote for the periodical removed whatever was dangerously revolutionary and retained enough that was still energetic in Enlightenment culture to circumvent repression and supply the middle class with a critical voice.

Another ideological development was the rise of autobiography as a lyrical rather than rhetorical genre. Spence, Godwin, and Thelwall used autobiographical narratives strategically to establish a morally authoritative ethos that would permit these Jacobin writers to express logos and pathos. In texts produced by Wordsworth and DeQuincey, however, autobiography is an end in itself, its own justification, as ethos subsumes logos and pathos. Romantic autobiography illustrates the loss and gain of literature's rise at the expense of writing. Although autobiography was congruent with individualism, it also was so socially leveling that the writing itself mattered far more than the writer herself; it was more socially leveling in fact than the Jacobin autobiographical narratives whose rhetorical status tied them to hierarchical social relations. When the middle-class public at the time wanted to entertain ideas about political economy and social justice, it turned to reliably moderate mediators like the *Edinburgh Review* rather than to the dissident public sphere of the 1790s.

Conclusion

> How many authors are there among writers? Author means creator.
>
> —Friedrich Schlegel[1]

Romantic ideology represses not just awareness of the socio-historical contingencies of individual creativity but also recognition of social creativity itself. If author means creator, then the plebeian public sphere authored Paine's *Rights of Man*, Thelwall's *Tribune* lectures, Spence's songs and pamphlets, and Wedderburn's sermons. These writings, however popular and exoteric in style, innovatively explored form, generic structure, and ideological conflict. The Jacobin writers did not use language instrumentally, although they did use it for communication and political effect. Jacobin writing at its best is also formally experimental, exploring the intrinsic capacities of language and literary conventions. According to T. W. Adorno, the turn from communicative writing to esoteric literature was a felix culpa born out

---

1. Friedrich Schlegel, *Philosophical Fragments*, trans. Peter Firchow, intro. Rodolphe Gasché (Minneapolis: University of Minnesota Press, 1991), 8.

of historical necessity: to maintain its critical power to speak truthfully about social injustice language had to reflect upon itself and retreat from public discourse that was irredeemably corrupt; the loss of a popular audience was a necessary price that had to be paid to insure the truthfulness that only autonomous literature could produce. Adorno identifies correctly the truth-content of esoteric literature but incorrectly assumes that communicative writing must always be false. Moreover, he paid little attention to the Jacobin writing produced before the structural transformation of the public sphere was fully in place. Reacting to the corruption of language and art during the age of Stalin and Hitler and then the Cold War, Adorno suspected all public discourse as untruthful manipulation. Only a retreat to esoteric art and the intrinsic powers of form and language could save writing from being subordinated to instrumental use by a murderous state or the culture industry.[2] Adorno, however, never studied closely the historical juncture where dissident exoteric writing enjoyed full expression while a nascent esoteric literature emerged.

As I hope I have shown, the great moment of British Jacobin writing did not collapse of its own inadequacies and contradictions; rather, such writing was coerced into silence and disguise. Its historical emergence, however, depended upon the conjunction of many cultural developments: the coexistence of a still strong oral culture with a sophisticated print culture; a politically insurgent, socially confident artisanate and middling class; the dominance of Dissenters in the London publishing industry; the labor-intensive rather than capital-intensive nature of printing technology; the absence of a fully developed police force and fully rationalized repressive apparatus; decades of Bible-reading, Sunday Schools, open-air Methodist meetings, and other forms of popular literacy; the rise of women in the fields of the novel and poetry; the coffeehouses; and perhaps most decisive of all, the growth of the literary market at the expense of patronage systems. The literary market permitted the revolutionary disruption of Paine's *Rights of Man*: a formally experimental work promoting ideas utterly incompatible with continued aristocratic rule found an audience far larger than literacy estimates had suggested were even possible. The ruling elite rebutted Paine with repression, propaganda, and a loyalist cultural offense. The repression

---

2. Adorno develops this influential idea in many different writings but I first learned it in "On Lyric Poetry and Society," trans. Bruce Mayo, *Telos* 20 (1974): 56–71; also in *Notes to Literature*, 2 vols., ed. Rolf Tiedemann, trans. Shierry Weber Nicholsen (New York: Columbia University Press, 1994), 1: 37–54.

Conclusion

and anti-Jacobin cultural counterrevolution were some of the pressures contributing to the formal qualities of the great achievements of Romantic literature like Wordsworth's *Prelude*, Blake's *Jerusalem*, Keats's odes and Hyperion fragments, Shelley's *Prometheus Unbound*, Byron's *Don Juan*, and Coleridge's philosophical prose. Jacobin writing and its public sphere — the periodicals, lectures, demonstrations, trials, political associations, meetings, pamphlets, street theater — directly and indirectly inspired some of the great achievements of the canonical Romantic literature, for which literary Jacobinism was a necessary context, and not a peripheral one.

I hope I have shown also that literary Jacobinism was intrinsically valuable even without reference to the more familiar Romantic masterpieces. Thelwall is especially important in this regard because inserting him into literary history highlights parts of the grid that are usually invisible. A Romantic before the French Revolution, an enlightener until his death, an unrepentant Jacobin, boldly experimental in both popular and "correct" compositions, Thelwall upsets some of our more complacent presuppositions. His social position as a middling-class intellectual forces us to pay more attention to the class that the Marxist historian R. S. Neale argued was the most politically insurgent in the early nineteenth century. Poised between the working class and the deferential middle class, the mostly urban middling-class artisans, tradesmen, shopkeepers, Dissenting ministers, and lower-level professionals (apothecaries, surgeons, clerks, journalists, etc.) were sensitive to economic stress, chafed under arbitrary restrictions, possessed enough economic independence from the upper-class landowners to defy their wishes, and had organizational skills and traditions powerful enough to generate a counterculture. The clash between the working class and the middle class, the conflict that defines Marxism, does not emerge in a fully articulated form until the 1830s. Even then much of the Chartist leadership comes from artisan ranks, not those of industrial workers (who do not assume a genuine voice of their own until the second half of the nineteenth century). Middling-class writers as a group share an opposition to Oxbridge culture in privileging the Bible over classical antiquity (Blake and Spence) or accepting the validity of English translations of classical texts (Keats and Thelwall); they revise democratically national myths, are constrained by the necessity of labor and struggle for the leisure to write freely, make use of popular culture (Keats's folklore, Blake's religious enthusiasm, Thelwall's oral "rhythmus") while revising conventional print-culture forms (Keats's odes and open couplets, Blake's epics and literary ballads, Thelwall's novels and blank verse). The struggle in Thelwall's career between writing and literature is evident as well in Blake's and Keats's. Blake eventually avoids literary publication altogether to avoid the pressures of false literary values institutionalized in the subscription system, reviewing practices, and patronage. Keats's repudiation of the egotistical sublime and yearning for a disinterested Shakespearean style are symptomatic of the conflicting logics of author-centered literature and socially centered writing.

The tenacity with which Thelwall clings to Enlightenment modes of thought does not seem foolish if one gives credence to Jürgen Habermas's analysis of modernity as an "unfinished" project. What seems most old-fashioned in Thelwall's enthusiasm for the *Monthly Magazine*, the *Panoramic Miscellany*, the London University, the Mechanics Institutes, and the nonprofessional scientific and learning associations presciently responds to the need for communicative action to mediate a fragmented culture. In the 1820s he did not follow Lamb, Hazlitt, and DeQuincey, who deepened Romantic subjectivism with literature ever more intricately inward, but reaffirmed an Enlightenment universalism chastened by experiences with repression and revolution. To bring together diverse aspects of what Habermas calls "expert knowledge" and connect it with the "life-world" and its own institutions is similar to how Thelwall imagines, somewhat grandiosely, the functioning of his 1820s periodicals.[3]

In the 1820s, when Thelwall was trying to sustain Enlightenment ideals, one can see the stresses under which Thelwall's own project was operating: he wanted aesthetic autonomy for art and freedom of inquiry for science but he also envisioned—as did Shelley and Blake—an integrative moment during which an emancipatory "truth" would emerge. If Thelwall thought polite journals like the *Monthly Magazine* and the *Panoramic Miscellany* could accomplish in the 1820s what lively plebeian and middle-class public spheres had accomplished in the 1790s, he was then mistaken. The fragmentation of the reading public described by Jon Klancher makes all but impossible the kind of noncoercive integration of social creativity imagined by Thelwall. Perhaps such an integration was possible in the 1790s but the road to the 1832 Reform Bill and the middle class's betrayal of universal suffrage and the working class was fairly well laid during the 1820s.

3. See Jürgen Habermas, "Modernity: An Unfinished Project," in Maurizio Passerin d'Entrèves and Seyla Benhabib, eds., *Habermas and the Unfinished Project of Modernity: Critical Essays on "The Philosophical Discourse of Modernity"* (Cambridge, Mass.: MIT Press, 1997), 38–55.

Conclusion

If ideologically Jacobin writing points ultimately to Chartism and other forms of working-class radicalism, Jacobin writing also points to allegory as a literary form and as aggressive interpretation. With the word itself born from catachresis and displacement, "Jacobin" characteristically destabilizes whatever it touches. Placed within the covers of Eaton's *Politics for the People*, canonical literature—Churchill, Dryden, Shakespeare, the Bible, Rowe, Pope, Goldsmith, Euripides, Smollett, Johnson, Gibbon, Milton— assumes democratic meanings it never had previously. These recontextualized extracts are made new by their physical location in a Jacobin journal, just as the Jacobin allegorist, like a bricoleur, borrows whatever is at hand that seems functional. As moveable extracts, these passages assume the quality of a "translation"—*translatio*—carrying from one place to another. In the *Statesman's Manual's* derogatory portrayal Coleridge defines allegory as "but a translation of abstract notions into a picture-language, which is itself nothing but an abstraction from objects of the senses."[4] Thelwall and Spence are zealous translators—of Latin, of standard into phonetic English—who delight in the capacity of language to be transferred from one place to another. Translation is dictated in part by the logic of popularization, of granting access to cultural capital that has been structured out of reach.

The allegorical mode also necessitates the reader's construction of meaning under conditions of ambiguity. What do Paine's "buds" mean? Thelwall's beheaded gamecock relates somehow to tyrannicide but how exactly is not certain. The Coleridgean symbol, on the other hand, provides semantic closure, uniting the particular and the universal, the temporal and the eternal, like *The Prelude*'s Alpine "woods decaying, never to be decayed," and the "stationary blasts of waterfalls" (1850; Book 6:626–27). If a metaphor is a "fragment of an allegory," in Coleridge's phrase,[5] then of course a symbol too can be translated and recontextualized. Why not? The only real difference between Wordsworth's stationary blasts of waterfalls and Thelwall's gamecock is that the former is a novel metaphor (deriving in part, however, from classical topoi such as Heraclitus's lesson about the river into which one

---

4. Samuel Taylor Coleridge, *The Statesman's Manual*, in R. J. White, ed., *Lay Sermons*, no. 6 of *The Collected Works of Samuel Taylor Coleridge*, Kathleen Coburn, ed. (London and Princeton: Routledge and Kegan Paul, Princeton University Press, 1972), 30.

5. Lecture 3, 1818, in Samuel Taylor Coleridge, *Lectures, 1808–1819. On Literature*, R. A. Foakes, ed., no. 5 of *The Collected Works of Samuel Taylor Coleridge*, Kathleen Coburn, ed. (London and Princeton: Routledge and Kegan Paul and Princeton University Press, 1987), 2:101. Coleridge's discussion of allegory here is much more sympathetic than the more famous passage in the *Statesman's Manual*.

steps never being the same) and the latter a more conventional one. Thelwall's gamecock is indeed attached to a "fable," another identifying characteristic of allegory according to Coleridge, but the alpine symbols in *The Prelude* are also part of a narrative, if not a fable (which is conventional rather than individualistic).

Jacobin writing is not entirely allegorical, of course, for there is a dimension that is mimetically realistic, most evident in the novels of Godwin and Wollstonecraft. The Thelwall apostrophe or the Wedderburn biblical digression, however, illustrates the way Jacobin writing as speech and speech as writing move away from realism to achieve emotional intensity. Thelwall's most carefully rendered mimetic representations tend to function also as allegory, as in his novels or opera. Even the conversational poems include numerous apostrophes and moments when particularities become allegorical. One such conversational poem, "To the Infant Hampden," from the 1801 *Poems*, for example, speaks of "a wilderness of wrongs, / A waste of troubled waters, whelming floods / Of tyrannous injustice canopied." While these lines echo parts of the Psalms (46:3, 32:6, and 69:2), the poem uses the gospel image of Jesus having no place to lay his head (Matt. 8:20, Lk 9:58) to lament the necessity of leaving Derby in 1797 to find another home. The diction and tonalities are all conversational but the figurative logic is allegorical and conventional (not religious, however).[6]

An allegorical logic is also evident in the characteristically aggressive mode of interpretation that is Jacobin. Provoked by Burke, whose example they imitated, the Jacobins turned symbols into fables. Instead of the aristocratic prospect symbolizing a hierarchical settlement of power, the land in Jacobin writing was instead "the people's farm," or the uncultivated waste requiring new agriculture, or a site where labor spoke of its history and way of life. Spence's parable about the squirrels and nuts exemplifies the Jacobin mode of interpretation: an observable, commonplace phenomenon gets translated into an allegory of injustice and power, as the squirrels have more rights to food than people. The allegorical mode is especially effective in translating abstract ideas about property into visualizable narratives.

Repression was surely a muse of sorts for Jacobin allegory, but one cannot be too sanguine about it; this repression largely achieved its goals. That the Jacobin allegories were invariably also "seditious," prosecutable, inter-

6. For a fuller reading of this and other Thelwall poems, see Judith Thompson, "An Autumnal Blast, A Killing Frost: Coleridge's Poetic Conversation with John Thelwall," *Studies in Romanticism* 36 (1997): 427–56.

Conclusion

twined with legal discourse, indicates the limits of aesthetic autonomy under which the writing was produced. Repression and government-sponsored loyalism were the means by which Jacobinism was silenced. Almost every Jacobin victory was also a defeat: Paine's *Rights of Man* sold spectacularly, but he was outlawed along with his essay; the treason trial defendants were acquitted but Thomas Hardy quit politics (his wife having died during a loyalist riot), the SCI and Friends of the People disbanded, and Thelwall himself dropped his LCS membership; Thelwall's lecture tour of East Anglia attracted hundreds but his supporters could not drive out the loyalist gangs that disrupted the lectures. An energetic and creative plebeian public sphere emerged and was then crushed, driven underground. The differentiated literary market that followed the 1790s exerted pressures on reading, writing, and publishing that made it very unlikely that there would be a repetition of the success of Paine's republican pamphlet. There was a moment, however, before repression was victorious, and that moment gave rise to a truly remarkable social creativity.

Index

Abbott (Chief Justice), 158–59, 199–200, 202
abolitionism, 95, 147–50, 241–44. *See also* slavery
Adorno, Theodor W., 289–90
Aeschylus, 184, 217
Aikin, John, 222
Alexander the Great, 143
Alfred (English monarch), 253
allegory, 10–11, 27, 257, 293–95
  autobiography, 268–87
  Burke, 45–50
  Daughter of Adoption, 241–44
  empire, 245–54
  Henry Cline, 193
  Incas, 235–40
  Jacobin, 165–66
  oratory, 203–4
  Paine and Shelley, 52–54
  Peripatetic, 211–19
  "Phenomena of the Wye," 229–32
  repression, 12, 16
  Thelwall's popular allegories, 111–25
  Wedderburn, 165–66
Althusser, Louis, 36
Altick, Richard, 7
anarchism, 5, 96, 165
Anderson, Perry, 34
anti-Catholicism, 49, 62, 162, 234, 251, 268
anti-Jacobinism, 11–12, 15, 27, 35–36, 40, 70–71, 83, 88–89, 257–61, 265, 279
Anti-Jacobin Review, 25, 125, 193, 245
antisemitism, 48, 49–50, 225, 234, 256
Aristophanes, 184
  The Clouds, 184
Aristotle, 143
Armstrong, John, 80

Arthur (legendary king of Britons), 248–51, 253, 255, 256
Ashraf, P. M., 103
Aulard, François-Alphonse, 23

Barnave, Antoine, 22
Barrell, John, 171, 175
Barruel, Augustin, 30
Bedford, Duke of, 57, 63, 70
Benjamin, Walter, 10, 162
Bentley, Richard, 179
Berri, Duke of, 198
Best, Thomas, 100
Bible, literary influence of, 12, 51, 74, 95, 103, 106, 109–10, 131–32, 133–34, 136–37, 143, 161–64, 211, 259, 282, 290, 291, 293, 294
  Amos, 96–97
  Exodus, 127, 141
  Isaiah, 53, 96–97, 105
  Jeremiah, 141
  Job, 53
  Leviticus, 105
  Luke, 96–97, 136
  Matthew, 136
  Numbers, 163
  Psalms, 99
  Revelation, 99, 101, 105
  Samuel, 55, 163
  Song of Songs, 147–48
  Tobit, 136
Bisset, Robert, 73
Blackett, Joseph, 279
Blake, William, 9, 30, 35, 61, 74, 106, 137, 187, 193, 207, 211, 217, 251, 253, 256, 281–82, 291–92
  "Black Boy," 148
  Jerusalem, 291

Index

blasphemy. *See* law
Bloomfield, Robert, 95, 279, 284
Boulton, James, 51
Breuer, Josef, 196
Brinton, Crane, 23
Brissot, Jacques-Pierre, 60
Brothers, Richard, 106, 140
Brougham, Henry, 287
Brunswick, Duke of, 27, 60
Brunt, John, 198
Brutus, 225, 237
Bunyan, John, 95
Burchell (court official), 189
Burdett, Sir Francis, 5, 7, 32, 187–88, 190, 198, 199
Burke, Edmund, 6, 13, 15, 24, 27, 29, 30, 52, 60, 74, 77, 81, 83–84, 101, 110, 130, 256, 274, 278, 286
   British Jacobinism, 43–50, 70–71, 284, 294
   Letter to a Member of the National Assembly, 48, 49, 168–69
   Letter to a Noble Lord, 24, 47, 48, 50, 56–57, 61, 64, 66, 70
   Observations on the Conduct of the Minority, 19
   Reflections on the Revolution in France, 20, 22, 24, 30, 43, 44, 47, 49, 70, 92–93
   rhetoric, 45–50, 70–71
   Third Letter on a Regicide Peace, 48–49, 169
   Thoughts on French Affairs, 24
   Two Letters on a Regicide Peace, 19, 46, 47, 48, 62, 65, 66, 68, 70
Butler, Marilyn, 11, 85, 95, 249
Byron, Lord George Gordon, 31, 207, 212, 265
   Don Juan, 212, 291
   English Bards, 281

Cadwallon (Welsh monarch), 246, 251
Cafarelli, Annette Wheeler, 13
Calhoun, Craig, 33–34
Campbell, Thomas, 251
Cannon, George, 155–57, 164
Carlile, Mary Anne, 163
Carlile, Richard, 5, 158–59, 164, 165, 198
Carlyle, Thomas, 23–24, 30

Cartwright, "Major" John, 32
Cato Street Conspiracy, 145, 155, 158, 164, 197–203
Caxton, William, 113
Cestre, Charles, 253
Chartism, 4, 34, 165, 291, 293
Chase, Malcolm, 31, 138
Chatterton, Thomas, 14
Chaucer, Geoffrey, 113, 216
Christie, Ian, 37
Churchill, Charles, 293
Cicero, 237
Claeys, Gregory, 5, 30, 76, 82–83, 131
Clare, John, 197, 207
Clark, Anna, 33
Clark, J. C. D., 37
Clarke, Samuel, 132
Cline, Henry, 193–94
Cobbett, William, 5, 32, 34, 77, 225, 228
   Political Register, 93
   Rural Rides, 226
Coleridge, Samuel Taylor, 2–3, 6, 9, 10, 11, 14, 21, 30, 36, 37–42, 56, 154, 165, 170, 193, 207, 210, 212, 216, 220, 221, 224, 231, 242, 254, 256, 258, 259, 264, 265, 277, 291
   Ancient Mariner, 144, 212
   Biographia Literaria, 21, 38, 39
   Christabel, 144, 250
   "Dejection" ode, 223
   Friend, 38, 40
   On the Constitution of the Church and State, 87
   Sibylline Leaves, 41
   Statesman's Manual, 293
   Table Talk, 242
Coleridge, Sara, 221
Colley, Linda, 17
Colquhoun, Patrick, 46
communism, 3, 5
Condorcet, Jean-Antoine-Nicolas, 28–29
Cooper, Thomas, 25
Courier (Derby), 221
Courier (London), 200
Cowper, William, 120, 147
Crabbe, George, 88–89
Critical Review, 275
Cruikshank, George, 202

Index

Cullen, George, 199
Curran, Stuart, 251

Danton, Georges Jacques, 179
Davenport, Allen, 145, 203
Davidson, William, 198
Davison, Thomas, 163
Defoe, Daniel, 135
DeQuincey, Thomas, 287, 292
Dermody, Thomas, 284
Derrida, Jacques, 87, 204
Dickinson, H. T., 16, 131, 132
Diderot, Denis, 237
Dinwiddy, J. R., 13
Dionysius of Halicarnassus, 73
Dissent (religious), 2, 16, 26, 39, 49, 94, 95, 103, 105–6, 130, 132–36, 140, 141, 143, 150, 157–58, 162–63, 165–66, 182, 187, 216, 220, 264, 280, 290, 291
Dominic (Catholic saint, Domingo de Guzman), 22
Donne, John, 13–14
Donohue, Joseph, 235, 239
Dryden, John, 185, 186, 217, 249, 293
Dundas, William, 176
Dyer, George, 5

Eaton, Daniel I., 47, 112, 211
   "The Goitre," 125–26
   Philanthropist, 93, 100
   Politics for the People, 12, 47, 93, 96–97, 101, 112, 115, 293
   "Republican Crop," 126
   "A Tale," 126–27
   trial, 94, 112, 115–18
Edinburgh Review, 84, 278, 287
Edwards, George, 200–201
Edwin of Northumbria (English monarch), 246–47, 251–53, 255, 256
Einion Glyd (Lord Elvel), 246–48, 249, 256
Eley, Geoff, 34, 94
Enlightenment, 16–17, 29, 56, 65, 71, 72, 80, 92, 93, 95, 97, 100, 103, 125, 129, 138, 141, 177, 183, 203, 206, 210, 211, 212, 234, 237, 239, 253, 255, 256, 265, 287, 292
Epstein, James, 31, 32

Erdman, David V., 25
Erskine, Thomas, 173, 174, 277
Euripides, 184, 293
Evans, Colonel, 188
Evans, Thomas, 108, 144–45, 197
Eyre, James (Lord Chief Justice), 35, 40, 171

Fair, Robert C., 165
Favret, Mary, 69
Feher, Ferenc, 30
Fielding, Mr. (state prosecutor), 115–16, 118
Fliess, Wilhelm, 196
Flower, Benjamin, 85, 261
Foster, Justice, 40
Fox, Charles J., 27–28, 50, 163, 264. See also Whigs
French Revolution, 2, 4, 20–30, 60–61, 65, 95, 217, 229, 237, 239, 240–41, 259–60, 265, 291
Frend, William, 5, 9, 30
Freud, Sigmund, 196
Friends of the People, 46, 98, 236, 295

Gagging Acts (Two Acts, 1795), 3, 5, 11, 42, 59, 60, 62, 66, 169, 184, 198, 222, 239
Gates, Henry Louis, 164
Geggus, David, 241
Gerrald, Joseph, 74, 177, 202, 248
Gibbon, Edward, 293
Gibbs, Vicary, 173, 174
Gilmartin, Kevin, 83, 142
Gilpin, William, 223, 228
Giraldus Cambrensis, 247
Girondins, 27, 28–29, 60
Glassites, 103, 135
Glendower, Owen, 245
Godwin, William, 6, 9, 13, 21, 30, 32, 35, 36, 39, 40, 76, 82, 96, 97, 130, 131, 135, 165, 182, 183, 186, 216, 241–43, 245, 261, 287, 294
   Caleb Williams, 12, 143–44
   dispute with Thelwall, 59–60
   Dr. Parr's Spital Sermon, 143, 258–60
   Fleetwood, 30
   Memoirs, 242
   Political Justice, 12, 85, 94, 96, 135, 211, 260

Goethe, Johann W., 10, 12, 212, 231
Goldsmith, Oliver, 96, 293
Goodwin, Albert, 46
Gordon, Lord George, 49–50
Gough, John, 196
Gray, Thomas, 95, 96, 223
Grégoire, Henri, 22
Grey, Earl, 263
Grumbling, Vernon O., 211
Guevara, Ernesto ("Ché"), 255
Gurney, Mr. (defense attorney), 116–18

Haberman, F. W., 191
Habermas, Jürgen, 8–9, 73, 79, 292
Hale, Justice, 40
Hall, Charles, 5
Hamburger, Philip, 172
Hampden, John, 206
Hardy, Thomas (d. 1832), 49, 65, 94, 168, 172, 173–74, 186–90, 199, 255, 265, 270–71, 295
Hardy, Thomas (1840–1928), 207, 248
Harrington, James, 105, 132, 143
Harris, Henry, 236
Harris, Thomas, 235, 239
Harrison, Gary, 211
Hartley, David, 132, 210
Harvey, Arnold D., 225
Haydon, Benjamin, 254
Hayley, William, 15, 251
Hazlitt, William, 5, 14, 31, 167, 292
Hearn, Francis, 34
Hébert, Jacques-René, 29
Hegel, Georg W. F., 65, 250, 256
Hengist (Saxon king), 246, 248
Henley, "Orator" John, 71, 179–80
Henry VIII (Tudor monarch), 57, 62, 63, 143
Heraclitus, 293
Herbert, George, 13–14
Herder, Johann G., 256
Hoagwood, Terence Alan, 13
Hobhouse, John C. (Lord Broughton), 32, 187–88, 198, 199
Hodgskin, Thomas, 145
Hofkosh, Sonia, 233
Holcroft, Thomas, 275–76
Holt, (Justice), 172
Homer, 251

Hone, J. Ann, 263
Hone, William, 134, 202
Hulme, Obadaiah, 245
Hume, David, 216, 251–52
Hunt, Henry "Orator," 5, 32, 162, 187, 198
Hunt, John, 201
Hunt, Leigh, 170–71
Examiner, 201
Hutcheson, Francis, 132
Hutchinson, Sara, 231

Imlay, Gilbert, 242
Imperial and Biographical Magazine, 275
imperialism, 206–7, 233–56
Ings, James, 198

Jacobinism, British, 1, 4–7, 9–11, 13, 19, 20, 289–95
  Burke, 43–50, 70–71
  French, 20–30, 161
  history of word, 21–30
  ideology, 30–42, 231–32, 259, 266
Jacques de Vitry (Catholic saint), 22
Janowitz, Anne, 102, 148, 215
Jeffrey, Francis, 63, 207, 278–81, 285, 287
Jesus, 74
Johnson, Joseph, 28, 85, 261
Johnson, Samuel, 95, 96, 135, 207, 293
Jones, Gareth S., 34
Jones, Robert, 246
Jones, Steven E., 125
Jonson, Ben, 186
  Sejanus, 186
Jordan, J. S., 85

Keach, William, 61
Keats, John, 74, 207, 291–92
Kelley, Theresa, 10
Kelly, Gary, 28, 34
Kennedy, Emmet, 23
Klancher, Jon, 7–8, 85, 220, 292
Knox, Thomas R., 132
Kotzebue, August, 239
Kroeber, Karl, 214

Lamb, Charles, 14, 292
Landauer, Gustav, 165

Index

Landes, Joan, 33, 34, 100
Landor, Walter S., 251
Langan, Celeste, 215
law. *See also* trials
  of blasphemous libel, 163, 171–72
  of sedition, 40–41, 171–72, 294–95
  of treason, 40, 144, 171
Leask, Nigel, 96
Lee, Janice, 245
Lee, Richard, 93
Lenin, Vladimir N., 36
literature, 8, 13–14, 54, 56, 83–86, 87–88, 92, 291–93. *See also* readers; Romanticism; writing
Liu, Alan, 246
Lock, F. P., 67
Locke, Don, 135
Locke, John, 80, 132
Lofft, Capel, 179
London Corresponding Society (LCS), 5, 6, 12, 15, 20, 30, 39, 46, 69, 85, 88, 121, 127, 129, 130, 165, 168, 172–73, 186, 188, 199, 227–28, 239, 240, 262, 264–65, 267, 270, 287, 295
  lectures, 180–83
  literary culture, 91–95, 263
  Moral and Political Magazine, 19, 34, 79, 93
  poetry, 95–102
  The Politician, 93
  Spence's songs, 102–11
  Thelwall's songs and allegories, 111–25, 253
Lottes, Günther, 5, 69, 96
L'Ouverture, Toussaint, 193, 241
Lovel (assassin of Duke of Berri), 198
Lowman, Moses, 105
Lupack, Alan, 250

Macdonald, Archibald, 116
Machiavelli, Nicolo, 132, 143
Mackenzie, Aeneas, 103
Mackenzie, Henry, 95, 271
Mackintosh, James, 35, 259–60
Magnuson, Paul, 264
Malthus, Thomas, 30, 80, 83, 84, 145, 260
Man, Paul de, 10
Manchester Herald, 100

Marat, Jean-Paul, 29, 217
Marmontel, Jean François, 236–38
  Les Incas, 236–38
Marten, Henry, 222
Marx, Karl, 41, 65, 73, 79, 82, 165
Matthewson, Matthew, 159
Maturin, Charles, 21
McCalman, Iain, 31, 49, 93, 138, 147, 155, 156, 157
McCann, Andrew, 181
Mechanics Institute, 86, 178, 292
Medici family, 143
Mee, Jon, 31, 32, 36, 102, 113, 165
Mendelssohn, Moses, 185
Mill, James, 237
Milton, John, 12, 95, 132, 206, 217–19, 229, 293
  Paradise Lost, 178–79, 217, 218, 229–30, 251, 261
Mirabeau, Gabriel-Honoré, 22
Montgomery, James, 251
Monthly Magazine, 84, 85, 210, 220, 222, 231, 253, 292
Monthly Review, 71–72, 73, 193
More, Thomas, 132, 143
Morganwg, Iolo, 261
Morning Chronicle, 98, 189, 200
Morton, Thomas, 235–37, 239
  Columbus, 235–37, 239
Moyle, Walter, 12
Murray, Charles, 201
Murray, James, 103, 132, 134

Nairn, Tom, 34
Napoleon, 32, 192, 239, 265
National Political Union (NPU), 187–88
National Union of the Working Classes (Rotunda), 187
Neale, R. S., 6, 35, 291
Nelson, Lord Horatio, 192–93, 234
Newton, Isaac, 132
Newton, Samuel, 135
Nicoll, Allardyce, 235

Oliver (spy), 162
Ollier, Charles, 170–71
Opie, Amelia, 147
oratory, 146, 155–64, 167–70, 178–90
Osmond, Thomas S., 191

Otway, Thomas, 186
    Venice Preserved, 186, 205–6
Owen, Robert, 145
Ozouf, Mona, 23

Paine, Thomas, 4, 5, 6, 9, 11, 15, 20, 28, 30, 31, 32, 34, 39, 40, 44, 76, 83, 96, 130, 165, 237, 245
    The Age of Reason, 5, 102
    Letter Addressed to the Addressers, 51, 54–55
    popular reader, 50–56, 92, 182, 186
    The Rights of Man, 7, 46, 51–54, 59, 91, 237, 289, 290, 295
Paley, William, 11
Palmer, Thomas F., 26
Panoramic Miscellany, 16, 86, 292
Parker, Richard, 226–27
Parkinson, James, 241
Parr, Samuel, 35, 259–60
Percy, Thomas, 282
Peterloo Massacre, 155, 170, 197, 199, 201
Pétion, Alexandre, 22
Petrarch, 218
Pfau, Thomas, 171
Phillips, Richard, 222, 240, 261, 266
Philp, Mark, 43, 97–98
Pitt, William, 19, 74, 176, 247, 263
Place, Francis, 5, 9, 178, 180, 187–88, 264–65, 270, 271
Plato, 87
Plush, William, 159
Plutarch, 12
Pope, Alexander, 67, 95, 207, 217, 293
    Dunciad, 179
Portland, Duke of, 141
Price, Richard, 22, 26, 50
Priestley, Joseph, 26
public sphere, 1, 8–10, 15, 20, 27, 44, 45, 53, 56, 58–59, 60, 65, 66, 68–69, 72, 84–86, 91–95, 286–87, 289–95
Puffendorf, Samuel, 132

Quint, David, 251

readers. *See also* literature; public sphere; writing
    Enlightenment, 71–72

literary canon, 217
middle class, 260–63
popular, 56, 103, 133–34, 182, 226–27
reader-writers, 16
Romantic, 87–88, 91–95, 277–78, 290–95
social class, 7–9, 85–86, 266–68, 284–87
Reeves, John, 180
repression, 1, 2, 3, 4–5, 7, 11–12, 13, 14, 20, 26, 41, 46, 50, 83–86, 88, 91, 94, 138, 237, 258–63, 290–91, 295. *See also* Thelwall, John: repression
Reynolds (spy), 162
Ricardo, David, 145
Richardson, Alan, 233, 251, 284
Ridgway, James, 211
Roberts, Captain, 190
Robespierre, Maximilien, 22, 23, 29, 65, 179, 259
Robinson, Daniel, 218
Robinson, George, 85
Robinson, Henry C., 213, 252, 265
Robinson, Robert, 26
Roe, Nicholas, 36, 222, 230
Rogers, Samuel, 251
Roland, Jeanne Marie, 28
Romanticism, 10–11, 13, 53–54, 56, 71, 83–84, 87–88, 92, 101, 154, 177, 211–20, 223–26, 229–32, 251, 253–56, 265–66, 268, 271–73, 278, 281–82, 291–93. *See also* literature; writing
Rousseau, Jean-Jacques, 23, 29, 47, 48, 50, 80, 82, 95, 223
    Julie, 48
Rowe, Nicholas, 293
Rowenna (Hengist's daughter), 248–50
Rudkin, Olive, 138
Russell, Lord, 57, 63, 185

Sandemaninans, 135, 260
Schama, Simon, 29
Schlegel, Friedrich, 288
Scott, Walter, 27, 30, 211
    Ivanhoe, 249, 268
Scrivener, Michael, 98
sedition. *See* law
Seneca, 225

Index

Shakespeare, William, 14, 68, 96, 186, 217, 218, 235, 237, 238, 281, 293
  Macbeth, 25
  Romeo and Juliet, 212
Shelley, Mary Wollstonecraft, 5, 9
  Frankenstein, 12, 28, 50
Shelley, Percy Bysshe, 5, 9, 31, 35, 154, 155, 170–71, 207, 224, 253, 256
  Cenci, 170–71
  "Hymn to Intellectual Beauty," 216
  Julian and Maddalo, 212, 216
  "Ode to the West Wind," 51, 53–54
  Prometheus Unbound, 61, 217, 250, 253, 291
  Queen Mab, 253
  Revolt of Islam, 28
  Triumph of Life, 74
Sheridan, Thomas, 236, 240
  Pizarro, 236, 239–40, 263
Sidmouth, Lord, 197
Sidney, Algernon, 96, 185, 206, 237
Sieyès, Emmanuel J., 22
Simpson, David, 17, 25, 211
Simpson, Roger, 249
slavery, 95, 113–14, 146, 147–53, 165, 193, 215, 233–35, 240–41, 243–44
Smith, Adam, 80
Smith, Charlotte, 95, 217–19
Smith, Olivia, 50–51, 75, 93, 97, 133, 138
Smollett, Tobias G., 293
social class, 6–8, 9, 12, 33–35, 41–42, 46–47, 50–51, 59, 74, 75–86, 87, 91–97, 102–3, 106, 110–11, 120, 123–24, 127, 130–31, 165, 180–82, 184, 187–88, 207, 225–28, 242, 264–65, 269–72, 289–95. *See also* Thelwall, John: social class
social democracy, 5, 131
socialism, 5, 131, 145, 165
Society for Constitutional Information (SCI), 46, 85, 179, 182, 295
Socrates, 71, 73, 74, 185, 225, 238
Sophocles, 184
Southcote, Joanna, 106
Southey, Robert, 9, 30, 31, 39, 40, 145–46, 170
Spelman, Edward, 73
Spence, Jeremiah, 103

Spence, Thomas, 2, 5, 7, 9, 30, 77, 84, 88, 92, 161, 167, 203, 211, 281–82, 287, 291, 293
  "Burke's Address to the 'Swinish Multitude,'" 110–11
  Constitution of a Perfect Commonwealth, 136
  Important Trial of Thomas Spence, 142–43
  "Jubilee Hymn," 103–6, 127
  life, 129–31
  Meridian Sun of Liberty, 130
  Pig's Meat, 12, 93, 96–97, 133, 145, 164–65
  Pronouncing and Foreigners Bible, 137
  "Propagation of Spensonianism," 108–10
  prose, 133–43
  Real Rights of Man, 133
  Restorer of Society to Its Natural State, 138, 139–42
  Rights of Infants, 136–37
  songs, 102–11, 289
  Supplement to the History of Robinson Crusoe, 133
  trials, 138–40, 142–43, 179, 258–59, 260
Spenser, Edmund, 186
Steele, Joshua, 191
Sterne, Laurence, 95, 210, 211, 212, 223
Stoddart, John, 197, 201
  New Times, 199, 201
Stormont, Lord, 54–55
Strutt, Joseph, 261
Swift, Jonathan, 95, 96, 132
Symonds, Henry, 211

Talfourd, Thomas N., 270
Thelwall, Cecil (Boyle), 245, 254
  Life of John Thelwall, 122, 168, 174, 257, 267, 273
Thelwall, Hampden, 247
Thelwall, John, 9, 13–14, 20, 30, 32, 33, 39, 40, 41, 44, 45, 47, 93, 94, 96, 97, 130, 131, 143, 154, 165, 291–93
  achievements, 5–7, 254
  allegory, 111–25, 193, 205–7, 211–19, 228–32, 235–40, 241–44, 245–54, 257, 268–87

Index

Thelwall, John *(continued)*
  dispute with Godwin, 59–60
  elocution, 15, 88, 167, 178, 262, 279, 285
  empire, 206, 233–56
  feminism, 241–44
  intemperance, 49, 70, 168–69, 174–78, 192, 200, 203
  labor theory, 15, 72–73, 75–82, 226
  lectures, 3, 6–7, 26, 31, 44, 62, 65–66, 77–79, 177, 180–90, 209, 257, 266–67, 276–77, 285, 288, 295
  life, 3–4, 221, 260–73
  oratory, 88, 167–70, 178–90, 203–4
  prostitution as metaphor, 62–64, 207, 272–75, 278–85
  repression, 3, 4, 5, 11–12, 16, 56–74, 84–86, 111–25, 130, 168–78, 180–90, 197–202, 209, 221–23, 226–32, 239–40, 245, 261–63, 276–78, 280, 285
  social class, 7, 59, 75–86, 120, 123–24, 180–82, 184, 187–88, 190–91, 207, 225–28, 242, 257, 264–65, 269–72, 278–87
  songs, 119–20, 172, 277
  speech therapy, 15, 88, 167, 191–97, 262, 285
  trials, 168–78, 182, 205, 257, 267
  Writings: *The Champion*, 6, 15, 146, 178, 191, 197–204, 221, 253, 262, 265, 267, 270; "Chaunticlere" allegory, 94, 112–18, 127, 155, 172, 173, 183, 206, 293–94; *Daughter of Adoption*, 146, 235, 240–44, 261, 274; *Democracy Vindicated*, 12, 234; *Essay on Human Vitality*, 80, 267, 275; "Essay on the English Sonnet," 217–19; "Execration," 283–84; *Fairy on the Lake*, 246, 248–51, 252, 253, 256; *The Hope of Albion*, 16, 207, 246, 251–53; *The Incas*, 16, 235–40, 251, 275; *John Gilpin's Ghost*, 120–25, 127, 173; *Letter to Henry Cline*, 16, 192–97, 214, 267, 285; *Life of John Thelwall*, 122, 168, 174, 257, 267, 273; "Lines Written at Bridgewater," 221; *Natural and Constitutional Right of Britons*, 87, 167, 168, 173, 175–77, 277; *Panoramic Miscellany*, 16, 86, 292; "Pedestrian Excursion," 220, 222–28, 231–32; *Peripatetic*, 16, 76, 80, 95, 194, 206, 210–19, 223, 231, 273–74, 275, 280; "Phenomena of the Wye," 220, 228–32; *Poems* (1787), 63, 275, 280–85; *Poems* (1795), 277, 286; *Poems* (1801), 14, 16, 143, 207, 234, 235, 246, 253, 257, 262, 278, 287; *Poetical Recreations of the Champion*, 14, 267–68; "Prefatory Memoir," 168, 240, 245, 251, 254, 257–58, 260–73, 283, 286–87; *The Rights of Nature*, 1, 19, 44, 62, 65, 74–77, 79, 80–82, 185, 226, 244; "Seducer," 282–83; "Sheepsheering Song," 119–20, 172, 206; *Sober Reflections*, 44, 56–65, 130; "To the Infant Hampden," 294; *The Tribune*, 3, 15, 34, 44, 77–79, 87, 93, 168, 169–70, 177, 182–86, 202, 209, 226, 234, 244, 267, 277, 285–86, 289; *Trident of Albion*, 192–93
Thelwall, Maria, 247
Thelwall, Susan (Vellum), 221, 247–48, 269
Theological Inquirer, 155
Thistlewood, Arthur, 155, 197, 198, 200–201, 203
Thompson, E. P., 31–37, 39, 41–42, 46, 220–21, 223, 228, 265
Thompson, Judith, 216
Thompson, William, 145
Thomson, James, 95; "Winter," 229
Tidd, Richard, 198
Tilly, W., 108
Times (London), 200
Tooke, Horne, 49, 85, 168, 173–74, 193, 269
Toussaint. *See* L'Ouverture, Toussaint
treason. *See* law
trials, Cato Street Conspiracy (for treason, 1820), 145, 197–203; Eaton (for seditious libel, 1793), 94, 112, 115–18, 262; Hardy, Tooke, and Thelwall (for treason, 1794), 65, 66, 168–78, 182, 198–99, 205, 267; Paine (for seditious libel, 1792), 54; Spence, 138–40, 142–43, 258–59; Thelwall (for sedi-

Index

tious libel, 1821), 201–2; Wedderburn (for blasphemous libel, 1819–20), 155–64, 202–3
Two Acts (1795). *See* Gagging Acts
Tyler, Wat, 216

United Irishmen, 263
Universal Magazine, 217–18, 275

Vergil, 251
Volney, Constantin-François, 12, 96
Voltaire, 216
Vortigern, 248–50

Waddington, Samuel, 155, 203
Wakefield, Gilbert, 85, 261
Wales, 195, 207, 220, 221, 222, 234, 240, 244–51, 252, 255–56, 261
Watson, James (Dr.), 197
Watson, Robert, 49
Watt, James, Jr., 25
Wedderburn, Robert, 5, 88, 92, 143, 146–66, 167, 197, 202, 203, 294; "Africans Complaint on Board a Slave Ship," 149–50; *Axe Laid to the Root*, 147; "Desponding Negro," 148–49; "Englishman's Domestic View," 150–54; *Forlorn Hope*, 147; *Horrors of Slavery*, 151; "Negro Boy Sold for a Watch," 147–48; oratory, 155–64, 289; poetry, 147–54; trial, 155–64
Wharam, Alan, 170, 175

Whigs, 2, 27, 120, 278
  Foxites 2, 27, 57, 239, 263
White, Kirke, 279
Wilkes, John, 132
Williams, Helen M., 28, 34, 251
Wimpory, J., 222
Windham, William, 221
Wollstonecraft, Mary, 9, 28, 30, 35, 95, 242–43 294; *Mary*, 242; *Wrongs of Woman (Maria)*, 28, 144, 242
Wood, Marcus, 102, 173
Wooler, Thomas J., 198, 201; *Black Dwarf*, 201
Wordsworth, Dorothy, 220, 221, 222, 224
Wordsworth, William, 2–3, 6, 9, 30, 36, 87–88, 91, 96, 154, 193, 207, 210, 211–15, 220–22, 224, 229–30, 231, 242, 246, 254, 256, 287; *Borderers*, 144; *The Excursion*, 4, 212–13, 277; "Goody Blake and Harry Gill," 78; *Lyrical Ballads* and "Preface," 179, 210, 217, 219; *The Prelude*, 2, 4, 56, 144, 194, 212, 214, 216, 231–32, 257, 291, 293–94; "Resolution and Independence," 212; "Tintern Abbey," 154, 214, 220, 222
Worrall, David, 31, 155
writing, 8, 13–14, 16, 54, 83–86, 278–87, 289–95. *See also* literature; readers

Yearsley, Ann, 95, 279
Yeats, William B., 61

www.ingramcontent.com/pod-product-compliance
Lightning Source LLC
Chambersburg PA
CBHW031545300426
44111CB00006BA/187